Mangaddicts: French Teenagers and Manga Reading

Youth in a Globalizing World

Series Editors

Vincenzo Cicchelli, *Ceped, Université Paris Cité/IRD*
Sylvie Octobre, DEPS – *DOC, Ministère de la culture and Centre Max Weber, ENS Lyon/CNRS (France)*

VOLUME 21

The titles published in this series are listed at *brill.com/ygw*

Mangaddicts: French Teenagers and Manga Reading

By

Christine Détrez and Olivier Vanhée

Translated by

Florian Berthé

BRILL

LEIDEN | BOSTON

Originally published in hardback in 2023.

This book was originally published in French as *Les mangados: lire des mangas à l'adolescence* by Éditions de la Bibliothèque publique d'information (Paris) in 2012 under ISBN 978-2-84246-154-6.

Cover illustration: Photo by Gracia Dharma on Unsplash. Public Domain.

The Library of Congress Cataloging-in-Publication Data is available online at https://catalog.loc.gov
LC record of the hardback edition available at https://lccn.loc.gov/2023010861

Typeface for the Latin, Greek, and Cyrillic scripts: "Brill". See and download: brill.com/brill-typeface.

ISSN 2212-9383
ISBN 978-90-04-70873-0 (paperback, 2024)
ISBN 978-90-04-54551-9 (hardback)
ISBN 978-90-04-54831-2 (e-book)

This book is printed on acid-free paper and produced in a sustainable manner.

Contents

Preface

Japanese comics have acquired a major place in France in the book publishing and distribution sector, in the digital dissemination of cultural content and in the practices of several generations of readers, from the late 1980s to the 2020s. The diffusion of manga attests both to the importance of Japan as an export pole for cultural products, and to the cosmopolitan recomposition of the repertoires and cultural imaginaries of the youngest generations in France (Cicchelli and Octobre 2018). While these fans were familiar with the uses of the Japanese media mix and its digital variations from an early age (Steinberg 2012), they also show a strong attachment to the traditional supports and gestures of reading (and collecting) black and white printed works. The power of attraction of manga is such in the world of books and publishing that many works of comics created by French, German, Spanish, Italian, American and Brazilian publishers, cartoonists and scriptwriters are presented as manga or one of their variants: "French manga", "euromanga", "global manga", "original-english-language manga", "Algerian manga" (or "DZ manga"), "Brazilian manga" (or "tropical manga"), "Filipino manga" (or "pinoy manga") to the point of constituting an entire field of "Japanese comics without Japan" (Brienza 2015). These hybrid mangas attest to a practical appropriation of the graphic and narrative specificities of manga, sometimes leading to publication in Japan, as is the case for rare French manga authors (*Radiant*, by Tony Valente). In such a globalized landscape, France stands out for the precocity and intensity of this attachment to manga (it is often presented as "the second manga market" after Japan, or even as "the other manga country"), but also for the diversity of comic book forms available there, and finally for the relative cultural and institutional recognition that "the ninth art" has enjoyed since the 1970s.

Such a worldwide and French success of manga is often attributed to explanations that are themselves globalizing: it is said to be the mechanical effect of the intrinsic properties and content of these comics, of the immediate charm of their "visual language", of the powers of emotional capture of their characters, of the bewitching capacity attributed to television and images, of the mental processes associated with transmedia or immersion in fictional worlds, or even of the supposed effectiveness of the globalized marketing of Japanese companies. In the media discourses of the 1990s, the relationship to manga was more widely characterized as a form of "hypnosis" or "optical gluttony", reduced to visual sensations located more in the order of nature and the innate than in the universe of culture. This physiological apprehension of Japanese comics was redoubled by the focus of public debates on scenes of combat, violence and bodily transformations, on images deemed scabrous and pornographic manga (Vanhée 2019). Manga and Japanese animation have also been associated either with a public of children and adolescents who are victims of the cultural industries, or, more recently, with cultural consumers and autonomous fans (Eloy 2022).

This book proposes to analyze in concrete terms the experiences, satisfactions and pleasures of manga reading among French adolescents by adopting a sociological perspective, attentive to the diversity of reading, to the plural identities of male and female readers, and to the variation of their socialization. It presents the results of an empirical survey conducted among teenagers enrolled in secondary school in France in the late 2000s and early 2010s, male and female manga readers aged 11 to 19 and from a wide variety of social backgrounds. Its purpose remains particularly relevant. The project of this survey was born at the crossroads of several research perspectives. First, it is part of an empirical tradition of studying reception, media uses and reading practices, particularly concerning works and genres characterized both by a strong commercial distribution and by forms of illegitimacy, such as sentimental literature, detective novels or fantasy. However, it embraces a whole range of media and practices related to manga, shifting the focus away from printed media and the closure of works to what circulates between media, fictional universes and linguistic and national borders. The reading of manga is in fact restituted in the practices and broader cultural trajectories of the young people interviewed, making use of quantitative and longitudinal surveys on the cultural leisure activities of French adolescents (Octobre, Détrez, Mercklé and Berthomier 2010; Baudelot, Cartier and Détrez 1999) as well as works from "fan studies" and academic literature on manga. This field has developed considerably since the 1960s in Japan (Kinsella 2000), and has been globalized since the 1990s, in connection with the departments of Japanese, literature, anthropology and sociology, with media studies and gender studies (Berndt 2010). These works have highlighted the multiple intersections of manga reading with the use of other media and with a range of leisure activities, cultural outings, and events: tourism (Sabre 2016), musical tastes, food (Reinhard, Largent, and Chin 2020), games, toys, and figurines (Brougère 2008), etc. They have led to a better understanding of the French reception of the multiple variations of the *Dragon Ball* franchise (Suvilay 2019), learning to read manga in Japanese middle and high schools (Allen and Ingulsrud 2009), the "domestication" of manga in the United States (Brienza 2016), the making of shojo manga magazines in Japan (Prough 2011), or the uses of Japanese media culture for pedagogical purposes (Ward-Black 2009). Often employing the notions of "participatory culture" and "convergence" (Jenkins 1993, 2006), investigations of Japanese manga and animation audiences have focused on the creation or reading of fan fiction or amateur manga, particularly by groups of female readers (McLelland, Nagaike, Suganuma and Welker 2015), on the cultural activities of male "*otaku*" and their representations in the media (Galbraith, Huat Kam and Kamm 2015), and on the "transnational" and digital aspect of these fans' engagement (Ito, Okabe, and Tsuji 2012). Compared to works focused on a segment of the editorial offer, such as shojo, on a specific type of amateur practice (fanfiction writing or cosplay) or on a single category of the public (fans or "*otaku*"), often based on content studies, our investigation is less compartmentalized and analyzes the constellation of amateur practices related to manga and the way they are distributed and invested in our population. It takes into account varying degrees of investment in the manga universe, and implements a biographical perspective. Manga constitutes here a means of capturing a crossing of adolescence (Mercklé 2017), its sociabilities and its emotions. It is a way to highlight what cultural practices, objects and tastes do to feelings and emotions, and what emotions do to each other's cultural repertoires, including the formation of tastes (Pasquier 1999; Chedaleux, Juan and Pillard 2020).

If the historical context of our investigation is specific, it nevertheless allows us to shed light on the situation observed in the early 2020s. We can indeed note that the current configuration of the manga offer stabilized in France in the second half of the 2000s. There are many similarities and continuities between these two periods from the point of view of the volume of sales of manga and their cultural value, or even the mode of access to these works, marked by the coexistence of significant distribution in book networks, wide dissemination of digitized versions of manga, and finally dedicated collections in public reading institutions. The end of the 2000s saw a peak in manga sales at the end of a decade of strong editorial growth. After a "phase of decline" between 2010 and 2014, this cultural sector experienced a "new euphoria" (Roure 2021) at the beginning of the following decade and returned to strong dynamism, including and especially during the Covid-19 pandemic and lockdowns (Bourlès and Nicolas 2022). The "culture pass" set up by the French government to support the cultural sector has also benefited manga (this sum of 300 euros granted to 18-year-olds has been largely used for manga purchases). In the 2020s, manga will benefit from an even stronger foothold in the global entertainment industry, notably through adaptations or the broadcasting of Japanese animated series on the Netflix platform and major investments by its competitors (Petit 2021), but also from a stronger synchronization with the Japanese publication rhythm, through the development of simulcasts of animated series.

This book thus allows us to look back at the adolescent generation which, in France, was the first to be exposed so early to a plethoric editorial and digital offer, to a constellation of amateur practices and easily accessible digital tools (Octobre 2014), whereas previous generations had to face not only strong media hostility, but also concrete difficulties in accessing manga (Vanhée 2019). It thus provides insight into the genesis of the current situation, shedding light on the differentiated logics of appropriation of this constellation of symbolic goods, and in particular the combined uses of reading print and reading digitized versions, since the activity of fansub and scanlation teams experienced, at the turn of the 2000s and 2010s, a high intensity in France, before Japanese and French publishers intervened to limit these forms of piracy and developed their digital catalog. This generation is also one of the first to have had access to a diversified and segmented offer according to multiple categories, including age and gender, well beyond the only male readership associated with comics. The teenage boys and girls interviewed during the first French manga boom lived through the heroic period when the characters of *Naruto, One Piece* and *Bleach* were still in the midst of their epic and fantastic adventures, but they also lived through the expansion of the supply of manga aimed at girls, which began in the mid-2000s and was illustrated at the time of the survey by the wide success of *Nana* (a manga about two young women and a music band in Tokyo) and the multiplication of "yaoi" or "boy's love" titles, featuring homoerotic relationships between male characters. Complemented by erotic and pornographic titles, this unprecedented diversity in the fictional and visual representation of gender, feelings and sexuality was an interesting element to study from the point of view of reception, as other surveys on young people's relationship to sexuality on the Internet have shown (Amsellem-Mainguy and Vuattoux 2020). At the time of the survey, manga is indeed marked by a growing anchorage in "girl culture" (Mitchell and Reid-Walsh 2008), in rupture with the targeting of a mainly male readership in previous decades (and in the universe of comics and comic books). It is not only shojo collections that develop for teenage girls, but also more specific and sexually explicit collections for young adults, and finally girls and women's magazines dealing with shojo, music and Japanese fashion at the same time. Alongside posters of Japanese singers and actors, the slogans of the publishers offer a map of feelings intended for young readers, from misunderstood love to sexual desire, with most of the time, on a colored full page, a heroine with big eyes staring at the readers or an embracing couple: promise of "skin-deep sensuality", "prelude to love", "romantic comedy of the year", "all the flavors of love: intense, bitter, full-bodied" (according to advertisements published in *AnimeLand* magazine, Vanhée 2019). The manga then invests areas of expressive culture allowing the display of one's tastes, echoing the clothing fashions derived from Japanese ready-to-wear brands and trends of Tokyo's urban youth, the outfits and looks of Japanese singers and musicians, and finally the practices of cosplay enthusiasts. These female versions of teenage subcultures are not only played out in the bedroom culture but also feed into street cultures and a whole commercial sector.

Finally, the supply of manga was characterized at this time by a growing embeddedness in "J culture", which emphasized the "consumption of difference", paving the way to the South Korean wave of Hallyu in the following decade (Cicchelli and Octobre 2021). For example, magazines specializing in anime/manga give an important and growing place to a Japanese culture whose definitions and contours vary according to the titles. The majority of them publish articles and reviews of the same range of contemporary Japanese cultural products: video games (mainly Japanese), music (especially contemporary Asian artists, genres and groups, from pop to rock to hip hop), cinema and Asian television series (dramas). In the wake of the magazine *Tsunami* (1992–1997), the magazines *Otaku* (2001–2006), *Japan Mania* (2002–2003) and *Japan Vibes* (2002–2008) have initiated and consolidated this Japanese editorial orientation, dealing with manga above all as a contemporary Japanese cultural and media production (and not primarily as a form of comics among others). *Otaku* is the "100% Japan, 100% Passion" magazine, *Japan Vibes* goes further and presents itself as "the 200% Japan magazine". The recurrent invocations of Japan contribute to making this country and its cultural industry an important source of legitimacy, and a pledge of authenticity, just like the United States for jazz (Roueff 2013) or hip hop (Hammou 2012). The Parisian festival Japan Expo has contributed to imposing this type of cultural expectations. According to its director, the festival aims to go "beyond reading-consumption" by opening "a window on Asian culture in general and Japanese culture in particular" (Pasamonik 2007). So-called cultural activities and spaces are thus becoming a permanent part of the organization and programming of these events, in connection with the growing investment of Japanese authorities and companies, cultural or sports associations. These exhibitors and activities thus contribute to unfolding some of the cultural references inscribed in manga and to making Japan a key to understanding this category of print. It was therefore also interesting to see the logics of appropriation of this offer marked by these indicators of "Japaneseness". It is thus a question of shedding light on the "incessant transformation of the offer of symbolic products" and the "temporality of tastes" (Bourdieu 1996, 160).

Now better known thanks to quantitative surveys conducted respectively in 2011, 2017 and 2020, the manga readership remains marked by a specific biographical and generational anchoring. As in our survey, in 2020 it is mainly pre-teens and teenagers who prefer manga, with the share of male and female manga readers peaking among 13-year-olds, before slowly eroding (Guilbert

2021; Vincent Gérard, Chaniot and Lapointe 2020). The attachment to reading is particularly strong for manga fans aged 13 to 15. The questionnaire survey conducted in 2011 highlighted the greater propensity of manga readers to become involved in amateur practices and communities, compared to other comic book readers (Evans and Gaudet 2012; Evans 2014). These are all aspects that we identified during our survey, conducted during the first manga boom in France. As the only survey of its kind to date, our survey, through in-depth interviews with middle and high school students, allows us to explore more precisely the reasons for their attachment to manga and the constellation of media and cultural activities that they associate with these books. These interviews also make it possible to trace the biographies of young readers, and to study the sociabilities and stages that underpin the beginnings of their journey as manga fans.

The national and cultural context of this survey is also very specific. The diffusion of manga was very early in France (as in Italy and Spain), first confidentially in the 1960s and 1970s, then on a much larger scale from the 1990s onwards. Parents and adults around our teenagers were socialized in a very different context, marked by the absence of manga or various moral panics about them. France also stands out for its strong diversity in terms of comics, since manga has been added to the Franco-Belgian comic books and US comics present since the beginning of the 20th century. *One Piece* became, in 2020, the second favorite title of adults, behind *Tintin*. Naruto was already among the favorite heroes of teenagers in 2010. Manga differs from other forms of comics by the frequency of its publication and its serialized fiction aspect. Like jazz (Roueff 2013) and hip hop (Hammou 2012), it is one of the symbolic goods produced abroad that have been very successful in France and have become part of the cultural hierarchy. The activism of French amateurs has contributed to shaping and enhancing their symbolic value: manga does not escape ordinary symbolic struggles and forms of cultural distinction, which are sensitive in the discourses and practices of young amateurs, their peer groups as well as their close friends and relatives. Today, manga can be a subject of discussion, controversy and deploration, without arousing moral panic or outright hostility.

Olivier Vanhée

Acknowledgments

This book presents a synthesis of the results of a survey conducted as part of a study program launched by the Bpi's Studies and Research Department, at the request of the of the Ministry of Culture and Communication. It was carried out by Christine Détrez and Olivier Vanhée, with the contribution of Cécile Touitou (Tosca consultants) for the mapping of the manga publishing offer in France.

Thanks to

Élise Benchimol, Marie Du Boucher, Raphaël Colombier, Julie Donjon, Nawel Guitoun, Lucie Jégat, Abir Krefa, Adrien Michon, Cécile Noesser, Safiya Panico-Djoued, Cécile Rodrigues, Marine Trégan, Pierre Zancarini-Fournel, for having conducted and/or transcribed interviews.

Férouze Guitoun, manager of the Max Weber Center at the ENS of Lyon, for his unbounded dedication.

Françoise Gaudet and Christophe Evans, Research Department of the Bpi, for their trust, their advice, and their wise rereading.

Sylvie Octobre and Vincenzo Cicchelli, for their interest for our work and their support to translate, revise, and publish it.

Tables and Graphs

Tables

Graphs

Introduction

> I think that as long as I have free time, I will read. As long as society gives me free time …
> Ah, he's got a big thing against society.
> But I've got nothing, stop it, he's a sociologist, he'll think: 'oh dear'
>
> MADJI and AURÉLIEN

∵

Just say the word "manga" and a whole series of colorful and often contradictory representations emerge: wide eyes and Japanese silhouettes, miniskirts and exoskeletons, garish colors or black and white, anime and printed books, onomatopoeias and introspective texts, mass production and avant-garde culture … The litany of the contrasting images would be long. The evocation of the public would arouse the same kind of various reactions: prostrated teenagers in front of television, computer or video games, teenagers disguising themselves with bangs in the eyes, skirts and lace jabots or even locking themselves in their room with bad quality paper books. And the risk they would become at best uneducated, at worst asocial and violent. Can we call them "readers", these young people who would forsake books, or even the Franco-Belgian comic strip, suddenly haloed by a legitimacy that has also been denied to it for a long time?

Since the 80's and its media panics against the broadcasting of Japanese cartoons in children's programs, the discourse has evolved but the debate remains passionate: should mangas be introduced in libraries? In school programs? Should the taste for manga be restricted, or negotiated with more "serious" readings, more "profitable" academically or more "enriching" personally?

More generally, manga allows us to understand in an empirical way the place of adolescents in a changing cultural landscape: on his work on moral panics, David Buckingham points that the lament of lost childhood is one of the most popular of the late twentieth century (2000). According to him, it is true that childhood has always been at the heart of the fears, desires and fantasies of adults, but in recent years, however, it has been invested with a growing sense of anxiety and panic.

But what are the real practices of these teenage manga readers? For, as we shall see, manga is a publishing sector that is doing well. Moreover, here is

 | DOI:10.1163/9789004548312_002

the second generation of French children to be confronted with manga and their animated adaptations: they know television programs—particularly on the new DTT and satellite channels -, printed albums, but also digitized versions, accessible on the Internet, of animated cartoons (subtitled by fansub teams) and even manga not yet published in France and translated by fans (scanlations, or "scantrad" in French). While a French manga culture is thus being developed, with its own memory, manga itself follows the trajectory of comics and detective novels before it: special issues, covers of cultural magazines, museum exhibitions, in a process of legitimation that brings about new distinctions. Thus, it is not insignificant that the Japanese media are worried about those children who now spend too much time "consuming" manga on the Internet or on their cell phones, and no longer reading them, and who would thus lose the skills, the "literacy" involved in this reading (Allen and Ingulsrud 2009).

This survey is therefore in line with a previous survey conducted by Erik Neveu and Annie Collovald on readers of thrillers. It shares the same qualitative methods: in-depth interviews with middle and high school students who read manga. Devoted to the reasons for reading, and therefore by definition to the readers, this survey is not about the reasons for not reading, the dislikes and rejections that could have been expressed by teenagers who are totally resistant to manga.

Another obvious common point is that this book concerns a publishing production that has long been stigmatized: like detective novels, like sentimental novels, like comic books before, manga has not always had good press, and the challenge is to shift the concern "from the book to the reader", to use Roger Chartier's expression (Chartier 1985). On another literary corpus, Janice Radway has thus shown the richness of the receptions, skills, appropriations deployed by the readers of sentimental novels (Radway 1984). And let us remember that cinema, at its beginnings, was marked by the same anxieties on their effects on the spectators.

Finally, this survey shares with Neveu and Collovald's book the concern to take the children's answers seriously. We think that attempting to explain choices, tastes, and behaviors is not denying the effectiveness or validity of the arguments put forward, in our case, by adolescents, and no hierarchy is posed between the kind of explanations. On the opposite, we have to be careful about enchanted discourses. Indeed, David Buckingham warns against the risk of focusing only on children's competences and appropriations, in a context of total social weightlessness. Our sociological approach aims to explain the variety of appropriations, depending, for example, on gender, social backgrounds, economic or cultural capital, or reading practices …

But what is a manga? This very question of definition, far from being simple and obvious, thus becomes a real issue. Indeed, as we shall see in the first part, it deals with the multiplicity of media, but also the positioning strategies in the French publishing field, and its literary and historical tradition. Thanks to this historical analysis, we will understand the variations in the symbolic status of manga. In this first part, it is important to outline the field of supply today in France. This mapping of the different poles of manga publishing, and its material factors such as publication frequencies and prices, helps to situate manga more precisely in the field of comics. The mapping of the manga offer obviously determines the possibilities of "choice" for readers, even if it does not exhaust it, with the recourse to forms of downloading or reading on screen, as we shall see in the practices.

Finally, to understand why a teenager read manga today, from detached practice to passion displayed in dress codes or musical tastes, we must proceed in two stages. On the one hand, manga "fits" perfectly into "youth culture". It is an easily transportable object, a support for nomadic reading. It can be inserted into a web of interests, including music, sociability, digital technology, and amateur practices. But this material adaptation of the manga object to the daily life of teenagers is not enough to explain the predilection for this or that title. Manga is also a support for appropriations (as understood by Michel de Certeau): our teenagers use their favorite series in a concrete way (they learn to draw or to do their hair, etc.) but also in an ethical way, and they identify with the characters. Not only do manga offer, like all readings, models of identification or repulsion, but also, reading can become a way of dealing with past experiences, a way of learning to manage and express emotions, and a way of taking part in the gender construction, between assignments, negotiations or even resistance. The aim is also for these teenagers to deal relationships to their age and their generation: by distinguishing themselves from adults but also from the youngest; by contemplating their own childhood with a certain nostalgia, objectified in the conservation and the rereading of childhood mangas, in the same way that the decorations of the walls of the rooms or the cuddly toys on a bed allow to keep for oneself and in oneself, the space of childhood.

Finally, are the cultural and reading practices of teenagers, here and now, exempt from these games of legitimacy, in a kind of free market where the "distinction" would not exist? On manga, and reading in general, not all teenagers escape the conflicts of legitimacy: if the criteria of distinction are particular to them, and do not often overlap with the principles of scholarly reading, mangas become, for some, opportunities to develop skills for which recognition is an important issue. For others, reading is more problematic, when their "cultivated" dispositions contradict the stigmatizing discourses heard about their reading: in the abandonment of reading, in the shifts from one corpus to another, in the way of answering the interview, positioning strategies are then played out which are not always easy. Thus, this survey, beyond this particular object that is manga, allows us to approach the answers to this question: why, today, does an adolescent read?

CHAPTER 1

What Is Manga?

In France, the books teenagers have the opportunity to read are to a large extent dependent on the national context of manga's reception. Only a small part of the Japanese publishing offer is selected by French publishers. In France manga are published directly in the form of bound volumes, available every two or six months, and not in prepublished weekly magazines, which is in use in Japan. When manga are imported into France, their original covers are often modified. Manga are translated and adapted into French and are sometimes subject to more substantial changes such as the reversal of the reading direction, changes in boards and frames or various types of "censorship". Even though the publication standards implemented from the 2000's on are more respectful of the original work and the reading direction, the relative recognition of manga is nevertheless associated with a number of changes such as an additive introduction, a body of footnotes or a glossary.[1] "Manga" does not refer exactly to the same media and reading experiences in France and in Japan, and the word "manga" does not have the same meaning for all the Japanese generations that use it: the Japanese born before World War II "define manga as a satirical comic strip or as a comic strip with a critical or political nature, published in the press"; "for the following generations, this word alludes to the Edo period's etchings" (Koyama-Richard 2007, 7). The bound volumes of specific titles are not referred to as manga but as komikku (in the plural form komikkusu) (Allen and Ingulsrud 2009, 3). The term "comics" has been used since the 1960's in the titles of some magazines, in particular those intended for young adults, so as to differentiate them from entertaining manga for children (Allen and Ingulsrud 2009, 42–46). In Europe and in the United States, manga is the standard term used to refer to the bound volumes distributed through bookshop networks, and manga is almost exclusively published in this format.

Nevertheless, even though these printed works are no longer subject to the mediations specific to the Japanese field of cultural production, a large part of the narrative, gender-related and graphical characteristics of manga, remains embodied in the formats' materiality made available in France. Moreover, outside the French manga publishing industry, Japanese manga and magazines

1 In the appendices, this book offers a glossary of the most commonly used terms related to the manga and the Japanese animation universe.

 | DOI:10.1163/9789004548312_003

are available in specialized bookshops, *via* mail order trading and in digital form on the Internet. Given the short time frame within which amateur teams of scanlation or fansub translate manga and on account of the competition among French publishers, France's manga publication calendar tends to be closer to Japan's publication calendar of bound volumes. Some chapters of scanned manga happen to be available even before the release of the Japanese magazine (Pigeat 2012) in which they are going to be published afterwards. The Japanese publishing and gender-related categories are used in France, even though they are likely to be reinterpreted. The specialized knowledge built in the Japanese field of the "manga critics" and the references, the products and the practices related to the amateur manga world and the "otaku culture", spread throughout the world and this spread has been and is still fostered by the Internet. The strategies implemented by French pusblishers are to some extent linked to the changes in the manga's symbolic status in Japan: the republication (policy) of "classics" by Osamu Tezuka, Shigeru Mizuki, Leiji Matsumoto and other famous mangakas, the forms of "heritage status" manga are subjected to (exhibitions, creations of museums and libraries, interventions of Japanese government agencies, as part of a cultural diplomacy taking from now on manga into account) are some examples of "legitimacy resources" that play a role in France. Manga is at the heart of the Japanese cultural industry (Bouissou 2010, 91–110) and is associated with a galaxy of media, forms of entertainment and "consumer culture".

1 "One Thousand Years of Manga" or "Sixty Years of Manga"? Definitions and Search for Origins

According to Brigitte Koyama-Richard, an expert in Japanese culture and a professor of comparative literature and history of art at the Musashi University in Tokyo, manga dates back to the previous millennium (Koyama-Richard 2007), whereas Paul Gravett, a journalist and a cartoon critic, argues that manga has been existing for a mere century (Gravett 2006). These widely diverging periodizations are associated with differing definitions of manga. However, they both fall within a search for the origins of manga. To a large extent, the current production of discourses and knowledge pertaining to manga is derived from the worldwide success earned by this kind of comic strips. Following an era (1980–1990) when public discourses dealt with "social problems" or "moral panic", this production is nowadays often driven by symbolic stakes of cultural recognition. Since the 1960's, there has been in Japan a secondary literature and a field of research dedicated to "manga studies" (Berndt 2010). Since the early

2000's, in France and in the United States, supporting discourses on manga are no longer confined to fans or the specialised press. Manga is indeed dealt with in mainstream or academic books, in dictionaries, encyclopedias, operation manuals and in illustrated books. The historical narratives build a traditional register of legitimization that ought to be roughly described here insofar as they embody the conflicting views associated with the term manga in France.

The writings of numerous histories of manga, in Japan and in France, are twofold: manga is either considered as fitting into the Japanese cultural traditions, the history of graphic arts and Japan's visual culture or it is considered as a step in the world history of comic strips seen as autonomous modes of expression, depending on how manga is defined. As Brigitte Koyama-Richard points out, in the Kojien dictionary of Japanese, "manga" is defined as follows: "1. Simple, humorous and exaggerated drawing; 2. Caricature or social satire; 3. Series of images building a story: comics". The term manga was coined by joining two Chinese characters and it literally means "aimless picture" or "quick draft". According to Shimizu Isao, an historian of manga, "manga" was originally the abbreviation for *manpitsu-ga* ("chaotic or sinuous essayistic writing") (Berndt 2009, 211). The term manga was used at the end of the eighteenth century in drawing or illustrated books such as *Mankaku zuihitsu* by Kankei Suzuki, published in 1771, or *Shiji no yukikai*, by Kyoden Santo, published in 1798, the popularity of which is said to have made possible for the term "manga" to gain public recognition (Kern 2006, 140). "Manga" refers to sketches, drawings or caricatures (Kern 2006, 142), or more specifically to "the fact of drawing all kinds of things *via* all kinds of techniques, and the collection of drawings produced in this process" (Miyamoto 2003). Random drawings are published and referred to as manga as well, such as the *Korin-manga catalog* (1817), published as the painter Ogata Korin died (Berndt 2009, 212), *Manga hyakujo* by Minwa Aikawa (1814) and *Hokusai Manga*, by Katsuhika Hokusai, that are drawing handbooks:

> A real encyclopedia based on images, *Manga* is a surprising set with more than eight-hundred pages, nearly four-thousand motifs, gathered in volumes published between 1814 and 1878. Representing (the) things and the living, human and animal, natural and surnatural world, *Manga* turns out to be a valuable iconographic record. [...] It would therefore be sketches the execution of which is based on inspiration, freely and without order, sketches quickly drawn on various subjects, rough outines, impromptu drawings.
>
> BOUQUILLARD and MARQUET 2007, 9–10

Hokusai's book is therefore a "drawing manual", a "collection of models" designed for "painters and craftsmen". The term manga does not only refer to a restricted category of books amid the extremely diversified graphical production characteristic of the Edo era, a time when poetry and calligraphic prose often mingled with painting.

The second meaning of manga is "comic and satirical pictures drawed in a simple style" (Miyamoto 2003). This short form of manga emerged between 1850 and 1920, that is at the end of the Edo era and at the beginning of the Meiji era. It fits within the tradition of the satirical press cartoons. Beside the one-framed press cartoons, all of the comic strips containing four or five pictures, either ironic or absurd, are generally lumped together under the generic term okashisa manga, or humoristic comic strips, and they still can be seen today in the major Japanese daily newspapers. This type of manga is characterised by its short form and the following role:

> Reading a comic strip must give rise to laughter in the broadest sense: this can be a smile, bitter laughter, burst of laughter, naughty or mocking laughter.
>
> TAMBA 1997, 171

This short form of comic strip has now found its place in magazines and press publications based on Western models. Japan experienced then a "publishing boom":

> The commercial dimension of the press activity can not be ignored. Newspapers are becoming products intended to make money. This requires to increase sales, lower prices, improve industrial manufacturing.
>
> LOZERAND 2005, 219–220

Political press cartoons and caricatures appeared then in press publications, and in magazines or specialized newspapers, such as *Japan Punch* (1862), *Marumaru Chimbun* (1877), *Toba-e* (1887).

In the 1920's and 1930's, a third meaning of the term "manga" began to spread, in reference to the comic strips published by the cartoonist Kitazawa Rakuten (1876–1955), who worked in the comic strip section of the newspaper *Jiji Shinpo*. In 1902, a column relating to the "manga news" (Jiji manga) was created as part of this newspaper. Between 1921 and 1931, Kitazawa's Jiji manga became a Sunday color supplement. In 1905, Kitazawa created his first own magazine, the *Tokyo Puck*, drawing his inspiration from the US magazine *Puck* and the *Rire* français, both humoristic weekly magazines. Kitazawa's Jiji was released two or three times a month and included texts in Japanese, Chinese and English, caricatures and a six-board manga by Kitazawa (Bouissou 2010, 39–49). In the 1920's, newspapers, that were topping off their empires, started to publish periodicals. Weekly magazines requested the popular authors' services, and popular literature soon became a decisive issue, both economic and cultural (Sakai 2000). Manga became an integral part of youth newspapers too and magazines entirely dedicated to manga began to be released. In 1908, Kitazawa Rakuten published *Furendo* (Friends), a color magazine intended for children only. Following this successful experience, he created in 1914 *Kodomo no tomo*, a periodical. Kodansha, the largest publishing house for youth, created the first full line of magazines for youth by launching *Shonen Club*, intended for boys up to junior high school (1914), then *Shojo Club* for girls (1923), and *Yônen Club* for the youth (1926) (Bouissou 2010, 44). Comic book folk heroes emerged in that era too, in various formats such as playing cards and dolls. Women's magazines such as *Shufu no tomo* (the housekeeper's friend) and *Fujin Kurabu* (the women's club) also released manga designed for their specific respective readerships.

In 1947, the publication of the comic book *New Treasure Island* (Shin Tarakajima) by Tezuka played a significant role in the creation of the story-manga, the "narrative manga" that gained a foothold after World War II. He favored storytelling over burlesque, sharpened the characters' psychological profile and set new standards in terms of esthetics, including cinematic techniques, such as variations in sightings and shots: whereas characters were often drawn full-length, in a head-on and centered way, Tezuka varies the points of view, uses a lot of zooms and displays a single action on several tens of panels (Hébert 2009). As far back as the mid 1950's, Tezuka built up his success with *Mighty Atom*, *Kimba the white lion*, *Princess Knight*, and mainly dedicated himself to producing sagas prepublished in various monthly youth magazines. There are numerous interactions between manga and animation in Tezuka's sources of inspiration and creation. In the 1950's and 60's, ties were established between the publication of magazines, the publishing of bound volumes, the broadcasting of cartoons, the production of full-length animation films, and the boom of derivative products.

The manga's materiality and the specificities of their "contents" are closely linked to the historical construction of the genre and to the manga production mode, which levelled off in the 1980's after two high growth decades.

2 Production Process and Manga Specificities

2.1 *The Effect of the Production Process*

The concept of manga that established itself in Japan after World War II and the very rationalized and competitive manga production process make it possible to understand the narrative structure and the graphical representations specific to manga. Manga "shares properties with most mass market consumer goods and its generic characteristics [...] is associated with a very low independence from the economic field. These characteristics result in a dependency on market conditions" (Boltanski 1975, 37). Some indicators pertaining to manga production and distribution show manga's dependency on economic constraints and on the audience's attitude. These indicators include harsh competitive practices and high frequency of publication, opinion polls in the form of vouchers (available in each publication) which readers can send back and that decide on whether a manga series will continue to be published or not; the weekly best-seller lists; a production built on a rational organization of teamwork ; the major role played by release managers (*tantô,* which are equivalent to English-language publishers); licence agreements and rights assignment with animation studios, advertising executives, broadcasters, toys or video games manufacturers whose role is to make the biggest profit possible out of a manga series or a specific character.

Manga's narrative effectiveness, which is in part due to this production process, is first and foremost related to the fact that manga are delivered on a weekly basis in magazines. In this respect, each episode has to be a focus with particular attention paid to the *hiki* (catcher) and the cliffhanger, a dramatic element the objective of which is to attract readers waiting for the next publication. Otherwise, sales may decrease due to the manga's declining popularity. This pressure also explains why the focus is on the most spectacular aspects of the narrative, including "fights with a knife, crowd scenes, natural cataclysms, love games and the appearance of monsters" (Groensteen 1993, 43). The concern for effectiveness is also illustrated by the narrative conventions meant to represent motion and speed (several movements are represented in one picture, speed lines focus on the action, blur effects are also involved in the process) (Sigal 2003, 222), the influence of cinematographic and visual codes makes it possible to emphasize relatability and participation in the action. The narrative and graphical structure is closely linked to the attention paid to the representation of the characters and the intensification of their emotions. The underlying idea is to foster an "ordinary" or "participative" reading based on the attention paid to faces.

Osamu Tezuka used and systematized some of the conventions implemented in the world of the North American animation that can be seen as absolute expressiveness codes. They include enlarged faces compared to the size of the body, big eyes, and « esthetics based on roundness ». Relatability is made possible through the fact that manga series unfold in the long run, with characters growing older and readers may witness their development starting from childhood, then adolescence and to adulthood. The production and reception of these manga, on a weekly or monthly basis, are associated with a complex layout of timeframes: *via* the plot developments, offering various disclosures, characters get older at the same time as readers, as new volumes are released. This enables a strong reader loyalty.

2.2 *The Categorization of Readers*

2.2.1 Targeting Readers

In France, manga are available directly in pocket size books (*tankobon*), and not in their original form of chapters in prepublication magazines. However, this logic, similar to that of serials, shows through when one reads the bound volumes compiling the chapters previously published in the press. Most publishing houses import the categorization and sequencing system for the target audience, another way of framing receptions and boosting sells.

There are three main types of specialized magazines which can be classified according to the target readership's age and gender: shonen magazines aimed at boys, shojo magazines aimed at girls, seinen magazines aimed at adults. A more forensic dividing would result in six types of manga: periodicals for children (*kodomo manga*), for young boys (*shonen manga*), for young girls (*shojo manga*), for older teenagers/young adults (*seinen manga*), for teenage girls and young women (*seijin josei manga*), for adults (*seijin manga*) (Allen and Ingulsrud 2009, 3).

2.2.2 Age and Gender Group: Segmentation and Hybridization

The categorization by age or gender does not cover a thematic categorization: the various literary genres such as the adventure story, the chronicles of everyday life, the sentimental comedy and humor, come in every type of publications and neither action nor romance or even horror are only intended for shojo magazines or shonen and seinen magazines readers (Suvilay 2006). Nevertheless, some consistent patterns can be identified in narrative mechanisms and character systems refer to the target readership: thus, the sex and age of the main character often match those of the target readers.[2] In the shonen publications, most of the time, the same narrative form is used with a great deal of variations, in particular in the publications of the *Shonen Jump*, the flagship magazine of the publishing house Shueisha:

> In order to attract a young male readership keen on action, the shonen genre relies on readily identifiable and nearly unchanging codes. The *nekketsu* ("boiling blood") genre is in the foreground. It is defined by a kind of golden rule: friendship, sense of effort, community spirit, self-transcendence [...] The earliest series of nekketsu manga were sports manga, such as *Captain Tsubasa* that glorifies the values associated with the *nekketsu* genre. However, it was later superseded by adventure and quest stories such as *Dragon Ball* and its direct successors: *One Piece* and *Naruto*. Recently, the sports thematic was extended to board games (*Yu Gi Oh!, Hikaru no go*), which significantly reinvigorated the genre. Historical narratives feature prominently (*Kenshin*), as well as investigation stories (*Conan*).
>
> RAYNAL, HAYEK and MEKO 2004, 34

There are two other types of shonen manga: humor and the sentimental comedy. Since the 1970s, sentimental shonen and seinen have been booming. In the 2000s "the new shonen" (*Full Metal Alchemist, D.Gray-Man, Death Note, Kekkaishi, Black Butler*...) focused rather on the characters' esthetical and psychological traits and offered a more straightforward approach of death, with stories taking place in dark universes, often gothic or full of shinigamis (Japanese gods of death), "whereas in shonens the focus was rather on action and characters who had died did not remaïn dead for a very long time" (Cino, Penedo and Méko 2010, 53).

A large part of the shojo production is characterized by "romance in all its forms: tragedy or comedy, ranging from historical narratives to the most mundane everyday life stories, from realistic stories to fantasy stories, from roman-fleuves to one-shots" (Raynal, Hayek and Méko 2004, 35). Even though the equivalent of the nekketsu also exists in the shojo genre, the genres range on a much broader scale than in the shonen. Shojo even includes horror manga (Nouhet-Roseman 2011, 140).

---

2 However, in some shonen manga heroines may be the main protagonists, for example in *Soul Eater* and shojos have been featuring male protagonists for a long time.

The distinction between shojo and shonen is not only about the polarity between action and sentimental relationships, and the sentimental comedies intended for boys and those for girls differ rather through "a number of formal features: point of view and gender of the main character, the tone used to deal with sentimental relationships" (Suvilay 2006, 167–168). In both genres, the main characters share similar traits: shonen and seinen feature "clumsy, shy, indecisive" trite boys, middle school, high school or college students with "no love experience and having experienced a great deal of sentimental failures" and "the seemingly ordinary and hopeful teenage girl". As a matter of fact, the narrative device of the "love triangle" is used as well in sentimental comedies intended for girls as in those for boys:

> The boy shonen hero, shy and not at ease with himself, faces two opposite and complementary incarnations of femininity: the unattainable beauty and the good friend. As for her, the girl is cute, but not very self-confident. She happens to be torn between two boys, one of whom is often charismatic, dark and mysterious and the other one is the unreachable buddy.
>
> JULÉ 2005

Manga is characterized by a dual process of segmentation and hybridization that Annie Collovald and Erik Neveu had noticed concerning crime literature (Collovald and Neveu 2004, 72). According to them, the specificity of crime literature is to offer the readers genres that are relatively distinct from one another and a significant mix of these genres at the same time. Humor can be found in adventure mangas, or horror in crime fiction manga. Some "markers" of a manga subgenre, such as *mecha* (Suvilay 2004),[3] can gradually invest in other genres, or mecha stories become more complex and incorporate more pronounced psychological or sentimental elements.[4] We can thus identify a process of psychologization in particular in the series *Evangelion*, which features a weak-willed and prone to introspection. The series *Evangelion* paved the way to characters that are "depressive and mired in their past, or carrying

3 Short for the English term "mechanics", mecha is a very common term in Japan. It refers to all the various machines, robots, but also vehicles, electrical or mechanical devices. In the Japanese animation where mecha is pervading, the *robotto anime* is a genre of its own. Generally, mecha refers to cartoons in which one or several giant robots appear. This genre of Japanese science-fiction initially intended for a male and teenage audience tends to spread to all anime productions".

4 The evolution of the robot anime genre is analyzed in the article by Bounthavy Suvilay. This has some similarities with the psychologization process analyzed by Éric Maigret about the superhero comics published in *Strange* (Maigret 1995).

a painful secret" breaking with the epic and manly heroism of the heroes of *St. Seyiia* or *Captain Tsubasa*" (Sigal 2003, 63–67). The hero's psychologisation is concomitant with their graphic transformation:

> No more big muscles, the new shonen hero is long-limbed (sometimes even skinny) and dark. […] A hero with a more tortured mind is likely to be prone to more soul-searching and therefore more blathering.
>
> BAHU-LEYSER and NAUMANN 2008, 8–9

Similarly, graphic codes previously devised and fortified in some subgenres may spread subsequently more widely. Some porn manga codes spread in sentimental comedies of shonen manga intended for teenagers, and the most popular shojo manga make occasional nods to yaoi themes,[5] suggesting ambiguous relationships between male characters. "Trends" periodically cross all genres, such as the theme of vampires or the occult. Several phenomena participate in this circulation of references, graphic codes and narrative formulas: the very harsh competition between weekly magazines; the circulation of authors between the different pre-publication magazines, from shojo to shonen, or from shonen to seinen; the successive or simultaneous creation of shojo, shonen, and seinen series by the same author; the circulation of the same series between several magazines, or strategies to broaden the audience, such as the one that consists in integrating male characters who meet certain standards of beauty favored by female readers (Vicky 2006, 243–247) into shonen manga. The shonen's renewal is also linked to the arrival of women mangakas like Hiromu Arakawa (*Full Metal Alchemist*) or Katsura Hoshino (*D. Gray-Man*). Since manga now has a long history and "classics", internal references and forms of parody, the manga readers' and creators' mise en abyme processes have also multiplied, targeting the segment of connoisseurs and otakus, and beyond, as evidenced by the success of the manga *Bakuman*, which features a schoolboy dreaming of becoming a mangaka.

2.3 *The Rise of the Manga Cultural Industry in Japan*

The very process of manga production inserts manga in constellations, in which television programs, magazines, the digital universe and music participate, all forming a powerful cultural industry.

5 Yaoi is a genre intended for female readers, featuring sentimental relations and sexual intercourse between men.

As early as in the 1960's, a very close link was created between the manga publishing, the TV animation, the industry of games and by-products, and advertising, laying the "media mix" foundations. The producers of anime often choose the titles that proved successful among manga readers or video games amateurs, so as to lower the risks taken on the animation market. Nevertheless, adapting manga into cartoons is not the only strategy implemented (Azuma 2008, 70):[6] a manga can also be adapted from a cartoon, a video game, a novel, or even an advertising mascot, as part of the secondary commercial exploitation of titles that proved successful. A visual and narrative universe, a large range of characters may circulate through all these formats, according to a fluid order and chronology. The plots depicted may vary depending on the broadcasting formats, in particular between manga and anime, in so far as different teams are in charge of the creation process in each case and because the production and broadcasting rates as well as the target audiences are not the same.

Beyond this repertory of virtual and drawn characters, a great deal of the animation world's professionals take part in the production and the manga recognition. Many mangakas, be they directors or chara-designers for instance, are recognised as artists, whose projects are followed by amateurs. The latter can also admire their works in *art-books*. In Japan, the dubbing of animated characters is also considered as a real artistic job: seiyus are popular characters who can win fame with songs. The interactions with the music industry (via generics, background musics, the singers' participation in dubbing, musicals adapted from succesful manga or anime, manga or anime dedicated to music) and TV series (dramas, TV series featuring actors who are sometimes singers and dubbers as well) have gained ground since the 1970's. These interactions between media contributed to make the musical style of the *visual kei** popular in France. These ties pave the way for "fan cultures" focused on "icons" along with various musical styles and fashions.

Since the 1980's, the links between successful shonen manga and video games have played a decisive role.[7] Adventure and fight manga are often transposed in the form of fight and adventure games (*Dragon Ball* and *Dragon Ball Z, Hokuto no Ken, Naruto, Berserk, HunterXHunter, One Piece, Bleach* … were adapted on a great number of video game consoles). The same goes for sport

6 Hiroki Azuma even says that "what is predominant now is the multimedia product. On the current market […], the "classic" order according to which an original manga is first adapted in cartoon, then in manufactured products and published fanzines, no longer applies".

7 In Japan, there are video games adapted from manga for girls. However, only a few of them were marketed in France.

manga. In most "beating" games, the narrative dimension is often outshined in favor of a characters' valorisation, their powers and their fights. The opposite trend consisting in a manga publishing house or an animation studio adapting a video game is frequent as well. More broadly, video games feature cinematic sequences similar to the Japanese animation or characters inspired by the manga aesthetics. Finally, a large range of Japanese computer games were also adapted in the form of manga, such as the "dating simulation games" which are simulation games the objective of which is to nurture a sentimental relationship with a female character, or the "visual novels" which are softwares designed for entertainment offering "illustrated stories". Games with more sexually explicit content (known as the *eroge*) were also adapted in animation series or manga.

Even though the spread of this format's constellation does not occur in the same order and on the same scale in France and in Japan, where formats are the objects of highly-developed and integrated forms of marketing, the interest for all these cultural products has gained ground in France. Of course, Japanese video games, cartoons and manga are the most famous formats. However, a more recent craze has been going on for Japanese forms of music and fashions pertaining to manga. In France too, manga are "embedded" in a wide range of media and by-products. As we shall see, the various supports involve mutual requests that have effects on the French contemporary teenagers' reading practices.

2.4 *Manga Spread and Reception in France: From Media Panic to Recognition*

The discourses about manga, in particular in the media, contribute to shape the receptions and the ways of reading, via a process of social construction of the audiences and public concerned (Proulx 1998, 10). In the mid 1990's, the "Manga phenomenon" and the controversies arisen about it reached a peak. *Envoyé Spécial, Lignes de mire, 52 sur la Une, Arrêt sur images, Nulle part ailleurs, La grande famille, Le monde de Léa, Déjà dimanche, Bas les masques, Tout est possible,* are examples of mainstream French TV shows dealing with the Manga phenomenon between 1994 and 1997, and half the topics concerning manga in the news were concentrated on these four years (according to a study conducted in the National Audiovisual Institute).

The production of discourses on manga fits first and foremost in a rationale for building a public matter. In 1996, an article published in *Le Monde Diplomatique* explained the "compulsive" reading of manga by the fact that they are easy to read and involve a "hypnotical suggestion":

> The style, surprisingly statical and syncopated, as well as the choice of angles, often compel the viewer or reader into a face-to-face encounter with characters the pain, resentment or bewilderment of whom we contemplate. The eyes' intensity and fixity are hypnotic and children are caught by these gazes staring at them with a snigger and that seem to want to meditate on them as the Gorgon once did.
>
> LARDELLIER 1996, 29

As of 1988, the French highbrow TV magazine *Télérama* expressed criticism against *Club Dorothée*, a famous youth TV program (1987–1997) that aired many Japanese cartoons on the main French private TV channel. The magazine blamed manga, considering them as a second-rate form of entertainment. *Télérama* blamed manga for being violent and stupid. They even used the slanderous term "japoniaiseries"[8] to refer to manga. In the wrtings of Liliane Lurçat, a psychologist, children's ties with TV and manga are described as an "enchantment", a form of "assented somnambulism" and an "emotional bombing" (Lurçat 1981, 1994, 1995). The publishing phenomenon arising from the large manga spread is seen as an unbridled proliferation:

> However, for one year already, Europe has been witnessing an invasion of comic strips (and cartoons) of a new kind: manga. Originating from Japan, they are characterized by a chronic violence, an appalling simplicity, and a disputable ideology. [...] Children are the main targets of this settlement.
>
> BOSCHE 1996, 14

In concrete terms, this public issue gave rise to a number of condemnations on manga and Japanese cartoons by the Audiovisual Monitoring Commitee and the Supervisory Commission of publications intended for young people. In 1996, five mangas were banned under article 14 of the law of July 16 1949 due to their "violent and pornographic nature". In addition to erotic manga, *Dragon Ball* was also seized by the Belgian police, and the representatives of the French publisher Glénat were interviewed in a criminal investigation opened by the public prosecutor's office of Brussels for "outrage of modesty", "child pornography" and "incitement to paedophilia" (De Muelenaere & Vandemeulebroucke 1997).

---

8 This pejorative term was coined in the middle of the XIXth century by joining the two French words "japonais" (Japanese) and "niaiserie" (silliness). It appeared once more in 2002 on *Télérama*'s cover in a special report entitled: "The Manga craze: art or Japonaiserie?" (n°2745, August 24 2002).

The reasons why manga were disapproved of are also cultural and aesthetic. Manga is considered as a mediocre commercial product and many people establish a hierarchy between manga on the one hand, and Japanese literature or Franco-Belgian comics on the other hand. "A beautiful aesthetic product" according to some people, "gaudy covers competing with bad taste, recycled paper with washed out colors, mediocre drawing" (Duval 1991) in other people's view ... A social labeling of the Japanese productions was thus elaborated, which made it impossible for them to integrate "the area of the European titles which had become that of the recognition and the cultural transmission between generations" (Maigret 1999, 251).

The first phase of manga's cultural trajectory in France was thus marked by media representations of manga readers seen as suffering from various kinds of pathology or addiction, attracted by sex and violence, bad taste (manga readers were even sometimes considered as illiterate). Based on interview surveys, the objective of our study is to compare the effective manga reception with the "fictions of audiences" created by some media.

Mapping the manga publishing offer in the 2000s also allows us to assess the processes of cultural recognition associated with the professionalization of this sector. Presenting the manga publishing sector is necessary insofar as the teenagers' reading practices are also determined by the existing offer and the "reading pacts" that it involves.

3 Mapping the French Manga Market

Contrary to other European countries, The French editorial market is characterized by a particularly diversified offer of cartoons. The French and European trend dates back to the 19th century, there has been US comics since the 1930's and manga came into being in the 1990's. For a long time, European and American comics were distributed as press products, and it was not until the 1970s and 1980s that the comic book format, distributed in bookstores, replaced the forms of serialized pre-publication of comics in "small formats" or in magazines distributed in newsstands:

> At the end of a half-century evolution that can roughly be traced back to the turn of the 1930s (with, in particular, the first Tintin albums), the comic book album became a specifically European cultural form that can be distinguished from Japanese and North American media.
>
> GABILLIET 2005

These changes in formats and channels of distribution were associated with the comics' cultural recognition's process, and the steady increase of the average price of a comic book. Thus, due to their format, manga are really different from European comic books and they are more similar to traditional popular French comic books or to pocket-format books (Lesage 2019). However, in France, manga are first and foremost bookshop products. In the 1990's, two magazines including the prepublication of manga were rather successful (*Kaméha*, published by Glénat, *Manga Player*, published by Média Système Édition), but subsequent attempts came to a sudden end (*Magnolia*, published by Tonkam, *Shonen Mag*, published by Pika, *Shogun Mag* published by Les Humanoïdes Associés, *Akiba Manga*, by Ankama Press). Even though some manga were released in the form of comic books, sometimes colored, in the French reading direction, such as *Akira* in 1989, or some works by Taniguchi, the pocket-format bound volume (that equals more or less to the Japanese tankobon format), distibuted in bookshops, with a "reverse" reading direction, is the most widespread format. For one series, the frequency of publication can be up to six to seven volumes every year. Thus, manga played a particular role within the field of the French cartoons, that was characterized in the 1990s by another series of changes (Beaty 2007): implementation of the international standard of the graphic novel, breaking with the comic book format "48CC" (48 pages, hard cover), rise of the "nouvelle bande dessinée" (new comic books) (Dayez 2004) within small publishing structures, followed by conventional comic books publishers. The manga publishing offer, as well as reading practices made sense in this renewed cultural landscape. Manga also contributed to reshape this publishing sector, giving rise to new formats and new topics within the French and European comics universe. In this process a "French manga" or "hybrid manga" emerged.

3.1 *Field Structuring*

In the 1990's, the manga sector was built around small-scale publishing structures created by amateurs or bookshops owners such as Tonkam, Végétal Manga, and Samouraï, medium-sized publishing houses (Glénat) or publishing houses specialized in pocket format books (J'ai lu). These publications, closely linked to the success of cartoons broadcast in TV youth programs (*Club Dorothée* on TF1, the main private TV channel; *Youpi, L' école est finie* on La Cinq, *Récré A2* on Antenne 2, the main public TV channel) bore the cost of the controversies regarding manga and Japanese anime, the break in transmission of la Cinq and the *Club Dorothée*. At the end of the 1990s, the gradual break in transmission of these cartoons caused a marked decrease in manga sales. In the early 2000s, the French manga publishing sector was characterized by a rationalization and a diversification of the offer and by a concentration of the publishing offer (repurchase of Tonkam et Soleil by Delcourt, of Pika by Hachette, of Asuka by Kazé and then by Shogagukan-Shueisha Productions, launching of the collection Kurokawa by Univers Poche/Editis). Thus, the early 2000s were marked by the transition towards a new publishing setup involving an expansion process in terms of titles published, publishers concerned and market segments. The two high-growth periods from 1993 to 1996, and from 2002 to 2006, were characterized by an increase in the number of titles published every year and in the number of publishers moving into the manga sector. The "peak in 2008, with nearly 12,5 millions of copies sold" (Guilbert 2011) was followed by a period of "stagnation, or even a drop in sales" (Walter 2011, 63). Anne-Laure Walter describes this "downturn" as the standardization of the manga sector "taking on all the features of a traditional publishing sector" (Walter 2010, 71). French publishers redirected their strategy by taking the following measures: rise in prices, tightening of the production and development of derivative products, republications to keep the bookshops' collections "alive", collector's editions of flagship titles, partnerships with the general press, targeting adult and young children readers, contracts with French, European and even Japanese authors, digital manga projects (Walter 2011, 64–68). In 2010, comics translated from Japanese, Korean and Chinese accounted for 38,76 % of the new comics released (Ratier 2011), that is "a little more than a third of total sales in volume, a little less than a quarter in value" (Guilbert 2011). Manga reissues have also been growing since 2004–2005, and the number of books dedicated to manga is also increasing, particularly manga drawing manuals, art books, "beautiful books" on the history of manga or dictionaries and didactic books.

In 2010, 39 French publishers published Asian comics (mainly manga, but also Chinese or Korean comics), against only 22 in 2004 (see graph 1 and graph 2 on next page).

The "big publishers" are the main publishers of French-Belgian comic books, they are opposed to the "alternative" publishers, who essentially publish "graphic novels". Japanese comics (manga) and American comics (comic books) are also distinguished.

In 2000, there were three times as many French-Belgian new publications as new manga and as many manga as graphic novels; in 2010, there were nearly twice more new manga than new alternative publications, and since 2006, the difference between the number of new manga published and the number of new comic strips published by French-Belgian publishers has amounted to nearly four-hundred, to the benefit of manga. However, the portion of manga is not as high as these figures suggest, if we take into account—in addition to new publications—new editions, which account for a large part of French-Belgian

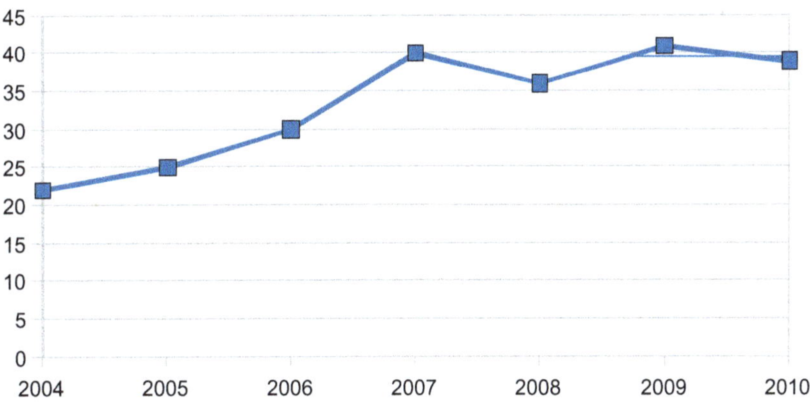

GRAPH 1 Number of French-speaking publishers having published Asian comic strips
DATA FROM THE ASSOCIATION DES CRITIQUES DE BANDE DESSINÉE (ACBD), ANNUAL REPORTS BY GILLES RATIER

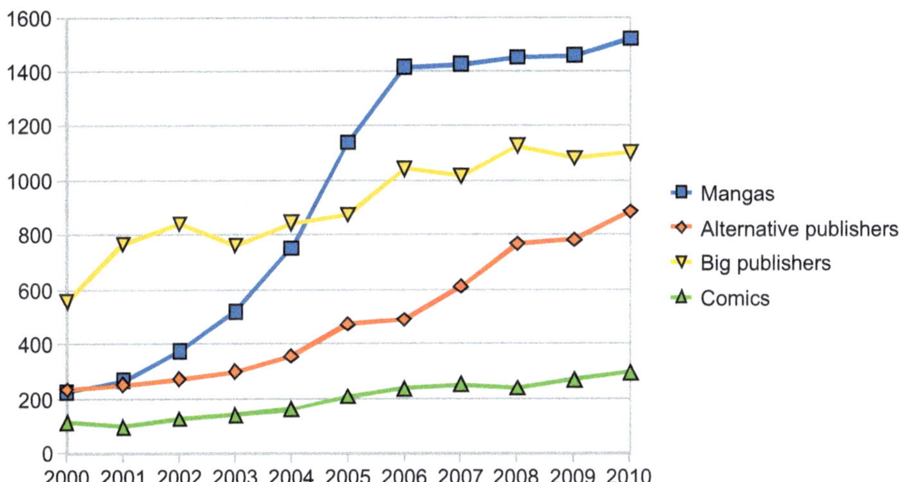

GRAPH 2 Number of new comic book titles published each year, by category
Blue line: mangas; yellow line: big publishers; red line: alternative publishers; green line: comics
DATA TAKEN FROM THE 2010 ACBD REPORT

publications. Likewise, the publisher's typology used for this chart does not really take into account the manga published by alternative publishing houses.

The latter include the collection Écritures published by Casterman, that favors short series, collections and one-shot publications (*The Magic Mountain* by Jirô Taniguchi published in 2007), the Lézard Noir, Vertige Graphic and

TABLE 1 Portion of manga in the comic strips market in France, trend 2001–2010 (%)

	2001	2002	2003	2004	2005	2006	2007	2008	2009	2010
Volume	9,6	11,1	18,5	21,9	27,8	34,2	35,6	37,2	35,6	34,4
Value	6,2	8	12,7	15,3	20	24,4	25,3	26,1	24,6	23

CHART BY XAVIER GUILBERT BASED ON LIVRES HEBDO/I+C DATA FOR THE PERIOD 2001–2010 (GUILBERT, 2011)

Cornélius, that publish a few manga intended for adults every year (in 2010, these publishing houses published two, three and five titles repectively).

A sales figures-based approach makes it possible to round out the above chart that focuses on the number of new publications. Ipsos and Livres Hebdo data allows for a distinction between the manga volume sales figures (number of copies sold) and the manga value sales figures (amount of manga sales). This shows that, even though the portion of manga increased sharply in volume and in value between 2001 and 2010, it showed contrasting trends, reaching a peak in 2008, followed by a downturn. The 2008's peak represented 12,5 millions of copies sold. Manga represents a larger part in volume (accounting for a little more than 33 % of the market) than in value (a little less than a quarter of the market), due to their cheaper price than that of comic strips books.

The chart below points out that, even though the comics' average price increased between 2006 and 2010, the manga's average price remained cheaper than the price of other comics and it increased less sharply. In 2011, the manga's price increase made it possible to mitigate the impact of the decrease of the sales volume on the total revenue.

3.1.1 Today's Publishers

Five manga publishers are being controlled by international major publishing and multimedia groups (Kurokawa/Editis/Planeta de Agostini, Pika/Hachette, Kana/Media-Participations, Panini, Kazé Manga/Shogagukan-Shueisha Productions), and they have the largest market shares. These groups' financial capacity makes it possible for them to negotiate with the Japanese publishers which corner the market (Shueisha, Kodansha, and Shogakukan) and to acquire the rights for the most profitable series (*Naruto, Death Note, Full Metal Alchemist* …). They often did that by implementing multimedia strategies or "cross-marketing" practices. Since the beginning of 2010, the Japanese

TABLE 2 Evolution of mangas and comics' average prices, 2006–2010 (Ipsos data)

	Manga titles	Other comic books titles	All comic books titles
2006	6,39	10,29	8,96
2007	6,58	10,87	9,35
2008	6,65	11,16	9,49
2009	6,78	11,48	9,80
2010	6,81	11,96	10,19
Evolution (2006–2010)	+ 6,6%	+ 16,2%	+ 13,8%

CHART BY XAVIER GUILBERT BASED ON IPSOS DATA PERTAINING TO THE COMICS MARKET (GUILBERT 2011)

publishers Shueisha and Shogakukan have been active in the manga French publishing sector, via their subsidiary Viz Europe, which repurchased the publishers Asuka and Kaze and launched the Kazé Manga publishing house. This strategic position is said to be linked to the manga sector's running out of steam in Japan:

> According to a Tokyo Research Report Institute report, sales decreased by 6,6% in 2009. This was the biggest drop in sales this sector had ever experienced in Japan since its birth. Pre-publication magazines sales alone fell by 9.4 %, which represented a 2-billion-euro loss. This loss of incomes explains why the Japanese publishers were eager to conquer the French manga market, the most important manga market outside Japan.
>
> WALTER 2010, 72

Alongside these "giants", medium-sized "independent" comic book publishers have made room for manga in their catalogs, creating collections or specialized labels (Glénat Manga at Glénat, Akata at Delcourt, Doki-Doki at Bamboo ...). Long established French-Belgian comics publishers have done the same, such as Casterman, since the mid-1990s, or the Lombard editions, in 2011. Since the early 2000s, small "alternative" or "independent" comics publishers have occasionally published manga titles, without having created a specific collection: Cornélius, Le Lézard Noir, Vertige Graphic, IMHO, Ego comme X, 12bis, Atrabile. Literary publishers have also positioned themselves in this specific sector of Japanese comics (Le Seuil, Picquier), as have publishers rather specialized in children's literature (Milan).

There are even small publishing structures entirely dedicated to manga, such as Ki- Oon, Tonkam and Asuka (before their takeover), Taïfu Comics, or publishers specializing in manhua[9] (Xiao-Pan, Paquet) or manhwa (Clair de Lune).[10]

Depending on their size and history, French publishers do not all have access to the same Japanese publishers' catalogs. Given their significant financial power, Kana, Kurokawa, Panini and Pika have been in a position to select titles from the catalogs of Shogakukan, Shueisha and Kodansha publishers for years. Other publishers benefit from their historical legitimacy and relationships established since the early 1990s (Tonkam, Glénat). The other French publishers negotiate with Japanese publishers who are also second-rate players on their national market, or with Korean or Chinese publishers. The publishers of alternative comics or literary publishers turn to the avant-garde magazines *Garo* and *AX* (Penedo 2011, 66–67).

Graph 3a and Graph 3b (next pages) highlight the domination of three manga publishers (Kana, Pika, Glénat), and the rapid reorganization of the sector, with, in two years, a change of order in the top three (Glénat is ahead of Kana, but also Ki-Oon ahead of Delcourt).

Sales remain highly concentrated on a few flagship series:

> Three series alone occupied half of the Ipsos/Livres Hebdo ranking for the period from January to the end of 2010: *Naruto* (Kana) took the lead with 11 ranked volumes; *One Piece* (Glénat) ranked 6th and *Fairy Tail* (Pika) 12th. [...] The concentration of sales on a few "hits" is such that only 17 series are present in the top 50 sales ranking.
>
> WALTER 2010, 82

Publishers are heavily "dependent on a small number of titles": 70 % of Kana or Glénat Manga sales are based on three series (*Naruto*, *Kyo* and *Death Note* for Kana, *Dragon Ball*, *One Piece* and *Bleach* for Glénat Manga). Given the importance taken by manga on the comics market, a considerable part of all these

9 Manhua: Chinese comic book; manhwa : Korean comic book.

10 The thirty-four publishers listed in 2010 are presented in detail on the Mangaverse website's status report 2010: http://www.mangaverse.net/html/bilan/2010/bilan2010.pdf.

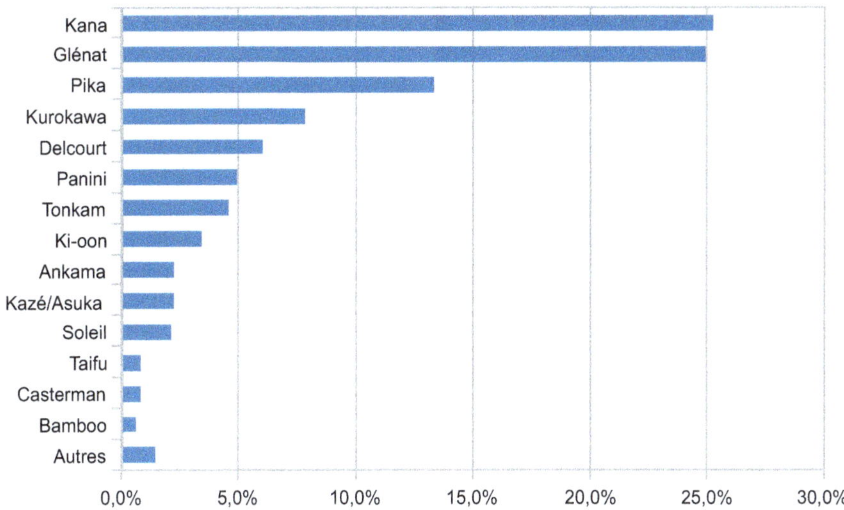

GRAPH 3A Composition of the market: distribution of publishers with a circulation of more than 25,000 copies
Manga publishers' share of sales volume in 2009
GRAPH BASED ON IPSOS/LIVRES HEBDO DATA, SUMMARIZED IN THE 2010 ACBD REPORT WRITTEN BY GILLES RATIER

groups' sales figures (24 % for Média-Participations, 37 % for Glénat) relies on this handful of titles" (Guilbert 2011).

According to Grégoire Hellot,[11] the average profitability of manga titles published in France has decreased in the second half of the 2000's: this period saw an increased polarization of this publishing sector, with blockbuster series on the one hand (*Naruto*, *Full Metal Alchemist*, *Death Note*), and series the circulation and profitability of which are much lower, and decreasing. There are thus "two manga markets" and distinct readerships. On the one hand, there are younger readers with reduced purchasing power, who massively follow the most popular series, with the erosion of this readership over time being compensated for by a continuous emergence of new readers. On the other hand, older readers explore specific segments of the publishing offer, continue with their reading trajectory beyond their middle school years and do not focus only on successful titles and genres.

11 Head of the publishing house Kurokawa (manga collection of Univers Poche), interview conducted in June 2008.

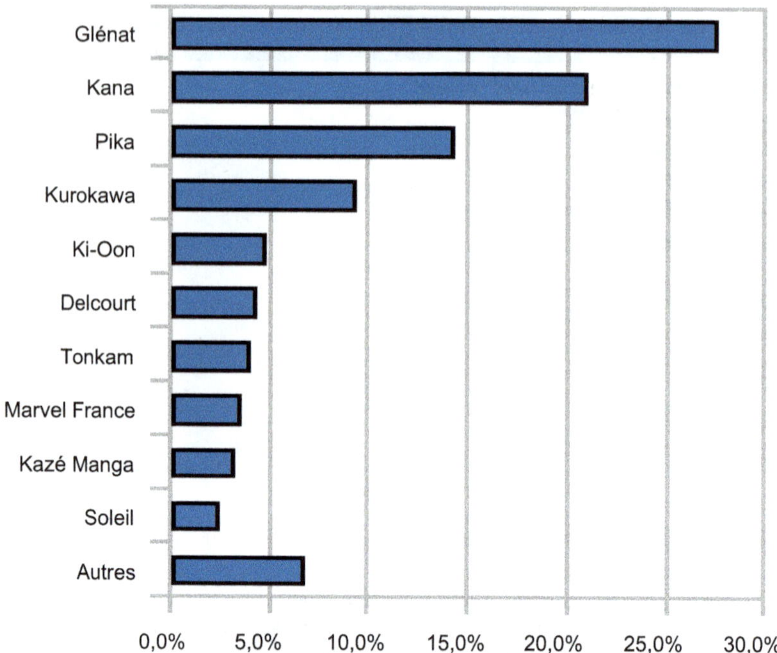

GRAPH 3B Composition of the market: distribution of publishers with a circulation of more than 25,000 copies
Publishers' share of manga sales volume (January-May 2011)
Reading: copies of manga sold by the publisher Kana represent just over 20% of the total volume of manga sales.
GRAPH BASED ON IPSOS DATA (WALTER, 2011, 64)

For many publishers, while shonen are still safe havens, the very high costs of acquiring the most popular titles and the leveling off of sales are resulting in further forms of segmentation. Some are exploring other categories of manga (seinen, josei, yaoi), in order for them not to be caught in the "pitfalls of the race for rights" (Piault 2005) that occurs when it comes to acquiring the most popular manga in Japan. The category of seinen manga is now widely used in the catalogs of most publishers and has multiple uses: seinen aims to support the trajectories of teenage readers coming of age or to attract an older readership, a fan of Franco-Belgian comics or graphic novels. The seinen makes it possible to offer teenagers or adults more erotic,[12] realistic, dramatic or violent content, alongside "author's manga" or "alternative" manga. The main publishers have initiated specific collections: Big Kana at Kana, Seinen Manga at

12 For example, the "Emoi" collections at Tonkam, "Iku Comics" at Soleil, "Senpai" at Pika, and "Pulp!" at Asuka.

Glénat, Gingko at Delcourt, Sakka at Casterman, Senpai at Pika. The published titles are "picked" from Japanese young adult magazines. More recently, the readers' targeting has become more accurate, between shonen and seinen, with "the launching of multiple *young* collection, a positioning that already existed in the manga offer, but which is now clearly labelled":

> This genre was born in Japan when a generation of authors felt the need to reach an older and demanding audience without making seinen (for adults).
>
> WALTER 2010, 76

This publishing category known in France as "young seinen" targets the audience of "high school and college students, that is people aged between 15 and 25", with "darker and more violent stories than in a shonen magazine" (Cino, Penedo and Méko 54).

In a sector long dominated by shonen, publishers have also extended their offer and "repositioned their catalogs" to conquer the female readership. Now, "shojo is becoming an ultra-competitive market with Japanese hits making it possible to make big money". In France, many titles such as *Fruits Basket*, *Nana*, *Otomen* or *Switch Girl* were very successful (Cino 2009, 91). French publishers are exploring other types of women's manga, drawing on Japanese publishing categories that have diversified (young ladies comics and teens love target high school girls and young women and have been incorporated between shojos manga for middle school girls and ladies comics for adult women, even though the boundaries between these manga categories and these age groups have themselves blurred). The josei manga offer, targeting college girls and young working women, has broadened and has benefited from significant recognition in France. The targeting of female readers has become more precise: the Lolita collection, published by Asuka, explores the "mature shojo" and "sexually explicit" world and is placed between shojos targeting 12–16-year-old and lady comics targeting adult women. This collection is aimed at "young women/girls who want to read sensual or even slightly erotic love stories" (Cino 2007, 90) (the collection, created in 2007 was stopped in 2009). The publishing niches that emerged have been, especially since 2008, yaoi and shonen ai (manga for girls featuring relationships between men, ranging from simple sentimental plots to explicit sexual content) (Cino 2008, 45). Tonkam, Taïfu Comics and Asuka have implemented such a publishing policy. In 2009, Asuka launched a yaoi manga prepublication magazine, *BexBoy* (Penedo 2010, 66). However, as Bruno Pham pointed out, in Japan as well as in France "classic shojos targeting teenage girls remained [...] very present in the manga production of the 2000s, with the fantastic and dreamlike vein playing a bigger role" (Pham 2011).

Given the increasing difficulties in accessing the Japanese market, some publishers have turned to the Korean and Chinese market to acquire the rights of series based on manga. However, after a strong expansion in 2003 and 2004, the number of Korean titles (manhwas) has greatly decreased, as readers often prefer manga.

Finally, French publishers may call upon authors themselves to develop collections of "French manga" and thus face the "translated manga" sector, sharing the same format and the same shelves. The publication labels are multiple: "French manga", "manfra", "euromanga", "global manga". The aesthetics of manga and Japanese animation influenced several authors of Franco-Belgian comics or comic books from the 1990s, and the labels "French manga" or "hybrid comic" appeared at that time. The use of this category became widespread in the 2000s and was the subject of a communication policy.[13] This sector is also developing in the United States and in other European countries (Germany, Spain, Italy) and feeds cross-translations. The "original English language manga" (OEL manga) category is well established in the United States (Cha and Reid 2005). The advantages are that publishers have a wider range of rights to the published titles, that the production of these titles is less expensive, but also that the authors are more available for tours, signings and promotional operations. Some French publishers, such as Ki-Oon, even work directly with independent Japanese authors.

In addition to the criteria of segmentation by age, sex and gender, there is sometimes an opposition, more specifically French, in terms of cultural legitimacy, between "author manga" ("manga d'auteur" in French) and "commercial manga". Some manga published in Japan in seinen magazines are presented in France as "manga d'auteur". According to Dominique Véret, the director of Akata, the idea is "to approach manga from very specialized and literary angles, by choosing intelligent titles and not B series". Against the use of the masculine gender, which has been imposed since the introduction of manga in France, Frédéric Boilet, an author of comics and the director of the Sakka collection

13 For example: Pink Diary, by Jenny (Delcourt), Dreamland, by Reno (Pika), L'immeuble d'en face, by Vanyda (La Boîte à Bulles), Vis-à-Vis by Miya (Pika), Sentai School by Florence Torta and Philippe Cardona (Kami), DYS by Moonkey (Pika). The publishers who launched specific collections are, among others Pika, Les Humanoïdes Associés (collection Shogun), Ankama (manga Dofus and collection Dofus Arena), Akiléos (US and Spanish manga), Gekkô.

at Casterman, even suggests reserving the use of the feminine gender for titles that are part of the "arthouse comics":

> It seems to me that a distinction could be made between the masculine manga, that is to say the Japanese comic book for teenagers in vogue, that of rights buyouts, the international market, the media phenomenon and French otakus, and the feminine manga that could be defined as a more mature, more universal and lasting Japanese arthouse comic book, rejected by the major international markets.
>
> BOILET 2001

While the use of the feminine[14] has not become widespread, the principles of legitimacy that underpin the distinction between masculine and feminine manga have been more widely widespread. Since 2003, a series of articles has been devoted to the feminine "arthouse manga", "adult manga" or "alternative manga" (in the following magazines: *9ème Art, Chronic'Art, Bang!, Animeland, Le Virus Manga*). As a result of the glorification of manga, "literary" titles adapted from Japanese novels are sometimes put in the spotlight, such as *Le sommet des dieux* or *Le temps de Botchan*. The legitimation processes involved are sometimes purely French artifacts, as Julien Bastide shows about Taniguchi:

> This mangaka works within the framework of mainstream pre-publication magazines, and thus has nothing of the cultural exception that one would like to see. Just like manga for teenagers, the seinen is well and truly a mass product. It is therefore impossible to oppose two registers in qualitative terms.
>
> BASTIDE, 2004

Thus, the manga *Quartier lointain*, considered in France as a literary manga, an intimist arthouse work, as opposed to commercial manga and their production process, was first released as a saga in a magazine targeting a specific socio-professional category, that of … office workers (Bastide 2004).

Even though from the 1990s the "authors' policy" ("politique des auteurs") first concerned the field of Japanese animation cinema, with the recognition of Hayao Miyazaki or Isao Takahata, it has extended to some mangakas that have been awarded prizes at comic book festivals, such as Jiro Taniguchi,

---

14 Translator'note: "The" in English can either refer to "le" or "la" in French. Frédéric Boilet suggests that a distinction should be made between LE Manga and LA Manga.

Shigeru Mizuki, Yoshiaru Tsuge, Osamu Tezuka, Naoki Urasawa. Some of these manga recognized by critics and the cultural press are published by literary publishers or publishers of alternative comics and they are singled out by their formats and material presentations: larger format (such as 15 × 21 cm, closer to the graphic novel or independent comics standards), high grammage paper, simplicity of covers. The differences of readership target are thus combined with differences in format and price, and sometimes in the classification in the bookshops' shelves (alongside European comics and not other manga).

The identification of the literary, poetic and plastic qualities of some manga titles contributes to their rooting in an artistic and/or comic book universe. Many adult readers with a high level of cultural and academic capital have discovered manga by appropriating this type of "legitimate" solicitation. Manga are also becoming established in libraries, media libraries and library information centers (Baudot 2010). The legitimation of manga as a genre and the generational renewal mean that manga now have a significant place in the reading practices and leisure activities of librarians (especially those under 40) (Benrubbi 2009). Other mechanisms have played an important role in manga's cultural and professional recognition, for instance exhibitions organized in libraries, cultural centers, museums and art galleries, but also conventions and festivals that associate manga and Japanese culture and attract a large audience, often families. There is a significant media coverage on manga when such events take place. On these events manga are a topic covered by the media. Traveling exhibitions also ensure a large widespread of "standardized" knowledge about the history of manga ("Manga in one hell of a state", "Discovering manga", "Better understanding manga", etc.). The "cultural entrepreneurs" who organize these events "popularize" manga and give it "visibility and dignity" (Collovald & Neveu 2004, 101).

3.2 *Outcome*

On the grounds of this set of criteria, it is possible to get an idea of the publishing offer. The first hub, which ties in with the "managerial-commercial hub" described by Erik Neveu and Annie Collovald (2004, 19), dominates the teenager manga market, via the publishing of the most popular series, in terms of sales and variety of multimedia supports. Most of them are major publishing groups with a large print run, the collections of which are mainly focused on shonen. More recently, shojo and seinen have been part of the publishing offer: Kana, Pika, Glénat Manga, Kurokawa, Panini, Doki-Doki, Soleil Manga. Grégoire Hellot, the publication director of Kurokawa, refers to/fosters a policy based on "entertainment" and "mass-marketing", targeting the "general audience". Stéphane Ferrand, the publication director of Glénat Manga, mentions the choice of "unifying titles": he says that Glénat Manga's publishing policy is the same as Glénat BD's, the publisher of *Titeuf.* One might add the French manga publishers to this category (Pika, Humanoïdes Associés).

The second hub consists of the medium-sized publishers providing a diversified offer and developing in parallel publishing niches or more specialized genres (shojo, yaoi, josei, manhwa, manhua ...), among which Tonkam, Akata, Asuka, and Ki-Oon (heroïc-fantasy). Those publishers play on their close ties with fans (via an active Internet policy, or by attending the meetings) and on the register of passion: Asuka, it is "manga in a different manner", Akata, it is "the true nature of manga", Tonkam stands up for "the manga passion".

Finally, the third hub is that of publishers or collections promoting a "legitimate offer" similar to the comic strip or the graphic novel: IMHO, Cornélius, Vertige Graphic, Atrabile, 12bis, Le Lézard noir, Ego comme X, Le Seuil, Picquier, the collections Sakka and Écritures at Casterman. The collection Sakka (meaning "author" in Japanese) is illustrative of this publishing policy aspiring to show "another side of manga". When the collection was first launched, an advertising promised the following: "When you read a Sakka, you're not reading manga." These publishing houses share some authors, such as Jiro Taniguchi, Shigeru Mizuki, Osamu Tezuka, Hazuichi Kanawa, Yoshiaru Tsuge, Kiriko Nananan, on their lists.

Recently, these distinctions have been blurred in so far as publishers now tend to develop shojo and seinen manga collections, along with "patrimonial" collections of manga "classics". For example, the manga by Osamu Tezuka are published by six different publishing houses, from Kana to Cornélius, Pika, Asuka and Tonkam. With the Bunko collection, Glénat, the publisher of *Dragon Ball* and *One Piece* aims to create "the Manga Pléïade" (Piault 2005). In 2007, Kana, the publisher of *Naruto*, also launched the collection Sensei, about "the manga masters". Therefore, it seems obvious that "these three hubs highlight key elements, however they do not make it always possible to attribute a steady and unequivocal position to every publishing house" (Collovald and Neveu 2004, 105). Just as the mainstream French-Belgian comic strip publishers created their own "alternative comic strip" label or repurchased independent publishing houses, the "managerial-commercial hub" publishers are now taking up to "alternative" or "traditional manga" publishing. Winning a prize at a festival, gaining recognition by the critics, having access to the general media or the cultural press are from now on key elements to acquire symbolic capital, even though the award-winning titles are not very profitable.

CHAPTER 2

A Reading Practice Embedded in the Youth Culture

Manga is therefore a diversified sector, constantly changing and restructuring. For sure, the structuring of manga categories, by age or gender, tends to steer receptions and trigger expectations. But what are the real receptions like? Reception studies, whether concerning literature, cinema or television, in France or elsewhere, have shown that it is not possible to deduce the readers' appropriations from the contents of the works. Similarly, the literary or esthetic "quality" of the products is not dependent on such or such reception at all. There is no match between the literary or esthetic quality of a book and the way it is appropriated. Readers may have a detached or identificatory relationship to the narrative, and an introspective and intertextual take on a best-seller. The first cannot be considered as a richer or more elaborate one, albeit it is more valued at school. Gérard Mauger, Bernard Pudal and Claude Poliak distinguished four types of reading (entertainment reading, didactic reading, salvation reading, esthete reading) (1999). However, it seems impossible to link any given type of reading to a specific kind of book. Manga, as we will see, lies at the intersection of these various reception modes, probably just like any other reading.

Taking an interest in the place of manga in the teenagers' leisure practices leads us to analyze more specifically the way they consider reading and the new media. Teenagers, as we know, read less than those of previous generations (Donnat 2009), and turn away from books as they grow older: at the age of eleven, 14,5 % of the respondents said they never or hardly ever read. At the age of fifteen, nearly half of the respondents (46,5%) said they read only a little or not at all (Octobre, Détrez, Mercklé and Berthomier 2010). The part of people that do not read comics rises during the same time, from 2 eleven-year-old children out of ten to six seventeen-year-old teenagers out of ten. Only periodicals benefit from a stable and massive readership.[1] By contrast, they are the first generation to be born with the digital revolution, which substantially changes not only the supply conditions but also the media, the ways in which they are consumed and appropriated, and perhaps as well the imaginary worlds and the references used in more "traditional" activities. Through these practices,

1 72.5% of 11-year-olds read at least once a month, and 78.5% of 13-year-olds, 75% of 15-year-olds and 70% of 17-year-olds do so.

 DOI:10.1163/9789004548312_004

be they traditional or not, teenage years are also characterised by a weaving together of both connections and autonomy, vis-à-vis parents and vis-à-vis the peer group, with these movements following different timelines: "homolatic" withdrawal (Moulin 2005 10–12) allows teenagers to detach themselves from the family filiation, to say, think and exhibit themselves as "young", and is part of the middle school years, before the development of individual "tastes" and practices (Octobre, Détrez, Mercklé & Berthomier 2010). Reading manga is also associated with these inter and intra-generational distinctions. Reading manga is a generation marker and a way to stand out from others, be they other literary genres' readers or even other titles' readers.

The first part of this book will look into the forms of embedding of reading manga into teenagers' spheres of interest and expectations, identifiable in their cultural and leisure practices: manga's accessibility and easy handling in various contexts, are one of the elements that make it easy to read in sofar as manga can be read anywhere at any time. Moreover, manga is part of a constellation made up of TV shows, music and computers, which characterizes the belonging to a specific generation. Last but not least, reading manga fosters sociability, in particular in middle school. On the one hand, peer groups play an active role in passing on the taste for manga, which is associated with pleasure and plays an integrating role in the "youth culture"; on the other hand, the reading experience provides critical resources to take part in the daily sociabilities and to support friendship interactions and relationships, both at school and on the Internet.

1 A Reading Embedded in Teenagers' Schedules

1.1 *Reading Easy and Practical*

Reading manga is embedded in various ways in the interviewed young readers' daily lives. Reading manga takes place in various temporalities and spaces and involves various mobile usage contexts. The manga's size, similar to a pocket book, makes it possible for teenagers to carry manga volumes in their school bags, just as some digital devices. Teenagers can bring manga in with them during their daily travels, and in particular while on their way to or from school. Manga are easy to read and esay to handle at the same time. While some readers admit having at first some difficulties getting used to the Japanese reading direction, they adapat quite quickly to it. When readers begin the second volume, they already have the required skills to read manga. As Hugo puts it:

> The first one is a bit hard because you get lost in the ... because the meaning of the images ... But then, as soon as you start the second one, it's ... easy.
>
> HUGO, 15, 10th grade, parents middle-school teachers

Through the explanations, provided in the paratexte, or through the intermediary of a big brother or sister, the necessary skills are acquired, to the point of then taking over Franco-Belgian comics ... upside down, like Célia or Estelle:

> *And, just a technical question, has reading upside down ever been a problem for you?*
>
> Uh, at first, it didn't bother me. But it was later, when I took a normal comic book, I started reading it backwards (laughs).
>
> CÉLIA, 17, 11th grade, mother an opera director, father a choreographer

> At first, we're sure we're bugging out a little bit. When I read my first manga, I got a little bit of difficulties, and then once you get used to it, it's a piece of cake. Sometimes I even read French comics in the original Japanese reading direction and only realized it after a while because it didn't follow the story.
>
> ESTELLE, 17, 12th grade, father a bank clerk, mother a school nurse

Even though not all manga titles are easy to read, and while some teenagers will insist on the concentration necessary to approach and understand other titles, a whole part of the production, according to teenagers, is characterized by the possibility of quick reading, accessible to all, as Maureen or Nathaniel point out:

> *And did you find them easy to read?*
>
> Ah yes yes yes, it's super simple. Yeah because language is, like, universal, it's super simple, there's no level, uh ... there's no complicated words, there's no ... No, it's really simple; everybody can read it.
>
> MAUREEN, 15, 9th grade, father a worker, mother an administrative officer

> Some are easier to get into. *Naruto* too, it's very simple. *Death Note* too, because *Death Note* is about the importance of human life, it's just: do we need the death penalty. This is what *Death Note* is all about. It's really easy to put yourself in the character's shoes. Most manga are easy to get into, are easy to.
>
> NATHANIEL, 17, 11th grade, raised by his mother, an employment office worker

This is particularly the case for some of the interviewed readers who read only a few or no novels at all. Kevin (13, father a machine operator, mother an accountant-secretary) is in eighth grade, reads very little, has only a few books at home, and says he is very reluctant to read all the books recommended for French classes. On the other hand, Kevin is an avid reader of manga, which he appreciates for their readability compared to other categories of printed material. The limited space for text, the role of the image in narrative, and prior familiarization through anime are all elements contributing to "the lowering of a series of cultural barriers" (Collovald and Neveu 2004, 174):

> It's a little easier to read than real books, because there are fewer things to read … It's easier than a book, you can look at pretty much what they do in manga, whereas in a book you can't see anything. You have to guess.

Nayir has some learning difficulties as well; he repeated his third year and is passionate about manga. Manga is one of the only categories of printed matter he associates with the notion of reading pleasure:

> It's the first thing I really liked about reading. It fascinated me right away, because it was the first thing I read. After that, I kept reading that stuff because I really liked it.
>
> NAYIR, 16, 9th grade, father a delivery driver, mother a housekeeper

Thus, the average reading time is about half an hour per volume, and everyone compares this speed with the time it takes to immerse oneself in a novel. Of course, the images are one of the elements that make reading easy, and Alexandre or Arthur also distinguish the easy access to manga according to the proportion of text and images they include:

> On the other hand, one manga that took quite a long time to read was *Death Note*. It takes me two hours to read a volume, because it's quite concentrated, a lot of text.
>
> ARTHUR, 18, 12th grade, father an executive, mother an accountant

> Reading *Bleach*, I can spend half an hour, and reading Reborn for example will easily take me an hour … because there are a lot of stuff to read in fact.
>
> ALEXANDRE, 17, 11th grade, parents schoolteachers

This speed of reading can also cause some trouble. When you start reading a manga on the bus just after buying it at the bookstore or the supermarket, your reading is most of the time over by the time you arrive home.

1.2 *Reading in Various Contexts*

Above all, manga seems to be adapted to the various temporalities of teenage days and weeks. The dynamism of a visual narrative, the serial aspect of the narration and the way in which manga is published are thus suitable for fragmented reading modes. In the same way that studies in media sociology have highlighted the adjustment of the narrative construction of some serial radio or television shows to distracted consumption in a domestic context (Le Grignou 1999, 108), the material supports and narrative structuring of manga allow for various reading contexts: very mobile and "interstitial", or in a silent room, throughout an evening or a weekend. Manga's various levels of organization, from the box to the page, from the action or humor scene to the whole volume, from the story arc that unfolds over several volumes to the whole volume, lend themselves to reading sequences whose duration can vary: from the ten minutes it takes some people to finish a volume during a first impatient reading or to reread a few particularly appreciated pages, to the rereading of a privileged story arc, to the "marathon readings" of some or all of the volumes of a series. The diversity of possible paths within a manga volume thus allows an adjustment to the temporal constraints of the adolescents interviewed. Paradoxically, it is even those apparently poor conditions for concentration and a traditional vision of reading that makes it easier to get into the manga universe.[2] Léo, for example, takes a school bus to go to his high school very early in the morning and reads manga for three-quarters of the day.

> *Do you bring manga to school, objects, or …?*
>
> Yeah, only manga because on the bus it's dark, you can't work, you can't do nothing. So, I always have a manga in my bag. It's the same thing when I arrive at school in the morning, I am in the very first coach arriving at highschool and my friends are in the last one. So, I spend a lot of time on my own and that's why I always have manga to read.
>
> LÉO, 15, 10th grade, father a commercial executive, mother a librarian

2 Léo considers supermarkets as follows: "For sure, it's noisier, but … it's precisely because there's noise around, that we manage to lock ourselves into the universe right from the start, you see. Whereas when you read alone at home, there's no noise, it's already quiet, so it's already … it's almost … In fact, in supermarkets, you can focus on your reading more easily."

Reading manga is a way of whiling away the hours. Léo reads them on the bus, or at the supermarket while his parents go shopping, Vincente (12) during office hours, Hugo (15) in the evening, when he doesn't know what to do. Cécile reads them in class, "instead of sleeping", or:

> When I don't have class and I don't want to go home and I have an afternoon off, I go to Part-Dieu, or the FNAC or Bellecour[3] or wherever and then I settle down. If I have nothing else to do, yes. If I don't feel like going home.[4]
>
> CÉCILE, 17, 1st year college student, father an executive, mother a private nurse

Reading manga, by investing these moments of transition or constrained idleness, constitutes a "bulwark against boredom", which "fills in the gaps between two activities" (Le Goaziou 2006, 59). However, reading manga is not just about these interstices, and it would be wrong to see them as a substitute for boredom or inactivity. Reading on the bus, when you have just bought or borrowed the latest volume of a title, reading in class so as not to have to break off your reading also points to a much less detached relationship than it might seem at first glance. The suspense caused by the time interval before a new volume is released or before it is possible to borrow it from a friend explains why teenagers are always looking forward to getting a new volume. Matthieu, Lydia and Clara express the thirst for reading manga, which turns out to be enrapturing according to Clara:

> When I bought some manga, I went home, it's borderline to read manga on the street (laughs). When I was in high school, I used to read in high school, in the corridors, in the courtyard. I even read in class (laughs). As soon as I had an hour of study, as soon as I had five minutes, I would read it. While waiting for the teacher in class.
>
> MATTHIEU, 17, 11th grade, parents architects

3 The FNAC is a French retail chain, created in 1954, and specializing in the distribution of cultural and electronic products to the general public. It is known to tolerate "free" manga reading in the manga shelves. Two main shops in Lyon are located in Bellecour square or in the mall near the Part-Dieu train station.

4 Cécile lives at her grandmother's place.

> Actually, what's good is that when you read manga, well, afterwards ... You can't stop, you feel like you're possessed in it, because in fact, you want to know what's next because it's too good.
>
> LYDIA and CLARA, two sisters aged 15 and 11, father a technical executive and mother a baker

> Sometimes I read it in class. I'm not allowed to, but sometimes I do (laughs). In French class. French is not too difficult, so I can take the liberty. In the courtyard, after eating. As soon as I have a new manga, I read it.
>
> MADJI, 19, 11th grade, father a bus driver, stay-at-home mother

Manga are also bedside books that people enjoy reading in the evening before going to sleep, or weekend books that people read by investing time in them. Reading in the evening is a strong symbolic marker (Cahen 2001). Hugo thus has his "record", having read "four volumes in one day, on a Saturday".

In the evening, Célia (17, mother an opera director, father a choreographer) picks "a tome at random, any serie", Jérôme (18, father an electrician, mother an accountant) "snatches a manga before going to sleep", just like Maureen (15, father a worker, mother an administrative officer) does, "quietly, all alone, without anyone around."

1.3 *Reading and Rereading*

As we already mentioned, manga, due to their structure, offer the possibility of various modes of reading. It is thus striking to see how widespread the practice of rereading is among adolescents, both in junior and senior high school. When they borrow or buy a volume, the first reading is quick and eager:

> On the first draft, we're going to be too enthusiastic or we're not going to look at it, I mean we're not going to be focused, we're not going to see the details.
>
> ASHKAN, 18, father a director of a clothing brand, mother a stylist

Then follows a second reading, so as to better grasp the details, as Laurent explains it well:

> In fact, when I read a manga volume for the first time, I read it quickly because I really want to know what's next, and then I read it again and

> again, to take a closer look at the little details I missed, to better understand the story, stuff like that. The first time, I read quickly to quickly know what happens, and then I read it again several times to catch the details I missed.
>
> LAURENT, 18, 12th grade, father an engineer, stay-at-home mother

Nadia (14, 8th grade, father a worker, mother a secretary) likes to reread the volumes she knows before going to sleep, because it "rocks" her, whereas Tom (15, 10th grade, parents middle-school teachers) "finds that when you read them a second time, especially when you've enjoyed them a lot, you appreciate them even more". The rereading also makes it possible to approach complex narratives, when "one is lost with the number of characters, depending on the tomes, at times, there are between fifteen and twenty characters ..." (Hugo, 15, 10th grade, father a middle school history teacher, mother a nurse). It makes it possible to be patient, while waiting for the novelties and also to anticipate, prepare the rereading of the previous tomes, so as to remember the subtleties of the plot, as it is the case for Arthur:

> Every time a new volume is available, I read one, and then, like, when there's a two-month gap, I'm like, 'Here, I'll read that whole series again'. Or sometimes, when I get to a book, what's ... Well, for example, *Until death do us part*, which I bought last Thursday, so it was starting up again, it's been two months, I don't think I've read them again. So, when I went back to the story, it ... I thought: 'Yeah, some parts of it, I don't remember too much' and everything. I thought, 'Well, this weekend, I'll read them all again'. There's five now, I'm reading the fourth volume. It's to remember the story and also, well, because sometimes I reread one from time to time, in the middle, because I like it.
>
> ARTHUR, 18, 12th grade, father an executive, mother an accountant

The rereading can also be punctual: a volume, a page, a privileged scene, a passage:

> Sometimes, if I liked the whole tome, I'll reread the whole tome, if it's a small passage in the tome that I liked, I'll reread that passage ... It depends.
>
> KADER, 18, 10th grade, father an industrial painter, stay-at-home mother

The dimension of the "narrative arc" (also referred to as the story-arc) offers intermediate reading sequences between the volume and the whole series, as Xavier explains:

> In fact, since I have finished all the series, I sometimes read passages again. Often the passages make up three or four books. And to reread them all in one evening.
>
> XAVIER, 17, 11th grade, father a firefighter, mother a childcare worker

Maele, when she walks by her library, "sees the book and says: 'I want to read that volume again'":

> I know what's going on in it, I know there are some funny scenes, others that are much sadder, or fight scenes and I think: 'What if I reread it?' And I start reading again.
>
> MAELE, 16, 11th grade, father a teacher, mother a counsellor

Rereading can focus on a favorite series, a "fetish" series according to Alexandre about *D.Gray-Man*, which one can eventually know "by heart", an expression that sums up both the incorporation of reading and its emotional importance: Océane (15) has read *Sailor Moon* eight times; Kayala (18) knows *Kenshin* and *Evangelion* "by heart"; Estelle (17) has reread *Love Hina*, *D. Gray-Man* and *Shaman King* "countless times"; Xavier (17) has reread the *One Piece* three or four times and all the *Naruto* twice, "for certain passages that I liked. But they're far away, so I'm re-reading them to re-appreciate". For Annabelle (16, 11th grade, father a bank executive, mother a consultant), who rereads the whole series as soon as she buys a new manga book, "it's *Tsubasa* who comes at the top of the list" and Nayir (16) believes he has read his series of *Naruto* "three or four times".

Rereading, a practice linked to childhood, is thus deployed by adolescents, whatever their social origin: it is on the choice of these titles reread that the distinction will be made. Serge Tisseron, in his psychoanalytical approach to comics, also stresses the importance of re-reading, which he brings back to the principle of the "fort-da" developed by Freud observing his grandson playing with a reel. Rereading and repetition would thus reassure the child, or the teenager, in moments of his or her life marked in particular by changes, identity wavering: "So I'm … too big for a child, too small for an adult", says Octave who is 17 years old. Without venturing into unfamiliar territory, we must nevertheless recognize the importance of these practices of re-reading among these adolescents.

2 A Reading Practice Embedded in the "Youth Culture" Constellation

While manga, because of their format and formal characteristics, are thus conducive to fitting into the varying timetables of adolescents, entry into the manga universe can be facilitated and guided by various forms of "thematic continuity" between adolescents' cultural practices and leisure activities. As mentioned above, the very process of manga production inserts them indeed into constellations involving television programmes, magazines, the digital universe and music, manga being at the heart of a powerful cultural industry.

2.1 *Cartoons*

Like Mr Jourdain, who writes prose without knowing it (in a play by Molière), teenagers saw Japanese cartoons adapted from manga during their early childhood, without identifying them as "manga". The links continue with adolescence, as the cartoons are available on some TV channels or on computers, either as downloads or streams. It is also surprising that they have never been stigmatized as being too childish or childlike. No doubt the terms anime or animated which are much more commonly used than "cartoon", are part of the possibility of continuing to watch these programs in middle school or high school, at a time when the issues around age are so lively. Numerous surveys, both qualitative and quantitative (Octobre, Détrez, Mercklé and Berthomier 2010) are available on this subject. They show how cultural practices are markers of age and of the "right symbolic size" (de Singly 2006) that one should have, especially towards others. Continuing to watch a particular series (Pasquier, 1999) that is too "babyish", playing with dolls or games, listening to music (Monnot 2009) can make you the subject of remarks and mockery which some Japanese cartoons seem to be spared. On the contrary, the interactions between reading manga and watching episodes are multiple[5] and vary according to adolescents. Their relationship with reading and their relationship with television are part of this interaction. Thus, for some adolescents, who are not much of readers, anime is more easily accessible. This is the case of Marianne, who, at age 16, is in the eleventh grade, but who does not like to read.

5 The selection criterion of the interviewed teenagers being to have already read at least one manga, we do not have, by principle, exclusive viewers of anime.

> Me, I prefer to watch them. I've never liked reading anyway, it's true that a manga is much easier to read, but I think it's better to watch, plus you have the voices.
>
> MARIANNE, 16, 11th grade, father a numerical control operator, mothera restaurant employee

Jérôme (18, repeats his eleventh grade, father an electrician, mother an accountant, both without a baccalaureate) prefers "to watch the series because sometimes [he] can't be bothered to read manga". Conversely, teenagers from the most culturally rich backgrounds are very contemptuous of the animated series, even though, as Félix (15, 11th grade, parents sculptors) does, they watch them probably because they are influenced by their relationship with television and the bad press they receive in their circles. Matthieu (17, repeats his 11th grade, parents architects) never watches them because he "finds that it spoils the charm a little"; Octave (17, 12th grade, parents sculptors) has "always preferred the paper version"; Laurent (18, 12th grade, father an engineer, stay-at-home mother) tried but he didn't like it, because he "prefers to imagine the characters in his head rather than see them in animated form"; Mickael (19, 12th grade, parents executives) prefers the paper version because "you can sit back quietly and listen to the music". However, these very clear-cut reactions are rather rare. For most, reading and watching are complementary practices, depending on the respective characteristics and temporalities of each medium:

> There are things that are weird, there are things that I prefer in manga, but there are times when I think that in manga it sucks and it's better in cartoons. And there are times, it's the opposite, I think: "This one is better in cartoon", and there are times when I think: "This one is better in manga". I find that in the cartoon for example, it's too boring, it lasts too long, they don't go straight through, they're clarifying everything, and while I find that in manga there are times it's the opposite, it's the manga version that explains too much.
>
> VINCENTE, 12, 6th grade, father a garbage collector, stay-at-home mother

Following and reading the same series also leads to comparison games between the two versions, a source of new skills thus operating on an intertextuality blurring the boundaries between media: Nayir (16, 9th grade, father a delivery driver, mother a housekeeper) watches in streaming the anime corresponding to the manga he reads, and appreciates both formats, "because sometimes there are parts that are cut in the anime, and the manga version focuses more on details".

Tom (15, 10th grade, parents middle-school teachers) watches *One Piece*, "because in fact the anime and manga are quite different. There are the big fights, the rather extraordinary things that come out in each thing, but otherwise … the approach is not necessarily the same. That's it, sometimes I compare". Maele (16, eleventh grade, father a teacher, mother a counselor) likes to "complete" her reading by watching the anime, because "sometimes there are stories that are included in the anime and not in the manga". For her, as for many, anime and reading complement each other perfectly, with the reading providing more details, while "we're not going to stop fifteen minutes the anime to watch everything" (Alexandre, 17, 11th grade, parents schoolteachers), while the anime allows you to visualize and get more emotions, thanks to the soundtrack. The question then does not arise in terms of preferences.

> *Bleach*, I started reading the beginning. And then the end, I watched the anime, because I'd been told that the fights, they were much more spectacular to watch than to read.
>
> LADJI, 18, 12th grade, father an electrician, stay-at-home mother

> It's true that it adds to the emotion, it's especially the soundtrack that does that. There are soundtracks that are absolutely magnificent and when you hear certain music with moments, passages that you know well, right away the emotion is stronger.
>
> CÉLIA, 17, 11th grade with a focus on literature, mother an opera director, father a choreographer

Anime also serves as a spadework for the final choice. Watching a few episodes allows for a preselection, before embarking on a reading that requires a significant time and financial investment:

> To discover a series, there is often an animated series based on the manga, so you can watch the anime to feel like reading the book.
>
> MAEVA, twin sister of Jérôme, 12th grade, father an electrician, mother an accountant

> In fact I never buy manga without knowing what it is before. I don't pick up a manga like that by reading the summary and saying to myself that

> I'm buying it. I never do that, I watch the anime first, and then I buy the manga.
>
> MARIANNE, 16, 11th grade, father a numerical control operator, mother a restaurant employee

Finally, watching the anime can keep the link with a series the volumes of which one stopped buying, because one has to choose between several series, or because the plot drags on and gets boring:

> First I read it, and then when I stopped reading it I watched it to at least follow the story a little bit.
>
> CÉLIA, 17, 11th grade, mother an opera director, father a choreographer

2.2 *The Digital Era*

The supply of anime goes far beyond French TV broadcasting—in fact, anime is mostly streamed on YouTube or Dailymotion, or downloaded from specialized websites, in original or fansubbed version (Dagiral and Teissier 2008). And this is but one aspect of how manga in a broader sense is embedded in digital culture and computer-related habits. Today's teenagers are one of the first generations who have grown up with computers and broadband Internet. For these so-called digital natives, computers are an integral part of daily life and coalesce cultural practices (Donnat 2009a; Octobre, Détrez, Mercklé and Berthomier 2010; Chaulet 2010). Not only does manga sometimes feature a technological, robotized universe which can echo this way of life, but the Internet also gives access to scanned manga (scans or scanlations) (Hee 2009) and to a variety of websites dedicated to manga.

Links to scanlation websites are extensively shared on teenage forums and blogs, and are easily accessible through mainstream search engines. Some of these websites are run and moderated by teenagers, which creates a closer connection with the readers. Cultural conventions such as language and interactional norms, the use of smileys, aliases and avatars (Béliard 2009), humor and self-staging forms are widely shared, although they involve a learning process. Marie (14, 8th grade, father an accountant, mother a housekeeper) mentions a practice commonplace among her fellow middle school students: reading, every Friday after school, the latest *Naruto* chapters uploaded by fan teams. Similarly, Jérôme describes his "little Friday night habit", to wit, reading the latest *One Piece* chapter online.

Reading scanned manga on the Internet serves different purposes: making an initial selection from the available offerings before a potential purchase, like

Noé (11, 6th grade, father a religious books publisher, stay-at-home mother), who reads the first pages of a manga in scanned version, "to know if it's good or not"; choosing, in the context of a tight budget, which manga to buy and which to follow only through scans; finding out what happens in the latest episodes before they are published in France; building up as big a collection as possible, like Pierre (17, 11th grade, father a postman, mother a retired schoolteacher), who has gathered 153 ongoing and 33 completed series on his computer, selected from hundreds of others; or—the finest distinction there is—, reading in English or in Japanese series unpublished in France. Marianne, Maele and Annabelle, for instance, are regular users of the Onemanga website, where English-language scans are uploaded. The availability of scans can therefore promote a compulsive, all-encompassing form of consumption, as is the case with Maele, who only memorizes the titles of those series she will eventually buy. Other teenagers, however, read scans out of passion for a given manga, when anticipation or suspense becomes unbearable.[6]

> *Which are the series that you read online?*
>
> Some of those that haven't been published in France yet. There are also quite a few that I used to read and which are now published in France. So, when I see them in FNAC[7] stores, I tell myself: it's not worth it, I already have them on my computer. I can't think of any specific titles.
>
> *Are those in English or in French?*
>
> I download either in English or in French.
>
> ÉLODIE, 18, 12th grade, father a biologist, mother a computer graphic designer

> *Do you read manga which haven't been published in France yet?*
>
> I do. For instance, in scanned version, you can read quite a lot of manga which haven't been published in France yet. Take *One Piece*. Here, they've published up to volume 40 or 42. On the other hand, scans of volumes 44, 45 and 46 are available.
>
> *So you're one step ahead?*
>
> Yes.
>
> *And do you read a lot of scans?*

6 Conversely, Nathaniel refuses to read scans because he does not want to anticipate on the plots: "Let's say that it spoils the story a little. So, after I've read a manga, I generally don't want to buy it anymore".

7 The FNAC is a French retail chain specializing in the distribution of cultural and electronic products to the general public.

> Only when I haven't read … when I'm done reading the published volumes and am waiting for the latest ones.
>
> NAYIR, 16, 9th grade, father a delivery driver, mother a housekeeper

> Sometimes, there are series that aren't so well known but that we read because we've heard about them. A friend of mine started reading a manga which hasn't been published in France whereas we read it online, it's called *Belzebut*. […] Sometimes we're just so eager to find out what happens next, we can't wait. With *Tsubasa*, for example, there are moments when you think: 'I need to know what's going to happen'. Same with *D.Gray-Man, Naruto*, all the series made up with a lot of volumes which you have to follow step by step.
>
> ESTELLE, 17, 12th grade, father a bank clerk, mother a school nurse

> Actually, it's when I'm tired to wait, I'm only reading one chapter from the whole book, just to … I won't read the whole book, because if I did, there would be no point in buying the book later, but I'll read a chapter so it … it teases me and I say to myself: "God, I need to buy this"
>
> LÉO, 15, 10th grade, father a commercial executive, mother a librarian

> *Nana* tomes are published really, really slowly, while people upload the latest chapters—say volume 1, Chapter 3 –, so I read them online, I don't wait.
>
> LEILA, 15, 10th grade, unemployed father, mother a janitor

Respondents rarely report qualms about reading scans and, when they say they 'know it's wrong', their admission of guilt sometimes appears addressed to the interviewer,[8] as do their convoluted justifications based on the idea that, if a manga has not been published in France, reading scans of it is not illegal. However, there can be practical obstacles to reading manga online. The most common problem is a limited access to a computer. For instance, Sophie (18, 12th grade, father a cook, mother a restaurant owner) often reads scanlations online, but has to compete with her four brothers for access to the

8 For instance, Maureen avoids downloading but the reason she gives for doing so is that her mother is an administrative assistant in a police academy: 'No, I don't download stuff. Or else I get told off: "it's illegal".—By who?—By my mother!—She doesn't want you to download things?—Well, not when it's illegal. Besides, she works at the police academy, so if I start downloading stuff … OK, we do download some things, I won't lie. But on the whole, I avoid doing it'.

home computer. The surveyed teenagers do not all have a personal computer with an Internet connection—one should not forget that social inequality does persist in the digital era, especially in terms of personal equipment. Some teenagers have access to a family computer or use computers in the library or at friends' homes. And although some of them find reading scans rather uncomfortable, it may be one of their few means of access to manga—take Nabil (18, 12th grade, father an employee, mother a home-nurse), for example:

> And then, a while ago, I discovered the benefits of the Internet and scans to get manga at zero cost (laughs).
>
> *And do you manage to read a whole scanned manga?*
>
> Mmh. But it's true that it's less nice to read, honestly, because I used to go read manga either in my bed or in the restroom. A quiet place, the restroom (laughs).

Reading scans takes some getting used to, given that chapters are not structured and split in the same way as they are in printed form, and that you must scroll down the pages on your screen. Tom and Nadia state that they cannot manage to read on screen. Similarly, Hugo (15, 10th grade, father a middle school history teacher, mother a nurse), who generally speaking keeps some distance from manga and enjoys reading detective novels and the classics which are part of his school curriculum, felt lost when a friend introduced him to scans, and gave up:[9]

> *And do you sometimes read scanned manga online?*
>
> No, because every time, I get lost. When I try, it … There's a page here and the next one is actually three pages further: I get confused, so I give up quite quickly.

Scans are not the only connection between the manga world and the digital world. Websites, blogs and webpages are dedicated to either manga in general or specific series. There, you can find information as well as ideas on what else to read. During the interviews, many readers mentioned chat forums, blogs, and publisher or fan websites as playing an important role in encouraging to read manga. On their websites, publishing houses give official information on

9 Those who reject scans do not do so out of repulsion for digital culture but as part of distinction mechanisms, which are sometimes subtle; see infra.

the latest releases and access to covers, summaries and sometimes the first pages of some books. Nevertheless, the most sought-after and followed advice often comes from web users and readers of the same age category or generation. Such advice is given through multiple channels: various chat forums—dedicated to manga but also online games or video games—; specialized websites where readers can post reviews of or comments on manga; streaming, download or scanlation websites. On this cultural influences market, some blogs are also reported as being authoritative sources or opinion leaders. Together, recommended or shared manga and anime, databases including summaries, pictures, excerpts, comments and reviews form a prescription system which teenagers can use to identify series they might like. Many readers take into account the popularity of a series or the download count of an anime to make a choice.

> *When you want to find a new manga to read, what do you do?*
>
> I look for the sites, I look for the sites first. But usually, for new manga, I don't have so much searching to do, I've found a website that gives you all the new ones, all the new translations that are released, every week. So, as soon as a new chapter is released, it is copied on this site. So I see, I go, I take a look. I read the chapter and keep it if I like it, or delete it if I don't.
>
> PIERRE, 17, 11th grade, father a postman, mother a retired schoolteacher

> There are manga sites or forums that recommend you manga, and this makes you want to read them. Sometimes I google 'manga' and look at the pictures, see if there's something I like on a graphic level.
>
> MAEVA, 18, 12th grade, father an electrician, mother an accountant

> I go online as often as I can. I read some mangas, I look at the pictures related to a given series. Or I take a look at the reviews.
>
> PHILIPPE, 14, 9th grade, father an executive assistant in a road transport company, mother a freelance nurse

Some of them even consider the Internet to be a more reliable and more comprehensive source of information than specialized magazines, mainly because websites are maintained by fans, while magazines would confine themselves to the more consensual series or would even give false information.

> *And how do you find information on manga? Do you read any magazines?*

Oh, no! No magazines, because, generally speaking, what they say is often untrue. Again, it's bound to the yes-Mr Nobody law, that is, the magazine will give its opinion, but at the same it'll try to use soft language, precisely to avoid losing readers. So, as a result, they'll say: it's good but there's this and that, whereas … So I look on the Internet.

MADJI, 19,11th grade, father a bus driver, stay-at-home mother

Celia (17, 11th grade, mother an opera director, father a choreographer) also mentions using chat forums to find new manga series matching her tastes:

And are there people who recommend manga to you?

Well, since I'm not necessarily so close to manga-reading people, or we don't really read the same genre … But it's true that you just have to ask, that's why such forums are somewhat good—when you ask for a bit of advice, you say more or less what you like, and then people try to find something that matches you based on what you said on manga you like.

Those community sites make it possible to share reading experiences, comments and assumptions on what is coming next (with a tab separating those who read the books of a given series on paper, as they are published, from those who are ahead thanks to scans). A wide range of personal creations around the manga are also shared, including drawings and fanfictions, where fans invent sequels or alternative stories featuring the same characters. While searching for information is a relatively mixed-sex activity, reading fanfiction appears much more frequent among girls, as does writing, a largely feminine practice.[10] Girls highlight the literary quality of some fanfiction works they read, as well as the humor of parodic productions based on well-known series. Reading fanfiction was Cécile's passion for years because "some stories are really well written. It's like novels, actually. And some are really very well made, so I've read them because there was a real story behind them. He'd created a world of its own, apart from the manga's universe, he'd just kept the

10 Fanfiction is a clearly feminized practice, as evidenced by the surveyed reader population and by the list of members signed in on specialized forums. About fanfiction dedicated to *Harry Potter* and for a theoretical approach, see François 2009. Historical research on fanfiction based around *Star Trek* and other American TV series also shows that this form of amateur writing is the preserve of women. This is especially true of slash fiction, where fan writers imagine romantic and sexual relationships between male characters (Bacon-Smith 1992; Jenkins 1993). For an analysis of fanfiction in the digital age, see Hellekson and Busse 2006.

characters and recreated his own universe. And I found it interesting, because it was really well written". Similarly, Marie (14, 9th grade, father an accountant, mother a housekeeper) "spend[s] [her] evenings on it, from 9 to 11.30 p.m.", and also writes fanfiction herself, as does Estelle (17, 12th grade, father a bank clerk, mother a school nurse), who reads "masses" of it because "there are writers … who write beautiful stories, which don't clash with the manga, and sometimes there are really good stories. It's always nice to read the stories that those people write". Coraline (17, 11th grade, father a worker, mother a cleaning lady) and Alice (14, 9th grade, father a skilled worker, mother a computer assistant), who come from a modest background, also enjoy fanfiction, as does Célia, 17, whose parents are choreographers:

> There's a site where I go to where lots of people write fanfiction, often with original characters they've created themselves. And, well, quite often the manga's characters are not even faithful to themselves, it's very badly made, often very amateurish, and … I've seen several of those, but still, there are some which are very well written, in a very literary way, it's interesting and, you know, sometimes it gives you a new perspective, new ideas, and also you can always find theories, ideas on the relationships between the characters

Video games and online games obviously form the last pole of the digital universe which manga is a part of. While some games transpose a given series or character on a medium other than paper or anime, the links between manga and video games are much wider, and include a narrative structure (the quest, fighting), a common universe (science-fiction, fantasy), possibly an aesthetic. In their study of students' cultural practices, Dominique Cardon and Fabien Granjon mention a similar "thematic continuity" about video games:

> In its very contents (heroic fantasy, war-making activities, sports simulation, manga universe), the game connects preference and taste structures which can be expressed on part or all of "an actor's system of practices, their constellation of cultural activities".
>
> CARDON and GRANJON 2002

For instance, Franck (17, 11th grade, father a cardiologist father, mother a healthcare network coordinator)finds it "brilliant to be able to reproduce the hero's attacks, in a way that is as spectacular as in the anime, to take him—often in fighting games—and make him fight against other characters from the series". Samuel (15, 10th grade, father a fireman, mother a childcare worker) plays *One Piece* on his PlayStation 2, while Théo (15, 10th grade, father a trainer in a transport company, mother a bank employee) plays *Naruto* and *Dragon Ball Z*. Although Xavier (17, 11th grade, father a firefighter, mother a childcare worker) plays *Dofus* as often as he can with his brothers, he did not get into the spin-off book series.[11] On the whole, however, video games based on a manga (such as *Naruto* or *One Piece*) are considered less interesting than the manga itself because they are more repetitive, 'tedious' and limited to one-on-one fights, unlike other games, such as *World of Warcraft* or *Final Fantasy VII*, much more focused on magic and fantasy.

> It's no story, it's just fighting. So, it's okay, but it still gets boring after a while.
>
> SAMUEL, 15, 10th grade, father a fireman, mother a childcare worker

> *Naruto*, basically, it's a game where you fight each other and you can always have fun loading a fight from the anime, but it's a lot less interesting.
>
> THÉO, 15, 10th grade, father a trainer in a transport company, mother a bank employee

Many surveyed female readers also play video games. This may reflect a generational effect, as gaming is becoming an increasingly mixed-sex practice. It should be noted, however, that those girls have brothers. Sophie (18, 12th grade, father a cook, mother a restaurant owner) has four of them, Maeva (18, 12th grade, father an electrician, mother an accountant) has a twin brother, Jennifer (15, 8th grade, father a veterinarian, stay at home mother) has two bigger brothers, and Ludivine (17, 11th grade, parents tax officials) and Maureen (15, 9th grade, father a worker, mother an administrative officer) have one, as does Juliette (18, 12th grade, father a doctor, mother a pharmacist), whose elder brother had a major influence on her socialization. Célia (11th grade, mother an opera director, father a choreographer) wants to become a video game designer and, at the age of 17, she has already charted the way to get there: she aims to study at an extremely selective school in Tokyo.

11 Xavier, 17, has two younger brothers (aged 15 and 12), and *Dofus* is typically played and read by middle school students.

2.3 *Music*

While computers and, above all, the Internet have become a fundamental fixture in teenagers' practices, every statistical survey shows that music undeniably is the other key element in secondary school students' tastes. Music gives children—especially girls (Monnot 2009)—the chance to engage their bodies from their late primary school years and becomes steadily more important as they get older, in teenagers' schedules but also as a means of self-expression. As such, it is an indicator of belonging to a community as well as a sign of distinction. This is all the more so because, as Dominique Pasquier has shown, the music industry itself is embedded into a constellation of interests, where the preference for a given kind of music is combined with certain dress styles or the practice of specific sports (2005). Linking manga to this may seem surprising. Through anime's credits, however, manga acquires a whole musical dimension.

Credit songs can be enjoyed on their own, especially because they often feature 'rock' rhythms, but their popularity extends to the singers or bands playing them and to the broader Japanese rock and pop scenes, with all their subgenres—J-rock, J-pop, visual kei, and so on. Apart from those clips aired on the Nolife channel and anime's credits, Japanese music styles still attract little media coverage, and the access to this musical world is a typical example of the so-called "digitamorphosis" of listening habits (Granjon and Combes 2007). Since the mid-2000's, however, record label and distributor networks have grown in France, and Japanese bands are scheduled in concert venues both in Paris and the rest of the country. Nevertheless, as with every other kind of music, identifying oneself as an amateur or, specifically, a fan of a given Japanese band or music genre is not neutral in terms of social and gender identities. Girls—with rare exceptions[12]—enthusiastically state that they like Japanese music or have discovered new bands or styles, and they display an in-depth knowledge of subgenres and band names. Caroline (14, 9th grade, father a shopkeeper, mother an insurance trainer) "now listen[s] almost exclusively to Japanese music ... J-rock, and some J-pop", which she got into through the opening credits of some anime (*Naruto* and *Bleach*, "which are nice, with a good vibe"). She can name the singers of bands such as "Home Made Kazoku, who make *Bleach*'s opening and ending credits" and "Asian Kung Fu Generation, who make the opening credits of *Full Metal Alchemist*", an anime she downloads. Fleur (19, 1st year college student, father an employee in

12 Cécile, who finds the singers too effeminate. For an explanation of such rejection, see infra, Chapter 3.

a security company, stay-at-home mother) does not miss one single concert by Japanese bands coming to France, and is willing to queue for hours to be in the first row (see portrait). Maele and Marianne prefer visual kei*, and Maele (16, 11th grade, father a teacher, mother a counsellor) warns: "I shouldn't get started on it, or else we'll still be sitting here tomorrow". She got into "the band's style and look, and the band itself". Nadia (14, 8th grade, father a worker, mother a secretary) has been a fan of the visual kei and sweet Lolita styles since she read *Nana* (a manga featuring a female singer as one of its main characters);[13] she even translates it in her dress and hair styles.[14] Nadia reads scanned versions of Japanese street fashion magazines targeted at female teenagers, such as *Egg*, and often brings pictures of visual kei haircuts she wants to her hairdresser[15] (see Portrait). Similarly, Célia who has a rather eccentric dress style, mentions many visual kei bands and likes about the genre that it combines a rhythm and a look:

> What I listen to? Well, a huge lot of visual kei. Originally, *visual kei* is mostly about style and music, which go hand in hand. Here, all my posters, they're *visual kei* (the walls of her room are covered with them). So, it really changes ... habits, say, completely, in that it's only about men, it's very androgynous, there are very few women in visual kei. And you get to see piercings, tattoos, a really incredible level of eccentricity. [...] Besides that, I like a bit of everything, mainly some metal, some goth, things like that, but I can get into absolutely anything.
>
> CÉLIA, 17, 11th grade, mother an opera director, father a choreographer

Anything, maybe not—for those girls, these music genres are part of a rock galaxy, as opposed to French pop music, or hip hop:

13 "I liked it because she was also a rock singer, and I liked their look too. And the music as well. Well, I downloaded the music from the bands afterwards".

14 For a historical approach to Japanese street fashion styles, see Macias and Evers 2007; Gomarasca 2002.

15 Specialized stores sell fashion items and clothing products from Japanese brands; many amateur designers find inspiration in the sweet or gothic Lolita styles; and, from the mid-2000's, fashion shows are included in festivals and conventions, such as Japan Expo. As analyzed by Angela Mc Robbie in the context of punk culture, such shops and designers form the commercial infrastructure supporting the development of a music and dress style (Mc Robbie 1989).

> I listen to all sorts of things, except hip hop and techno, or tecktonik, I don't like those. I also don't like French chanson, because it sucks. Christophe Maé, that guy drives me crazy, I don't like him.
>
> NADIA, 14, 8th grade, father a worker, mother a secretary

> I only listen to Japanese music, I don't like French pop music, I really don't. In fact, what I don't like is following what everyone does. Like Rihanna, I find it more or less OK actually, but honestly, it's what everyone listens to so I get fed up with it, it's just too much of a hype.
>
> MARIANNE, 16, 11th grade, father a numerical control operator, mother a restaurant employee

Those female teenagers with such asserted tastes, and especially distastes, are more likely to attend high school than middle school. They also come from middle class to privileged backgrounds—among teenagers from the upper class, rock has become a distinctive taste, in stark contrast with rap and R&B. Nadia might seem like a counterexample, being the daughter of a skilled worker and a lower-level civil servant; however, her parents exhibit high aspirations for her social advancement, notably through education (for instance, they enrolled her in a new middle school, much more privileged than the local one she previously attended). In this context, for Nadia, distancing herself from the tastes of working-class girls (French chanson, R&B) is certainly also a way to work towards a higher social standing. Estelle, 17, who is in grade 12 and comes from the middle class, introduces a new distinction by opposing J-pop to J-rock. She knows several J-rock bands and links them to 'old rock', an extremely distinctive genre:

> By the way, I listen a lot to all the OSTs [original soundtracks], the music from manga, that is.
>
> *So you listen a lot to J-pop, to Japanese music?*
>
> Not so much to J-pop, Japanese metal for example I quite like, Japanese female singers who sing old-fashioned songs, I think it's called A cash, I can't remember exactly …
>
> *Do you listen mostly to Japanese music or to other types of music?*
>
> I find a sort of balance between everything, I listen to that a lot, but what I really like is old rock as a whole. I mean Nirvana, The Beatles, Queen, The Police, all that.

By contrast, Maureen, who not only comes from the working class (father a worker, mother an administrative officer) but is also younger (15), exhibits tastes based on clearly different criteria and concerns:

> *Have you ever listened to Japanese music?*
>
> Yes! I don't know the names, but it's got a good vibe. We even have what we call Japanese rap, because a cousin of mine, he has a Japanese song on his phone, it's so funny, it's all over the place. Also, I had a friend in middle school who loved Japan. And so she had some Japanese music. There was this woman, she was tiny, so pretty. She was an amazing singer. I can't remember her name. She's famous over there ... What else? Credits too.
>
> *And do you like it?*
>
> Yeah, I do. It's lively. Yeah, it's original. Different.

In this opposition between hip hop and rock, one might expect that upper class boys would embrace J-rock as well. Distinctions are not only social, though—they are also used to reaffirm one's gender. Such boys therefore dissociate themselves from J-rock in accordance with two principles: rejecting fandom, stigmatized as and for being a feminine attitude,[16] and the importance attached to looks.

> Everything related to music, I stopped, well, I still listen to some of it, it's ... I like listening to credits, I put the music on my MP3 player, but that's it. I won't try to know more about specific artists.
>
> LAURENT, 18, 12th grade, father an engineer, stay-at-home mother

> Some female friends of mine ... Well, they're not close friends, they're acquaintances, anyway, I know some girls, for them, it's not just about manga, they're into everything about Japanese culture, music ... That I find it a bit annoying, I don't like the Japanese music style at all.
>
> FRANCK, 17, 11th grade, father a cardiologist, mother a healthcare network coordinator

Most of all, J-rock is considered not 'hard' enough by young men who are into metal or punk.

---

16 See Chapter 4.

For example, my buddy really likes Japanese music, so I like it but not so much, it puts me out a little, it does get tiresome. I really enjoyed J-rock for a while, but I stopped listening to it. Also, he listens to this stuff a lot and he listens to a lot of soft rock as well. And that ... that I can't stand.

FÉLIX, 15, 11th grade, Octave's brother, parents sculptors

Do you listen to Japanese music?

Yeah, kind of. In the *Beck* series, they'd given out a CD by a Japanese band that I like. I also listen to Japanese punk. And to other bands, mostly Korean, which aren't bad either.[17]

MICKAEL, 19, 12th grade, parents executives

Here too, comparing with what working class readers say reveals what is at stake in these choices and displays of tastes. For Ladji and Nayir, Japanese music is no rock music; it is credits music.

And you became interested in Japanese music?

Oh yeah, well I liked it in *Naruto*, it was always the closing or opening credits, I put them on my iPod and all ... Also *One Piece*, I don't know anything about this manga but I have all the music on my iPod. And even knowing nothing about this manga, I like the music, I don't know why.

LADJI, 18, 12th grade, father an electrician, stay-at-home mother

Do you know any Japanese bands?

I do. There's The Gazette, there's Myavi, Nightmare, Asian Kung Fu Generation ... um ... All those manga credits, that's how I got to know the bands.

Have you listened to J-music for a long time?

To J-pop, yes, for a very long time, since I started watching manga on TV.

NAYIR, 16, 9th grade, father a delivery driver, mother a housekeeper

---

17 Here, distinction is made by mentioning punk and Korean bands. The statistical survey carried out on the sample showed that when, in high school, girls become interested in rock music, boys migrate to punk and metal (Octobre, Détrez, Mercklé and Berthomier 2010). Since the early 1990's, K-pop (Korean pop music), Korean TV series and Korean fashion have become very popular in Asia. This phenomenon is known as Hallyu, the Korean cultural wave (see Cicchelli and Octobre 2021).

As we can see, through their ties with music—in particular rock music—, manga provides teenage readers with means to implement their complex distinction strategies in the music world.

2.4 *The Fantastic and the Sentimental*

World of Warcraft, The World of Narnia, Harry Potter, Twilight, Final Fantasy ... Game consoles and computers, movie screens, and the often voluminous tomes of novels are full of wizards' guilds, worlds populated by elves or, on the contrary, strangeness in the cracks of everyday life. The infatuation for fantasy is real among teenagers, and even though our study is not about trying to explain the taste of teenagers for fantasy and its vampiristic declension, we see nevertheless the characteristics of the genre which can be involved: a world apart where one escapes, characters, sometimes teenagers, endowed with extraordinary powers or exceptional courage, communities helping each other or tearing each other apart, ordeals to overcome, where the hero fights gods, malefic creatures and his own inner demons, in infinite declensions since Homer's *Odyssey*. Whether one sees in them, like Serge Tisseron, a way to cope with a time in life full of uncertainty, and/or, perhaps more prosaically, a way to continue the action and adventure books of elementary and early middle school, to finally go on dreaming, manga are part of these tastes for a magical elsewhere, or for the mysteries hidden behind the most realistic cities.

The fact that manga are part of the fantasy universe can lead some teenagers to read manga. Prior familiarization with a reading pact or with specific hobbies brings about a circulation between various supports. Some narrative devices in hero- fantasy novels or "cycles and series in genre literature" (Besson 2004) are thus similar to the narrative style of some manga: setting a team of characters with magical powers, a guild or team that has to overcome a number of ordeals, the role of flashbacks, analepses, and prolepses, the attention paid to the coherence of a fictional universe, expressed by specialized lexicons, maps, and encyclopedias or "special guides". Coraline (17, 12th grade, father a worker, mother a cleaning lady) likes the fact that "every character has some kind of magical power, has a supernatural force", and she "seeks out fantastic manga". She is far from being the only one, and the taste for "fantasy", "magic", "powers" is often put forward as a primary explanation for the taste for manga:

> [*Fairy Tail*] It's fantastic, there's magic ... It's a guild story, they're part of a group where there are magicians, there are fights between the guilds ... I mean it's very fantastic, it's not a hard fight.
>
> MAEVA, 18, senior year in high school, father an electrician, mother an accountant

The fantastic, everything that is fantastic. Everything like *One Piece*, *Naruto*, *Bleach*.

PIERRE, 17, 11th grade, father a postman, mother a former schoolteacher

And what did you like about Sakura?

There are powers. Well, that's not like ... there is adventure, and magic too.

JENNIFER, 15, 8th grade, father a veterinarian, stay-at-home mother

Rave ...

It's the story of a young man. It's a completely different fantastic world, I think that's what I liked. It's a bit like a magical world, I wouldn't say elves, but they have some special powers, that's really what I liked. [...] *Bleach* and *One Piece*, I think that the fantastic part of the manga, that is to say, not like every day, the part a bit magical, is really what interested me the most.[18]

LAURENT, 18, 12th grade, father an engineer, stay-at-home mother

When asked about their favorite reading, the teenagers we interviewed made a clear distinction between fantasy manga and "realistic" manga. *Nana* or *Peach Girl* are, for example, sentimental comedies that take place in a realistic setting (a love triangle in a school for the latter, the life of two young women sharing a flat in Tokyo for the former), whereas *One Piece* or *Bleach* clearly take place in a fantasy universe where the characters are endowed with magical powers, superhuman abilities. While practices are often much more complex than these gendered attributions[19] may suggest, the girls of working-class origin we met are much more often fond of 'sentimental' manga, while boys, as well as girls of more favored backgrounds and/or oriented toward scientific areas, prefer fantasy. Among our teenage readers, manga is most often articulated with the reading of *Harry Potter*, The *Lord of the Rings*, *Eragon* or *The Emerald Knights* ... It is also this taste for fantasy that, for Jennifer, Philippe[20] and Yohanna, explains their preference for manga and not for 'traditional' comics.

---

18 Laurent's comments also show how reaching high adolescence can somtimes meangiving up fantasy, then categorized as more 'childish' reading, or even as too consensual and commercial a taste. See Chapter 3.

19 See Chapter 3.

20 For example, according to Philippe (14, father an executive assistant in a road transport company, mother a freelance nurse), who compares his practice of reading manga and comic books such as Asterix or Lucky Luke: "I enjoy reading manga more. First of all, manga is more surreal. And then the drawings are better than in comics".

What kind of books do you like?

Fantasy. Fantasy is anything that has to do mostly with wizards and the Middle Ages, I mean we'll say knights, the mixture of the two. I've read Feist's *The Apprentice*, the whole Pug the Apprentice series, there are 17 volumes (laughs) and 500 pages per volume. And *Eragon* too, do you know it?

And do you read them in the comics format?

Trolls of Troy, and *Lanfeust of the stars* and *Lanfeust of Troy* too.

BASTIEN, 15, 10th grade, father a biologist, mother an engineer

Can you name a book that influenced you in your childhood?

In my childhood? *The Lord of the Rings*. It was my cousin, who had lent me some mangas, who read them to me before going to bed at night. She's a brave girl (laughs).

KALAYA, 18, 2nd year of preparatory science classes, parents executives

I read all the *Harry Potter* books. When I have one, I read a lot. The second *Eragon*, I read it in 15 days.

XAVIER, 17, 11th grade, father a firefighter, mother a childcare worker

Fantasy, science-fiction, that kind of stuff. I read ... what's it called? Brooks, Terry Brooks, otherwise, there's also Jeff Cléments, there's Christian Grenier ... Fabrice Colin ... Ewan Colfer ... the one who wrote *Finalwen*, what's his name? Eric Lown, Stephenie Meyer ... Who else is there? ... Shoot, I lost the name ... There's also O'Connell, there's ... I happen to have read anything fantasy related ...

What do you like about these fantasy stories?

The fact that this is totally detached from the world and that it involves magic, fight, and so on ... This is what I like about it.

ANNABELLE, 16, 11th grade with a scientific focus, parents executives

Those I read recently ... I read something, it was a bit fantastic in fact. It reminded me of *Bleach* for that matter. He was the Spook's apprentice, someone chasing away the wandering souls. And even though I am no believer, I like this story about wandering souls getting to the other side. I am really fond of Greek mythology. I really like it and that's why it also reminds me of *Bleach*. For example, the Greek mythology says that souls, you have to put gold coins on your eyes when you burn a body, to pay the ferryman, because they say that a river pulls two worlds apart, so one has to pay so you have to pay the ferryman to take you to the other side.

TOM, 15, 10th grade, parents teachers

2.5 *Reading and the Book*

It may seem paradoxical, after the digital and musical world, to take reading as a teenagers' unifying principle that would benefit manga. As we already pointed out, reading is a practice that statistically decreases as young people grow older: 33.5 % of eleven-year-old children say they read everyday, and when they reach the age of 17, only 9% of them read. 11% of eleven-year-old children say they never read a book at all and 46.5% of 17-year-old teenagers never read a book. Nevertheless, to those who read, reading is a practice involving emotions. About 40% of readers say that they would miss reading in case they had to stop reading. When asked which practice they like the most, computer, sport, music and arts are ranked higher than reading, however reading is ranked higher than TV and video games. As we have seen with fantasy, the reading pacts favored by some readers can serve as "bridges to circulate between different cultural worlds" (Cardon and Granjon 2002) and between different media and modes of expression.

This is also the case with crime literature: Jennifer (15, 8th grade, father a veterinarian, stay-at-home mother), a fan of this literary genre, discovered at random on the shelves of the library where she was borrowing the manga *Detective Conan*, and enjoys the the way the plots of that manga are solved. It was funny to notice that when she was asked to sum this manga, she ended up by calling the hero … Arsène Lupin.

Connections can also be established through magazines. Specialized magazines include the manga in the world of women's magazines for teenagers, with a marked orientation towards Japanese media culture: the magazine *Japan Lifestyle* has columns on Japanese singers and bands, fashion, accessories … Élodie tells how she became interested in the manga *Peach Girl* after seeing an ad in a "magazine of stars".

For teenage book readers, the manga is just a way of exploring the readership offer. Philippe (14, 9th grade, father a commercial executive, mother a freelancenurse) discovered "a new literary genre", "a new style of writing". Jennifer "read a lot of novels" and wanted to "change to see and start manga": "And I started reading one or two or three and then I kept reading". Xavier (17, 11th grade, father a firefighter, mother a childcare worker), a big reader, started because he had nothing left to read: "I thought, why not. I read them, but it's actually jsut to read any stuff".

The relationship between reading manga and reading novels thus varies according to the previous reading level of adolescents. For readers of novels, manga follows previous tastes and interests, of which it is just another, lighter, easier declination, but which could not be sufficient in itself.

> *And what about you, what is the reason why you kept reading manga?*
> Because I like it! (Laughs.) I like reading a lot
>
> MAEVA, 18, 12th grade, father an electrician, mother an accountant

> But reading only manga, it would irritate me too much after a while. When I was a child, yes, well, I must still have a few left, but … I'd like to read that from time to time, but that wasn't it either … I still preferred reading novels.
>
> CÉLIA, 17, 11th grade, mother an opera director, father a choreographer

> Everybody says … everybody says it's good, because since young people today don't really like to read anymore, this is really the … this is the perfect book to … to enjoy reading, knowing that it's a bit boring over time when you read a bit too much. Some people, they're quite …, they really only read that, most of them only read that, but sometimes it changes, I don't only read that. What's good is that it's only pictures, it's a bit different from traditional books where it's only text, where you have to picture the scene in your head, it's … it's in the pictures and with the text … but then you don't have to read only that all the time because it doesn't bring much but from time to time to have fun … you have to read something else I think, otherwise
>
> HUGO, 15, 10th grade, father a middle school history teacher, mother a nurse

These last two examples also point to the internalization of legitimacy judgements, particularly among children from culturally endowed backgrounds, which, as we shall see, can act explicitly as a strategy of distinction. While this is not the objective of Hugo, whose parents are both teachers, and whose first purchases of manga were requested "to please his parents" who wanted to buy books for him, his comments clearly show how he was socialized to various kinds of readings.

For readers of novels, manga reading is not a substitute for this reading genre, except, in the following excerpts, for Kader, whose comments suggest that he tends to overestimate his children's reading practices. For children or non-readers of novels, reading manga has opened up other horizons, and for some, acts as a reconciliation with reading. Kevin (13, 8th grade, father a machine operator, mother an accountant-secretary) reads them thanks to his brother, who told him: "It's a little easier to read than real books, because there are fewer things to read". Hacine (15, 9th grade, father a textile company manager, stay-at-home mother) believes that since he started reading manga, he reads faster the books the schoolteachers ask him to read and, above all, he can understand novels better, even though this skill does not lead to a real taste for novels.

> *So, your father is happy that you like manga?'*
>
> He'd rather I read novels, but he's still happy for me to read you know. He thinks I got used to it, now I'm getting used to reading so I can take a novel and read it well while … I mean the novels I'm asked to read in middle school. I mean I read them fast actually. I can read very quickly. But if I understand the story. It used to take me four weeks! Now I don't even take three days.
>
> *But do you like it?*
>
> Reading?
>
> *Yes, reading novels, I mean?*
>
> No, really no. I can read novels, but if I like what I read … For example, *Harry Potter*, I've read everything.
>
> HACINE, 15, 9th grade, father a textile company manager, stay-at-home mother

> I used to be really into novels, I really was, it's not a joke, I promise. Afterwards, you know, I discovered manga, it was all about manga. Before, I was a great reader of novels and all that, but then, you know, from the moment I discovered manga, that's it.
>
> *What kind of novels did you read?*
>
> Novels … you know, when you're a kid, you know, *Robinson Crusoe* novels, you know, the classics, when you're a kid, you read them. Or maybe, like, Scary Me, Goosebumps, stuff like that. That's what I'm talking about. And then there were the manga, and that was it. Now it's manga, manga, manga, manga.
>
> *Aren't you still reading novels?*
>
> No, except the ones for school, you know. I'm asked to read … Oh, I've just read *Les Misérables*, and *Illusions perdues*, you see. Yes, I liked it. Although sometimes, you know, *Illusions perdues*, have you read it? You see it's not … You know it's long, it's not very interesting, the printing press … But I read it. Then you worry that I went to read manga. Come on, I had to read manga. I've almost never been into comic books, you see. I was into novels, then it was manga.
>
> KADER, 18, 12th grade, father an industrial painter, stay-at-home mother

But it is rather with the "traditional" comic strip that the competition seems the hardest, at the expense of the latter: Théo and Samuel (both 15 years old) quit reading comic strips. Above all, manga seems to fill a void in the field of comics in the opinion of teenagers who identify them as too childish:

> *And French comics, don't you like them?*
> No, because comic books are for kids. Comics aren't too interesting.
> LYDIA, 15, 8th grade, father a technical executive and mother a baker

> I think comics haven't adapted … There are comics for children or for adults, there's no age range in between.
> LÉO, 15, 10th grade, father a commercial executive, mother a librarian

> Well now I almost … I didn't read a lot of books. I used to read mostly comics, now I only read manga and no comics at all. Comics were boring. Now I read manga.
> SAMUEL, XAVIER'S brother, 15, 10th grade, father a fireman, mother a childcare worker

> French comic books I haven't read any for a long time. I had made a collection, it was *Le collège invisible* and it's already been a long time, it's been two years since I made it and I've read them. But it's true that now that I read manga, I read practically no more comics. I read Obelix, Asterix, some classics.
> THÉO, 15, 10th grade, father a trainer in a transport company, mother a bank employee

In a broader sense, it is also the relationship to the book, to paper, which is put forward by those who prefer published manga to scans or anime. For Maureen, the printed manga gives more freedom to the imagination,[21] for Jérôme, the predilection for the printed manga is justified by its better quality,[22]

---

21 "I prefer books [to anime]. Well, there's more suspense, actually. It's like we get the picture: the drawings, how things are going, whereas in the cartoons everything's already … they've already chewed us up. We see and we don't imagine too much."

22 "I still prefer to read a book, it's much nicer … the quality on a book is much better than on the Internet."

for Leila by practical reasons.[23] While, in Théo's opinion, the printed manga allows a greater flexibility in the temporality of reading,[24] Tom, whose both parents are teachers, "enjoys carrying a manga in the hands", Pierre, the son of a teacher, considers it obvious that "everyone prefers the book", Célia, whose parents are an opera director and a choreographer, "when she reads something, [I] prefer to have it in [my] hands, it's the same sometimes you can also find books on the Internet, but [I don't] like that", Kalaya, whose parents are executives, "prefers to have the paper in her hands", like Félix, whose parents are sculptors.

But the relationship between scans, anime and print does not end with a simple preference, often linked to family socialization, for print. Hierarchies are created by the degrees established between the various media, which are objectified in the purchase. Buying manga makes it possible to select it, to elect it, and in particular to reread it. This is where lies the importance to possess a lot of manga.

> I also read scans on the Internet, most often series that I know will not be available in France or in about ten years. Then afterwards, as it released in France, I try to buy it there, because I'm interested, and then I like to be able to say that it's mine, that I own it.
>
> MAELE, 16, father a teacher, mother a counsellor

> Well, actually, I prefer to buy them because I know they're mine and I can come back to them several times, and two weeks after I give them back, uh, I'm not really interested. I prefer to keep them, take my time, read. Understand the story. And then, yeah, keep them at home.
>
> HACINE, 15, 9th grade, father a textile company manager, stay-at-home mother

The importance of owning is associated with a specific relationship to the book,[25] but also the importance of objects as an expression of the self, especially in the bedroom's materiality. The shelves full of collections, the posters

---

23 "Because when you scan, you never know which is the left or the right page. Let's just say, it's never very clear."

24 "The thing with anime, given that it's on the computer or on TV, when it's on TV, it's not when you want, when it's on the computer, you can put the videos on but sometimes you have to turn off the PC, you can't stop in the middle and then you have to start again, it's complicated. But with a book you can make a break and resume right after the moment where you stopped."

25 However, for teenagers from the most culturally rich backgrounds, manga is not necessarily a "book" worthy of the name, and worthy of being bought. See Chapter 4.

displayed on the walls, are part of this bedroom's culture, which is primordial in childhood and adolescence (Glévarec 2009). The evolution of its decoration, toys and furniture could be read as so many successive mutations of the growing child. Some of the readers dedicate specific times to reading manga, in the personal space of their room. In this regard manga will also fit materially into this culture of the bedroom: Nathaniel (17, 11th grade, raised by his mother, an employment office worker), who admits that he is "a bit manic", covers his manga, washes his hands before reading them, and refuses to lend them … Célia (17, 11th grade, mother an opera director, father a choreographer) does not like to lend them either, nor does she "move" them around, so as not to damage them. Caroline (14, 9th grade, father a shopkeeper, mother an insurance trainer) arranges them by size, "takes very good care of them" and is rather reluctant to lend them: "I have a friend who doesn't take care of them at all and I never lend them to him". Annabelle (16, 11th grade, father a bank executive, mother a consultant) "tries to arrange them by author, if not by format, because some are a little higher than others. It's important to keep them, because [she] can't bear to throw a book in the garbage". Kalaya (18, 2nd year college student, parents executives) gathers the "same editions together": "Behind, there are those that I no longer read, in front there are those that I read, and I arrange them by series. In order of volumes".

These manga libraries, often shared between brothers and sisters, make up an objectified cultural capital. The universe of manga and Japanese animation thus offers, in the form of material objects or digital content, numerous supports for personal expression, fitting in the personal and domestic spaces of the room.

> *Is it important for you to keep them?*
>
> Yes, I think it's nice to have the whole collection. It's true that I put them in a special place. On the cupboard when I get back to my room.
>
> *And the other books, do you put them away too?*
>
> Further away, I pay less attention to them.
>
> THÉO, 15, 10th grade, father a trainer in a transport company, mother a bank employee

> So, I bought all the *Dragon Ball* (laughs). Here you go. I bought all the *Chrno Crusade*. Then I bought all the *Death Note* too. I also follow *Kurokami* and *Till Death do us part*. This is in manga tomes. And concerning those which are not in anime, yeah, there's Final Fantasy VII, which I bought. So, there's *Full Metal*, *Chrno Crusade*, GTO, *Elfen Lied*, *Dragon Ball*

> ... There's a lot of them anyway. Yes, so that's three series at the same time, actually. And I read three of them until the end, I think. At the beginning, actually, I only started with *Full Metal*. So here it is, at the beginning ... As eleven of them were already released, I bought them two by two, every month, so it was going pretty fast, and after a while, when they were released every three months, I said to myself: 'Well, maybe we'll start another one ...'; in the meantime, I might as well buy other manga. And so, a buddy introduced me to *Chrno Crusade*, so I bought *Chrno Crusade*. Afterwards, when I finished it, it was the *Dragon Ball*, after the *Death Note*, it was my girlfriend who introduced me to it, etc. And so right now, I've got three in progress. Till death do us part, it's actually, it was, well, on Manga Sanctuary, they had put the first twenty pages of the first two volumes, I started reading, I liked it, so I bought them. So, I bought them. That's it.
>
> ARTHUR, 18, 1st year college student, father an executive, mother an accountant

> *Do you sometimes resell some of them?*
>
> No, I never did that. I also look at the size of the series, when there's a manga title that attracts me, I prefer it to be short, to make sure I can buy them all ... I've already put a lot of money into this...
>
> *Don't you ever borrow one?*
>
> No, I don't borrow them. I borrow from a mate because he's buying the latest One Piece and I like to read them. But I usually buy everything.
>
> *If we lend you one you like, will you buy it afterwards?*
>
> Yes, I think so.
>
> JÉRÔME, 18, 11th grade, father an electrician, mother an accountant

It is remarkable that many people, even though they have already read the manga on the Internet, in the library, in supermarkets or because they borrowed it from friends, decide to buy it, to have it. Possession is thus socially marked: prices obviously contribute to it, as does, no doubt, the importance given to print in family socialization. For example, Océane, from a working-class background (father an electrician, mother a housewife), borrows her manga because she "doesn't have much money", but buys video games ("at forty euros each") and owns three game consoles. Lydia and Leila don't see the point of buying a book at all:

> No, I don't buy because it's better to borrow some because when you buy, it's useless because you read them but then.
>
> LYDIA, 15, 8th grade, father a technical executive, mother an employee

You bought all the Nana?

No, I didn't buy them all. No, because they have them in the library and besides, I don't see the point of buying seven euros for a manga that you read in seven minutes ... It's a bit of a waste.

LEILA, 15, 10th grade, unemployed father, mother a janitor

However, family socialization alone cannot explain the relationship to possession: while Jérôme is a collector, Maeva, his twin sister, does not see the point of buying manga which she can borrow from her friends.[26] Conversely, Maureen, from a working-class background, buys manga and, in a sentence, informs that the books in her room are about the only books in the home at all.

How do you store your manga in your room?

Well, actually, it's simple. There's a side to it with the books the teachers ask us to buy, all that. And then there's a row of manga, and then there's the Chair de poule at the front. And then there are all my *Naruto*, in order of their release date of course. And then there's *Dragon Ball Z*. Because in books, what we have at home is mostly the ones I have. And then there are others, but they're not ours.

Is it important for you to have them with you, to keep them in your room?

Yeah, but then if you have to lend them, I lend them, no problem. Because I like to see what I read. Some people don't believe me that I've read all this.

MAUREEN, 15, 9th grade, father a worker, mother an administrative officer

For Maeva, for Ashkan, for Cécile, whose whole relationship with manga is imbued with a legitimate bad conscience (see Chapter 4), above all, a manga is not worth buying, unlike a novel.

I never buy manga. Either I have the scans on the Internet, or I borrow them, or I have a cousin friend who is a fan of manga, so when I go to his place I read them, and he lends me some. But that's just the way it is. It's just that I like having a library with my books, manga it's not serious. No (laughs), it's not that, it's that, maybe it's the lifespan of a book, maybe

26 "I've been the one who's been the one who's been recovering. Because I don't buy too many manga in fact ... I prefer to be lent the show, I read it, and then I give it back. Because a manga is not really ... enfin, a manga I will not read it all the time, what, enfin ... So that's why, when we start a big series, I do not want to buy because I know that there are already thirty or forty volumes that have already been released."

> it's more profitable to buy a book than a manga, because the manga, I'm going to read it quickly and the book, it's going to take me some time and I'll be able to reread it. I do not know why at all, but I am much more attracted to buying a book than a manga.
>
> ASHKAN, 18, 12th grade, father a director of a clothing brand, mother a stylist

Ashkan is a very good highschool student. He got very good marks at the written examination and good marks at the oral examination when he took the French Baccalaureate. He masters specialized knowledge of literature and commentary techniques, and has a real personal taste for literature, including one of the works on the program, Les liaisons dangereuses. For him, novels are more "profound" and "lasting" than manga. He attaches no importance to owning manga, on the contrary to books, which represent for him a long-term investment, for which there are forms of capitalization, both material and symbolic. Here we can see a contrast between readers for whom reading manga is only a superficial hobby, and readers who attach great symbolic importance to manga and engage in building up personal collections. Through the objects they own, a form of self-projection takes place, a mirror also held up to others, parents, brothers and sisters of all ages and different genders, but also visiting friends. It is noticeable that some boys, as we will see, only read shojos on the Internet, but would never consider buying them. Similarly, others read hentai (pornographic manga) only online and do not want to buy them. Bastien, Célia, Laurent resell the series of their youth (notably *Naruto*) but continue to follow them in anime …

But buying manga is expensive.[27] Laurent (18, 12th grade, father an engineer, stay-at-home mother) estimates the cost of his collections at around two thousand euros, as does Félix, a sum he estimates he has spent in three years. Owning them leads them to adopt various strategies: most of them select, thanks to scans and possible loans, in the library or from friends. Some decide to give up or resell a collection they no longer like, as Laurent, who keeps buying *Naruto*, almost out of habit rather than because he likes it. Bastien (15, father a biologist, mother an engineer) has resold the *Naruto* he owned and watches them in cartoons now. Célia (17, 11th grade, mother an opera director, father a

27 "But concerning printed manga, I prefer to first learn about the manga itself, the story and the characters before buying because you know, when there are many volumes and it's expensive to buy them all. Because you don't realize that, you think about it is, the price is six, seven euros per volume, on average. It can cost more depending on the format, and uh after a while, when there are some manga that have about thirty volumes …" (Célia, 17, mother an opera director, father a choreographer).

choreographer) has resold the *Full Metal* and stopped buying the *Dragon Ball* to buy the *Saiyuki*, and Félix would be ready to resell the *Naruto*:

> But other titles like *One Piece*, never.
> *It's important for you to own them, to keep them?*
> *One Piece*, yes, it is a sacred book to me. *One Piece* is on a pedestal.
> FÉLIX, 15, 11th grade, parents sculptors

Siblings often divide the purchases between themselves, like Laurent and his brother, who follow seven series (*Rave, Dragon Ball Z, One Piece, Naruto, Love Hina, Negima, Air Gear*), Samuel, who shares the purchases with his two brothers (he follows *One Piece*, one of his brothers *Rave*, and the other *Naruto*), Xavier who buys *Naruto* while his brother follows *Rave*, or Annabelle who does the same with her sisters and cousins.

> In fact, my big sister has them too, and my little sister started reading afterwards, when she saw that we were reading them, it spread to the whole family ... so I have my sisters reading them. Each one has her own series
> *It's in a shared library?*
> No, it's not a shared library precisely because my sister keeps her manga for herself because she has series that have been successful too, Fruits basket for example, then there's Ceux qui ont des ailes and also, the *Gals*, it's perhaps less wellknown, it's in ten volumes. The *Urukyu*, that's not wellknown at all, but I don't remember the author. Yes and then my little sister for the moment, she only owns two series and that's some series she saw on the Manga channel, it's *Vanilla & Chocolate* I think.
> ANNABELLE, 16, 11th grade, father a bank executive, mother a consultant

Above all, the manga circulates, is exchanged, is borrowed in the friendship networks, on the bus, in the schoolplayground ... In this respect, manga is embedded into a central dimension of the middle and high school years: friendship networks.

3 Friendship Networks

In adolescence the peer group plays a key role. Adolescence is a time when one wants to be autonomous and tries to distinguish temselves from their parents in particular (de Singly 2006). The tastes shared with those of the same age group make up the necessary limit towards younger brothers and sisters, towards the one one used to be, but also towards the older generation. The pole of gravity shifts from the family sphere to that of peers, with whom adolescents, as they get older, go out more often, exchange more practices and have more chats (Octobre, Détrez, Mercklé and Berthomier 2010). However, manga, thematically, materially and symbolically, makes it possible to weave these bonds of sociability, to feel like being part of a community of shared interests. As a matter of fact, many of these series feature gangs, guilds, groups (*One Piece, Naruto, Dragon Ball, Fairy Tail, Vampire Knight*, etc.), in fantasy universes, or at least friendly relationships, sometimes in school contexts similar to those of teenage readers, middle school, high school, boarding school (*Love Hina, GTO, Otomen, Switch Girl*, etc.). However, this relatability, to which we shall return later, is doubled by the concrete inclusion of reading practices in the teenagers' daily lives, particularly by the advice, exchange, talks they involve, and the making of common references, a kind of cultural background : the most popular manga titles, such as *Dragon Ball, Naruto, One Piece, Nana, Death Note*, define the outlines of a common youth culture likely to provide the symbolic benefits for integration into peer groups, at a distance from family identity assignments (Maigret 1995).[28] The sociability issues specific to adolescent social spaces are thus at the heart of individual reading practices, and provide a reason to read them, or to continue this specific reading practice.

3.1 *Exchange Networks*

The creation of exchange networks about manga is a sign of their symbolic and affective role in the leisure economy of these teenagers. The interviews we conducted testify to the intensity of the material exchanges that take place around manga. Private sociability and book loans circuits (Burgos, Evans and Buch 1996) are sometimes very carefully organized. Xavier and his brother Samuel, Nicolas, Hugo, Tom and Théo are a group of friends aged between 15 and 17 who live in nearby villages and attend the same schools. They arrange to exchange manga among one another, which is not easy in the rural areas they live in. They share the series to be purchased and discuss the manga they read on a daily basis, especially during their long school bus trips. They have set up a manga exchange network in high school. Hugo (15, 10th grade, father a middle school history teacher, mother a nurse) evokes the organization of this sharing

28 Éric Maigret points out that manga allow a game of intergenerational distinction and "provide new weapons in the struggle of ages and generations", while Franco-Belgian comics "form a stable base for intergenerational exchange" and are now part of the references (and libraries) of parents (or grandparents).

in which the rhythm of personal reading (and reflection) is intimately linked to the rhythm of collective exchanges, and contributes to the development of a common culture:

> As soon as we get ... As soon as we get one, so we read it. And then we ask if you're interested. We say, 'I just got the latest *Full Metal Alchemist* or the sequel to the series I'm doing right now. I'm going to get it back, so if you're interested, I can lend it to you, I'll bring it back tomorrow,' or 'I have it right here in the bag' if I just got it back from someone I've already borrowed it from. [...] When I have one, I try to read it as quickly as possible, so that I can pass it on to others. And we do exactly the same thing. Since the others do the same thing to pass it on to us, to pass it on to me, to pass it on to others. So, we try to read it quickly and then I take it back once I get it back. To get a better grasp sometimes.

A large part of the readers read manga that they borrow from friends. Each series they follow is linked to the particular emotional relationship they have with another reader. Théo (15, 10th grade, father a trainer in a transport company, mother a bank employee) borrowed the *One Piec*e from his friend Samuel (15, 10th grade, father a firefighter, mother a childcare worker), the *HunterXHunter* from a classmate. He draws on various spaces of inter-acquaintance: old friends from primary and secondary school, friends from his village, friends from high school, cousins. Within these sociability networks, readers are famous according to the manga collections they own. The very constitution of all these manga libraries is a collective issue, based on a distribution of purchases among friends. This system of exchange with friends is evoked by all the schoolboys we met:

> Yes, we actually lend them to each other, we take them to school in packs of five and we exchange them. Yes, for example, one of us has a series the others are interested in, he lends it to one of us who lends it back, and we give it back to its owner and so on.
>
> ALICE, 14, 9th grade, father a skilled worker, mother a computer assistant

> *Who are you exchanging your manga with? Male or female friends?*
>
> Both, frankly, both. There are about five girls who lend me manga and about three or four boys who do the same.
>
> *And you guys always trade in secondary school, never outside?*
>
> In secondary school, it was only during schooltime.
>
> MAEVA, 18, 12th grade, father an electrician, mother an accountant

> As time goes by with all the friends I have, we lend each other the series. There must be five or six of us to exchange with. Right now, I've got about a dozen series to watch.
>
> ALEXANDRE, 17, 11th grade, parents schoolteachers

Marie (14, 9th grade, father an accountant, mother a housekeeper) also exchanges manga in secondary school, and her network even includes supervisors and teachers.

> *And so, in secondary school, you exchange manga a lot?*
>
> Yes, we lend them to each other. For example, if one of us got a new volume. There was even a proctor who lent me all the *Death Note*, and I lent him other manga to try. I lent him the *Full Metal*. I even lent some to my French teacher to try. She wanted to try, I lent her a crime literature series and a fantasy show. She preferred the crime literature series. But the first thing she told me was that there was a spelling mistake.

Just like borrowing from a library, where some volumes have disappeared or are not available when one would like them to be,[29] the exchange system is not flawless at times, especially when one has to wait until it is one's turn, and one is dependent on the others' reading pace, when one would like to reread a volume, or when moving out takes one away from the usual network, as is the case with Laurent. Xavier, when leaving the boarding school of his high school, has lost his exchange network and therefore cannot continue the *Full Metal Alchemist* series. He tried to integrate his big brother's, but doesn't share the tastes of those other readers, "people who read trash stuff. A series with a lot of blood in it".

---

29 Océane (15, 9th grade, father an electrician, mother a housewife), who only reads borrowed manga, thus has an erratic practice: there are many series whose beginning she did not read ("*Naruto*, I had tried to read but I started with number 19 so I understood nothing"), or which she interrupts because the last volumes are not in the library. So, for *One Piece*, "the only problem is that it goes from 14 to 41, so I try to wait until there are 15, 16 to be able to read them". She also explains that she reads more shonens because the library does not have a lot of shojos. So, she knows many titles, which she would like to read, but can't find them ("*Tsubasa*, they're not there, they don't have them here, that's a pity"). Likewise, Vincente (12, 6th grade, father a garbage collector, stay-at-home mother) would like to read *Fairy Tail*, but has "not read many of them because at the media library they are rarely available, everyone borrows them", and could not read numbers 36 and 24 of *Dragon Ball*, which are now sold out.

> Coralie and Estelle are two friends who widely shared their manga readings in secondary school, the latter providing the former with manga that she bought in quantity. Estelle and Coralie enrolled in two different high schools, and no longer have as many opportunities for interaction and exchange around manga. While Estelle (17, 12th grade, father a bank clerk, mother a school nurse) has an enduring passion for manga, and has found other partners in her new high school, Coralie found herself isolated in her high school and gradually gave up reading manga. Nadia (14, 8th grade, father a worker, mother a secretary) also lost touch with her friend from middle school, each of whom was attending a different high school.

The exchanges obviously have an economic reason, in that they make it possible to follow several series at the same time. However, there's more to it than just saving money. In fact, the circulation of objects is associated with discussions and advice, and helps to forge links between friends.

3.2 *Discussing Manga*

Éric Maigret opposed the majority of adolescents, who were rather hostile, resistant or indifferent to manga, to small groups of fans, united within their classrooms by their common reading practice (1995). As a matter of fact, the exchange groups bring together at best a dozen or so friends (about four or five for Sophie, five or six for Hugo and co), except for Marie whose "whole class except three" reads manga. But within these small groups, most often mixed, discussions are intense, advice is given, comments and hypotheses are made ... Reading manga is a resource for many readers that is used in daily interactions, within siblings and groups of friends, in the same way as sports or video games, with which it is often linked. Hugo and his friends discuss "every morning when they arrive, and at lunchtime": they discuss "the characters", "the nonsense we see in them" and make assumptions about what happens next. Every time a new issue of *Naruto* is released, Ladji also discusses, "we didn't expect this, we would have preferred this, we would have preferred that. We imagine what will happen next". For Nayir and his friends, making hypotheses allows them to wait for the next episodes, and they all admit to "debating" a lot.

> What did you think about which volume, which character you like, what do you think will happen next?' Often, we share our opinions on what will happen next, and sometimes it is interesting because we realize that we were right or wrong. So, we talk about it again and then we laugh.
>
> NAYIR, 16, 9th grade, father a delivery driver, mother a housekeeper

Do you remember the last conversation you had about this?

Maybe yesterday or the day before. We had talked about *Les chevaliers du Zodiaque* [*Saint Seiya*] we were comparing our astrological signs with theirs, and then we actually laughed about it. I remember when we didn't yet have all the revelations that had been made about Tsubasa. There's a character that's quite mysterious in the manga, and we used to wonder a lot about him, you know, 'Why is he like this, what's going to happen to him, what's his past, why does he react like this when you talk to him about this person or that person'. We made assumptions and realized in the end that we were all wrong, which was fun.

ESTELLE, 17, 12th grade, father a bank clerk, mother a school nurse

An Example of a Hypothesis Developed between Félix and Octave

"*You're making predictions about what's next?*

Yes, that's it. It's more about the characters, how the story develops, what's going to happen. For example, *One Piece* right now, it's a turning point, we were talking. He was saying to me: 'Maybe there's a rumor, he's going to make a temporal ellipse'. And I talked about it with Félix for a long time and he said: 'Yeah, why do you think that?' And then we came to the idea that yes, he's going to have to do that, and my brother and I said that he's going to have to do a time ellipse. Now you can see it on the scans, they're at volume 60 or so. All of his crew that he put fifty volumes forward, was scattered all over the world, the hero suffered a big shock and we don't know how he's going to get back up, he can't spend two volumes going like 'everybody gets back together' it's going to look very heavy, he's going to have to do an ellipse with either at the end they get back together or at the end they get back together, he grew up a little bit the hero and there will be flashbacks to show how he found everyone, either in relation to the hero who is a little bit dumb, not a little bit dumb but is a little bit lousy at finding his bearings, and sometimes a little bit lousy at getting himself organized, he is a little bit lousy on his island training and it's his crew that will have found him, they will explain how they found him. But I don't think he can do that for two volumes, but rather for one volume."

The discussions, which are recurrent for all the teenagers we met, are accompanied by advice on this or that reading series, which act as a kind of readership solicitation, with the peers acting as concrete role models for the readers, and some considering themselves to be "less well-informed". Quoting a distinction made by Fanny Renard in her thesis on the reading of high school students, we can consider that these solicitations are part of a "logic of communion: issued by close relatives, themselves readers, these solicitations are supported by the constitution of common references and common practices". This type of solicitation differs from a "logic of prescription", implemented by holders of professional authority, and an "incentive-based logic", implemented by parents or adults in the child's circle (Renard 2011). The members of the friendly network combine incentives and advice with practical support for the first readings, even just by making manga available and transmitting the basics of "reading skills".

Many of them mention that their friends' and classmates' advice acted as a multiplier effect on their reading practices. This peer group is a system of monitoring and information on the latest news, a cultural influences market that feeds the collective craze for some manga:

> *There was a time when you started reading more manga?*
>
> There, I have to say quite a lot, because, as time goes by, with all the friends I have, we lend each other the series.
>
> ALEXANDRE, 17, 11th grade, parents schoolteachers

The group is united on the basis of common interests and readings. These shared references, whether they are lines we know by heart, gestures (Maureen and her brother have a greeting with their hands, a "check" inspired by *Dragon Ball*), jokes from manga[30] or simple chats, allow for keeping alive the daily sociability around common concerns. As Catherine Monnot has shown with regard to songs and reality TV shows, or Dominique Pasquier with regard to the series *Hélène et les garçons*, adolescents' cultural and media consumption often includes a collective dimension, and these entertainment experiences are used to stimulate and fuel interactions on various social scenes, "so as not to be rejected or out of step with the peer group" (Monnot 2009). The "symbolic milestone" of entering middle school, and then high school, thus implies putting a distance between practices considered too childish or familial, and taking a model from older adolescents, or young adults. The constraints linked to horizontal socialization encourage these adolescents to appropriate manga

30 "In *Naruto*, when Kakashi is late, he always comes out with the same excuse: 'Excuse me for being late, but I had to save a grandmother who was about to be run over'." (Nayir, 16, father a delivery driver, mother a housekeeper).

that belong to this peer culture, which allows them both to "reassure them about their identity", and to "strengthen ties within the group", or to participate in "the rich social life within the school" (Monnot 2009), without these practices necessarily being regular or made up of personal tastes.

Many sociologists have analyzed the processes of "conversion of informal cultural knowledge" into "social ties" (DiMaggio 1987; Erickson 1996). Within the world of manga, the series that benefit from the highest media visibility, particularly through a television broadcast, can play the role of "common cultural currency", in the context of the forms of inter-knowledge and "weak ties" that unite middle and high school students in their schools or classes. Series such as *One Piece, Dragon Ball, Naruto, Rave, Vampire Knight, Full Metal Alchemist, Soul Eater*, among others, play this role in readers' social networks. Most of the time, these are the most popular series: the widely shared references make it possible to build cultural complicities, by sharing jokes, memorizing certain lines, multiplying allusions and comparisons with characters. For Nathaniel (17, 11th grade, raised by his mother, an unemployement office employee), *One Piece* is part of the "convivial" series, which he distinguishes from series for "connoisseurs", such as *Evangelion*:

> *And it's a pretty popular show?*
>
> Yes, it's very well known. It's very popular because it's friendly. There's no mystery, there's no … Unlike *Evangelion*, it's easier to approach. *Evangelion*, you have to rack your brains to understand some actions, whereas *One Piece*, well it's fluid what, the characters are instinctive … I mean, they're funny what, they're endearing. Sometimes you can even relate to them. For example, Luffy, he eats all the time, you can say: 'I'm like him too, I'm eating all the time and I always want to eat'. That's good. That's good.

This has to do with the manga's "relational uses", to put it as James Lull expressed this idea in his study on the social uses of television (Le Grignou 1999, 108). Manga reading can "facilitate communication" by providing common references and convenient topics of conversation. Manga reading can be a resource, an opportunity for interpersonal contact. Xavier, Samuel or Alexandre clearly express this sociability issue that guides their reading:

> *What do you think you got out of reading manga?*
>
> To have a good time. To have something to talk about with other people who read it.
>
> XAVIER, 17, 11th grade, father a firefighter, mother a childcare worker

> And if not, well, the fact that you can already talk about it with your friends, it's, to start discussions, it's interesting.
>
> ALEXANDRE, 17, 11th grade, parents schoolteachers

> *And you feel you've learned things by reading manga?*
>
> No, not too much. It provides topics of conversation with friends and it keeps you busy.
>
> SAMUEL, 15, 10th grade, XAVIER's brother

Conversely, not knowing what the main subject of conversation in the peer group is, makes it to some extent difficult to be part of it or to build an affinity with the peer group members. Nathaniel (17, 17,11th grade, raised by his mother, an unemployement office employee) told us how a friend of his, who is resistant to manga, has finally got into it. Hugo (15, 10th grade, father a middle school history teacher, mother a nurse) is the last of his group of friends who started reading manga, to take part in conversations, almost constrained and forced. His friend "advises" him to read *One Piece*:

> At first I didn't ... I didn't like it too much, and then one day he told me ... he gave me *One Piece*, he said: 'Read it', I read it.

Maeva's words also reflect the prescriptive power of peer discussions, and perhaps the risk of being ostracized for those who resist (Pasquier 2005), if only by excluding some of the everyday sociabilities:

> It's true that I have friends who read manga and others who don't. It's a subject of discussion, so it can set other people apart when we talk about it. They are not familiar with so they feel a little.
>
> *And what do you do in such cases?*
>
> Well, then we talk about something else! Or we try to get the person to read it. If this is somebody who really doesn't like manga, we won't force them either ... But we'll keep talking about it.
>
> MAEVA, 18, 12th grade, father an electrician, mother an accountant

However, having skills can also be a way of distinguishing oneself, of being considered as part of the group, the adolescent being thus divided between the will to integrate, to blend in with the group, and that of standing out, within the group itself, especially from the second half of the secondary school onwards (Le Bart 2004). The reference to the same series can fuel a logic of distinction, which is often based on the anticipated knowledge of the continuation of the plot by the readers who consult the scanlations. This is a process in which "the logic of affiffiliation is sometimes associated with a competitive logic aimed at knowing more, better, faster than peers in certain areas" (Renard 2011, 276). Within his group of friends, Samuel (15, 10th grade, father a fireman, mother a childcare worker) is recognized as the most legitimate reader, as a "pioneer" and manga lover. Hugo, Tom, Xavier and Théo refer to him as the one who knows it best, and Hugo refers to him every time he cannot answer a question ("no, but otherwise, uh these questions, I think that when you go to see Samuel, you'll get more information because I'm not really … I've read only *One Piece* so far").

He was the one who introduced them to *One Piece* and who got them to be familiar with *One Piece*. Besides he is the only one within the group who is from a working-class background, all the others being of intermediate background, rather marked towards the cultural pole, and the distinction that he draws from his competence perhaps comes to compensate for this social deficit.[31] Among his friends, Nathaniel (17, 11th grade, raised by his mother, an unemployement office employee) is also the one who is the most passionate about manga. He himself has been "initiated" by two of his former college friends, and he in turn introduced *One Piece* to his high school friends. Nayir (16, 9th grade, father a delivery driver, mother a housekeeper) calls himself "the specialist"; Marie, 14, from a working-class background, is also the "pro" of the group and invests time to keep this position which allows her to discuss manga with the supervisors, and even with her French teacher. The value of this cultural capital and how it can be transformed into social capital within the group in a place where they have to meet criteria of school legitimacy (Marie is "average", Nayir is repeating a year), given the fact that most of them are from working-class background.

> Jé, he's on the same level. No, one notch below. Cause right now he's trying to come up with manga names, and every time I know them. They're having a little trouble finding a manga I don't know.
>
> *And how do you get all this knowledge?*
>
> I read magazines, and I type on the Internet to see the scans and the episodes. I spend a lot of time there, so I often get scolded by my parents.
>
> MARIE, 14, 9th grade, father an accountant, mother a housekeeper

31 Samuel's parents are firemen and child care workers. Hugo's are a teacher and a nurse. Tom's parents are teachers, Théo's parents are teachers in a transport company and a bank clerk. Théo is also Xavier's little brother, but he is the who gives him advice.

3.3 *A Way of Connecting with Others*

While manga is a medium for conversation within a previously built peer group, nourishing already existing bonds, it can convey the integration of a shy or unknown teenager from the middle school. Nathaniel (17, 11th grade, raised by his mother, an unemployement office employee) describes himself as uncomfortable speaking and with others, but he acknowledges that manga is one of the few areas in which he can be very talkative and sociable. Hacine, Océane and Estelle relate to characters who are rejected or hazed at school because they have experienced it, especially in elementary school. And the discovery of manga in middle school has gone hand in hand with integration into groups of friends. For Hacine, the practice of reading manga fits totally into forms of friendly sociability, from reading advice, collective visits to bookstores, manga exchanges, daily chats, and even shared and collective reading of some titles, such as *Naruto*:

> In fact, when I was young, I was rejected by my friends … like him. Now it's good. Well, actually, ever since I started reading manga. […] Sometimes, on Wednesday afternoons, we go to someone's house and we exchange books, we read them at each other's houses, and we actually talk. We talk.
>
> HACINE, 15, 9th grade, father a textile company manager, stay-at-home mother

> *What do you think you got out of reading manga?*
>
> How can I put it … I mean, you know, you get interest in something, because I remember, when I was in the sixth grade, I didn't have a lot of friends, I was pretty dark actually, and when I started reading manga, it opened the door a little bit to a more fantasy world and I really needed it at that time, and I started reading that, and by reading that, I started meeting people who had the same interests as me. Now I'm very surrounded by friends with a common interest. I would say it's brought me a little bit of sociability. Yes really that's how I made friends. Not really in middle school, it's from my tenth-grade year in fact.
>
> ESTELLE, 17, 12th grade, father a bank clerk, mother a school nurse

The taste for manga thus makes it possible to break down some barriers, to create or boost knowledge:

> There's a friend in my class, Augustin, I wasn't talking to him specifically and it was just one day I saw him with a manga and I asked him what it was and it was *World of Warcraft* in manga and he said: 'I know a lot of manga, I've had a lot of manga and if you want, I can lend them to

> you', and that's how I read them. And that's how I made him my friend. Augustin, since he went to middle school elsewhere, he knows other manga readers and I told him that if they ever wanted to read *Bleach*, he could ask me to lend it to them, because if I lend it to them and then, in exchange, they can lend me others, so it helps to make acquaintances.
>
> THÉO, 15, 10th grade, father a trainer in a transport company, mother a bank employee

> *Did you make friends because of manga for example?*
>
> Well, yes well, for example, my friend, it's because we talk about manga.
>
> OCÉANE, 15, 9th grade, father an electrician, mother a housewife

> *And this girl, how did you come to talk to her about manga?*
>
> Actually, she was the only girl in my class. And she was drawing manga, so I was like, 'Do you like manga?' and she was like, 'Ooh, yeah', and we started talking about manga. In the class they called us 'the two crazy people' because I love manga and she loves manga too.
>
> PIERRE, 17, 11th grade, father a postman, mother a retired schoolteacher

The case of Estelle testifies to a relational circle based essentially on the taste for manga:

> *In your circle, do you know many manga readers?*
>
> Yes, I do. A lot of them. My circle of friends is based on that in fact. We all have that in common. That helps us a lot. We can always share our opinions on series, discover new stuff, it's really interesting.
>
> ESTELLE, 17, 12th grade, father a bank clerk, mother a school nurse

The possibility of recognition via the manga universe is the pathway to the creation of virtual communities, such as forums on the Internet, or the attendance of festivals and conventions dedicated to manga, where one is sure to meet people like oneself, to find oneself among one's own, and where, as Estelle says, "one feels less weird". Specialized shops, conventions and festivals are other social scenes where shared knowledge of manga facilitates contact and informal interaction. Discussions on forums, where comments, advice and hypotheses are exchanged, as in face-to-face discussions, can then give rise to real encounters, whether friendly or amorous (Arthur met the woman who became his girlfriend there), the lowest common denominator here being a taste for this or that series. Virtual sociabilities are often intertwined with "IRL" ("in real life", or "DVV" in French—"dans la vraie vie") forms of encounters, *i.e.*

with "physical" interactions, especially at conventions. For some, these exhibitions are an extension of already existing sociabilities, broadening them to geographical horizons or people from a different age, while also focusing on the most popular series, such as *Bleach*, *Rave*, *Naruto* or *One Piece*. In this way, Laurent (18, 12th grade, father an engineer, stay-at-home mother) builds hypotheses, posts comments, and shares advice:

> Most often, we talk every time a new volume is released. We all go to the forum and exchange our opinions on what we think is going to happen. We compare our theories and then we see what happens. But not all the time. Afterwards, there are manga about which you can't build too many theories.
>
> *So, you participate, you write, you post some …?*
>
> Yes indeed. I'd say, like, four, five times a week. I like to come up with my own theories but it's never good. I'm always out of it. I have MSN and mobile phones of several people on the forum and sometimes we meet. […] But if we met on a *Rave* forum, we all love *Rave*, but I discovered *Bleach* and *Naruto* thanks to them. I had heard about them but I had never tried reading them. They lent me the ones they had and I liked it and that was it.
>
> *How often do you two meet in person?*
>
> I would say every other week or once a month, just to exchange the new manga we bought.

But for other readers, especially the most skilled ones, who happen to have "heterodox" tastes, blogs and discussion forums are the main market on which to place speeches about one's reading, and therefore an incentive to read. Interactions with members of the daily environment often cannot lead to the emergence of such a linguistic market, since some of the peers do not master the cultural codes and sometimes esoteric references that are prized by manga lovers and connoisseurs, or since interactions in middle and high school are limited to the most popular series. Thus, Madji (19, 11th grade, father a bus driver, stay-at-home mother) considers the forums as the only place to discuss manga with connoisseurs and to escape sweeping generalizations:

> Only on the Internet, because [in my town] it's really a mess. People, they all really have their own opinion about manga, that is to say they know a manga, they say to themselves: 'I just like it, I don't care about the other ones'. And for example, we will try to talk about manga with them, they are always right, we are always wrong. Or they're usually people who are

predjudiced about manga even though they never read any, or they just saw the cover, and they immediately criticize it, like: it's ugly, the script, it looks too ugly because it's about a clown, so it's not interesting, or things like that. So, in my opinion, [in my town], it's really … But if not on the Internet, you meet a lot of people who are like me, who have watched it for a long time, and it's interesting to exchange our opinions. That makes a lot of people: I must have about the three hundred contacts who talk about manga. Usually, I find their address by pure chance, by playing video games. For example, I put a manga nickname, and then someone calls me and says: 'Is this the manga?' I say 'yes', and he says: 'Go ahead, we'll talk about it on MSN', and then I give him my address, and then we discover our tastes.

As Omar Lizardo points out, two types of conversion between cultural capital and social capital can be distinguished (2006). The first corresponds to the consumption of popular cultural forms, which, through their wider social distribution, provide the material for everyday sociabilities and support the less particularized interactions. Reading rarer and less accessible manga can, by contrast, function as a form of "particularized cultural capital", linked to more exclusive sociabilities. The example of Nathaniel (17, 11th grade, raised by his mother, an unemployement office employee) testifies to the constitution of more specialized masculine sociabilities around another kind of series rather reserved to "connoisseurs": the cult series *Evangelion*, and the manga featuring robots or cyborgs in science fiction, or manga multiplying winks to the "otaku culture" and parodic references to other manga. For these series, it is more diffifficult to find readership sociability partners in one's immediate environment, and discussions and contacts take place in a privileged way on the Internet, or with friends met through specialized sites. Contrary to the popular series, these forms of virtual sociability can also be built from a more distinctive corpus of manga titles. For Marie, a schoolgirl, the Internet represents the only space for discussion about yaoi manga, which she does not dare mention with her peers, let alone her parents:

Did you read a lot of these?

There aren't many of them in France. I think it's still taboo. So, all I can read are one-shots, collections. […] My parents, they don't even know I read this kind of stuff.

Because …?

I'm afraid of their reaction.

Do you know other readers who like this?

> No, I don't. But on the Internet, I can talk about it openly without being judged. There are sites that specialize in this.
>
> MARIE, 14, 9th grade, father an accountant, mother a housekeeper

4 Manga-Related Hobbies

While it is possible to shed light on the practices of manga readers by bringing them back into social networks, this principle is also valid for amateur activities. Amateur practice has a central place during childhood and adolescence: through the time explicitly devoted to it, through supervision in clubs or associations, or during the middle and high schools' lunch breaks, or in children's leisure time, it requires an extremely important temporal and symbolic investment. Practicing an artistic activity is thus one of the areas of activity that remains stable in the timetables of children from early childhood to adolescence. It is also one of the activities that generates the strongest attachment, increasing with the years, since while 52% of 11-year-old feel that they would miss it very much if they had to stop doing it, 66.5% six years later. Amateur drawing makes it possible to reconcile both concern for the group and family disappointment, since it is often done, and increasingly with age, with friends, and the search for autonomy and expressiveness (Octobre, Détrez, Mercklé and Berthomier 2010): drawing is a good example, which is done for oneself, to decorate one's room (a third of 11-year-olds hang a drawing of themselves in their room, and they are 25% six years later), but also, very often, to be shown to friends, or even to be put online on a blog or a forum.

The spread of the digital era does not upset this adolescent commitment to amateur practice. Only some of them are trying new tools, which offer new possibilities, especially in terms of video, photo editing or music.

However, teenagers find in the manga a support of expressiveness. These activities show varying levels and forms of investment in reading practice: not all of the teenagers we interviewed engage in manga-related activity, and those who do are characterized by more intense interest and reading practices. These practices are part of specific forms of sociability in which boys and girls engage in different ways.

4.1 *Drawing: A Mixed-Gender Activity*

Drawing is one of the activities most invested by readers, who copy or creata things, based on their reading. Drawing invests their free time and moments of boredom, sometimes even during classes. While manga themselves offer a great deal of possibilities, there are also manuals to learn how to draw in manga style. Célia "recopies manga images", relying all the same on manga drawing manuals, Océane has learned to draw characters through decal and has two manuals, Nayir borrows these books that "have helped him on the details" from the library. "Fists folded, hands closed and all that", and Maureen is inspired by the models suggested by the Canson covers bought for the visual arts course in middle school.

Among the teenagers, almost the majority tried to draw and they are more or less confident in the quality of their works, like Kader ("I try but (laughs), how can I say, I'm not very gifted") or Vincente ("I bought myself a book to draw manga and all that, I try, but it doesn't necessarily give results, sometimes it's a complete waste [...] how can I explain it, I find that it doesn't look like what I wanted so every time I start over and then sometimes I go on and do it"). Thus, drawing is practiced both by girls and boys, some of them just reproducing while others will try to develop their own style.

> *You told me you drew. I'm interested in this, when did you start?*
>
> Since I was a little boy. I was already drawing and I turned to manga; but I do a bit of manga mixed with Tim Burton's universe because I'm really attracted by this universe ... I take white and Indian ink, and I draw on sheets.
>
> FRANCK, 17, 11th grade, father a cardiologist father, mother a healthcare network coordinator

> In class. I think it's a bit sad a table like that, to put a little drawing on it, it brings life. Manga all the time. I only draw Itachi, I don't know lately, I only draw him. On all the tables, there was a sharingan, I had to. It's because I'm bored in class. Otherwise, when I have a sheet of paper, I do it on my paper. But when I don't have any sheet of paper, I'm so bored, I'm going to leave like that, I'm going to make one line, after another, after that I'm going to do what comes into my head, I'm going to finish it. At the end of the next class afterwards, it takes up the whole table, I can't erase it anymore. The poor cleaning lady, she'll come behind me, she'll insult me and then that's it.
>
> MOUSSA, 18, 12th grade, father a doctor, mother a pharmacist

Drawing at recess, like Océane, who "draws during recess because she doesn't have much to do", also allows you to show others that you are drawing. Océane (15, 9th grade, father an electrician, mother a housewife) says that almost the whole school has seen her drawings, and that "they say it's good". Maureen gives her drawings, especially on her friends' birthdays. Franck has created a blog where he puts them online. Coraline scans them, then makes small photomontages. Nayir shows them to his friends and to his art teacher to get some advice. Octave, likewise, shows them to his friends. The drawing practice is mixed and crosses the middle school's borders, its inscription within the community of manga readers perhaps allowing an activity that was until then strongly attached to childhood to continue.

4.2 *Girls: Cosplay and Fanfiction*

4.2.1 Cosplays

While all the boys tell with a mixture of fun and nostalgia that they used to play *Dragon Ball Z* in the playground during their elementary school years, this physical appropriation of manga does not last after they have reached the sixth grade, as Ashkan (18, 12th grade, father a director of a clothing brand, mother a stylist) puts it well:

> When you're in middle school you do no, you can't … you stop.
>
> *Were you ashamed afterwards?*
>
> Ah no, not ashamed, it's just that in middle school, you don't do that anymore, otherwise you are seen as a social misfit.

A practice related to manga, however, allows for the use of the body: cosplay, which consists of dressing up as a manga, cartoon or video game character at conventions or festivals. During conventions, cosplayers can take part in contests and parade on stage, play little sketches, or go for a walk giving 'free hugs' to visitors or other cosplayers. It's all about seeing and being seen, and the show is put on by visitors and organisers alike. However, this game of self and appearances is mostly practiced, among the teenagers met, by girls.[32] While some boys talk about it without being aggressive, many of them look down on this exhibition of the self, which is all too characteristic of "groupie behavior".[33] This is not without problems for Célia (17, 11th grade, mother an opera director, father a choreographer), who had in mind a cosplay inspired by a manga where two characters merge: her friend could not do the other character, because of the costume (open bolero on bare chest), so she asked her cousin and her cousin's best friend. Neither one wants to complete the duet. Célia, Ludivine,

32 The photos of cosplays listed on the sites cosplay-world.com or france-cosplay.fr, such as the attendance at festivals and conventions, however, testify to a quite significant male practice.

33 See Chapter 4.

Ariane, Estelle are thus enthusiastic practitioners of cosplays, for which they make their costumes, both by buying pieces and by sewing them.

To make a costume requires money (ready-made costumes are very expensive), but above all time. Maeva and Nadia would have liked to dress up for a cosplay but didn't get around to it in time, Juliette would have liked to but has "neither the patience nor technical skills" to make the costume, and Célia and Ludivine think, make sketches, gather their costumes months in advance, leaving the costume on display on a mannequin in Célia's room.

The type of cosplay teenagers prefer depends on the series they like the most, but also on their sel-confidence and the way they view their own bodies. Madji (19, 11th grade, father a bus driver, mother a housewife), one of the only boys who doesn't make fun of cosplay, says:

> When we go there, there are cosplay contests, it's pretty cool to see that there are people who are able to do cosplay. I just wouldn't be able to do it yet.

Coraline (17, 11th grade, father a worker, mother a cleaning lady) plans to do it, but with her best friend, "or else I won't do it alone", Océane (15, 9th grade, father an electrician, mother a housewife), a very shy high school student, selected the disguise of a *Bleach* character (a long black and red tunic), while Ariane (16, 12th grade, father a metal worker, mother a secretary), an extroverted high school student, chose the relatively naked outfit of a video game heroine. Parents also play a role in "setting limits", for example, on the size of skirts or the cut of necklines. The skills used in cosplay are traditional skills: sewing, fabric cutting, do-it-yourself work, and several of the readers interviewed made use of their family circle in the making of a costume. Ariane's father is a metal worker and he helps her make the (wooden) swords of her warrior characters (see Portrait). Célia and her best friend thus make cosplays together, disguising themselves as Allen and Kanda, a couple of friends in *D.Gray-Man*, who happen to be brawlers just like them. For them, cosplay is more like theater than disguise, since it's all about putting themselves in the characters' shoes and playing the playlets they wrote.

> *Okay, so Kanda is the one she compares you to.*
>
> And Allen's the one I compare her to, so we got to get into the characters' shoes. [...] Yeah, because that's what cosplay is all about, you have the costume, but on the other hand you really have to be in the character's skin and know him.
>
> CÉLIA, 17, 11th grade, mother an opera director, father a choreographer

Many activities organized during conventions also require the ability to put oneself in the picture, to express oneself and to "go wild". Karaoke with cartoon credits or "J-music" (Japanese music), dance video games ("para para", "DDR" or "Dance Dance Revolution"). Some quizzes or blind tests on manga, music and animation also have similarities with a show, closely linked to the mastery of "manga culture". Thus, in a game often organized in a convention, participants on stage have to jump forward or backward to answer yes or no to the question of the host, and in another game, they have to swallow a bowl of noodles if they do not know the right answer to a question. These animations often refer to the organization of television games ("Questions for an otaku", "Who wants to win manga?").

Portrait of Ludivine, a Manga and Cosplay Fan: "My Mom Takes It Well. I Mean, It's Sewing! It's Better Than Doing Drugs"

Ludivine is in a literary section in high school (11th grae), and her parents are tax officials. She likes to read books a lot, even if she regrets that the school pressure linked to the French literature test at the end of her schoolyear prevents her from reading beyond the program. The interview was conducted before Ludivine went to a cosplay photo session with her friends, the sessions taking place in the "most beautiful" places possible in Paris: the Trocadero, the Louvre, the Bercy park, the Buttes Chaumont ... She used to read three or four mangas a day, but due to lack of time, she has slowed down her reading rhythm, but she still reads them "all the time". Ludivine discovered manga in the fourth grade, with *Naruto* that a friend had lent her. At the time, she appreciated the action, the characters, and the fact that she was discovering "a new kind of book". Passionate about this series, where she preferred Sakura, the clumsy young girl she identified with, as with all the clumsy young girls typical of manga, she then dropped out, finding that the rhythm of *Naruto* was running out of steam, and above all, that this manga had become too well known, too commercialized, and that "when it's too commercialized, too derivative, to see it everywhere by dint of it ... it's disgusting". Ludivine likes to stand out by looking for and finding unknown mangas, not yet published in France, and knows a lot of titles. She prefers the Clamps' mangas, especially for the quality of the drawings, which is one of the criteria she mainly uses to explain her likes and dislikes. Ludivine has developed a passion for cosplay over the last two years: she used to be a spectator, but thanks to a friend, she started herself. Since then, she assiduously frequents the shows, and takes part in competitions, on average once every two months. She was preselected for a cosplay contest, where the Clamp mangakas themselves were the jury. She lost, but she is very proud to have met them. She also won a "small" contest.

Ludivine sews her costumes herself, both because the ones available in shops are of poor quality and in limited choice, but also because, according to her, in France and contrary to Japan, the personal making of the costume is a way to show her investment and her passion, since "you make your costume and you're proud of it, you show what you can do in fact. Instead of just wearing something you bought. She has already dressed up as a schoolgirl, and the next costume will be inspired by *07 Ghosts*, "it's fights that take place in churches with monks ….": she will be dressed up … as a nun. But she is most often inspired by the outfits of a manga she loves (*Black Butler*), which she follows on the internet, in subtitled version, and in particular the costumes of "maids, servants"…, in reference to the character of the little maid, very clumsy and shy, like her …

The cosplay represents an important budget, since it is necessary to buy the fabric, but also "a wig, lenses, make-up and all that", that is to say approximately 100 euros by costume. She spends all her pocket money for those accessories. Every night, Ludivine goes on the web to discover new things, and sews her costume for the next convention. This manual and traditionally feminine activity has two contradictory effects: it is a source of mockery for some of her friends, who assimilate it to "a grandmother's activity", but it also legitimizes cosplay in the eyes of her mother: "My mother takes it well. I mean, it's sewing! It's better than doing drugs, or …! (laughs)". Her father is more reluctant, especially because he fears that she will expose herself too much, thus sharing common prejudices about cosplay, where "it's pretty much frowned upon. When you think about cosplay, you see mostly images of young Asian girls, not very dressed, to please, with photographers who are really looking for young girls … But it's not that in fact!". Nevertheless, he lets her do it, especially because Ludivine knows how to set limits herself, and her father trusts her, since he knows "that I'm old enough to know if I'm going too far or not". Thus, Ludivine avoids costumes that are "too sexy": "I avoid them in the sense that I set a limit to decency. But I don't hide behind a veil or under a cape: I look for the beautiful costume, whether it is covered or not. Afterwards, it depends if it suits me too". Ludivine is among the youngest cosplayers, and she appreciates that this practice allows to cross the usual borders of ages, since "it's a passion that brings people together, which makes it easier to discuss with other people. The practice of cosplay has transformed her taste for manga into a real passion, which she cannot "leave aside", since according to her, with cosplay "it is another dimension". She says she is really passionate about it, unlike her two older brothers who, if they know about it, have a more distant relationship with it than her. Her room is thus full of pieces of fabric, manga DVDs, and *Black Butler* posters have replaced those of *Naruto*.

But this physical appropriation can even go beyond disguise and amateur practice, and become a lifestyle. For example, Nadia (14, 8th grade, father a worker, mother a secretary) is dressed and does her hair according to the manga fashion, and has gone from the "emo" style, rather rock and punk, to that of the "gothic Lolita", much more "dollish", to use her terms. Likewise, Estelle (17, 12th grade, father a bank clerk, mother a school nurse) dresses as a gothic lolita, with "some gothic lolita gowns that you can wear in real life and not get a weird look on your face". Caroline (14, 9th grade, father a shopkeeper, mother an insurance trainer) ordered an outfit from China via the Internet, "it's a mix of gothic and lolita, so it's often black and white. There's lace. Gothic side because it's rather dark, and lolita for the shapes and the lace". Her first attempt to wear this dress was on the last day at middle school. As a result, she was banned from the school. Like Nadia, she wears her dress on Saturdays, when she walks around town with her friends. Marie (14, father an accountant, mother a housekeeper) is also very fond of the gothic lolita, which she distinguishes from the "traditional gothic ... the sweet lolita, the industrial gothic".

Not being able to afford a whole outfit, because "it costs too much", she "gets two or three items to customize her jeans". Maele appreciates the "visual kei" look, because it is "offbeat" and she likes "this offbeat style that doesn't pay attention to what people might say about it afterwards". Célia (17, mother an opera director, father a choreographer), who had already started the gothic look "a bit" before reading manga, now sometimes turns to the gothic lolita, especially inspired by the visual kei.

4.2.2 Fanfictions

In a completely different vein, fanfictions are also predominantly invested by girls, both as readers and as authors (François 2009). The fanfictionss consist in writing manga scripts or stories based on an existing series or character. They can then be posted on blogs or specialized forums, or put online on personal pages. The hierarchies worked out in the fanfiction universe testify to the important weight of school judgements and skills: SMS writing is despised, spelling mistakes and forms of writing are deemed naïve, the emphasis is put on the writing work ... However, contrary to school, there is no binding framework imposing all these prescriptions, and a large place is given to fanfictions written in SMS style, with a great deal of dialogues in "theatrical" style and authors who stage themselves expressing their emotions in the stories they write.

Several of the female readers interviewed have "posted" their fanfictions on a specialized website (fanfiction.net or fanfiction.fr). Others, like Marie (14, 9th grade, father an accountant, mother a housekeeper), simply write them in a notebook, or even imagine them. Caroline (14, 9th grade, father a shopkeeper, mother an insurance trainer) doesn't publish them but has her friends read them. These fanfictions are often read mainly by friends from high school or middle school, even worked out together, like Coraline does with her friends. Writing and reading allow one to share enthusiasm for a series, but some young authors take this practice seriously. Élodie (18, 12th grade, father a biologist, mother a graphic designer) carefully proofreads and spends many hours writing. She plans to start writing original fictions. Similarly, Océane (15, 9th grade, father an electrician, mother a housewife), who is writing a manga, which she draws on a story she created, would dream of being published: "In any case, I'll try later."

> *Do you publish them on the Internet?*
>
> It happens, in particular when I was happy with what I wrote. The last one I published on fanfiction.net was very successful, which surprised me a lot. I think I'm close to fifty comments, and they all say they liked it very much, that they found it very funny. It's always a pleasure! It was about *D.Gray Man*. But since I have a lot of friends who do this kind of stuff, we usually ask one other for advice.
>
> *And you think you've made progress?*
>
> Yeah, because when I look back at the stuff I wrote, I think, 'Damn, I wrote that!'
>
> ESTELLE, 17, 12th grade, father a bank clerk, mother a school nurse

> From time to time we do fanfics, we take the same characters, and then we change the story a little bit, but with the same characters. We just change universes. Sometimes secondary characters, we make up a story of their own. Just for fun. The last time was about *D.Gray Man*, we invented that the main hero had to participate in a cosplay, so he had to disguise himself … He had to disguise himself as a zebra … Each character disguised himself as an animal. One of them ended as a platypus. … with the same friend who's been writing them and having me read them for the last five years. On TV shows, or bands that we both follow. Sometimes it's funny

> because we can make them do anything because we're the authors … It's situations … that may never be developed … we can really do what we want … situations that we would have liked to happen, and that don't happen. I've got six in progress, none completed. I don't publish them, I'm having a friend read them … but I haven't finished it either, it's really the first stage.
>
> MAELE, 16, 11th grade, father a teacher, mother a counsellor

The writing of fanfictions is generally more represented among girls. Yaoi can even be seen as an exclusive domaine for girls insofar as the writing of yaoi or slash fiction is despised by the majority of the male readers we interviewed.[34] For example, below is Estelle's personal page on the fanfictions website, which gathers together the three amateur stories she created, which are mostly shonen aï fictions (*i.e.* fictions featuring sentimental and love relationships between men, but without sexual or pornographic content, contrary to the yaoi).

> *Age*: Physically, 17 years old. Mentally, 4 or 5.
>
> *Chinese zodiac sign*: Sheep.
>
> *Location*: Planet Earth.
>
> *Particularities*: Incredible memory for useless details, no sense of direction, dreadful black humor.
>
> *Focus of Interest*: Manga, books in general, video games, rock, drawing.
>
> *What I like*: Chocolate, the smell of mint, grey, penguins (how can they be so adorable?), punk-rock, artbooks, yaoi fanarts, yaoi manga, yaoi fanfics (yaoi, you know! XD) [emotikon], […], the OST [original soundtrack] of *Tsubasa Reservoir Chronicle* and lots of other things unrelated to each other.
>
> *What I hate*: Coffee (I just hate it!), those who complain all the time about being alive, the utopian fanfictions ("Oh what a wonderful world it is Bill" … It makes me feel like throwing my PC through the window), bright colors (like candy pink or fluoresecent yellow …), the ringing of my alarm clock and many other things that I won't mention cos' the list would be too long …
>
> *My fanfictions*: *Tsubasa Random Chronicle*: OS [one-shot] series, mostly KuroxFye. I don't have much to say on this fic. Usually, they're just ideas that come to me all of a sudden.

34 See Chapter 3.

> *Once Upon a Time*: My first TRUE fanfiction on this site. I am dying to write a fic on TRC [*Tsubasa Reservoir Chronicle*] with fairy tales as a main theme. I grabbed the first idea that came to my mind and started to write: unfortunately, I'm finding it harder and harder to finish it.
> *Artificial Love*: Probably the dumbest fanfiction I ever wrote! XD Still, I hardly ever had so much fun writing a fic on *D.Gray Man*. KandaxLavi.

So, Estelle wrote three stories inspired by the following manga and cartoons: *Tsubasa Reservoir Chronicle* and *D.Gray Man*. These three amateur stories are classified "T", meaning that they are not suitable for children (the site includes classifications and American signage system), and fit into the "romance" genre. The first is an "OS", the other two have six and seven chapters, respectively. In the last fanfiction (Artifical Love), the acronym "KandaxLavi" means that Estelle invented a love relationship between the two male characters Kanda and Lavi, heroes of the manga *D.Gray-Man*. In the first fanfiction, she writes a story about the male couple Kuro and Fye. Estelle says the following about "Artificial Love":

> This fic is a shonen aï: that is to say, it features couples where both protagonists are men! If you don't like it, don't read it! The main couple is LavixKanda, and I would certainly add a little AllenxLenalee: these are my favorite couples and I find that there are not enough of them on: 'If you don't like these couples, you just have to click immediately on: Back to the previous page'.

These fictions still contain erotic scenes and are a particular form of "poaching" consisting for young female readers in appropriating manga intended for boys by distorting the gender relations of the original story. Here is an example of an "erotic" passage written by Estelle. This kind of passage can be found quite often in the fictions written by schoolgirls:

> He was being touched by another man, lying helplessly and forcibly in front of him. It was supposed to be disgusting!
> So why is it so good?
> Lavi's tongue, which drew burning streaks on his chest, triggered a heat in him that was far from unpleasant. His large hands, which held his wrists tightly, now only managed to make the situation even more exciting for him.

More generally, many female readers of shonen manga for boys are very sensitive, in their amateur writing practices as well as in their reading mode, to the identification of male "couples" likely to have a love relationship. Usually the participants of the site fanfiction.fr introduce themselves by declaring their "favorite couples", as Estelle does, about such or such manga (for example: "*D.Gray-Man*: Unquestionably, LavixKanda U_U Otherwise, I like very much the AllenxLenalee or the TykixAllen. Recently, I also took a liking for the couple MaryxMiranda", "*Naruto*: There are many XD. I like the SasuNaru, the GaaraxLee, the SasorixDeidara or TobixDeidara (it's sometimes hilarious XD). I don't hate the NaruHina, and I also like the IrukaxShizune couple (although it's VERY hard to find T-T)" or "*Death Note*. Like many fangirls, I support the LightxL U_U couple but my favorite couple will always remain MattxMello"). Then there are also the hated couples ("*D.Gray-Man*: I don't have any especially: I've always had a little trouble with the AllenxKanda and the LavixLenalee, but nothing more"; "*Naruto*: SasuSaku and NaruSaku, without the slightest hesitation!"; "*Death Note*: LxMatsuda, and all couples that involve Misa in general"), and she concludes with a warning: "I mostly write shonen-ai fics shonen-ai, so don't be homophobic!".

4.3 *Anime Music Videos and Role Playing Games* (*AMV and RPG*)

Among the readers interviewed, girls and especially boys, the manga reading experience is often combined with another type of amateur writing that unfolds on the Internet: participation in "RPG forums", an intermediate practice between writing fanfiction and online multiplayer video games. RPG, an acronym for "role-playing game", refers to a category of video game in which one has to play a character (like those that can be encountered in *Final Fantasy* for example). Aurélien and Madji compare this practice with role-playing games, which are also mainly practiced within male peer groups. Here, the users of a forum dedicated to a manga define their characters, and interact on the various topics of a discussion forum, through interactive forms of writing. This practice, with which the interviewers were not familiar, emerged in many interviews.

> I spend time on a PR forum, role playing, putting myself in the shoes of a hero, and it's on *Fate/Stay Night* again. The universe is too big, and really, it's interesting to play with other characters, just to write a story, knowing that you're not necessarily the master of the story, but you know that you can make it your own by playing with other people who have more ideas. It's a bit collective, actually.
>
> MADJI, 19, 11th grade, father a bus driver, stay-at-home mother

While the RPG is the rather masculine counterpart of the writing of fanfiction, the making of amateur video clips ("Anime Music Video"), from former Japanese cartoon lines and musical titles, is a practice which also allows to mix several foci of interest and to highlight computer skills. For instance, Arthur (18, 1st year college student, father an executive, mother an accountant) puts clips made from *Full Metal Alchemist* on Dailymotion, based on a track of the American group *Sum 41*, trying to respect the "synchronization". He discovered these video clips on Dailymotion, "with manga sequences, and you put a music, you paste a music, and you put sequences, so I made some on *Full Metal* and *Chrno Crusade*. I either made videos like that, or I tried to make a trailer, for *Chrno Crusade*, and one for *Full Metal* as well". When he hears "good music", Arthur often says to himself: "Well, that could go with this kind of anime, or it would fit well with this passage, what could I do afterwards, with the rest". Arthur thinks that making AMVs is pretty easy, and he's improved thanks to amateurs' advice:

> We have a software, we import the video file, we do cutouts, so it's … Then we use overlay effects, transitions, flashs. We're going to change colors, things like that. After that, it's mostly about knowing how to use the software itself, but otherwise, no specific skills you see.

Arthur does not participate in AMV contests, but advertises his AMVs on several forums. Madji, on the other hand, has learned how to make AMVs by asking for advice and "constructive criticism" on several specialized forums. On his Youtube channel, he uploaded six videos that he made from the animated *Fate/stay night* or *Air TV*. He also "remastered the opening of *Tsukihime*". Madji presented two AMVs during the contests organized at the Japan Expo festival. In 2007, his AMV wasn't selected but entered in the "You have talent" category.

4.4 *Blogs*

Blogs are another form of investment in amateur practice, where the taste for manga, the sociability of peers, and the digital era skills come together. Among the teenagers we met, blogging is neither a gendered nor a differentiated social practice. Félix (15, 11th grade, parents sculptors) created a forum dedicated to *One Piece*, where he took the name of one of the characters of the series. Franck too created a forum on which he posts his drawings, with a little sentence next to them which "reflects well what [he] thinks when [he] drew this drawing!". Océane (15, 9th grade, father an electrician, mother a housewife) also created her blog, taking the nickname attached to it as domain name ("I wanted to call it Ichigo because Ichigo is a bit my nickname, I mean it's the nickname someone gave me, I was rather against it but well, so I had written, but as it was already taken I wrote Ichigo****"), where she posts the episodes of the story she's writing. Ariane (16, 12th grade, father a metal worker, mother a secretary) also has a blog; like Alice, who writes articles there to discover the yaoi manga genre.

While some of these "screen writings" can take the academic form of a summary or presentation file, it should not be forgotten that these blogs are also used for self-presentation, for interaction with Internet users and friends (often listed in the links), mixing text, image and sound (one's favorite pieces of music can be streamed on the blog's presentation page, for example). Alice's friends are the first to react by leaving comments on her blog, and she published photos of her cosplays. A last type of writing on the Internet is the participation in discussion forums or MSN interactions: the interactive dimension is more present here, the language is more oral, the references remain quite implicit, and the emotions are transmitted through the use of emoticons. In the interviews the importance of exchanges with friends was emphasized and these pages allow to capture them live. It's about asking for reading advice, but also sharing one's impressions of a series. Thus, Laurent and his friends often meet on Friday evenings on a specialized discussion forum (on the *Rave* series), and they talk about their readings. Laurent (18, 12th grade, father an engineer, stay-at-home mother) gives his opinion on volumes 23 and 24 of the manga *Rave*, then, three months later, on volume 26, after having taken his French baccalaureate:

> *Re: Rave Volume 23*
>
> I found the 23 not bad … but I think there wasn't enough action!!!! In the 21st and 22nd, the fights follow one another, and I think that the 23rd is a kind of 'relax' tome …
>
> We don't learn a lot about Elijah and the story doesn't go very far. But it's good to have a funny tome from time to time to 'chill out'
>
> *Re: Rave Tome 24*
>
> A superb volume, not quite as good as the 23rd for my taste but still … Just as everyone else, I liked the little jokes at the beginning.
>
> Am I mistaken or is Hiro getting more and more perverse? I have the impression that the volumes are more and more 'hot' and that the girls' breasts became much bigger compared to volume 1 xD.
>
> Otherwise, I think it's too much to take 3 months to translate a little tome of nothing at all … They'd better work instead of thinking about the next time they're going to raise the prices
>
> *Re: Rave Volume 26*

> I just read it! I didn't want to read it before because I had my French A-levels and I'm sure it would have bothered me and disturbed me
>
> Yes, and we still don't know who is the guy who massacred everyone in the big ship and that Shuda is afraid of ... We don't see Shuda or Julius in this tome ... I also found the tome great in terms of drawings but a little less good in terms of story. Yeah, or else we realize that Hardner is a really crazy guy ... he wants to destroy the world to temper his ambition ... completely sick guy xD
>
> I'm a bit disappointed in Huma's defeat (I'm sure he's not dead, it would have been too easy) because I thought he was going to destroy everything when he ... blew a fuse ... I'm also saddened by what I found out about Belnika, it's a pity that it ended like that for her ... I find Hardner's power a bit exaggerated. He's able to regenerate himself (isn't that cheating then?), to summon trees by going back to the past and to control them ... I find him a bit overpowering anyway

These teenagers talk about the volumes they read, but they also give their opinion on the covers of the Japanese volumes that have not yet been translated. They also talk about the concrete aspects of reading: budget, pocket money, supplies, and also "reading at FNAC",[35] evoked with humour by Laurent ("me at FNAC, they don't let us sit down. They may hope that we'll break down and stand for hours on end, but no! The madness of the manga acts like valium on the physical pain") or the hard reality of the courses ("in tenth grade, in the 2nd quarter, I had 9.9 average in French XD I begged my teacher to round up to 10... nothing to do!!!! So, I was offended and I didn't do anything in her class until the end of the year, I was getting all the way to the bottom and I was talking about basketball and computer and manga with my buddy ^^").

Rave series discussions focus a lot on the female characters' figures or the comparison of the strengths and powers of the different categories of characters, especially the male characters' muscles. On the forum, battles between two characters are organized to find out which character is the strongest, or the most endearing or funny. Laurent thus votes for the Musica character who "flirts with the chicks, but gets often knocked back". These teenagers, most of whom are male, are also aware of the sentimental relationships between people, and also discuss their favorite "couple": a "topic" is about "the most beautiful couple", *i.e.* "the male and female characters who would go best together".

---

35 The FNAC is a French retail chain specializing in the distribution of cultural and electronic products to the general public.

It is possible that these interactions mediated by a discussion forum make it easier for these boys to express their emotions and comment on sentimental relationships, whereas this kind of talk is more difficult in face-to-face interactions in peer groups. Even though most of the discussions deal with manga readings, political topics are also discussed (here, the French presidential elections), or even their dreams. While some people occasionally comment on spelling mistakes, the key here is to master the codes of interaction and humor on a teenage discussion forum.

Portrait of Ariane, "Part-Time Otaku and Geek"

The interview with Ariane, 16 and a half years old, in 12th grade (applied arts section), took place during a "manga culture convention", shortly after the prize-giving ceremony of the cosplay contest she had just participated in. Ariane was dressed as Lycus Claine (long pink hair wig, long blue dress with a slit and low neckline), one of the heroines of the Japanese animation series *Gundam Seed*; she received the third prize in the "individual cosplay" category. Contacted through the forum dedicated to this manga convention, she was accompanied by her mother (employee in a real estate agency), who explained that her husband (a metal worker in an industrial bodywork company) had "a little more difficulty" accepting his daughter's fashion show activities and the outfits she wore during cosplays. Ariane did receive help from her father to make the plywood sword she used for her previous cosplay ("He helps Ariane when she does her cosplays to make her weapons, it's a real team effort!"). Ariane's mother intervenes to "establish a certain number of rules": "I tell her to be careful, she's into her own thing, she doesn't necessarily realize how others look at her. So, I try to tell her, if she has short clothes, to put a long coat over them. [...] If she's a little low-cut on top, I tell her: downstairs, you close everything (laughs). She's 16 and a half, that's my way of protecting her". In addition, Ariane's mother is "not embarrassed because I, my little brothers and sisters were raised on *Goldorak*, myself in high school, I watched *Candy*, so it was already the beginnings of manga".

Ariane discovered Japanese animation and video games thanks to her older brother ("I watched *Dragon Ball Z* with my older brother when I was 5 years old"), she then watched *Card Captor Sakura* and *Sailor Moon*. It is in middle school, in fourth grade, that she invests more in the "manga culture". She watches a lot of "manga in the original version with subtitles", thanks to a friend who introduced her to *Naruto* and to her older brother, who is "into anime and downloads and watches them all the time": "he's the one who introduced me to a lot of series like *Gundam Seed*". Ariane's younger brother is also a fan of manga, Japanese animation and video games, and Ariane refers to "a family of geeks" (this is the caption of a photo posted on her blog, where the three siblings, on Christmas Day, are all behind their laptops, testing their gifts, video games and anime). Ariane introduces herself on her blog as a "part-time otaku/geek, Asian music addict (my MP4 is my drug)". Ariane mainly watches anime in streaming on Dailymotion. In the same way, since the fourth grade, she reads mostly mangas by "squatting" the shelves of the FNAC[36] or Carrefour supermarket ("Manga, I read them when I have hours of hole, at the FNAC, for free, I'm a parasite (laughs)"). Ariane owns few mangas and anime DVDs, and therefore does not exchange them with her friends "because we all watch on the Internet, and read at the FNAC". She bought some manga with the "book card" financed by the regional council, and her Japanese pen pal sometimes sends her manga titles by mail ("She sent me the last *Nana* three months before its release in France"). If Ariane remembers that "the first manga I took in Japanese reading, I started to look at it in the French reading direction, it was *GTO*", she quickly got used to it. In order to be able to read manga in Japanese and to follow more closely the news of video games and Japanese fashion, she now takes Japanese courses with the French National Center for Distance Education, and can decipher some manga: "Often, manga, as it is a young target, there are small hiraganas, in very small, next to the kanjis".

Like her parents, Ariane is a very weak reader: "I don't read French comics at all, I don't like reading novels. I can only read manga, but otherwise, I really liked Baudelaire, *Les Fleurs du Mal.* Ariane's father "doesn't read at all", but according to her mother, who reads little and "likes novels that are easy to read, like those by Danièle Steel", Ariane nevertheless spends a lot of time "with her nose in her course books" and gets good grades. This success means that Ariane's mother leaves her free in her leisure activities, from video games to manga to cosplay: "As long as her studies don't suffer, there's no problem. On the contrary, it's her way of getting her nose out of the books, because otherwise, she would be always with her nose in the books. It's a very good and healthy escape". Manga reading is not central to Ariane's interests, which combine video

36 The FNAC is a French retail chain specializing in the distribution of cultural and electronic products to the general public.

games, Japanese animation, visual kei, fashion, "computer aided drawing" and finally cosplay. Ariane has read *Vampire Knight*, *DNA Angel*, *Full Metal Alchemist*, *Yu Gi Oh*, *Saint Seiya*, *HunterXHunter*, *Jigoku Shojo*, that is to say shonens and shojo taking place in fantastic, sometimes horrific universes. Her favorite mangaka is Kaori Yuki, whose *Vampire Host* and *Ludwig Revolution* she read and enjoyed. In the field of anime, Ariane's tastes are very marked by her brothers' influence: she appreciates mecha titles like *Gundam Seed* or *Code Geass* or "slightly violent" series like *Elfen Lied* ("it's a diclonius, a newly discovered species, with horns, which have vectors, invisible arms as sharp as razor blades, they have them from the age of 3 onwards and they are enemies of the human race"). Ariane recently saw the anime *Samurai Champloo*, she was taken with the "charm of the katana fights", and "loved the many unlikely situations they find themselves in, and also their struggle to find food or pay for food". She also read and watched the series *Pandora Hearts*: "I flashed on the drawings when I read the volume 1", as well as on the publisher of the anime: "SQUARE ENIX obliges! Its universe corresponds to me (fantastic, childish but also mysterious and a bit scary). A bit like a gothic version of *Alice in Wonderland*. I've only seen it in anime for the moment, and I can tell you that the OST is MA-GNI-FI-CENT!". Ariane used to follow "*Naruto*, *Bleach*, when it wasn't yet trendy, in eighth grade, but now after 160 episodes, I'm bored, I can't keep up with more than 160 episodes". In general, Ariane "avoids following too much" manga and anime, "because it eats up time" and she has many other interests and extracurricular activities.

While she doesn't enjoy strictly "realistic" manga and romantic comedies, Ariane did enjoy *Nana*, "because it takes place in the world of music". Ariane is indeed passionate about Japanese music, fashion and cosplay. She discovered cosplay in the fourth grade: "I was at a Japanese products exhibition and sale in M***, and there were people who were cosplayed. I had already seen pictures on the Internet, and I went: 'ah, I didn't know that existed in France!'". Ariane then started making costumes of her favorite manga, anime and video game characters, to the point of taking sewing classes every Saturday morning for three hours. She also has a sewing machine at home ("sometimes I do things outside of class to get ahead a little"). Ariane participates in cosplay contests and parades in all the conventions of her region in southern France, and during the Japan Expo festival. She has put online, on her blog and on an English-speaking website specialized in cosplay, the pictures of her costumes and her "performances". She often uses the services of professional photographers, during the Japan Expo or in agencies in her city. Ariane has embodied female and short characters from *Final Fantasy* (Rikko from *Final Fantasy X*, Lightning from *Final Fantasy XIII*, Stephie Timitt from *Final Fantasy VIII*, Yuffie Kisaragi from *Final Fantasy VII*, Nyu from the anime *Elfen Lied*), or anime and manga characters, in low-cut dresses (black lace for Amane Misa from *Death Note*, long slit dress and pink wig for Lycus Claine from *Gundam Seed*). Ariane recently cosplayed a singer from the Japanese band DIO. These are all her favorite characters (or singers), and Ariane has won several awards in competitions (individual cosplay prizes). During conventions, she is often accosted to be taken in pictures, and multiplies the activities while being cosplayed (quizz, DDR dance game). Ariane is currently working on her next costume, that of Meer Campbell, the heroine of the anime *Gundam Suit Mobile Seed Destiny*: she made a cape during her sewing classes, is still looking for a "one-piece white swimsuit" and is considering selling old toys at a fair to be able to buy "THE wig I need for my Meer! cosplay at the ebay cosplaywig store". She would like to play Rosso, a *Final Fantasy* heroine, whose costume seems too complicated for her at the moment. To show her different costumes, Ariane recently organized a small parade on a platform in front of her mother's real estate agency. She also has many jobs as a hostess, as a model for fashion shows and as a participant in beauty contests. Ariane loves the "Japanese gothic Lolita" style, she buys many clothes and accessories on the websites CD Japan or Fanplusfriend Garden. She also loves Tim Burton's movies and visual universe and would like to buy "the red dress of *Alice in Wonderland*". But Ariane does not hesitate to frequent satirical websites that stigmatize those who "show bad taste in dress/makeup/hair".

It is while playing *Final Fantasy* that Ariane discovered Japanese music, first Jpop and then Jrock, notably thanks to the credits of *Full Metal Alchemist*: "I was looking for music, and I found Kodakumi, from *Final Fantasy II*. After that, I looked for other Kodakumi's songs, I discovered Ayumi's music, I went into Jpop, and I discovered J rock afterwards with mangas like *FMA*. And visual kei since high school". Ariane informs herself mainly on Internet ("Jmusic europa" website) and a little in the press ("I receive *Planète Japon* every three months where there is a section on it.") Ariane likes Kanon Wakeshima a lot, "the cute gothic lolita who sang for *Vampire Knight*". Ariane quotes a lot of bands ("Ayume Masaki, Hikaru Tada, Dio, The Gazette, Ayage, Versailles, L'Arc en Ciel too") and attended some concerts (Anna Tsuchiya, Dio, The Gazette,

Miyavi, Plastic Tree, Kanon Wakeshima, X Japan ...). On her blog, the titles of these Japanese artists are played in a loop, next to Lady Gaga or Muse. Ariane writes that Anna Tsuchiya, interpreter of the songs from the anime *Nana*, is "the female personality I would most like to be like. She is a singer, an actress, a model ... And she is successful in all three fields. And she's so classy. She was the first Japanese star I saw in concert and it was sooooooooooo good". Ariane also loves dramas (*Vampire Host*, *Nobuto wo Produce*), her favorite being *My Boss My Hero*, in which "the singer of the band Tokio" plays. Ariane also enjoys video game music, and has attended several concerts where instrumentalists, sometimes cosplayed, play the credits or background music of cult video games such as *Final Fantasy*, *CastleVania*, *Silent Hill* or *Zelda*.

Ariane has in her room "a lot of figurines, blinds, posters, stuffed animals, mangas and especially *Final Fantasy*". Her blog and Myspace page reflect her multimedia interests: Ariane posts trailers of video games, movies or anime that she has "flashed on", "a lot of Jmusic", photos of herself in cosplay and her "creations on Photoshop". She describes herself as a "fan" of Cloud Strife, the main character of *Final Fantasy*, but also of Takanori Nishikawa, actor and singer of Jrock, and of Tetsuya Nomura, video game developer for the Japanese studio Square Enix. Next year, Ariane plans to enroll in a school of visual communication with a multimedia option, then to obtain a higher diploma in applied arts, with an audiovisual communication option, "to become a freelance graphic designer" ("character designer, that would really kick me"). For her drawings in class, her Photoshop creations, Ariane "draws her imagination" from the world of "Japanimation" (video games, manga, Japanese anime, cosplay).

5 Readers' Careers

5.1 *Discovering Manga*

Based on these elements, it is then possible to trace the readers' careers, where the common age calendar will be broken down with nuances according to the gender and social origin of the children.

Children most often discovered manga through cartoons they watched during the first years of primary school or even during their last kindergarten's year. In their minds these cartoons are not anime adapted from manga. For boys, they are part of the constellation of figurines, trading cards like *Pokemon*, and playground games, where they imitate the powers and actions of their heroes.[37] The initiating manga for boys is *Dragon Ball*, which they begin to read in middle school:

> When I was a little kid and I was watching *Club Dorothée*[38] on TV, I must have been five-six years old, I was watching *Dragon Ball Z* in *Club Dorothée* and that's when I began liking manga because *Dragon Ball Z*, I was a fan at the time.
>
> *You had figurines, cards ...?*
>
> Figurines stuff like that yeah, and I may have had three-four posters when I was a kid.
>
> *Until what age?*
>
> Elementary ... It's like *Pokemon*, yeah big *Pokemon* period too! *Pokemon*, I was a fourth- or fifth grader, I was 10–11 years old.
>
> ASHKAN, 18, 12th grade, father a director of a clothing brand, mother a stylist

> *And you got a liking to manga after watching anime on TV?*
>
> Well, yes, I had already seen them but I didn't know they were manga, but otherwise I started to know that I read manga before I knew that anime were adapted from ... So, *Dragon Ball* in the third grade.
>
> FÉLIX, 15, 11th grade, parents sculptors

While many girls began their reader's career with cartoons, those who watched *Dragon Ball Z* were mostly those who had an older brother (Maureen, Juliette, Alice, Nora, Ariane), a twin brother (Maeva) or a cousin (Maureen, Nora). Leila watched *Princess Sarah*, Marie *Detective Conan* (in fifth grade), Jennifer *Detective Conan* and *Sakura*. Estelle (17, 12th grade, father a bank clerk, mother a school nurse) directly relates her reading of *Sakura* to the cartoon she loved as a child, as Marianne (16, 11th grade, father a numerical control operator, mother a restaurant employee) does with *Sailor Moon*:

---

37 For a historical analysis of the ludic principles and forms of *Pokemon* or *Yu-Gi-Oh* marketing, see Brougère 2008; Allison, 2006. For ethnographic investigations of the uses of these toys and games based on Japanese cartoon characters, see Ito 2010; Montmasson-Michel 2020.

38 See Chapter 1. The *Club Dorothée* is a famous youth TV program (1987–1997) that aired many Japanese animation series on the main French private TV channel (*Dragon Ball*, *Sailor Moon*, etc.).

The first manga I read? *Dragon Ball Z* (without hesitation).

Did you see the cartoon before?

Well, actually when I was little, I had a tape, and we listened to it, it was actually an audio tape, and we would listen to it in the morning to wake up, and we would hear *Dragon Ball Z*. It was my mom in the morning, she'd put this on to wake us up

MAEVA, 18, 12th grade, father an electrician, mother an accountant

Dragon Ball Z. Well, I didn't actually get the advice. It's because I used to stay a lot with one of my cousins, and he's really into it. He's got the whole collection, he's got everything. And it's true that since I stayed with him, I watched, and I liked it. Oh, yeah, I was really young at the time. And then when I could read, well, I started reading. Slowly but surely.

MAUREEN, 15, 9th grade, father a worker, mother an administrative officer

Remember when you first discovered manga?

Not really, because my brother was a fan for a very long time, since the *Club Dorothée*; of course, I watched since I was very little, but it didn't mark me that much and then, about the age of 10–11, I remember the first manga I read was Love Hina and then, well, it was on. It was my brother who passed it to me, I don't remember why I agreed to read it anyway, but I know, as usual he always insists on my discovering what he likes.

JULIETTE, 18, 12th grade, father a doctor, mother a pharmacist

When did you discover manga?

Well since I was a little girl, because my brothers were already reading manga. It was the *Dragon Ball*, in tomes, from the moment I could read. Well, before that, I was looking at the pictures, but … it was mostly because my brothers were reading me, so I wanted to read it.

NORA, 16, 11th grade, father a school teacher, stay-at-home mother

So let's say that when I was little, I used to watch every *Sakura card hunter* on TV, with a lot of my friends, and one day I found out that they had made a manga where Sakura was the heroine, and it wasn't the same story at all. I was a bit surprised, I wanted to try it, and I liked it very much from the beginning.

ESTELLE, 17, 12th grade, father a bank clerk, mother a school nurse

> *Sailor Moon*, I talked my brother into buying them, because I've loved *Sailor Moon* since I was a little girl. I started with the cartoon at *Club Dorothée*, when I found out there were manga too, I was like: 'Ah mum, I want that for my birthday. I want this series so badly'. That's how I started, and then the next thing you know.
>
> MARIANNE, 16, 11th grade, father a numerical control operator, mother a restaurant employee

Thus, Juliette, Nora and Maureen are three cases of socialization with particularly influential older brothers, having initiated them to manga, video games, computers and, in the case of Maureen, karate, and these incentives were even reinforced by a circle made up of males too (cousins, friends of their brothers). However, for many of them peer socialization resonates with a significant person who introduced them to manga. Being often older, these cousins, brothers or sisters offer as well role models readers can relate to, as well as advice and books where to start the reader's journey: an older sister for Noé Maele or Fatou, a cousin for Annabelle's or Cécile, cousins for Matthieu and Élodie, with whom they spent time during holidays, a twin brother and an older brother for Maeva, an older brother for Franck (Marc, whose influence is such that he constantly refers to him during the interview), for Moussa (this brother is nicknamed "the Jesus of manga" by Moussa's friend, Nabil …), for Kevin or for Alexandre, who in turn take advantage of the advice given by the brothers' friends …

For others, the initiator may be an adult, such as a librarian: this is the case of Kader, or Lydia. In addition to this explicit incentive, the school libraries can arouse curiosity about this or that title. Pierre found his first manga in the library of his college. As for Océane, she came across a copy of *Sailor Moon* on the library shelves at the age of nine, which marked the beginning of her career as a manga reader.

> I was 14 years old when I discovered, well, it was Caroline [librarian] who introduced me to manga. I started with *Dragon Ball Z*, then it was *Dr. Slump*, *Tekenshino*, *Olive and Tom* [*Captain Tsubasa*]. Manga, yeah, this is where [the media library] I discovered. It's thanks to Caroline. One day, we were talking, and you know, the subject came up. And then I'm like, 'Yeah, I'd like to see what it's like', she gave me some and I started reading, I liked it. And then, I'm stalking her every week. I'm like, 'Caroline, there's something for me, there's something for me?'.
>
> KADER, 18, 10th grade, father an industrial painter, stay-at-home mother

> It was in the library of my middle school, there was a manga that I liked and then the librarian of my middle school, she asked me to come to the library to look for this manga book. And when I came, I couldn't find it and when I saw that there were other manga, well, I thought, I read and then I got interested. It was Fruits basket, it was *Fruits Basket* ... Already, it was her who showed me, I just read the series I mean just uh the first series and then I read the others but uh I read the others, I read until the end.
>
> LYDIA, 15, 8th grade, father a technical executive and mother a baker

Those, like Laurent (18, father an engineer, stay-at-home mother), who didn't watch cartoons, started reading *Dragon Ball* in middle school, because "at the time, it was quite trendy, I mean there were quite a few who watched *Dragon Ball*, almost everyone". So, even though Laurent says he came across his first *Dragon Ball Z* volume "by chance" in a supermarket, this chance is totally due to his desire to do like his friends. In the same way, Samuel (15, father a firefighter, mother a childcare worker) had never watched a cartoon before, but in middle school (in eighth grade), he received his first manga (*One Piece*) as a gift from his aunt, a librarian in a school library, and then went on (leading his older brother Xavier, until then a very big reader of Franco-Belgian comic strips,[39] in this reading). Estelle (17, father a bank clerk, mother a school nurse) also started reading manga when she was in seventh grade, because she "had always more people around me talking to me about it" and she discovered that the cartoons of her childhood were adapted from manga ...

However, discovery does not necessarily mean love at first sight, and as far as reading is concerned, one must "learn to love".[40] It can be assumed that the motivation and even the material supports that make it possible to continue despite a bad experience are linked to the importance of the peer group.

> *And* Naruto, *how did you discover it?*
>
> At first, in the world of manga, I noticed that people kept quoting *Naruto*, we talked about *Naruto* all the time. On the internet, in real life, in manga magazines, so, out of curiosity, I thought: 'I'll try'. And then it's weird, because I hated the first one. And it wasn't until I read the rest that I really started to like it.
>
> ESTELLE, 17, 12th grade, father a bank clerk, mother a school nurse

---

39 "I've read them six or seven times, every series. It was the *Tintin* first. But I didn't read those many times. The *Lucky Luke*, the *Asterix and Obelix*", collections belonging to his father.

40 In his study of the "genesis of the use of marijuana for pleasure", Howard Becker (1963) shows that learning the technique, locating the sensations, incorporating the taste for

> I mean, the first time I've read *One Piece*, I didn't like it. I didn't actually get hooked, that's just why. It was a friend who introduced me to it, he had the 13th tome, I read it like that, and then I really didn't understand the story, and then, and then I wasn't … interested more than that. And then at one point I reread it …, yes I didn't even have to start with the first one, I reread it, I found this magnificient and I just liked it more and more, and I wanted to buy some more. I know the very first time I didn't like it.
>
> FÉLIX, 15, 11th grade, parents sculptors

> *Naruto*, I tried to read it but I started with number 19, so I didn't understand it so I said: 'Oh this sucks' and everything … And then, I said: 'Why do people say it's so good?' So, then I tried to read and then I liked it very much and then I started reading other volumes.
>
> OCÉANE, 15, 9th grade, father an electrician, mother a housewife

Fatou (24, 12th grade, father a oultry farmer, mother a shopkeeper) shows how necessary it is to accompany a new reader in this way, and how much, as Becker showed, taste is the result of a learning process:

> Most of them don't know how to read it, because you have to read it backwards and everything, so some don't know yet, you have to tell them, explain to them that it's like that and everything, so that they can be into it. As far as I'm concerned, my roommate, she didn't know how yo had to read it, she said … She thought it must be diffifficult to read it backwards and everything, last time I explained it to her and I told her a little bit about *Paradise Kiss* and everything, and I showed her how to read and everything and then I went back to the library and I borrowed the … I borrowed eight volumes of *Nana*, I brought them, I didn't have the time to read them yet but she read them, every time she came to borrow the other volume and everything, finally I think she got a liking to it, even … now she reads a lot.

5.2 *High School as a Confirmation*

Being part of the adolescent culture in all the components that we mentioned, reading manga is concretized as well as in the next stage: middle school,

effects are linked to interactions with experienced members of the smokers' circle, seeing and hearing them, and being able to see and hear them.

especially from the fourth grade. The teenagers then start to read more and more, and to watch a great deal of series. The middle school period is thus marked by binge watching, and manga plays a big role filling both the gaps in the teenagers' schedules and their evening relaxation times. Between reading and rereading, some read several volumes per day (five per day for Madji), and follow several series at the same time. Moussa (18, 12th grade, father a doctor, mother a pharmacist) thus bought the thirty-seven volumes of *Death Note* in one go, which he read in four days, as if he was 'possessed', to use his own term. The supply varies according to social origin and the passion invested in reading manga, from reading in a library or reading exclusively on scans, most often in a combination of buying a few series, circulating in exchange networks of about ten people, reading on the Internet and watching anime, learning almost physically to read standing or sitting on the floor along the shelves of hypermarkets and the FNAC:[41]

> There are armchairs, but there's one for about fifteen people who spend their afternoon sitting in them. I remember one time, well, there were some free armchairs that I hadn't seen, I mean I didn't know if we were actually allowed to read. There's this big security guard coming up, this big black guy, about six feet tall, and he says, 'Hey, there's a chair there'.
>
> FÉLIX, 15, 11th grade, parents sculptors

Boys follow on with other "fighting" manga, according to Laurent (18, 12th grade, father an engineer, stay-at-home mother), such as *Naruto*, where action and fun are mixed (*One Piece*, *Bleach*, etc.), and girls most often associate shojo and shonen, insofar as those who have been socialized with brothers or cousins sometimes develop an aversion to shojo[42]. Friendly socialization, such as sharing reading manga with siblings, gives them the basis to maintain and develop. Octave got back to manga when his little brother, Félix, started reading manga, as did Xavier with Samuel, the siblings offering room for discussions, thus supporting the manga-related activities.

5.3 *Turning Points and Career Endings*

While the successive middle school stages bring teenagers together, the high school years involve two ways to pursue one's career as a manga reader, whose

41 The FNAC is a French retail chain specializing in the distribution of cultural and electronic products to the general public.

42 See Chapter 3.

relationship to *Naruto*, the manga flagship of the middle school years, crystallizes the differences among readers. Indeed, those who remain *Naruto* followers are distinguished from those who explore other titles during high school, rejecting Naruto as the very symbol of commercial manga.[43] Nevertheless, the distinction should not be understood only in terms of classical legitimacy. The idea here is to distinguish oneself from others, from the group, of finding one's "individuality", one's "authenticity". Teenagers' objective is then to distinguish oneself by reading less well-known, less consensual manga after the "*Naruto* period" or *Dragon Ball*, as Estelle calls it, before exhibiting the range of one's knowledge:

> There was a time when I was into *Naruto* like the majority of manga readers. So, *Shaman King* I mentioned it. One that didn't really stand out in France, which is called *Tsubasa Reservoir Chronicle*, by the Clamp, so I read a lot of the works by the Clamp or Ken Akamatsu's works, also, you may not have heard of them: *Love Hina*, *Negima*. As for the humorous side, I generally like it a lot. The *Death Note* too.
>
> ESTELLE, 17, 12th grade, father a bank clerk, mother a school nurse

> Well, it's mainly because when I was in ninth grade, I was following the trend, and when I reached highschool, I wanted to discover new manga by myself, so I flourished a little.
>
> *And what was the trend in ninth grade?*
>
> Well, it was *Dragon Ball Z*, you know. Everybody was reading that, right?
>
> *So, what's that you found out on your own?*
>
> So, there are many manga … The first one was *Rave*, it's a manga that nobody knows. I really discovered some unknown manga, which I started to like. Most of the time, I was the one who went to the supermarkets, who leafed through the books and discovered by myself.
>
> LAURENT, 18, 12th grade, father an engineer, mother a housewife

The challenge here is to distance oneself from the dominant state of mind, from what is "fashionable", particularly for adolescents from privileged backgrounds or who, through their knowledge of manga, aim to develop a cultural capital recognized in the friendly and generational sphere.[44] In this regard, stopping watching children's series, such as *Naruto*, as opposed to "psychological" series,

---

43 See Chapter 4.
44 See Chapter 4.

is a way for boys who continue reading to notify their evolution in terms of maturity.

At the end of high school, two paths are open to readers: to continue reading, especially for boys from working-class backgrounds, who were born with a passion and have developed expertise and skills in the field, such as Madji, for example; to stop reading, arguing a lack of time due to pressure from school. Coraline (17, 12th grade, father a worker, mother a cleaning lady) "doesn't read that much anymore", because of her baccalaureate, because she is not currently watching a series anymore, because her friend left … Kalaya (18, 2nd year college student, parents executives) plans to give her collection to her little cousins, or to sell it at flea markets.

Stopping, paradoxically, as Matthieu shows, is still a sign of belonging to one's age, when he remarks "we all tend to stop": it is a question of leaving behind a practice that may be judged, in turn, as too childish, too marked by the middle and high school years, when one is heading towards adulthood. At the beginning of the interview, Matthieu said he had stopped reading manga for several years, but the biographical recomposition suggests that he in fact quit reading only a few months ago … And even then, it is only a question of abandoning new series, since he rereads those he owns. In the same way, Kalaya at first declared she did not to read any more, then she admitted reading only the ones she owns, then she said she bought only *Full Metal Alchemist* … But Juliette, just like Cécile, already sees herself as a non-reader:

> Yes, for a while, yes, I did read a lot of them. Afterwards, for sure, I had less time, for sure, I stopped starting new series and then I finished just the ones I had when they were released. Well, it's worse and worse I no longer watch my series until the end, I don't even have time to read them anymore, because of school, I have many other focus of interest.
>
> *And when was the time you read manga the most?*
>
> I'd say it was in ninth grade, tenth grade, about three or four years ago … But it's possible that after a while, I'll get tired of reading manga, reading with pictures like that, I'd rather just focus on novels … we'll see!"
>
> JULIETTE, 18, 12th grade, father a doctor, mother a pharmacist

Manga, due to the materiality of their supports, their very specific mode of expression, but also the temporalities of their publication and the material devices ensuring their availability and circulation, are part of the teenagers' shared references. Their format is handy, they are easy to carry anywhere, easy to read during recess, in the bus or, discreetly in class … Their construction allows readings with variable dimensions from reading a volume, a narrative arc or a page, to rereading either in the bedroom or elsewhere. Above all, they offer the possibility of sharing a common cultural currency in the peer group, since "a cultural good should not be reduced to its mere material accessibility" (Passeron, 1991).

As a matter of fact, the 15-year-old teenagers just as the 18-year-old teeangers recalling the time when they were 15, tell similar reading experiences.

The reason why teenagers seem to be so fond of these readings may have to do with the fact that they are building issues that go beyond the desire to be "trendy". Getting a closer look at what they tell us about the pleasures of reading could make it possible for us to understand what can be played out and developed, both between friends in the playground, but also in the space of the bedroom and moments of solitude, around a book … What if, when they talk about manga, teenagers were talking about themselves?

Portrait of Fleur, "So Much Into Flowers That She's Got Powers"

Fleur, 19, is a first-year university student in English and Japanese. Her father was born of Chinese parents in Mauritius, where he obtained the equivalent of a baccalaureate in economics before studying economics at a French university. He is a consultant in a security company. Her mother is unemployed (no high school diploma or higher education). Fleur has been keeping a blog for years, which makes it possible to follow her evolution as a reader.

Fleur discovered the *Sakura* cartoon on television in elementary school, but at the time it was "just another cartoon, a little more serious for the age group", with "more complicated plots, a little less superficial". Fleur then decided to buy the *Sakura* manga, but she "didn't really care if it was a manga or a comic, well a normal series". It is while going to the manga bookstore of a shopping mall to complete her collection of *Sakura* that Fleur was attracted by the cover of volume 3 of the manga *Rurouni Kenshin*, of which she has a very precise memory. She came back the next day to buy volume 18 (the only one available). It is above all the graphic style of this manga that attracted her. Fleur specifies that she "remembers almost every cover of every volume of this series". Fleur follows several series that are lent to her, or that she reads from time to time at friends' houses, without necessarily being able to reread them. On the other hand, she likes to reread the mangas of her personal collection, which she has carefully built up and which now counts between 200 and 250 mangas.

Fleur hasn't started any new series for several months and continues to follow "the ones that are still in progress", that is to say "pretty much always the same shonens". As for her favorite manga, she combines reading online and buying the bound volumes, because "in general, I read the first chapters in scanlation, and if I like them, even if I've read the whole series, I'll still buy a manga out of pure respect for the author", and to follow "manga that have not been released in France, like *Dogs*, by Sumomo Yumeka", and other titles that are "not super well known". Fleur's limited budget sometimes forces her to stop buying certain new series, such as *Naruto* or *Nana*, and she carefully selects the titles that will join her collection: "the good thing is that, in the end, I'm proud of my manga collection. For the past two years, Fleur has been reading manga mostly on weekends and during the vacations, "because I really have more time during the week". She read more frequently in middle school and early high school. Fleur owns five DVD sets of anime and watches a lot of dramas.

Fleur especially enjoys action and adventure shonen. *Naruto* was "a crush", which she does not deny, since she "fell back into a *Naruto* crisis". She bought all the volumes of *Kenshin*, also enjoyed the manhwa *Chonchu*, and the manga *Shinsengumi imon Peacemaker*, a shonen about a 15-year-old boy who learns to become a samurai to avenge his murdered parents. In high school, Fleur finally adored *Death Note*, of which she read many chapters in scanlation before the French edition was released. She was first attracted by the "captivating" drawings, was "scotched" by some of the plates, then fascinated by the plot and the debate on Good and Evil. Fleur also appreciated the "evolution of the characters" and their complexity, which she perceived better during her re-readings. Because of her attachment to the character of L, Fleur had a hard time reading the chapters in which he dies ("I was sad as hell when I read it and I had a hard time, it took me two months to read chapters 59 to 62"). Fleur also followed the anime, "very well done" but feels that "the manga is much better than the anime, deeper, prettier to watch". She can't wait to see one of the film adaptations of this manga ("my conscience can feel the marketing stunt, the fangirl in me won't stop squealing!"). At 17, she writes on her blog that she's looking for "anything related to *Death Note*: a fic, a fanart, an icon, a wall, a statue with the face of L, a candy in the shape of L (mouahahah XD), one of the mangas, the movie, anything you want …". Fleur likes shonens and video games of action and adventure but she doesn't like "harem" shonens like *Love Hina*: "I didn't like it at all, one guy for ten chicks in fact, the kind of manga I don't like too much". She hates "fan service for fan service's sake" in this manga, but appreciates this kind of wink in GTO ("it depends how it is inserted in the manga"). Her middle school friends introduced her to shojos and seinen titles. In *Gundam Wing*, she didn't like Helena, "the character that everyone adored: I don't like characters who are always adored, who seem to be liked by everyone, who aren't really human, basically", as well as "characters who are too perfect". She did like Sojiro in *Kenshin*. Fleur likes this character so much that she "knew all of Sojiro's dialogues by heart, plus Yumi and Sano's in volume 16 (a crazy person I tell you)". Fleur also feels close to Shikamaru, and declares herself "affected by the shikamaru syndrome, which makes me say: "and galère ..." when I see something to do ...". If few shojos have marked her, Fleur nevertheless appreciates *X* and *Tsubasa Reservoir Chronicle*, by Clamp, "one of the authors' collectives that have reconnected her with the shojo genre". She has also read some josei manga, such as the American edition of the manga *Sapuri*, by Mari Okazaki, which recounts the sentimental adventures of a 27-year-old woman employed in an advertising agency. In high school, Fleur's French teacher introduced her to seinen manga titles, such as *Monster* or *The Walking Man*. Fleur also likes "Tsutsui's manga", *Duds Hunt*, *Manhole*, *Louisette*. On a forum, Fleur advises shonen for their "crazy fights" and seinen for their "serious storylines" or their "sick storylines". In *Death Note*, she notes that "the fights are intellectual and the script is to open the window to check if you can fly ... After that, you have to like good intellectual masturbation". She also recommends *Leviathan* and MPD *Psycho*, "terrible seinen" and "trash".

It was while searching on the Internet for a fanfiction on the manga *Gundam Wing* that Fleur discovered the genres of shonen ai and yaoi. When she was 14 years old, she visited a site focused on yaoi and left enthusiastic comments to the administrator of the site ("I love your site, it's really too good! Keep it up! I encourage you with all my heart"). She also offers to send her yaoi "fics and/or fanart". At 15 years old, she participates in several forums specialized in yaoi and "boy's love", where she presents herself as a fan of "yaoi, bishis and sake", who likes "as much *uke* as *seme*". On one of these forums, when a topic of discussion is launched on "your favorite yaoi couple", she likes to imagine the possible male couples: "there are too many bishi to choose from in each series". So, Fleur has been reading *doujinshi* (Japanese amateur manga), yaoi manga, like *Gravitation*, but prefers "more adult stuff like *Fake* or *Kizuna*" (*Fake* tells the sentimental adventures of two policemen of the New York police station, *Kizuna* the love story between two students struggling with the

Japanese mafia), "boy's love" manga by Kasuza Takashima, and yaoi fanfiction, and she is very sensitive to the "yaoi" dimension of the popular manga she reads, like *Gundam Wing* or *Sakura*. In this last manga, she finds that Yukito and Tora form "one of the most beautiful yaoi couples, absolutely adorable!". Fleur has also made some forays into "the yaoi world of *Harry Potter*". When she was 17, one of her favorite yaoi fanfictions featured Arthur Rimbaud and Paul Verlaine; a friend wrote it and dedicated it to her ("holy crap, that's so beautiful!"). Fleur herself wrote a fanfiction based on *Gundam Wing* and a "shonen-ai" fanfiction based on the manga *I'll*, a scene between two basketball players after their training ("I pull vaguely on his arm so that he comes closer to me and lean before putting my lips gently on his. It took me like that [...] He tries to disengage but with my second free arm, I catch his second wrist and prolong the kiss. But it all has to end sometime, and I end up letting go of him before backing off"). Finally, Fleur participated in an online fanzine "intended to promote stories and artwork dealing with female or male homosexuality, but also with bisexuality and, sometimes, heterosexuality". Three years ago, Fleur came into contact with female yaoi manga readers through a discussion group on the Yahoo site, and regularly participates in meetings of this group of "yaoists", which she specifies is "more of a manga fan meeting, and as they liked yaoi more, it's more of a theme". They eat Asian food and exchange advice on manga ("it's a bit hard to say, but they know more about manga than I do"), music (Japanese boy bands) and literature (one of them introduced her to authors like Neil Gaiman and Terry Pratchett). Fleur also appreciates dramas, "especially Japanese and Chinese", she finds that the acting has "a certain charm", and she can appreciate "super flowery" stories and identifies with her favorite actors (Masanobu Ando and Ryuhei Matsuda).

Fleur chooses a manga according to the drawings, and according to its notoriety on the internet, a real "word of mouth" according to her. She spots the "trends" in the Livejournal communities or specialized forums she frequents, and the series that generate the most drawings on DeviantArt. A friend sent her a link to "scanlation *dojinshi* on *Naruto*", and Fleur discovered Sumomo Yumeka, who is now one of her favorite authors, for the fineness of her line and the sweetness of her stories. Fleur looked for information on several mangakas, to understand their artistic trajectory and their way of drawing, and to find advices to help her in her own artistic and professional orientation. She particularly appreciates the author of *Naruto*, who knew how to persevere ("he has not said to himself by snapping his fingers: 'yeah I'm going to become that"), and who persisted to manage to draw the hands and the feet.

Fleur started drawing in the fourth and fifth grades, before discovering manga, "to decorate her pink-covered poetry notebooks" and to "illustrate the different stories she writes", such as a "mini-series about a horse", or a story inspired by the American comic strip *Elfquest*. The discovery of the manga *Kenshin* in the sixth grade was "a trigger": "I started drawing seriously at that time. I made tons of copies, mainly of Sojiro Séta from the manga". Fleur copies characters from *Gundam Wing*, *Sayuki* or Clamp's manga, but "frustrated by copying", she also creates original characters, which she works on for years and sometimes uses to illustrate her fanfictions. In the fourth grade, she discovered the MangaStyl website while searching the Internet for technical advice and drawing tutorials, then "kakis" (programs that allow the creation of drawings online) and drawing software (Photoshop). In the third year, her production is mainly dedicated to *Naruto* fanarts and to the influences of Clamp, Kaori Yuki and Kazuya Minekura. She loves art books. In the private catholic school where she was educated from kindergarten to high school, Fleur was perceived as "the girl who loves manga": "when you draw, in my school, it's more like: woaaaaaaaw, you're a rebel in life XD. (…) If you draw, you're an artist, you're apart and they kiss your ass". In high school, Fleur is known as a "visual kei fan" and in this "mini-society in itself" she admires the 12th grade boys: "my high school still has the mentality of middle school, except for the 12th grade students, who were too classy. They were too strong … and … and all the guys were potential bishis, super intelligent, and too classy". In her class of English-Japanese at university, "there are a lot of *otaku*, I might as well say it clearly". Fleur's younger sister also likes manga: she doesn't buy any but reads Fleur's. The two sisters also share an interest in video games and especially *visual kei*.

After falling in love with *Naruto*, Fleur's passionate discovery of *Death Note* encouraged her to resume drawing. Her taste for the mangaka Shirow Mina, who drives her "crazy especially because of the black/white flatness of the comics, the dynamism of the drawings" makes her "want to make comics". Fleur then participates in a comic book fanzine with Parisian friends, whom she met on a forum and whom she only meets at conventions and festivals, on the sales stand of their association. She proposed drawings for the first issues of the fanzine. On the advice of a friend, she then got involved in another forum, a "platform dedicated to amateur cartoonists, comic artists and mangakas" whose objective is to help amateurs to "set up their project and publish them in the fanzine sphere". Fleur created a 29-page comic strip for the special issue on fantasy. Fleur also illustrated a friend's script for another special issue of her fanzine ("the fanzine so much into flowers that it has powers") and created a comic for a special issue of the fanzine dedicated to "shonen ai".

Fleur went four times to the Japan Expo, once to the Japan Addict (Strasbourg), to the Chibi Japan Expo, to Paris Manga, and she also attends conventions in her region. She often goes there as an "exhibitor" with the team of her fanzine. Fleur likes cosplaying "at other people's houses", but says she is "too lazy" to do it. Fleur estimates that she has met "70% of her acquaintances on the Internet". In addition to her Facebook page, she maintains a LiveJournal blog and several pages on the DeviantArt website, where she publishes her drawings and fanfiction; she also participates in many forums gathering amateur artists, yaoi or visual kei enthusiasts. On her Deviantart site, Fleur has mentioned, on a "map of influences", the names of the artists and mangas that have inspired her. In this stylistic patchwork, popular shonen (*Kenshin*, *Naruto*, *Death Note* and *Gundam Wing*), more specialized Japanese mangakas and illustrators (Shirow Miwa, Sumomo Yumeka, Inio Asano, Hiroyuki Asada, Minekura), Chinese and American artists influenced by manga (the *Elfquest* series, Jo-chen, Benjamin), American comics, Japanese video games (*Final Fantasy*), but also Japanese bands (Plastic Tree, Dir en Grey). Fleur is indeed also passionate about Jrock, since the beginning of high school when she read *Nana* (she listens to Miyavi since the age of 14). For her 17th birthday, Fleur made a fanart in which she makes her self-portrait with Neji, her favorite character from *Naruto*. She also created many fanart about her favorite Japanese bands (Plastic Tree, Dir en Grey, Miyavi, Mucc, Kagrra ...). The comments on the DeviantArt site are generally positive: "You have a pretty lively pencil. We can see that you don't draw from yesterday"; "Your drawings are really dynamic, the poses are natural and supple". She tries to vary her influences, notably by reading comics and French-Belgian comics, so as not to have "a stereotyped drawing". In high school, she initially wanted to study art and drawing. In her final year of high school, she attended a selection interview at a private school that offered "refresher courses in applied art". She was accepted but finally preferred to study languages at the University, notably because of the high cost of the art school ("4000 euros, 5000 euros a year, for three or four years"). She chose "Japanese because I was interested in the language, not just in music or manga".

Fleur's passions are intertwined: it was on an amateur drawing site that she got advice on visual kei music. Since the beginning of the year

2000, the organization of tours of Japanese bands in France has given a new dimension to Fleur's passion for Jrock and visual kei, allowing her to realize a dream that she considered inaccessible a few years before: "I remember that before 2005, one of my big dreams as a fangirl was to see the Dir en grey (and only them) in concert, while I was getting used to the idea that a small metal band like them would never come to our country. The result is that I've seen them for the second time". She writes detailed reports on her blog about the concerts she attended with her sister and a group of friends since she was in high school. She saw the Japanese band Dir en Grey three times in concert, twice the singer Miyavi. She also attended concerts of Kagerou, Mucc, DIO-Distraught Overlord, An Café, Plastic Tree, L.M.C. and some others (Anli Pollicino, Keisha Ono, Yaneka …). This passion is expensive, the Parisian concerts requiring an organization and important expenses ("it was necessary to buy the train tickets (and we broke), the place of concert, to know where to sleep and the incidental expenses. It was very tense"). Fleur usually arrives very early in the morning to be among the first in line and spends the whole day waiting: for Miyavi's concert, she joined two friends who had spent the night in front of the concert hall around 7am; for An Café's concert, she arrived at 4am, to be ahead of the fans arriving with the first subways. Tensions between fans were high in the queue, and Fleur often complained about the "bullies", "the ever so uncivilized fans" who tried to pass her or "glared at each other and obviously criticized each other …". As soon as the concert hall opens, the challenge is to get to the front row as quickly as possible, and the concert experience is very physical: Fleur is often "pinned against the barrier", "obliged at times to elbow her way to the front because [she] has difficulty breathing". Fainting is frequent. At her first concert, Fleur was given advice by a fan she had met on the spot, "tips like following the movement during pogos or how to get a good seat". Fleur later gave some advice to novices who felt uncomfortable in line or during the concert. She sometimes launches into "pogos", takes up the choreography of the singers, starts "headbanging" on the most rocking songs, like at the Plastic Tree concert: "I headbanged so much that my neck still hurts and since Dir en grey, I hadn't been so sore and I hadn't gone so wild. At one point, I straighten up and then I started to rock back and forth, completely disoriented, I had gone too far [laughs]". The outburst of enthusiasm was collective: "We chanted Miyavi's name and then we hit the ground with our feet, we clapped our hands. In my corner, everyone was hysterical and seemed to know the words by heart. It was scary". The expression of emotions is also very intense. At Miyavi's

2008 concert, Fleur saw "quite a few people crying in the audience (and not just girls ... hmhm ...)". She has found herself in tears on several occasions, such as at the An Café concert ("It makes me laugh, I've always laughed at people who cry at concerts and now it's my turn"). And while Miyavi covers an old song they listened to in high school, Fleur and her friend "hold hands and, like idiots, start to cry". While Fleur's attitude is that of a "fan" (she also loves the fleeting contact with the singers during dedications: "he gives me back my album, I hold out my hand, a second little smile of the I'm-too-cool-baby type and he shakes my hand with a firm grip and yet another nod ... And I must admit, I left his hand with regret ..."), she is very critical of "the fan community, too superficial" and too attached "to the look": "you see them arriving, they are all dressed as eccentrically as possible, but just to show off, it's not necessarily because they like it: well, it's a concert, I can show off". Fleur defines "the fangirl syndrome", a term she claims in other places on the site: "There is everyone who ran, and then screamed like fangirls, they were there screaming, as if they were gods passing by, but I also like, during a concert I scream, because everyone, screams is normal, but sometimes they really have no restraint, it's quite shocking, the concert of DIO, there are still some who clung to him, well to the singer, it was quite indecent anyway. Personally, I don't like that aspect very much".

Since high school, Fleur says she is "more of a visual kei fan than a manga fan", especially because listening to music fits more easily into her schedule, "since it's music, you put it on and you can work on the side". She is influenced by visual kei groups in the field of clothing, "but more, the visual kei which is sober" that only connoisseurs can spot and which relies on the choice of patterns (tartan, plaid) and on an art of assembling clothes bought in "normal stores". During the summer vacations, she plans to "start sewing (...) in relation to clothing, to inspire me a little bit with everything that is visible, without necessarily being super eccentric".

Fleur also describes herself as "a big fat forum *rpg* addict", and has also played a few mmorpg, like *Ragnarok* and *Dofus*. She also loves the game *Samurai Warriors*, especially for the "bishi" character that she plans to "fan-art". Fleur loves literature, "Oscar Wilde and Rimbaud at the top of the list and then Poppy Z. Brite" (she would like to be offered "the super mega beautiful and expensive collector's book with lots of stuff about Rimbaud, his life, his works, his letters, etc.", and "the Rimbaud Verlaine DVD"), but also children's literature (by Jonathan Stroud, by Ted Van Loeschout). She had loved Ovid's *Metamorphoses*, read at school. She has just finished two novels by Haruki Murakami. She read the

French-Belgian comic books read by her father at a very early age and still reads them very occasionally, “when my father lends them to me and I find them good”. Fleur’s father does not read manga, and at first “he didn’t like it very much”, but he is curious about his daughters’ reading. Her mother “doesn’t read much”, but “is a little interested in the music we listen to, my father too, just to see what we’re doing”. Now “obliged” to study Japanese history for her classes, she often relates what she learns in civilization classes to manga or *Samurai Warriors*. Fleur has already read about the history of manga, but she is “not really very interested”; she has tried to read manga by Osamu Tezuka, because he is often presented as the “God of manga”, but she did not like these mangas, and she has forgotten the titles. Fleur would like to “travel the world” and especially go to Japan as part of her English-Japanese studies. Fleur also “really wants to go to China because my father is Chinese so I’m more interested in that than going anywhere else”. Fleur is very attracted to China, loves Chinese cartoonists, gives Chinese names to her favorite original characters, but she doesn’t “know my family on my dad’s side, I don’t really know where they are”.

CHAPTER 3

Reading Manga

And why do you read manga?

I haven't done enough philosophy to be able to answer that question. No, frankly, what you're asking is big

∵

Getting close to the heart of receptions, where the emotions, sensations and thoughts experienced when reading, watching a film or a series, listening to a tune of music, are worked out, is certainly not simple, and requires an uncomfortable reflexivity to avoid the tautological 'I love because I love' answers. While tastes and colors are not supposed to be explained, the words of teenage manga readers nevertheless allow us to understand why manga can gain a place of choice in their practices and sociability. Gérard Mauger, Claude Poliak and Bernard Pudal distinguished various ways of reading and expectations invested in reading: entertainment reading, didactic reading, salvation reading, aesthetic reading (1999). As surprising as it may seem, on the part of adolescent and on a production that is often deprecated, the pleasure of reading manga, whether one is passionate or not, is a combination of these various dimensions. Reading to while away the hours, for escapism, to laugh and cry, to admire and dream, or on the contrary to recognize and understand oneself, reading to learn about the world, Japan, oneself and others, reading to be of one's own age and gender, etc., such are the big recurrences, which are translated in various ways according to the series and the readers. This process occurs according to the series, but not according to any overarching principle that would classify titles according to their contents, the hierarchy of which, devised according to aesthetic or semantic legitimacy criteria, would correspond to a hierarchy of receptions and appropriations, each reception being the linking of a title with a reader, according to the characteristics of the latter and his expectations.

 | DOI:10.1163/9789004548312_005

1 Entertainment

1.1 *Enjoyment*

When we ask teenagers why they read manga, their first answers emphasize the notions of entertainment. Thus,"the need to be entertained" is an essential reason to read. It wobbles between reading against boredom or downtime, and reading for entertainment associated with a real pleasure ... the essential foundation of how reading is learned at this age (Baudelot, Cartier and Détrez 1999, 140). Manga is both a form of relaxation and entertainment:

> It entertains me ... it's my leisure time ... I'll work and then I'll read a manga, it will relax me. It's really my leisure time, where we relax, have a good time and have fun.
>
> MAEVA, 18, 12th grade, father an electrician, mother an accountant

> It's really for uh for relaxation, for uh ... it's really for leisure ... It's distracting.
>
> HUGO, 15, 10th grade, father a middle school history teacher, mother a nurse

> *And would you miss it if you had to stop reading?*
>
> Well yeah, because, when I have free time, I either paly on my computer or I read manga, so if I don't read you know, it's still going to be like: what am I going to do?
>
> NADIA, 14, 8th grade, father a worker, mother a secretary

Small readers such as Nayir, Noé or Léo, for whom manga is almost the only category of printed matter they read, emphasise the pleasure they get out of simply reading. Manga is above all a "pleasure reading":

> *What do you think you got out of reading manga in general?*
>
> General knowledge, and also a lot of pleasure. I mean things that I wouldn't get from reading other books.
>
> NAYIR, 16, 9th grade, father a delivery driver, mother a housekeeper

> I read them to pass the time ... I read them because I like them ... they're ... they're the only books I can read.
>
> LÉO, 15, 10th grade, father a commercial executive, mother a librarian

> For fun you know, I like it, it's … it's relaxation. Well, it's true that I don't really like reading big … literature. For example, one day I wanted to start reading The Lord of the Rings, as I had really liked films, I've been trying to read it for four years now, and I haven't even finished the second one (laughs).
>
> ARTHUR, 18, 1st year college student, father an executive, mother an accountant

Nayir's comments show that, as in the case of the detective novels analysed by Erik Neveu and Annie Collovald, "accessibility is directly and strongly associated with pleasure": the idea of a "lack of a cultural entrance ticket" is not associated with less pleasure, or with a low investment in reading practice (2004, 174).

1.2 *Escapism*

Entertainment can then be understood in its two meanings, in the sense of the French philosopher Pascal, entertaining oneself also means getting out of one's everyday life and to escape. This escape is made possible by the very accessibility of reading, which does not hinder imagination and daydreaming.

It is also facilitated by the universes staged, be it fantasy, intrigues with a historical background, or scenes from Japanese daily life. For Cécile (17, 1st year college student, father an executive, mother a freelance nurse), "the goal associated with reading manga is not to learn something. It is above all to escape" and Kalaya (18, 2nd year college student, parents executives) appreciates that "it clears the mind". Maureen (15, father a worker, mother an administrative agent) likes manga to "take her out of reality", as does Pierre (17, 11th grade, father a postman, mother a retired teacher), "because living too much in the real world is a bit boring, so it's good to get out of it a little once in a while", or Matthieu (17, 11th grade, parents architects), who reads "to imagine things other than his tiny life". The pleasure is the same as "watching TV" for Bastien (15, 10th grade, father a biologist, mother an engineer), to have "a world of escape".

But escape is not a luxury. It is necessary and allows for breathing, moments of putting school pressure aside, or troubles, be they big or small. Thus, for Laurent (18, 12th grade, father an engineer, stay-at-home mother):

> Since about the eleventh grade, it's true that I've been really interested in manga, I had to find a passion when it … when things were not going well in my life, I had to … I had to have a hobby to … to forget all that, now that it's better, I don't feel the need to live it so deeply.

The story has to be captivating, to allow readers to escape from reality and everyday life: the plots, based on twists and turns, as well as the suspense, which puts you on the edge of your seat until the next volume, according to the well-known "cliffhanger" principle used by the soap opera and television series scriptwriters, serve this logic, which means that manga readings are made in one go, even if you have to reread them later, or on scans, because you can't wait to see what happens next. Seriality is indeed a characteristic of the way manga is told and published, contributing to a narrative tension that contributes greatly to the reading pleasure in its very dimension of frustration. If Xavier criticizes those who take frustration too seriously, his remark on some of his comrades shows the strength of this frustration: "It's meant to have a good time, it's not meant to feel bad waiting for the next one".

This reading pleasure also accounts for the widespread practice of sharing hypotheses and theories, which have been shown to fuel forums and discussions in middle school courses. The importance of suspense explains Xavier's preference for manga over novels, and Arthur's preference for manga over traditional comics.

> *Is the type of story different?*
>
> Yeah, because *One Piece* always ends with suspense. Whereas *Eragon* when it's finished, it's a period that's over. Whereas *One Piece*, we know there's gonna be a sequel. We know that they're going to go to this place or that one afterwards.
>
> XAVIER, 17, 11th grade, father a firefighter, mother a childcare worker

> In a comic book, usually what you see is that in each volume there's a story, so there's for example, there's gonna be an investigation, there's gonna be … For Tintin and Snowy it's gonna be an investigation, for the Smurfs it's gonna be a story. Whereas a manga is … several volumes, it's actually a complete story. I prefer when the story lasts than when it's summed up in 40 pages or so.
>
> ARTHUR, 18, 1st year college student, father an executive, mother an accountant

> *And you know why you kept reading it?*
>
> Well actually, I like it because it's stories, it follows. It's in several volumes, or chapters, I don't know what you call it; and I like it. We're really into it. Because we always want to know what happens next
>
> MAUREEN, 15, 9th grade, father a worker, mother an administrative officer

> That's why when I read at night, it's not great because finally, I end up going to bed really late. That's the problem with manga, it's that even when you know the story you still rediscover a little bit, even though you know what's gonna happen, so you know that the sequel goes on, so you think I'm gonna stop there, but they always manage to make sure that the end of a volume is not the end of a story, so you're forced to continue the next manga, when you think I'm going to stop, you think I'm not going to stop in the middle of the manga, it's going to bother me to put a bookmark, and then it goes on and on.
>
> FÉLIX, 15, 11th grade, parents sculptors

The series read by teenagers last for dozens of volumes. They are paradoxical insofar as they are made up of successive episodes, most of which we don't know when they end, even though we know for sure that there will be an end which is always postponed. This explains why many teenagers dislike short or medium-length series, the end of which comes too quickly, or tank series, the end of which is sometimes "botched", "fizzles out" and is "open" according to Cécile (17, 1st year college student, father an executive, mother a private nurse), who feels then "left hungry for more", either because it leaves the reader alone and abandoned ("in fact you're sad that it has to have an end", according to Félix):

> For example, I'm going to say *Satan*, it's a manga that I find great, I mean it was going to be a long stuff, except that they have finished it in sixteen volumes, we're going to say about volume 12, they explain in their world that there are twenty-four ... there are twelve angels and twelve demons, they're super-powerful people, and in volume 12, we know three, and in volumes 14 and 15 we know all the others, so basically, it's an abrupt end, it's not very interesting. In the end, they rush the end and it becomes ... everything goes to shit.
>
> FÉLIX, 15, 11th grade, parents sculptors

Conversely, when the story drags on or the episodes become too repetitive, readers can pick up the phone and stop following the series, like Matthieu, who stopped *Naruto*, then *One Piece*, which "doesn't stop ... Often the series, they're good until between the fifth and tenth volume, and then it stretches, it stretches, it stretches, it's ... it gets boring". Nayir stopped *Bleach*, "because the story's kind of the same every time. They're always going to fight the same people". Kalaya (18, 2nd year college student, parents executives) also quit watching "the *Shaman Kings*, because afterwards it's not very interesting anymore, nothing happens anymore".

Just like the descriptions in the novels, some readers, who are generally rather weak readers, skip the overly descriptive parts or even the flash-back parts, which can be recognized in the grey background of the pages, and which slow down the pace of the action too much to their taste.

> Because some of them are not very interesting, in the books there are grey pages, dark grey pages, in fact they tell the past of the characters, that's … that's too long. It's not that it's not interesting but pfff …, it's that they cut the fight to tell the story of a character and then they come back to the fight, and we're … we can't wait for them to resume the fight so we're not really interested anymore but it's … it can be quite good, but it mustn't be too long, because there was a tome where it was just that, and then otherwise uh suspense, because they cut in the middle of a fight at the end of a tome and then you have to … you feel a little compelled to read the next tome.
>
> HUGO, 15, 10th grade, father a middle school history teacher, mother a nurse

1.3 *Laughing: A Serious Matter*

Another meaning of entertainment is humor. As we know, laughing is a serious matter, especially when you're a teenager. The importance of humor at this age was highlighted by psychologists and psychoanalysts (Kamieniak 2009). Serge Tisseron considers humor as one of the keys to understanding teenagers' taste for comics in general (2000), humor allowing, according to him, to cope with ambivalence and separation. Humor is also seen as one of the principles of appropriation of new media (text messaging, SMS, Youtube …) (Metton-Gayon, Aziz, Paris and Jost 2009). Humorous books and comic strips, and comedy shows are also at the top of the list of teenagers' preferences (Octobre, Détrez, Mercklé and Berthomier 2010).

The importance of humor can be noticed at several levels. It can be seen in the functions ascribed to manga as a whole, in comparison to other cultural media; within the manga website offer readers' preferences then often shift to manga genres and titles designated as humorous, to such an extent that it has become an indigenous category, "humor-manga"; the scenes and situations readers enjoy in manga, and which they preferably re-read, are largely those that are considered as the funniest ; finally, humorous lines are the ones that seem to be the most easily memorized and quoted, both in peer interactions and in the interview situation. In his analysis of "manga laughter", Jean-Marie Bouissou underlines the essential role of "marriages of humor":

> Japanese cartoonists know how to marry humor, like fantasy, with very various genres. These combinations, which are quite rare in our comic strip universe, brought something new that contributed a lot to make manga appealing. These combinations allow hitherto unseen script variations, but even more so, they make it possible to convey scenarios that, without humor and burlesque, would seem 'too much': too dark, too banal, too moralizing.
>
> 2009, 27–30

This variation of comedy within the most diverse genres of manga is indeed what explains its unifying character as well. Humor is mentioned as much by lovers of adventure and combat shonens as by readers of sentimental shojos. Bastien or Ludivine thus underline that manga always have a humorous dimension in their eyes:

> No, in fact, the advantage in manga is that even the incarnation of evil, they are nice characters. They are quite funny, they are to be taken with a pinch of salt, you know. You can't take them at face value. Manga always has a sense of humor.
>
> BASTIEN, 15, 10th grade, father a biologist, mother an engineer

> In all manga, you find a little humor, there's ... In shonen, there's a lot of humor. And in shojos too.
>
> LUDIVINE, 17, 11th grade, parents tax officials

Manga "that combine humor and fighting", to use Laurent's words, are popular, as the fight only makes sense in connection with a comic dimension. In the same way, only their humorous dimension makes the shojo acceptable in the eyes of Cécile (17, 1st year college student, father an executive, mother a private nurse).

> *You still compel yourself to read a few shojo?*
>
> When you put it like that, yeah. But in fact, generally speaking, there's a lot of humor in it. There better be some, otherwise I won't get hooked at all.

Lack of humor, conversely, can cause a manga to be less appreciated, like *Naruto* or *Dragon Ball* in the eyes of Nathaniel (17, 11th grade, raised by his mother, an unemployement office employee):

> *Dragon Ball* too, that's a bit what irritated me, like *Naruto* too a bit, is that the beginning is quite humorous, and then as time goes by, well the pages are less and less humorous. You know in *Dragon Ball*, there aren't a lot of texts, but then, there are even less. It's just Bim! Bam! Boom! it's just onomatopoeia. And in *Naruto*, it's just fighting between Naruto and Sasuke. It's more … Whereas in most other series, there is … *Evangelion*, it's a purely serious series, from the beginning, it's serious, so I like serious series, but sometimes, there is a little touch of humor, stuff like that. And what I like in a series, first of all, is humor.

1.3.1 Burlesque and Situational Comedy: A Comic Pattern of "Degradation"

Certainly, the comic dimension of the told scenes is hard to transcribe. However, when asked for examples of scenes that particularly made them laugh, the teenagers we met mention recurring patterns: the comic of burlesque degradation (Flandrin 2021), very present in the adventure and action shonen, features characters who are mocked due to their clumsiness and stupidity. In the dramaturgy of shonen manga, the hero is often a clumsy, naive and inexperienced teenager. Even though the hero goes forward in imaginary and fantastic universes, he nevertheless gets closer to the reader by his age.

The social forms of ridicule, shame, belittlement that he experiences are motives of the shonen comedy, and while this humor works among teenage readers, it may be because a connection can be made with their own social experience. In this regard the anti-heroes are the source of comedy, because they are too small, too clumsy, too coward:

> *Fairy Tail*, actually, it's a guild of wizards, and they're actually not very good. They suck, they're totally lame. And they're actually trying to get by. For example, she summons a mermaid to help her and the mermaid actually goes to her and says: 'Oh no, it's my day off so I gotta go!'
>
> ANNABELLE, 16, 11th grade, father a bank executive, mother a consultant

> Mostly it was just fun. It's a manga full of humor. Some scenes are a bit ridiculous, the characters very … either goofy or … In fact, there are several types: either goofy or, a bit like Naruto, a bit silly, but who believe in it. And the third type is more like lazybones, who are always jaded but who do anything. For example, Ueki's hero, well, he's Ueki, he's always stoned, and stuff happens to him, but he doesn't even realize it.
>
> NORA, 16, 11th grade, father a school teacher, stay-at-home mother

> Otherwise, in *Naruto*, he makes mistakes, he hits himself when he runs too fast.
>
> CORALINE, 17, 11th grade, father a worker, mother a cleaning lady

Scatological humor is obviously an inexhaustible comic resource, when characters find themselves diverted from their noble quest by their bodily needs, or their sexual desire …

> The one who makes me laugh the most is *Naruto*, because for example, I give a random example, a fight and then all of a sudden, Naruto farts, so it makes me laugh.
>
> VINCENTE, 12, 6th grade, father a garbage collector, stay-at-home mother

> There was a passage where Luffy is on an island full of enemies and at that moment there's Zorro who is ready to fight the enemies, and Luffy, he just had a big party the day before and he just drank a lot and he walks right into the middle of the fight scene, and he says 'pee', because he has to go to the bathroom.
>
> THÉO, 15, 10th grade, father a trainer in a transport company, mother a bank employee

> And in *GTO*, he's a big pervert, and I really enjoy it (laughs)!
>
> NABIL, 18, 12th grade, father an employee, mother a home-nurse

1.3.2 Nonsense and Absurd

In all these examples of burlesque comedy, we can clearly see the importance of the body, displaced, outraged, almost independent of the character which it belongs to, in strange situations that perhaps allow teenagers to cope with the discomfort and anxiety related to their own body that they sometimes perceive as strange and alien to themselves. Thus, the power associated with scatology and humor linked to sexual allusions take on meaning in daily, family, school and social life, where bodily manifestations must be concealed (Elias 1969), and where the body is only socially experienced in its wiping away (Détrez 2002). Graphical codes strengthen the comic objective of situations, when they are shared by adolescents, who learn to see and read signs, as important as the lines or actions drawn, the effects of which they are reinforced in the process. The drawings depict the disorders, particularly in their bodily expression, using metaphors in the true sense of the word: we remember the characters in Tex Avery who literally run away, or who, subject to great sexual emotion, have their jaws dropping, their eyes popping out of their heads, and so on. Humor is born from this figuration of metaphors. One of the comic elements specific to manga is also the use of the graphic style of the SD (abbreviation of "super deformed"), and the symbols used to express the embarrassment of the characters witnessing the clumsiness of their companion. Examples of this phenomenon are the "drop of embarrassment", the "vein of anger", the "pinched eyes of effort" or the hair undone (Sigal 2006).

1.3.3 Comedies in a School Setting: Satire and the Subversion of Authority

Situational comedies play also a big role. Next to the islands and fantastic worlds, some manga depict more specifically the relationships between students, and between teachers and students, in the school context: *Love Hina*, or *GTO*, to name only the most popular ones, provide obvious humorous contexts. Keitaro, in *Love Hina*, failed the entrance exam to the prestigious Todai University in Tokyo three times, and Nora enjoys his character as a "loser". Above all, the success of *Great Teacher Onizuka*, the thug turned professor, with his unacademic teaching methods, illustrates the carnivalesque principle of the reversal of values, where the dunce teaches, and legitimate and serious characters are mocked. The transgressive value of carnivalesque inversion, and the role it plays in "authoritarian" contexts, has been highlighted, especially in the case of popular cultures and socially or politically dominated categories (Bakhtine 1968; Scott 1990). While in the classroom, we are far from the coercion used on black slaves, South American peasants or the living conditions of the people in the Middle Ages, the inversion of roles and situations of authority is nevertheless obvious.

> I mean, *GTO* tells the story of a former hoodlum who becomes a teacher, using methods that are not at all up to standard to teach his students. I liked it, it made me laugh a little.
>
> NATHANIEL, 17, 11th grade, raised by his mother, an employment office worker

> *And what do you like about* GTO*?*
>
> Well, it's the high school world, the humor ... A former thug who becomes a teacher, that's quite bold, it's out of the ordinary.
>
> MADJI, 19, 11th grade, father a bus driver, stay-at-home mother

1.3.4 Humor in Coming-of-Age Comedies: Comical Variations on Romantic and Sexual Relationships

Sentimental relationships are another theme that is the subject of humorous declensions. These are mainly sentimental comedies that take place in schools, intended for both girls and boys, but this sentimental dimension is also present, to a lesser extent, in the adventure and action manga mentioned above. The range of relationships between girls and boys, the stages of sentimental life, from the birth of love to the formation of a couple after love has been declared, feed a repertoire of comic situations, based on misunderstandings and the clumsiness of the characters involved. Jean-Marie Bouissou sums up the main specificities of this type of humor as follows:

> A repetitive situation comedy based on emotional and/or sexual imposed figures that the reader knows by heart: the shy boy's indecision in the face of the multiplicity of panties in the wind, the zany chance that makes the first love declaration fail a thousand times, the thrashing of the libidinous male by the female he desires, the misunderstanding just before a slap in the face, the epistaxis (nosebleed) gushing out in front of the accidentally disclosed female nudity, the misplaced erection of a boy that a sadistic screenwriter forces to share the room of the girl he secretly dreams about.
>
> 2009, 30

As in some American comedies for teenagers (teen movies), comic effects in manga are produced by staging some "first time rituals": first declaration of love, first sexual emotions, first feelings experienced ... While these rituals are subject to different codes in Japan, which include a ritualization of the declaration of love that seems to be more state-of-the-art and which only occurs after a fairly long period of time, the readers interviewed, however, are very sensitive to the comic staging of the lack of experience and difficulties in adjusting to these codes and in mastering relationships with the other sex. These mangas also deal with the diffifficulties in mastering one's body and emotions. Many readers referred to the humor of manga like *Love Hina* ("*Love Hina*, I read them all too. It's pretty funny, because it's about a guy with big tits and an ugly guy who gets chased by those big-titted girls. [laughs]", Kalaya), *Negima* ("He's a 12-year-old boy who's going to teach girls who are 16 years old. So, lots of goofy stuff, uh, stuff like that" according to Hacine), which are sometimes referred to as "harem" manga, featuring a clumsy boy who, by a set of circumstances, happens to be surrounded by pretty young girls, which gives rise to a whole bunch of misunderstandings.[1] The *School Rumble* series thus accumulates misunderstandings linked to a sentimental imbroglio within a high school class ("The story is actually a trio in love, but who precisely ... There's a girl that is in love with a boy, but the boy doesn't love her, because he prefers curry [laughter]", according to Nathaniel). But sentimental relationships are also a source of comedy in manga like *Naruto*, where the love chain is visibly less tragic than in *Andromache* (by Jean Racine).[2]

> It's funny because Sakura, she loves Sasuke, and Sasuke doesn't, and it's Naruto who loves Sakura. And they're actually in the same group. It's funny, because when Sakura asks Sasuke to date her, Sasuke coldly answers 'no', while Naruto, he's always there acting like a gentleman. And he's always the one who gets the beating instead of Sasuke.
>
> NAYIR, 16, 9th grade, father a delivery driver, mother a housekeeper

As for *Step Up Love Story*, it is more explicitly centered on the discovery of sexuality, and the main character's setbacks in this respect:

> *Step Up Love Story*, I liked it, it's rather funny, because there's the personality of the hero ... I don't know, it's weird, it's funny. He gets married to a woman, by an organization, it's a marriage ... And except he's precocious, so he always arrives first, let's say (laughs). And the woman, she almost never gets anything, so actually, it's just ... He's just trying to get better, stuff like that. And then there's the personality of the brother, who is always yelling at his brother, stuff like that. Then, at work, he's surrounded by pretty girls but he can't because he's faithful to his wife. And then there's his wife's sister who also excites him a bit. It's quite funny.
>
> NATHANIEL, 17, 11th grade, raised by his mother, an employment office worker

Finally, a theme also arouses laughter, which, as we shall see, works as a gendered reminder of order: that of transvestism. Experiences of cross-dressing or the blurring of gender identities form a scriptwriting element and comic effect

---

1 Scenes that allow "fan service", *i.e.* "useless sequences that show female characters in very sexy postures or framing" (Animeland n°94, September 2003, p. 69).

2 Orestes loves Hermione, who loves Pyrrhus, who loves Andromache, who loves her husband Hector who died ... Which, for *Naruto*, results in "there is Naruto who loves Sakura. Sakura who loves Sasuke. But Hinata loves Naruto, Kiba loves Hinata ... Sasuke hates Itachi. Itachi hates his father." (Marie).

used in a large number of mangas. This device causes a great deal of misunderstandings, as shown in Rumiko Takahashi's famous manga, *Ranma ½,* the hero of which, a high school student, turns into a girl as soon as he is contact with cold water. There are a lot of vaudevillian situations based on gender stereotypes and the concealment of identities. Ludivine and Nathaniel mention the humor of the manga *Otomen*, a shojo featuring a boy who shows all the outward signs of virility at school, but who is in fact himself a shojo lover, loves sewing, interior decoration and cooking:

> In *Otomen*, for example, there's a lot of humor, because he's an otomen who has to hide the fact that he likes feminine things, so he pretends he's a tough guy and all that, but he gets into a lot of situations where he's sewing or making food, so there's a lot of stuff like that.
>
> LUDIVINE, 17, 11th grade, parents tax officials

> *Otomen* that too, by name. I read the first chapter, I had a little booklet. The story made me laugh a bit (laughs) because he's a guy, he's a man, well, he's a high school student, he looks quite virile, but when he's at home, it's all pink, there's a lot of cute little things, when he sees something cute, he goes totally nuts. It's kind of funny, but I haven't read the whole series.
>
> NATHANIEL, 17, 11th grade, raised by his mother, an employment office worker

> In *One Piece*, yeah I remember, it wasn't in those volumes, they were in their boat fishing and instead of catching fish, they caught a … a transvestite, that's what … yeah that made me laugh, with the big words, ah we caught a transvestite, that makes me laugh!
>
> HUGO, 15, 10th grade, father a middle school history teacher, mother a nurse

> And so, it's quite funny how he fights with attacks … His attacks are quite funny, when you meet him he was in a tutu, swans on his shoulders, completely ridiculous
>
> FRANCK, 17, 11th grade, father a cardiologist father,
> mother a healthcare network coordinator

Humor has various degrees of legitimacy, within the manga universe as in all written productions. Thus, Madji (19, 11th grade, father a bus driver, stay-at-home mother) got into a debate with a pupil of his class about comparing the humorous aspects of manga … and Molière. We notice indeed here to which extent manga brings Madji a cultural capital that he then tries to value in comparison with more legitimate cultural references. Grasping subtle humor also becomes a skill, which is given only to experts who can identify the references.

> Exactly, we had a debate in high school, or like we were saying that Molière ... It was Molière, I think. In fact, there was a guy in my class who said manga would never be at Moliere's level. And we argued about it. And, in the end, I found only one manga that would be Moliere's level, namely *Adieu Monsieur Desespoir* [*Sayonara Zetsubo Sensei*]. It's meant to be funny, it makes daily life experiences look ridiculous. Like when he's negative, he always says: 'I want to kill myself, I'm going to kill myself'. He takes a rope, he wants to kill himself. It takes particular themes, it makes them bigger just to make it ridiculous. It's really quite funny. You know, for example, there are manga that are mean to be funny, but the problem is that the humor is always the same, or it's based on other anime, that I don't find it innovative. As long as these are subjects taken from other manga, or it's for example, we take a manga, and we make fun of it, I don't think it's funny, because in the end, I find it insulting, for one thing. And worse, sometimes it's badly done. Humor is not interesting enough, not enough, and when it takes subjects of life, it's already more interesting. [...] Humor too, as in *Sayonara Zetsubo Sensei*, where humor is sometimes quite subtle, and you really need to have good knowledge or a good vision of things to understand humor.

Similarly, Tom contrasts manga, such as *One Piece*, where humor is "first degree", with those where the humour is more subtle: "It's pretty simple humor. It's not really what they intended to do. It's first degree".

1.3.5 Plays on Words

Caroline (14, 9th grade, father a shopkeeper, mother an insurance trainer) also appreciates the "fresh, childlike humor" of *Yotsuba, AzuMangaDaioh*; Yohanna (16, 10th grade, father an engineer, mother a sales representative) says he laughs at "nonsense", Kalaya (18, 2nd year college student, parents executives) calling "dumb" what makes her laugh. In this scale of legitimacy, plays on words, and especially the authors' mises en abyme are put forward more by adolescents from privileged backgrounds:

> [*YakiTate Japan*] Uh, basically it's a little bit simple, so they're bakers, but when you see people's reactions when they eat the bread, well, that's really fantastic, and well, they often put little notes in there, because basically,

it's in Japanese with subtitles, and there are notes to explain a little bit, but some words are misunderstood. The main character is not very very clever, I would say, and when we ask him to make a croissant for example, the Japanese pronunciation is "kloassan", and "-san" is also a suffix to say Mr. or Mrs., and he understood "Kloa-san", Mr. Kloa, he didn't understand that we were asking him to make a croissant, so he calls his family at the other end of Japan to ask them: "Who the hell is Kloa-san?" Well, finally we have to explain to him exactly what it is because he doesn't know much about baking, he knows how to make it but he doesn't make too much, so he often confuses words and you know (laughs). Well, that's why there are the notes, that's why it's explained, because it's true that it's one of the basic elements of manga humor."

CÉLIA, 17, 11th grade, mother an opera director, father a choreographer

The French translation, when they translate names they don't make too much effort, it's a bit strange stuff like 'Cherry Flower', or 'Liar', names like that are often related to the character—that's funny in manga too, usually, in France, apart from *Gaston Lagaffe*, the characters have a very trite name. When you translate, you can see that the author makes humor out of the names, it's funny. Usob, uh Usob means liar, in *One Piece* … Usob, hence his name, he spends his time lying, a real coward […] the author plays on little tricks like that. […] One time, it was so huge, an anecdote in brackets, that the character was vaporized by a sort of column of lightning, the character caught in it, everyone is sad: 'Oh, he's dead', etc., and he arrives, he goes: 'But who died'. And everyone turns around: 'Ah but, how did you get out of it?', and he scratches his head, and he says, 'Author's Facts'.

FRANCK, 17, 11th grade, father a cardiologist father,
mother a healthcare network coordinator

Tezuka, it's a little bit more childish, but the funny thing is, he adds himself to the comic book.

MICKAEL, 19, 12th grade, parents executives

1.4 … *and Crying*

For sure manga make you laugh, but they also make you cry. This other form of participatory reading, which thus engages physical reactions, is recurrent in interviews. Girls admit to it more easily than boys do. They confess that they sometimes cry as well, but to a lesser extent, given the social norms of masculinity (see below). The death of a character is experienced emotionally, and crying is part of the pleasure, as Marianne points out in relation to the dramas, for whom "it's so easy to cry that it's not even funny" or Nabil, who remembers crying and says: "It was good". Leila, for example, was "shocked" by the death of a character she "loved" and she says that "it feels like a void without him afterwards". Although it is easier to cry in front of an anime or drama than when reading a manga, there are many examples where the emotion was so intense that it caused tears. The precision of the memories of these scenes is an indication of this emotional involvement.

> Yes, I often cried when I was watching manga, that's for sure. I know I'm not the only one, by the way. Sometimes, when a character you love very much dies, or is in dire straits, you are more or less moved.
>
> *And do you remember anything that happened?*
>
> *Naruto* is one of the first manga I read, and I wasn't at all used to sad situations in comics, given that before that I read classic French comics. I think it's in volume 4, there's a character called Haku that I liked a lot and who had a really sad death, let's put it that way, and I remember that it moved me a lot.
>
> ESTELLE, 17, 12th grade, father a bank clerk, mother a school nurse

> The end of *Count Cain*, it is magnificient and at the same time so sad. The main character, Cain, dies, but the last picture is so beautiful, it's in an explosion, and as he's in a very glassed-in place, there are a lot of pieces of glass around him; it's arranged so that it looks like he has some kind of wings. It's magnificient, but to such an extent that it just grabbed my throat and I cried.
>
> MARIANNE, 16, 11th grade, father a numerical control operator, mother a restaurant employee

> *Dragon Ball*, that's special. This manga is a religion. I was reading, I was crying. When I saw the end, I wanted to cry. When he took the other one under his wing, to go teach him, the black one, Majin Boo …
>
> *And Love Hina, did you like it?*
>
> Yeah, I thought it was good. I don't know why. I was going through a tragic time (laughs). No, I don't know why, it's not bad. I thought it was a little … No, there was too much emotion in it. As soon as I read, I was with the character, I cried with him, it was good.
>
> NABIL, 18, 12th grade, father an employee, mother a home-nurse

> Yeah, the black guy, I could see him flying away, I don't know, I started crying for about thirty minutes. All the most beautiful manga are the ones that make you cry at the end. For example, *Elfen Lied*, it killed me. I don't know, the little girl who was mean in a wheelchair, I mean the crazy one, with several arms, yeah, that's it, she's mostly the one who gets tortured, in short, the redhead, it made me sad at the end … *Dragon Ball Z*, Son Goku, he's the one who dies all the time. He was always making me cry that idiot.
>
> MOUSSA, 18, 12th grade, father a doctor, mother a pharmacist

> I don't necessarily read dramatic manga but let's just say that *GTO* upset me because the hero dies at the end (laughs). I must have cried for hours and hours, and it still happens when I read it.
>
> LÉO, 15, 10th grade, father a commercial executive, mother a librarian

The ordeals experienced by the characters have effects on readers, and involve a quasi-bodily reading, between tension and suspense to know the end, which compels to continue the series without being able to turn off the light. Laughter and tears are experienced as an integral part of the reading pleasure.

2 Relatability

Humor and entertainment have far more elaborate functions than might seem at first glance. By laughing at the characters, their clumsiness, their embarrassment, readers also laugh at themselves, and the embarrassing situations their heroes have to deal with undoubtedly make it possible to trivialize, to play down episodes that have happened or could happen. The school grounds obviously offers a context teenagers can relate to, even though the more fantastic worlds where teenage characters most often go forward, can also work, metaphorically, on this dimension. In these "unusual encounters" (Petit 2008), Michèle Petit underlines indeed the role of metaphor in reading experiences, understood here not as a figure of speech, but as a figuration of one's own experience, through displacement into other contexts, times or places. It is in a Japanese novel, whose shared references are striking with manga, that one could find a literary exhibition of this metaphorical importance. Thus, Haruki Murakami, recalling in Kafka on the Shore that the labyrinths were originally those of the bowels in which the Etruscans read the future, and thus an exteriorization of the meanders of the interiority, puts in the mouth of one of the characters the key to understanding the magical forests, the worlds populated by spirits that populate his novels, Miyazaki's cartoons … or manga:

> What we call the universe of the supernatural is none other than the darkness of our own minds. Long before Freud or Jung shed light on the workings of the unconscious in the 19th century, people had already instinctively established a correlation between the unconscious and the supernatural, considered as two dark worlds. It wasn't a metaphor. […] It was probably impossible for people at the time to think of the two worlds of darkness in different terms. Today it's different. The outer darkness has cleared up, but the inner darkness remains. What we call ego or consciousness is the tip of the iceberg: the most important part remains buried in the kingdom of darkness and there lies the source of the contradictions and deep confusions that torment us.
>
> Around your mountain hut there was real darkness.
>
> Exactly. The real darkness still exists there. Sometimes I go there only to contemplate it.
>
> MURAKAMI 2006, 306–307

Of course, the comments of teenagers do not reach such a degree of psychoanalytical elaboration … Some of them remain do refuse any idea of identification, because of the unrealistic aspect of the worlds depicted in manga:

> No, I've always been realistic on this subject!
>
> BASTIEN, 15, father a biologist, mother an engineer

> No, well I can't … it's … it's … it's completely unreal, you can't … you can't imagine … […] or except that I lived on an island when I was a kid, the beginning could seem real, because the character ends up on an island.
>
> HUGO, 15,10th grade, father a middle school history teacher, mother a nurse

> But you still have to be realistic, it's not … it's not possible.
>
> VINCENTE, 12, 6th grade, father a garbage collector, stay-at-home mother

> No, it's too fantastic. It's so fantastic, it has nothing to do with the real world.
>
> XAVIER, 17, 11th grade, father a fireman, mother a childcare worker

Moussa, likewise, rejects any idea of identification, to which his friend Nabil retorts that it's because there are no black heroes in manga, and that Freud would retort that he identifies ... unconsciously.

> Maybe it's because there are no black heroes. But subconsciously there are. Yes, Freud said that about manga ... No, I'm just kidding.
>
> NABIL, 18, 12th grade, father an employee, mother a home-nurse

> Yeah, probably. Besides, try and find a black Japanese guy.
>
> MOUSSA, 18, 12th grade, father a doctor, mother a pharmacist

These few teenagers thus oppose the fantasy reading pact as an obstacle to identification ... But the most astonishing thing is undoubtedly the number of those who, conversely, implement identification strategies, whether admiring or empathetic, whether they are directed at them, their friends or the everyday life.

As Éric Maigret points out about the world of American comic book superheroes, a world that is apparently just as far removed from the daily lives of teenagers, "the world of superheroes, made up of fights where you never get seriously injured, of gathering between friends, of conflicts between friends, also seems particularly relevant to children, for whom it irresistibly eminds of schoolyard fights and their climate of physical and psychological insecurity" (1995). The construction of the self thus goes beyond the mere identificatory dimension, which makes one recognize oneself in such or such a character, even though this dimension exists, focused around the comparison with the personality trait of a character, or an ideal identification with a "perfect" character.

2.1 *The Various Facets of Identification: Admiring*

The notion of identification is part of the common sense, and Martin Barker reminds us that the history of this concept is marked by "the hold of behaviorist psychology and psychoanalysis: it has mainly been used rhetorically in public debates on the media's effects, in statements on reading, and has been little tested empirically" (2005). The term identification encompasses a multiplicity of facets, as shown by the typology of the five models of identification outlined by Hans Robert Jauss, which distinguishes "the admiring identification", with the perfect hero, the model, "the example that must be followed", and "the identification out of sympathy" with an imperfect, more common hero, "belonging to the same species as the spectator" (1978, 165). Jauss still mentions the cathartic identification, the associative identification and the ironic identification. Each of these modalities of identification is characterized by a reference character type, a receptive disposition, and norms of behavior. Like Jauss, Marie or Laurent clearly distinguish two modes of identification to characters:

> *Do you have any favorite characters?*
>
> Darren Shan. Cause I think we have a little bit of the same taste. He likes spiders, anything creepy. They're often endearing, they each have a different character. Actually, our favorite characters, we relate to them. Either we recognize ourselves, or it's the way we'd like to be. For example, Itachi, in *Naruto*, he is straight. He is straight, he is not afraid.
>
> MARIE, 14, 9th grade, father an accountant, mother a housekeeper

> In every manga, I have a favorite character. Either it's our model, or we identify with the character, it depends.
>
> LAURENT, 18, 12th grade, father an engineer, stay-at-home mother

The admiring identification is thus particularly vivid in some teenagers fascinated by the superpowers, the "smart" attitudes, the intelligence or the charisma of the hero. Kader (18, father an industrial painter, mother a housewife) appreciates that Tsubasa "brings out something beyond us" and says to himself "it would be nice if I was like him, you see. You know, sometimes I promise you, I tell myself: 'I would like to be like this character'". Léo (15, father an executive, mother a librarian) likes Allen Walker, by *D.Gray-Man*, "because he has style", just like Maureen:

> I can't remember her name. It's in *Naruto*. She's, how can I put it, basically the leader of the ninjas. And she's the one who says, 'Well, you're gonna do this, you're gonna do that, you're gonna get so-and-so … you're gonna train …' I like her because she's the one with the most power, I mean she's the one who has power over others.
>
> MAUREEN, 15, 9th grade, father a worker, mother an administrative officer

But more often than not, and especially in privileged circles, it is not the "perfect" heroes who are chosen as favorite characters, on the contrary. For example, Annabelle (16, 11th grade, father a bank executive, mother a consultant) stopped watching the series *Fate/Stay Night*, because 'the hero tries to be one, and therefore, it gets on my nerves'. Or else they must have dark sides and ambiguities … Most of these heroes are ambiguous characters who had to cope with a very troubled family past, and therefore have multiple inner flaws. What arouses attachment therefore, is often the inner suffering that hides behind a mask of apparent strength and determination. Laurent thus expresses his interest for one of the main characters of *Death Note*, and for the two brothers heroes of *Full Metal Alchemist*:

> *And do you have any favorite characters who marked you ...?*
> Yes, the character in *Death Note*, the first detective, because in fact there's a calm, serene side to him. He's introduced to us as the greatest detective of all time, and he's a teenager who has some weird, strange quirks, so we get attached to him. And so that's why, and even when he dies, we ... well, it's not ... we still remember him anyway. There's this one, there's the ... the brother in *Full Metal Alchemist*, Edward Elric. Those are the two characters that really made an impression on me.
> *And the Elric brothers, why?*
> Well, because first of all, they're two teenagers, and they're ... they're ... I mean, no, you can't even get close to them, identify, but ... I don't know, it's a character who has a personality, who ... And so ... I think you have to read several manga to get attached to this character. I mean when you know his personality, it's interesting.
> LAURENT, 18, 12th grade, father an engineer, stay-at-home mother

Like him, Ashkan's (18, twelfth grade with a focus on scientific area, parents clothing brand manager and stylist) favorite character is "the beast-looking guy Nugen [...] but on the other hand he's hyper-sensitive too". Annabelle (16, 11th grade, father a bank executive, mother a consultant) likes Haru, a *Fruits Basket* hero who "has a kind of dual personality". As for Ludivine (17, parents tax officials), she prefers Sasuke, who in *Naruto* is "a dark and gloomy character":

> It's often the tortured characters that are the most impressive ... In *Black Butler*, it was the same, this 12-year-old English lord who lost his whole family, and who has no one next to him, who pushes everyone away, and that's a lot of characters like that.

Another "offbeat" admiring identification is the one that focuses on the secondary characters, somtimes considered as more interesting, less unidimensional than the hero. These "discrepancies" can be read as a greater sensitivity to psychologization, especially in the privileged circles (Maigret 1995; Cotelette, Détrez and Pluvinet 2007), a sign of distinction in terms of both age and gender, which we will come back to later. But the distinction can also be a way of distancing oneself from too obvious or naive identifications, or too obviously heroic, as Maureen expresses it well when asked if she prefers main or secondary characters: "Secondary! Because everybody likes heroes and that pisses me off. They're not necessarily the ones who, I mean the story doesn't necessarily work because of them you know. Because they're not alone. So, yeah, the secondary characters", as well as Alexandre: "I have to say that it's rarely the main character actually. The main character, we take too much care of him".

2.2 *Recognizing Oneself*

On the contrary, the empathetic identification is rooted in a common point, either psychological or physical, with a character: the clumsiness, impulsiveness, bad temper of the characters, which we have seen to which extent they were at the principle of comic, thus allow to recognize themselves, and to smile about it. Nabil prefers Trunk (*Dragon Ball*) "because he was small, and he was a bit like [him]" (laughs). Tom likes Zorro in *One Piece*, because "I'm a bit like him, actually. I'm not very sociable, I kind of keep my distances with other people, but when they need help, I'm always there for them". Nathaniel likes Onizuka (GTO), Urd (*Ah My Goddess*) and Levi (*Reborn*), "impulsive" characters like him, and Terrence (*Dreamland*), because "he's pretty much like me: he's always upside down. I'm like him, in class (laughs), I'm half asleep".

Salim (19, father a mason, mother a cleaning agent) identified with Piccolo in *Dragon Ball* "because sometimes I'm quite lonely, sometimes I like to be alone, like him". Marie (14, father an accountant, mother a cleaning agent) loves tomboys "like her", just like Maele, who in *Ranma* prefers Akane, "because she looks like me, she doesn't let herself be taken in, she is like me. It's because she's a real tomboy too clumsy in love … in fact I always wanted to be a martial arts professional like her. That's why I like her". Coraline (17, 11th grade, father a worker, mother a cleaning lady) relates to the hero of *Love Hina*, "because he's very goofy, and well I'm a bit goofy too", just like Ludivine (17,11th grade, parents tax officials):

> *And the characters you identify with?*
>
> It's rather the clumsy characters (laughs) who are a bit out of place all the time!… The classic character of the female manga. It's very often clumsy or shy girls, things like that … who have a hard time either talking to boys, or in class who always make a blunder, things like that. Here, the character that marks me the most is in *Black Butler*; it's the character I dress up the most. In fact, it's the 'maid' in quotation marks from the mansion, who's very clumsy, who can't see anything, who's shy and that's it. There is a possibility of identification yes. I identify quite a lot with

> her: I'm just as clumsy as she is (laughs) and there are moments when I find myself in situations that can be similar!

Léo (15, 10th grade, father an executive, mother a librarian) even manages to intellectualize this process of identification:

> I think I adapt myself to almost every character, because you can recognize yourself in almost every character concerning some traits of characters, so you get attached to everybody, I think that's also the goal of the manga [...] it's a caricature, this is a bit far-fetched, it will never exist but that's what's interesting, because it's excessive and we laugh about it, even if we know we have those features in real life to some extent, we laugh about ourselves and we question ourselves.

Manga then becomes a reading grid, of oneself and of others, and the friendly sociability can even elaborate games of comparison between one and the other. Kalaya (18, 2nd year college student, parents executives) compares her best friend to a *Fruits Basket* heroine, who is also extremely clumsy. Comparing herself to the characters in *Fruits Basket* was a game between Estelle and her friends. Coraline finds in *Naruto* her little brother, just as "insolent", Alexandre and her friends compare themselves to the characters of *D.Gray-Man* and *Reborn*, "as well on the temperament side as on the physical side" even if physically, it is more complicated "because of the hairdo"... Maureen compares one of her friends, who wears long, black and straight hair, to Sasuke. Similarly, Célia and her best friend both compare themselves to the *D.Gray-Man*'s characters, Kanda and Allen. The resemblance based on their characters is heightened when it comes to their friendly couple, since, just like these two friends, they never stop teasing and arguing. They have even pushed identification to the point of disguising themselves as cosplayers (just like Ludivine disguising herself as a clumsy little maid to whom she compares herself), one as Kanda, the other as Allen, and playing an argument scene ... intensified in real life by an argument in the locker room ...

> But for example, *Saiyuki* and *D. Gray-Man*, I'm compared to the same kind of character. In *Saiyuki*, the main character, Sanzo, who's a monk but smokes, drinks, shoots anything and has a really bad temper: I'm compared to that character, apparently, I have a bad temper (laughs). And in *D.Gray-Man*, he's a really cold samurai who doesn't like anyone

> and doesn't hesitate to attack his friends to get them to leave him alone (laughs). I am compared to this character (laughs). By my best friend. But it works both ways because I compare her in *Saiyuki* to a character who only thinks about eating all the time ans who is really childish. And to the central character in *D.Gray-Man* who is also quite childish, very smiling, and only thinks about eating so (laughs). There are times when it's true that it corresponds to me, especially because, in both manga, the two characters have the same relationship : one hits the other, and there are often arguments, well we do it in a more friendly way but it's true that it's like that ... […] And in the dressing rooms, well, as usual, we argue a little bit, and well, it's friendly but for us it's natural, and then some people say : 'Yeah, a real Allen-Kanda fight' (laughs).
>
> CÉLIA, 17, 11th grade, mother an opera director, father a choreographer

The comparison between manga and daily life, outside of oneself or one's friends, can also relate to scenes and situations one has either experienced or observed:

> Sometimes you meet little idiots in the street who play smart with you, sometimes you ... It's like in manga, you see people who think they are stronger than the others, who want to play smart with you, it's the same thing, in fact it's to take them down a peg or two, because all the time you have to ... you can't let yourself go, people come to you all the time, they look down on you, they think they're I don't know who, so uh me that ... so uh me I think that ... I think that sometimes, what you find ... there, you find real things that you find in manga and in real life.
>
> SALIM, 19, 12th grade, father a mason, mother a cleaning agent

> I don't know anymore. It was while I was waiting for the subway. Yes, very interesting situation. There's a girl who gets groped by a pervert and in manga it happens all the time. You see the great reference, already. I'm not going to help her, I'm just thinking of manga, that's all.
>
> CÉCILE, 17, 1st year college student, father an executive, mother a private nurse

Another element is obviously central to the process of identification: there are many series that feature a child growing up and becoming an adolescent. This is particularly the case for the most popular series that children discovered in kindergarten or primary school through cartoons, such as *Dragon Ball Z* or *Naruto*. Just like Harry Potter, "Naruto grows up with them". This is, moreover, explicitly what Maureen says ("It's already changing, and we're growing with it"). Ashkan and Nayir emphasize the interest of seeing the character grow:

> In the ones I liked, like Naruto for example, you see it starts when he's little, when he's really little, then when he's average, preteen, and it ends when he's preadult.
>
> ASHKAN, 18, 12th grade, father a director of a clothing brand, mother a stylist

> Naruto, *do you still like it?*
>
> Yeah, 'cause it's actually getting more and more exciting. He tells stories when they're little, and as they get older.
>
> NAYIR, 16, 9th grade, father a delivery driver, mother a housekeeper

Manga thus provides a grid for reading the problems or issues experienced during adolescence. These ethical and practical expectations explain why Leila stopped reading "fantasy", declaring that she now prefers "realism". In *Hana Yori Dango*, Maele and Marianne liked the description of the heroin's distress, which leads her to commit suicide, because "it reflects reality to some extent. Because you don't have to look far to find people who are cutting their wrists, not necessarily because they are persecuted, but for other reasons". Stories of "tortured" teenagers, diffifficulties in love affairs and betrayal of friends, situations which undoubtedly echo daily questions even if Caroline, Maureen and the others do not say so explicitly:

> In *Comme Elles* [*Anoko to Issho*], it's the same thing, teenage girls and then, since it's adolescence, they all go through passages that aren't very ... well, we'll say it. All their relationships with boys, how they get away from each other. It's very realistic, so it's nice to read. Setona Mizushiro, who acted in *Ace*, *X Days*. So, her manga are shojo, but it's the same, with tortured teenagers, we'll say. That's interesting.
>
> CAROLINE, 14, 9th grade, father a shopkeeper, mother an insurance trainer

> *Do you pay attention to the emotional relationships between the characters?*
>
> Yeah, but this, on the other hand, could be realistic. Pretty much, yeah. Because there are stories of friendship where one has betrayed the other ... love stories ... but it's ok, it's not too slushy either, eh? Exactly, this, on the other hand, it could be real. It's not boring. [...] When you see the adventures that happen to them ... It's a bit like us ... in life, at school ... we fight, we don't fight ... Because it's the same, they also have fights. Then

> maybe it's unconscious, but for example I know that there are friends you can count on, and others you can't.
>
> MAUREEN, 15, 9th grade, father a worker, mother an administrative officer

Safya is also an emblematic case of this "interested" reception (see Portrait below). Safya is a 15-year-old girl who wears the veil. Until recently, she only read shonens borrowed from her brother, and she discovered the shojos thanks to her female friends. She reads a lot of them, particularly for their description of adolescent sentimental relationships and their staging of the first questions about sexuality, which she probably cannot talk about in the family setting (Cahen 2001): Safya is thus a fervent reader of *Switch Girl*, which tells the story of a high school girl, who is apparently a very good student, but much less well-behaved in the private sphere. The manga is accompanied by letters to the editor, in which the mangaka answers young girl's questions, relating both to her own sentimental life and to "practical" advice on love and even sexual matters.[3] Last but not least, the love triangle, a recurrent narrative scheme in manga, very often evokes the issues raised by adolescent love relationships: Octave finds there "the girls who (very strongly) can't make up their mind, who are a pain in the ass, who need four or five manga before saying 'yes', and then 'actually no', yes, and then 'in the end actually no', so there yes, we recognize right away". Matthieu was very touched by *Blue*, and by another manga the title of which he forgot, but which according to him, staged "realistic" sentimental relationships.

> It was a love story, and they break up, and ... but by life what, they're separated by life, but it's not ... they don't decide to break up. And they just meet up in the end, before the woman died ... And yeah, that really moved me. On top of that, at the time, I was a little upset, it was last year ... And yeah, it moved me a lot. These two manga, it's really something that you can ... I mean ... everyone could have experienced this.
>
> MATTHIEU, 17, 11th grade, parents architects

As for Salim (19, 12th grade, father a mason, mother a cleaning agent), his embarrassed words suggest that this 19-year-old man is in actual fact a transient lover ...

---

3 Which makes it the female equivalent of *Step up love story* for boys.

> Sometimes I read little stories, uh, how can I say, that moved me, sometimes I see characters who … how can I say, who have the same kind of problem, so sometimes it touches me a little bit.
>
> *And in which series is it?*
>
> In *Ranma ½*, when everybody is trying to conquer Adeline [Akane] while Ranma is crazy about her so that I … that I identify with him a little bit because I understand him on the other hand.

Arguably the most difficult thing for boys today is not to have access to sexual representations, through traditional and digital media, or boyfriends, but to talk about feelings and love. As a matter of fact, if we consider the topics of discussion between boyfriends and girlfriends, at the age of 13, 73% of girls talk about discuss feelings with their friends, compared to 48% of boys. At the age of 15, 89% and 61% respectively, and at the age of 17, 92% and 73% respectively. The subject is therefore not taboo, far from it, even for boys, but less frequently discussed at home.

Thus, as Matthieu sums up about *Blue* ("she is a woman who is gay, and it is about the acceptance of herself, and the others' point of view, I mean how to accept the others' point of view"):

> It's really something that everyone can experience. Well, yes, well, I'm a teenager, I wonder about everything, and I like to discover this kind of things.

Portrait of Safya, a "Switch Girl"

Safya, a ninth grader, has been reading manga for two years. Her father is a nurse's aide, her mother does not work, she has an older brother aged 17, two sisters aged 10 and 9 and a younger brother aged 1. She would like to become a child psychiatrist ("I know child psychiatrist, it's complicated, otherwise I would like to be a history teacher"). She started reading *Naruto* on the Internet two years ago, after seeing the cartoon. She learned how to find scans from her "buddies". Safya borrows and reads mostly manga from the local library next to her middle school, in a disadvantaged urban area. She complains about her sisters, who "steal" her manga and annoy her "because they want to read everything". Finally, she says that her parents "are a little annoyed because sometimes, I only bring this stuff home when I come back from the library". Safya knows few other manga readers in her school, as Japanese manga and cartoons are more likely to be mocked. However, Safya believes that manga "is better drawn than comics, the drawings are better". She also finds that "stories are better explained in mangas". She repeatedly emphasizes the ease of understanding of manga such as *Ueki's Law* and *Fruits Basket*. Safya comes to the library primarily to borrow or read manga, which she often reserves in advance, but she is also interested in children's novels or certain bestsellers. Her favorite authors are Meg Cabot, who wrote the ten volumes of *The Princess Diaries*, and Stephenie Meyer, author of the *Twilight* saga. Safya spends a lot of time reading ("my mom gets mad about reading, she thinks I should go out a little more"). But Safya doesn't like the books she studied in French class: "They're too much like 'the flower is slowly blooming', and that annoys me. There's no action, I want action". Safia first read several shonens, such as *Naruto*, *Ueki's Law*, *HunterXHunter* and *Ranma 1/2*. She describes herself—and is identified by those around her—as "a tomboy", who "loves fighting" and "boy manga". She points to her older brother's influence on her tastes, but admits, however, that she has changed since that year: "now I had to change, because it kind of pisses off the teachers". Safya is also starting to get tired of *Naruto*, "because it goes on a bit too long". She is more sensitive to the dramatic aspect of shonen than to their humor: "some of them made me really sad but not so much funny. There is one who dies and that made me depressed, in *Ueki's Law*". She also loves reading *Naruto* fanfiction ("I read it all the time, it's the same characters but for example, it's when they're on vacation"). Safya does not draw, and she finds it "too complicated to do a blog: I don't have time, I'm terrible". She tried to put online a fanfiction she had written about *Naruto*, "but it didn't work: not enough people said bravo, so I stopped, I said: 'oops, that's lame'. It was Naruto coming back from his training with Jiraya, and they were all going to go on a mission, and they were going to meet three new characters, I invented the three new characters. It didn't work well enough. I've been looking, I haven't found any yet on other series than *Naruto*". Safya's preferences are divided between shonen and shojo, *Ueki's Law* and *Fruits Basket*, and during the same interview, she sometimes prefers shonen and sometimes prefers "a little" shojos.

It is indeed very recently that Safya's friends from high school made her want to read "manga for girls": "some of them started to read manga for girls, they told me: 'yeah it's good'. I said, 'Well, I'll give it a try', and I liked it". She feels that romantic relationships are "well portrayed", and girls' manga is now among her favorite reads. Safya shares less manga reading with her older brother ("it annoys him because it's manga for girls, he doesn't like it very much"). She sums up *Fruits Basket* this way: "it's a family that is cursed and there's a girl who tries to help them to end the curse. And in the end, everyone is happy". Safya is following three shojo, *Global Garden*, *Nana* and *Switch Girl*, her favorite manga of the moment: "it's a girl, when she's at home, she doesn't pay attention, she's messy, and on the other hand, when she's outside, she pays attention to her". Safya, who wears black pants and a veil, thinks that there is "a bit of a comparison" between her and the main character of the manga, a 17-year-old high school girl who is very good at school, popular and a model in public (when she is in "ON mode"), but very messy and casual when she is at home ("in OFF mode"): "we think a little bit: yeah, it would be nice to be like her". The high school student, Nika Tamiya, has all the trouble in the world to keep her "OFF mode" from being discovered by her classmates, but appreciates being able to stop playing the game of appearances of the proper and popular girl at home. Everything gets complicated when she falls in love with a boy. Safya also started *Nana* a week before the interview date, and she prefers "the one who rocks, the other one is too nic"". But if she sometimes imagines herself in the situation of the characters ("I say to myself: 'but why does she do like that, why doesn't she do that'…"), Safya considers however that "it does something else than recall people and situations lived. That's why I like it, it really does something else for me". Safya also enjoys the adventures of the two witch heroines in the shojo *Chocola & Vanilla*, who must leave their magical kingdom to go to Earth, "seducing as many boys as possible to get hearts".

Safya would like to go to a high school next year "to do Japanese" ("It annoys my mother because she thinks I only want to do it because of the manga"). However, she specifies that she "doesn't live only for that" and doesn't have any posters in her room.

2.3 *Ethical Receptions*

Identification can also be projective: teenagers all tell about childhood scenes, alone in the bedroom or together in the playground, imagining themselves with this or that power, "the superpowers that make you dream when you are 10 or 11 years old, like the Jedi" (Kalaya):[4] dreaming of "flying like Dragon Ball Z" (Matthieu), of getting out of a difficult situation, "at some point there's a kid pissing you off, telling you: if I was super strong …" (Félix), or to escape

4 "And Son Goku, he had a great little cloud that allowed him to go wherever he wanted. So that's what everybody wanted."

from school thanks to "multicloning as in *Naruto*: if we didn't go to school, we would have the clone" (Nayir). It's amusing that Félix, who says he no longer does it, talks for ten minutes about which magic fruit of *One Piece* he would like to have. As Coraline puts it in a nutshell, "every manga reader has always imagined himself in a situation with the hero".

But as they grow up, the projections are of a different kind and involve more ethical reflections. The manga that causes the most comments of this kind in the words of the teenagers we met *is Death Note*, where the hero finds a notebook that gives him the right of life and death, since he only has to write down the name of someone so that they die. He then decides to use it to exterminate criminals who have gone unpunished. This manga raises questions about good and evil in the minds of teenagers who mention it, and the justice thus rendered in an individual and personal way. Many, like Matthieu, are bewildered: "What would I have done in his place? Would I have thought about that? Would I have done it that way?":

> After a while, I felt a little like banging my head, because it was actually getting on my nerves. I said to myself, if I found a notebook like that, on the one hand I would be tempted to kill criminals, and no, I don't want to be considered as a murderer, and I think it's better to leave it to the justice system even though it's not quite right sometimes. He's not wrong, the one who looks like the bad guy, he's got a good heart if you want. It starts with a good intention, but to reach his goal, it takes murder. After that, you have to deal with your own conscience and morals.
>
> MAELE, 16, 11th grade, father a teacher, mother a counsellor

> When you look at the hero, someone great, loved by all, I always say to myself: 'What would I do in a situation like that?'
>
> AURÉLIEN

> It's true that he's one of the few who did that to me, with *Death Note* ... It's true that we ask ourselves the following question: what would we do in that case? I know that for *Death Note*, the question we're asking ourselves right now is when does good turn into evil. Because in the beginning he acts for good, against a justice system that he considers to be rotten. So, he decides to do his own justice, but in the end, it's less and less fair. The question is, what would we have done in his place, how would we have done it and why would we do it. Things go pretty fast in this series.
>
> ALEXANDRE, 17, 11th grade, parents schoolteachers

The quality and dynamism of the fights are an important but not sufficient dimension for these readers. Many of them underline the limits of *Dragon Ball Z* or *Naruto Shippuden* in this respect: fighting for fighting's sake is of little interest, but must be based on the values of honor and the characters' commitment to the defence of moral values, according to the nekketsu's own reading pact. This term means "boiling blood" and refers to the shonen manga which are based on the values of courage, sacrifice, the idea of surpassing oneself, loyalty and friendship. Théo (15, 10th grade, father a trainer in a transport company, mother a bank employee) finds "the honor of the samurai" in manga and "finds it good". Moussa (18, 12th grade, father a doctor, mother a pharmacist) also emphasizes "the notion of honor, it's there all the time". Ladji appreciates the altruism of Naruto, who "always tries to go further just to protect others, whereas Sasuke, it's just for a personal interest: to kill his brother". Estelle (17, 12th grade, father a bank clerk, mother a school nurse) also hates Sasuke because she has "always been very opposed to the concept of vengeance, revenge and all that" and was "really shocked". As for Nabil and Célia, they almost have philosophical overtones to bring up their favorite passages:

> Ippo [from the manga *Hajime no Ippo*], I actually like him, it's because basically he's a student that is not … He's shy all that, he works, he has no friends, he goes home, he goes to help his mother, since his father, he's dead. And then he discovers boxing, and in boxing he learns how to fight all that. I liked that, his transformation, you see his courage and everything, it's beautiful. Every time he thinks of his mother, I find that magnificent … […] What I like, I don't know, it's reflection sometimes. It's not so much the fight but what they usually fight for and all that. I don't know, I think it's beautiful. I mean, they never fight for fun.
>
> NABIL, 18, 12th grade, father an employee, mother a home-nurse

> But I remember in *D.Gray-Man*, there's one of the exorcists who betrayed the congregation of the shadows to save his life. In those cases, an exorcist who betrays … God becomes fallen in a way, becomes a creature who dies within 24 hours, but before dying, destroys everything in his path. And Allen wants absolutely to save him, to a point where even at times, you feel like telling him to give up … But the will that some characters have, and their attachment to life, because I think that's what it's like with manga … People can forget the attachment to life, and the value of human life. And when you see characters who are so attached to it, who absolutely want to save a character they don't know, because Allen never met him, never spoke with him, but he absolutely wants to save him

> anyway, and already there it's more interesting than in a film where we kill anyone … So having reminders like that, remembering how important it is to live, and how important life is … Well, it's true that there are a lot of manga that have this as a recurring theme. […] In the manga, it's still beautiful, you want to say 'give up', but they go on anyway. Yes, it's very much the will that works in manga, the characters who have the will to go all the way, because that's what makes them where they are when you read them.
>
> CÉLIA, 17, 11th grade, mother an opera director, father a choreographer

The characters' behavior can be interpreted ethically as well, or in relation to realism, especially in the case of sentimental relationships and love betrayals. Thus, Leila (15, 10th grade, unemployed father, mother a janitor) is very critical and finds that "it wasn't what she did the chick" because "at some moment she goes with one, at another moment she goes with the other one. That's not realistic, you don't just change your mind like that. Let's say, she'd been with a guy for six months and in one day, it's over".

It is also striking that the comments focus on sentimental relationships, much more than on the erotic aspect of some manga, whether it be the "fan service", which refers to the staging of young people girls in underwear,[5] or the more explicitly pornographic manga. While moral panics have often taken hold of these features of manga, by considering them as their main characteristics, what teenagers say instead, marks an interesting sense of personal boundaries. Only Madji is passionate about "hentai", but this passion goes beyond the mere interest in seeing pornographic scenes. In the list of titles on offer, the "pornographic" titles are not known, or elicit laughter, but have not been read.[6] While it could be argued that teenagers would hide this reading, the list was suggested at the end of the interview at a time when readers could be quite reassured that there was no moral judgment from the people conducting the survey. Manga "in panties" was thus deemed to be boring, even too commercial. As for the hentai, they elicit shocked and ethical reactions from these teenagers, especially those from privileged backgrounds. Thus, many people think, just as Nabil does, "that wanking in front of a manga (laughter), frankly, is nothing one can be proud of", or even that it is "unhealthy".

5 Or any element that refers to a cliché or a code specific to a manga genre: a robot fight for mecha fans, an allusion to sentimental relationships between boys for yaoi fans.

6 However, some readers are familiar with this term and have seen hentai images, or excerpts from pornographic anime, even though they don't read manga.

But *Love Hina*, and all that, now I know that if I watched it again, I wouldn't like it. A lot of things like that, so finally, he had us juggling for fourteen volumes about the same things: the heroine hitting the hero because he sees her in her panties or stuff like that ... For fourteen volumes, it's really annoying. In the end it gets a little boring. The series, since it's the popular that wins, the big series now, it's like in Japan, it's really big fans of panties you know: now, they only show that. So now, there are only series like that, and I don't like it.

MADJI, 19, 11th grade, father a driver, stay-at-home mother

Have you ever been confronted with manga that you weren't attracted to at all?

Yes manga ... uh, hentai, I think that's what it's called. It's very much about ass, it's not ...

You're not attracted to it.

I'm not attracted to it. Well, I don't see the point. I've already seen it, but well, it didn't interest me.

MATTHIEU, 17, 11th grade, parents architects

Love Story is mainly to teach young people how to ... how to make love. It's techniques in order not to ... how to say ... It's like a little ... It's to learn, in fact. It's for us to learn. It's the only one like that. I nerver encountered any others like that. But it's not intended for adults, it's for children under 16 years old, you've seen the pictures and everything, it's not ... There's nothing perverse in it, it's not ... It's not like the hentai, the hentai is mostly centered, it's perverse. Even if there's stories next to it, it's mostly perverse.

PIERRE, 17, 11th grade, father a postman, mother a retired school teacher

Okay. Have you ever been shocked or embarrassed by situations in manga?

It depends which manga. So, when you look, just for your personal, general culture, when you look at a porn manga, called hentai, you're afraid.

Is it really shocking?

Have you ever seen a woman on whom the sex of a man grew?

Did it shock you?

Yeah, it was pretty shocking, all the more so that the image was pretty disgusting.

CÉCILE, 17, 1st year college student, father an executive, mother a private nurse

2.4 *Seeking Comfort*

While we can wonder what we would have done in the hero's place, conversely the hero can help us to know what to do, what to think, how to react, or simply to feel less alone in a given sitaution. So, analogies are no longer the result of a character trait or a physical aspect, but of experiences, most often painful, lived in the friendly, sentimental or family space. Some people directly relate an episode or series that touched them to a biographical element. For others, the links emerge from an allusion, or in an embarrassed silence that suggests pain that has not yet healed. Thus, Fatou, who, at the age of 24, decided to go back to school and is in her final year of highschool, remains very modest about her biographical journey. However, she accounts with ardour for her passion for *Paradise Kiss* or *Mademoiselle Oishi* [*Sukuna Hikona*] and especially for the heroine, who returns after years of wandering and resumes her studies, as well as her unfinished, undeveloped sentences about the need to continue on her path, to mourn her loss. This gives a glimpse of the identificatory principles that go beyond the mere fact that she resumed her studies.

> In *Paradise Kiss*, I like … the … the character of the girl, but uh sometimes I like to compare her to me because, concerning her ideas, she looks like me and everything else … well it's more like actions or what she does. She runs away from home, because … (laughs softly) because her mother didn't want her to, her mother didn't understand her reaction and everything, and uh, then she decides to stop studying and she comes back, and so on and so forth. […] *In Paradise Kiss*, I thought 'she went back to school finally to retake the exams' and everything, I thought 'it's the same, this is what I'm doing now' […]. It's not that she looks like me, not at all, it's just that it's the … it's the … it's the reaction … Miss Oishi, it's just that, after the tragedy, her friend gets killed there, she's … she's rather … how do you say, after mourning, she has regained a taste for life and she continues to do so, but she always remains herself … It's rather her behavior that reminds me of mine, even though the drama aspect, it's true … not the drama of her kind, but another drama (almost inaudible voice), it's comparable
>
> *You feel like you learned something from reading manga?*
>
> Oh, learning things no, but I think it's not in manga that we're going to learn things, it's more about my own mistakes but well, it's true that in manga, we always find them, we say: 'Yeah, it's better to do that than that, yeah'.
>
> *Do you have examples of situations where it's better to do that?*

> Yeah, in *Paradise Kiss* (laughs), I thought it was better to go back to school and decide to work somewhere, and then in *Mademoiselle Oishi*, I thought: 'You can't be mourning forever, it's better to go back to your normal life and move on instead'.
>
> FATOU, 24, 12th grade, father a poultry farmer, mother a shopkeeper

In the same way, Leila repeatedly insists on what distinguishes *Nana* from the other shojo: shojo are wrong to depict a world that is all pink, too happy, and therefore far from reality, whereas *Nana* shows a "realistic" world, that is to say a hard world. Leila is 15 years old, her father is unemployed, her mother is a janitor. Even for those who do not directly relate what they read to what they are and experience, manga can also be the object of "readings of salvation" (Mauger, Poliak and Pudal 1999) and allow, through the appropriation of an imaginary universe, to work on the patterns of their personal experience and to deal with painful situations. In the memories of writers, in the actions of associations working with children who have lived through trauma and experiences of mourning, abandonment, imprisonment or hospitalisation or daily misery, Michèle Petit shows how much reading makes it possible to "resist adversity" (2008). The situations of distress that some of the teenagers we met tell about, more or less explicitly, and which, on the whole, seem less dramatic, are nonetheless, for those who experience them, sources of real life pains. Some teenagers find answers, support and comfort in reading manga, and look back on the experience.

Situations of isolation and loss of self-confidence, are a recurring narrative sequence in shojo and shonen manga. However, Olivier Galland's statistical survey about the depreciation felt by young people testifies to their particular sensitivity to various forms of ostracism, and above all "to attacks on their self-image" (2006). Océane herself makes this connection between her personal experience and the fictitious universe of *Fruits Basket*, in which Kisa is rejected by the pupils in her class. Océane compares this situation to the one she experienced when she was in primary school, before she entered middle school. She has the impression that nobody loved her and never spoke to her:

> I don't know why everyone hated me and I never knew why. I was made fun of because of my haircut and stuff like that. And in *Fruit Basket*, Kisa's story, it was so sad, it reminded me too much.
>
> OCÉANE, 15, 9th grade, father an electrician, mother a housewife

Hacine or Laurent evoke the same type of experience, in primary school for Hacine, in middle school for Laurent.[7] Marianne (16, 11th grade, father a numerical control operator, mother a restaurant employee) also draws a parallel between the bulling experienced in middle school by Makino Tsukushi, the heroine of the manga *Hana Yori Dango*, and the pains she felt in middle school.

> In my case there are, strangely enough. Tsukushi's situation, at the very beginning, it made me think of a situation in middle school, because she was a bit harassed by everyone else, which I was a little bit. In fact, she rebelled against those who persecuted her, and so did I. When I watched the drama, I thought, 'Well, she did what I did'.

Another recurring situation in the manga universe is that of the loneliness of a hero in whom no one believes: the devaluing look and negative judgments made by his circle have an impact on the self-esteem of this unexperienced character. Nayir (16, 9th grade, father a delivery driver, mother a housekeeper) has been very marked by the beginnings of the manga *Naruto*, when the hero is about 12 years old. Naruto must first face the contempt and the distrust of the inhabitants of his village, because he has a "fox demon" in him. No one believes in his ability to become hokage (the most powerful ninjas in the village). Nor gets Naruto good results at the academy where he learns the ninja arts. In fact, he is one of the only students who fails the exams to obtain the rank of aspiring ninja (*genin*). For Nayir, this situation is "indirectly" similar to the one he experiences in middle school. He repeated his third year and feels abandoned by teachers who don't believe in him:

> *Do you ever read manga that makes you think of situations you've been through?*
>
> Yeah, but indirectly, actually. When, for example, in Naruto, there's no one who wants to help him become hokage, while everyone underestimates him. I felt a little like him at school because I repeated a year. The teachers, they didn't do much to help me, so I felt a bit like that.

Sometimes, the teenagers we met established links between the series they watch, their favorite characters and their own experience, in particular in their family circle. This is the case for Fatou, but also for Nathaniel. The latter

7 "It's true that for a while I didn't have any friends so, uh, I was very focused on everything that was Japan, on everything that was manga".

never knew his father, who left the family home shortly after his birth. He was brought up by his mother and grandmother, in a female environment, and says in the interview at the end: "My mother is employed at the Unemployment Office … And I don't have a father". This passionate reader repeatedly insists on father-son relationships in the manga he reads, notably in *Evangelion* and *Get Backers*. One of the two main characters of *Get Backers*, Ban Mido, is 18 years old. He was abandoned by his father and raised by his grandmother, "one of the last great witches in Europe". Nathaniel insists on the confrontation between Mido Ban and his father:

> *Get Backers* is the story of two young men, Mido Ban and Amano Ginji, who are professional reclaimers, in fact. … Now the plot is that Mido Ban, he has found his father. And he wants to fight him because his father abandoned him when he was little. And that's it.

The analogy between Nathaniel's and Mido Ban's family configurations is clear, but its analysis is complex and runs the risk of over-interpretation. However, the recurrence of reading stories that evoke the father's figure does indicate that this is a relatively stable interest and pattern of appreciation for Nathaniel. Actually, he repeatedly evokes other situations of abandonment and isolation, even though the protagonists are not a father and his son. *Evangelion*, Nathaniel's favorite series, features a solitary and introverted hero, Shinji, who has a difficult relationship with his father. At the age of 14 at the beginning of the series, Shinji is invited by his father, whom he hasn't seen since the age of three, to join Tokyo-3, the fortress capital of Japan, rebuilt after a gigantic explosion that devastated the earth. Nathaniel's proximity to Shinji is sensitive on several levels: like Shinji, Nathaniel describes himself as a lonely boy with little social contact, and he too has been more or less "abandoned" by his father:

> *What did you think of Shinji?*
>
> He's a typical charcter in fact, because he takes up everyone's … let's say existential questions quite well, because he doesn't know why he lives. He doesn't know why his father called him back, and he wants … He doesn't know what to do, actually. He's pretty unsure about what he's doing, he's … he's not very good at socializing either, and here we go … He actually dreams of a world where he's actually all alone. He's kind of weird because he's lonely. That's what I'm saying.

Nathaniel mentions a passage that was particularly trying for him and that he could not manage to reread. It is a fight scene in which Shinji feels betrayed by his father:

> *And why did you find it difficult to read the end?*
>
> Because one of Shinji's best friends, Toji, is chosen to be the pilot of Evangelion, except that the Evangelion he's flying is actually an angel, so Shinji has to kill the angel, but except that if he kills the angel, he also kills the pilot. So, he doesn't know what to do, he doesn't want to fight. And his father launches a dumi system, it's actually a kind of … A self-pilot actually, but very violent, which makes the Evangelion go out of control, and kills the angel, kills the angel, and kills the pilot, Toji at the same time. So, Shinji feels betrayed by his father, so he runs away, but it's mostly because of that that I have trouble reading the rest.

Cécile (17, 1st year college student, father an executive, mother a private nurse) too has a bad relationship with her father, which she experiences as a form of absence: at the end of her interview she quietly points out the fact that her father has been sleeping with a great deal of men since his separation. She gets on extremely badly with him, only seeing him on weekends when he has child custody. Her conversations with him are, according to her, limited to asking him to put the Internet on, or asking him for money. Cécile says she hates shojo, and any description of sentimental relationships, because "yes, you'll excuse me, but when you read a book and find yourself confronted with the harsh reality of the couple, it's crazy". She develops an aversion to the visual kei, not so much because of the music, but because of the way the singers look:

> Their music itself, I don't know, I mean, I've listened to it sometimes but I didn't get hooked on it because … when you see them … they're all guys … you can doubt they are.

Above all, his comments on the yaoi, these manga staging sentimental relationships between men, are extremely searing:

> What I find disgusting in the manga, is that there's a lot of yaoi, between boys.
>
> *It's very successful?*
>
> A lot, I don't know why. It's very successful. The manga, when it's two boys together, right away, it's magnificent, it's beautiful. It's a big hit. In fact, there's a bunch of girls who are totally into this: 'It's cute, two

> boys together'. All right, yeah. In manga only, it's actually disgusting. It should be.

Finally, she prefers manga featuring heroes … killing their father.

3 Right Age, Right Gender, Right Manners

Manga shows teenagers overcoming challenges. This initiatory journey offers hooks to identification, in particular via the models proposed and the exemplary situations described. The publishing offer itself seems to determine categories from which the adolescent, according to his or her gender or age, would draw: shonen for young boys and seinen for older ones, shojo for girls. But not all teenagers conform to these categories, and the paths they eventually take say a lot about how one becomes a boy or a girl of one's age depending on one's social background in particular. Having the right symbolic size, having the right gender does not mean the same thing to everyone, and judgements about manga shed light on the construction of self in adolescence.

3.1 *The Role of Age and Generations*

Reading manga, for these teenagers, as we have seen, works as a resource in the network of sociability. This integration into the peer group is a way to detach oneself from parents, and manga is a sign of generational belonging. As Dominique Pasquier pointed out about the television program *Hélène et les garçons*, the taste for manga among these teenage readers opposes the majority of "adult" discourse pertaining to them. Thus, "we can also think that children have tried to forge for themselves […] a universe of their own, a different universe from that which their circle offers them, or even a universe forbidden to adults" (1999, 31). This "new game of intergenerational differentiations" also arises "at a time when cleavage media such as comic strips and television were losing overall their power of identity and protest for young people accustomed to living with them in the family circle and to knowing that they were being consumed by adults" (Maigret 1999, 243). Admittedly, the vast majority of parents is not frankly hostile to manga: alone, among the approximately sixty adolescents we met, Hacine's mother formally forbids him to read manga at home. Parents from working-class backgrounds (or parents with a low level of diploma) can even see their children's taste for manga quite favorably, since at least they read … Hacine (15, 9th grade, father a textile company manager, stay-at-home mother) thus started reading manga because his father urged him to read more. To use Kader or Leila's own words, their parents "don't care". Nayir's parents (father a delivery driver, mother a housekeeper) encourage him to read manga, which for them "are books". Coraline's mother, who arrived at the end of the interview with her daughter (Coraline said earlier that her father, a worker, never reads, and her mother, a housekeeper, very little, especially true stories about war), says this:

> It's true that he likes it. It's also nice to have several interests, to always focus on the same thing, to be able to read something else as well. But I still find that young people read much more … I mean, we're in our 40s anyway. But the books, as I always say, they devour them. I always look at the number of pages and if it's written very small, to say it's been as long as possible, because it's frightening, it's a hell of a budget. So besides sometimes they read two series at the same time, so … we can't always provide all the books. So, it's true that if we have the opportunity to exchange.

In more privileged backgrounds, reactions vary from benevolent indifference to forced and deprecated tolerance, depending on the cultural and economic capital endowment and the age of the adolescents. Parents from middle or privileged backgrounds but whose capital is rather economic, and who are themselves weak readers or readers of police or comic books, arbitrate with the time spent reading these manga, or the money spent. It is also these parents, who most often also try to read them.

> They think I spend a little bit of time on what, but they don't necessarily think it's such a bad thing sometimes. They think it's more about Japanese culture, for example.
>
> YOHANNA, 16, 10th grade, father an engineer, mother a sales representative

> They thought that … at first they said it was good, that it opened us up to something else. Now that we read them again, they say it's always the same thing.
>
> XAVIER, 17, 11th grade, father a fireman, mother a child care worker

> My mother told me that it can't be that bad, since I love reading them. She keeps telling me that one day she'll have to try a series.
>
> *Have you tried getting your parents to read some?*
>
> I've given it a thought but I don't know what to suggest them to read so that they like it, I was thinking about *Death Note*, but we have to get into it right away.
>
> ESTELLE, 17, 12th grade, father a bank clerk, mother a school nurse

And your parents, what did they think of the manga? They didn't stop you?

No, they didn't stop me at all. No, because, well, at the same time, I buy them for myself. No, they don't tell me anything. No, they're just teasing me, but that's all. (laughs).

ARTHUR, 18, 1st year college student, father a commercial executive, mother an accountant

Well, sometimes they say: it's a little too violent, in general, but otherwise, it's OK, they don't say much.

And they tried to read some?

My father never did, my mother read the *Love Hina*, all the *Love Hina*, and then she stopped, nothing more.

CAROLINE, 14, 9th grade, father a shopkeeper, mother an insurance trainer

Contrary to Coraline's mother, parents from culturally rich backgrounds do not consider manga as "real" reading.[8] However, they do not vehemently oppose it either. It should be pointed out that their children are very good pupils: the "fulfilled" contract on the school level thus undoubtedly leads to tolerance of leisure activities, but without these parents trying to share or "understand" their children's tastes: they never tried to read manga ... This is how the evolution of Élodie's parents, for example, an excellent pupil in the final year of secondary school, can be understood:

At the very beginning, I remember I only bought this, they told me: 'Read something else'. Now they just don't care.

ÉLODIE, 18, 12th grade, father a biologist, mother a graphic designer

This position of tolerance, more or less afficted, is very common among parents from the cultural pole: Félix's mother (a sculptor) "finds it useless" but doesn't "bother him too much either". Alexandre's parents (school teachers) "are not necessarily very receptive", do not forbid him but "just ask him to read something else from time to time". Tom's family (15, 10th grade, parents teachers) doesn't like manga: "They don't read manga, and we never talk about it". So, everything is based on a form of covenant based on trust, as Célia explains:

My parents never really told me anything about it, because some people take it so seriously, it can become very obsessive, but personally it's

8 See Chapter 4.

> reading like any other reading, it's something I like a lot, but it's not ... that does not destroy my life so ... My parents know that I read it, and every once in a while, when we go to a store, we buy some stuff, and they agree to buy me a book. But after that, it's my thing, I'm kind of good with it. It's a bit like video games, okay, I don't want to spend too much time on them, but after that, I buy my own games, I'm the one who gets by with that.
>
> *So, they never interfered to control what kind of manga you buy?*
>
> No, they feel I'm responsible enough. For me, that's what's important, to establish a relationship with my parents based on trust. They let me look at the films that I want, they let me read the books that I want. So far, there hasn't been a problem with that.
>
> CÉLIA, 17, 11th, mother an opera director, father a choreographer

So, manga does not bring about a violent conflict among generations, even though the remarks and reflexions, in privileged circles with a high cultural capital, as we shall see, are bearing fruit, in a more or less insidious way. The parents' positions actually reproduce the differences in educational modes according to social backgrounds, and the place given in these circles to the children's "leisure" activities (de Singly 2006).

Nevertheless, even parents who try to read manga, mostly in popular or intermediate circles, do not hang on, read a few volumes and give up. Manga, even without being the source of open conflits, is thus labelled as "matter of young people", whether parents encourage or regret it. Thus, Maureen's mother read some *Dragon Ball Z*, but did not continue. Xavier's father "read twenty pages and stopped", and Yohanna was no more successful:

> *And did you try to get them to read it?*
>
> I tried, but ... My mother, it's not even worth thinking about. She can't even read a silly comic book yet, so ... If she can't do that, she can't do it. And then my dad, I tried, he gave up halfway through.
>
> *What was that?*
>
> *Full Metal Alchemist.*
>
> YOHANNA, 16, 10th grade, father an engineer, mother a sales representative

Even teenagers feel that manga is not for their parents, who, to begin with, are too old to have the required skills, such as the ability to read "backwards". Manga is thus a generational marker, even when it is accepted and admitted by parents, "a thing for you, a thing for young people" (Matthieu, 17, 11th grade, parents architects):

> Well, I've tried to initiate them, but I can't. Already, they can't read the other way around, and it's not their style at all; they find it a bit grotesque. And then it is not at all what they're used to reading, so they didn't get hooked.
>
> LAURENT, 18, 12th grade, father an engineer, stay-at-home mother

> Because otherwise, my mother once tried to read a manga, but it disturbs her too much to read the other way around. Already, you have to start with the right page, read from right to left, and then after the page, you have to take the habit of turning it in the opposite direction, it's been too upsetting to her. Then my father, he's too old school … he doesn't mind me reading it, but he'll never get into it.
>
> LÉO, 15, 10th grade, father a commercial executive, mother a librarian

> Well, no, he didn't really get into it. At the same time, I was annoyed because it took him three days to read one.
>
> FÉLIX, 15, 11th grade, parents sculptors

> The stories are not the same and then, in quotes, she was raised with all the comics like *Achille Talon*, *Gaston Lagaffe*, *Blake and Mortimer* … But she has nothing against.
>
> MAELE, 16, 11th grade, father a teacher, mother a counsellor

> It's too much change for him, it's too weird … For my mother too, it's true that the only manga she can read is *Princess Sarah* and *Candy*.[9]
>
> MARIANNE, 16, 11th grade, father a numerical control operator, mother a restaurant employee

Léo is not sure that once he becomes an adult, he will continue to read manga:

> Yes, I will, I will continue to read some for a while, but it's just going to be a fad and it's going to pass at some point I think. I don't think it's going to replace comics. Well after I don't know, we'll see, but I think manga, they're not necessarily adapted for adults because for adults there are just porn manga so.

9 Concerning that topic, Maele, who was present at the interview, said "it's as light as … but it's already good".

3.2 *Age Matters*

In our corpus, the youngest manga reader is 11 years old (in sixth grade). The oldest is 24 years old (in 12th grade). Some of our respondents are 18 years old, but are already 1st or 2nd year college students. Even if only by these examples, age is not just about the number of candles on a birthday cake. In readers' careers, the "boom" occurs during the second half of the middle school years. Yet some readers go on reading manga in high school, whereas one of the main strategies for "growing up" is to distance oneself from the practices of the youngest (Lahire 2004), a challenge that is all the more thorny when one crosses the thresholds represented by entering middle school or high school. In the words of some readers, one can see the risks of being despised incurred whether the mockery is focused on a series (*Naruto* is in that regard the perfect scapegoat), or on gender in general: manga can be seen quite rapidly, as Bastien (15, 10th grade, father a biologist, mother an engineer) points out, as "something for children", and Fatya regrets that "the others make fun of it, they say it's childish":

> *And have you ever disagreed with someone about a manga?*
>
> Well … I liked *Naruto*. But some people think it's bogus because they say it's a bit babyish. … Besides, now it's the kids, not really the kids I mean but the little ones who read *Naruto*.
>
> MAUREEN, 15, 9th grade, father a worker, mother an administrative officer

It should be noted that Maureen, who is at the critical stage of entering high school, found a compromise to keep following the adventures of Naruto: she no longer buys them, but watches the anime, because these are "the new episodes, where they are grown up" and that "we can say they're babies, but there's some good stuff, eh". This transfer is particularly interesting, because it shows that mockery is not only due to peers. Maureen could very well buy *Naruto* and not tell anyone. So, this is a "self-distinction from oneself", as opposed to a "self-distinction from others".

Like Matthieu (17, 11th grade, parents architects), who, after having despised manga of yesteryear as "pre-teens", adds:

> Preteen, but that doesn't stop me from reopening them from time to time'. But hey I mean now I know them, it's just for me … At night, I can't fall asleep, I think of something else … here.

So, for those who want to continue reading manga, it is a question of making this reading "matching their age". While the physical evolution of the characters has already been underlined, as for Naruto, in the process of identification, here, the teenagers will insist on the psychological evolution of the characters, and their maturation in the course of the volumes, which would be reinforced by the "maturity of the drawing": better drawn, the characters would also gain in thickness, in depth, in short become adults, and their readers as well within the process.

> It depends on which manga, but in general, yes, we often feel an evolution of the character. Either he becomes more mature, or there are bad guys who become nice, or there are people who become bad, that's quite common too. Already, you can feel it because as the manga goes forward, the author's features improve or change, so already there's a physical change that is necessarily noticeable. So yes, in general we realize quite well that there is a certain maturity that develops.
>
> ESTELLE, 17, 12th grade, father a bank clerk, mother a school nurse

> *Samouraï Champloo*, it's not a physical evolution, it's rather an evolution in the way the characters think or in the way they think about each other'. I think that in almost all of them, there is a relationship like that, when a series is developing, it has to, otherwise there's no interest. If the situation is the same all the time, it's not really interesting.
>
> ASHKAN, 18, 12th grade, father a director of a clothing brand, mother a stylist

> Sakura's going to change, too. At first, she was a bit crazy, but then she'll become much more serious. Naruto too, he's going to change completely. At first, he was a little crazy, and he's going to get a lot more serious, and he's going to want to win. He will think more about his actions, instead of acting unconsciously. Otherwise in all manga, the characters change, that's the good thing about manga.
>
> CORALINE, 17, 11th grade, father a worker, mother a cleaning lady

Another way to grow up with manga is to turn to other genres, and become more competent. This is the case of those who explicitly focus on seinen, a category intended for adults. Thus, Noé (6th grade, father a religious books publisher, stay-at-home mother), a particularly precocious eleven-year-old child, is proud to say that he gets his supplies two out of three times "from the adult shelve" of the library, as opposed to the "7 to 11 years" shelve, which poses a sensitive problem of those who belong to the upper limit, and are in fact integrated to the lower limit. In order to distinguish themselves from these "children's" manga, a label that is often attached to manga that they no longer read, some will put in the spotlight the much more psychological aspect of the manga they read: in this case, it is a question of thinking about serious subjects, such as death, or 'more philosophical' themes, such as those that Arthur

(18, 1st year college student, father an executive, mother an accountant) finds in *Until death do us part*, noting "that a year or two ago, I wouldn't have been interested". For others, it is the level of violence in some titles that allows them to be classified within the "informed" public[10] category:

> *And it's very different from* Naruto*?*
>
> Uh yes well yes, it's different, because for example, we see in this book cut-out heads rolling around on the floor. It's different from Naruto, because *Naruto* I think, it's more intended for young people, those who want to have fun doing ninjutsus in the courtyard, or whatever. Anyway, in *Naruto*, there is less blood
>
> LADJI, 18, 12th grade, father an electrician, mother a housewife

> It's rather for the adults, it's a little more violent. It's for an informed audience. It's forbidden to children under 16. Because it's much more violent. You see the violent scenes where they're cutting off arms and stuff like that. It's also an interesting story, but it's a lot more complicated than the other manga.
>
> NAYIR, 16, 9th grade, father a delivery driver, mother a cleaner

> This manga, I would consider it for adult. Because children's manga, for under 16, are quite protective. They won't show the bad aspects. There'll be no blood or wounds or ... We'll barely see a bruise. There's fighting, though, that's all there is. So ... Whereas in the adult manga, it's really ... When the guy gets his arm cut off, he really gets his arm cut off. And there are a lot of details. [...] Here, we see that the authors have done studies in this field, because ... well already, to make a guy hang with his guts, you have to know where they are located.
>
> PIERRE, 17, 11th grade, father a postman, mother a retired schoolteacher

Annabelle (16, 11th grade, father a bank executive, mother a consultant) points out that she shares her three years older sister' s tastes, and not those of her younger sister, who is three years younger. She likes manga that is "dark", "complex", "weird", without a "happy ending", which is a proof of a more mature reading for her. Célia (17, 11th grade, mother an opera director, father a choreographer), likewise, considers that she has moved from the fantastic to the

10 The distinction between psychology and violence will also be a way of exercising the socially differentiated learning of virility, see below.

psychological. Juliette, at the age of 18, realizes how far she has come and she notes that "when [she] I started, [she] I never thought I [she]'d read Tezuka". Caroline (who is only 14 years old) now reads manga by "Mari Okazaki, who is an author who makes manga for adults, which are more mature".

That doesn't stop 18-year-old Jérôme (11th grade, father an electrician, mother an accountant) from sticking the little *Dragon Ball* figurines from his childhood on his Playstation and laughing about them during the interview. The risk of being taken seriously if you have figurines stuck on your Playstation or if you play Pokemon cards is certainly much less important at 18 than at 13 or 15, when you might be suspected of really liking it. At 18, even nostalgia is allowed, those childhood years are objectified in the manga collections, about which Juliette notes that they're "memories" and that she "can't get rid of them".

Célia, 17, is "nostalgic" about *Sailor Moon*, and Kader, 18, about *Gunnm*, that he rereads from time to time ... While the narrator of in *Search of Lost Time* found the sensations of his childhood by leafing through the book by *François le Champi* that he had loved so much, young people today, at the end of high school, look back with nostalgia, sentimentally re-reading a shabby copy of *Naruto* or *Sakura* ...

> *Are there any titles that you didn't like before, that you wouldn't like now?*
>
> I don't know. Honestly, I don't think so, because even if I read more, well, I still have a nice memory of it. So no, I think I'd still like it.
>
> MATTHIEU, 17, 11th grade, parents architects

> Dragon Ball, I still like it but I just find it less interesting. But there are no titles that I used to like and that I couldn't read anymore, no. Even the comics I read when I was younger, I read them again because I like them.
>
> ASHKAN, 18, 12th grade, father a director of a clothing brand, mother a stylist

4 Getting One's Gender Straight: Boys, Fist Fights and Little *Nana* Girls

Abnormally enlarged muscles for some, short and low-cut outfits for others, violence and sentimentalism, such could be the reductive image of masculine and feminine long conveyed in manga. Our objective here is not to conduct a semiotic study of the representations of masculinity and femininity in manga: the most stereotyped production possible would in any case mean nothing concerning its effective reception and the appropriations. It is moreover in dialectical terms that this relationship must be thought of: according to their characteristics, boys and girls, from such and such social background, of such and such an age, will select this or that series, or read it in such and such a way. But conversely, this series, this way of reading it, will contribute to making boys and girls from such and such social background or of such and such an age.

4.1 *Boys and "Beating"*

The titles read by the male teenagers interviewed are mostly shonen and a few seinen, while the reverse is not true: the girls read as many shonen as shojo. Among the popular titles among the male teenagers met, action and adventure shonen such as *Naruto*, *Death Note*, *Bleach*, *Rave* or *Fairy Tail* were mentioned. Ladji (18, 12th grade, father an electrician, stay-at-home mother) evokes manga 'in beating mode':

> Well *Death Note*, that's the only manga I ever liked that wasn't in beat-up mode, yeah. Because otherwise, all the others I've seen, yeah, it was just beating.

Some older high school students distinguished themselves by expressing a taste for manga described as 'trashy' or violent. Ladji's, Moussa's or Samuel's and Kevin's opinions are thus emblematic of a masculinity based on violence, either understated or not according to their age and agonistic relationships:

> From the very beginning of the book, there's a guy getting his head cut off. And it's a manga or a character, it's a jackal, and he's paid to kill people. [...] Oh, that was a friend of mine, he told me: 'Yeah, I saw a manga, it's too much. It's kids ripping out hearts, batati patata ...' I'm like, 'Wait, let me see!' I watched it, I liked it, I read six volumes in a row. It's just intensive cutting, in the whole manga. People say: 'Yeah, hello', they cut one another. 'Yeah, hello', another one, they cut one another. Two pages long, the guy, he stays home, he's doing push-ups, one-finger pull-ups (laughs). And then he goes outside: 'Well, where's the guy who cut me, I'm gonna cut him', and that's it.
>
> LADJI, 18, 12th grade, father an electrician, stay-at-home mother

> *Baki*, I liked it, it was quite violent. It's brand new, only a few people know it. In fact, it was a child that was the son of the greatest martial arts champion in the world. He's a demon actually, his father, and then he will try to beat him. And it's really violent fighting. There you go, I recommend it to you.
>
> MOUSSA, 18, 12th grade, father a doctor, mother a pharmacist

[*One Piece*] *And what do you like best?*

Well, the fight scenes and the comedy scenes. The scenes where they talk a lot, it's a bit annoying.

SAMUEL, 15, 10th grade, father a fireman, mother a childcare worker

[*Samurai Deeper Kyo*] *And what made you want to read it?*

It was because there was a fight. In manga, what I like is violence. I don't really like police stuff.

KEVIN, 13, 8th grade, father a machine operator, mother an accountant-secretary

The taste for fighting is or has been shared by all boys. Many, like Kader, naturalize this interest in fighting by the fact that they are "boys", and ascribe one genre to girls and another to boys, even if they are not familiar with Japanese terms. For Pierre, the manga for girls, "it's a lot of love, a bit of action, manga for boys is a lot of action, a bit of love". Félix (15, 11th grade, parents sculptors) believes that manga for boys are "more combat-oriented, and not too many thinking", while "for girls, so more sentimental stories".

The exacerbated violence is nevertheless one of the limits that some teenagers set, especially those from privileged backgrounds, such as Laurent (18, 12th grade, father an engineer, stay-at-home mother), for example, who believes that he is "into fighting but not into gore":

I'd say the manga's a bit gory, I don't like it too much. I've been advised a few, I read them but I didn't like them very much. Too gore manga is not my thing. I can't remember the title. No, I did well to forget it by the way (laughs). The heads are cut off, you can see blood and stuff like that. Well, it's not really my style.

Learning one's gender involves adhering to the principles of masculinity, but also distinguishing oneself from the practices of the other sex.[11] Thus, their reaction is very strong when we assume that they may have read manga "for

11 Here we share Martine Court's hesitations about the widespread idea that "children adopt behaviors characteristic of their sexual class in order to build or maintain a sexual identity": "To adhere to this idea is to postulate that children necessarily wish to be assimilated to persons of the same sex as themselves, without questioning the social conditions of possibility of this desire. The desire to be perceived as a girl or a boy is not universal. It is in fact constructed in the interactions that the child experiences and has experienced with the agents of socialization present in his or her environment" (Court, 2010, 232). It is the study of these interactions that this paragraph addresses.

girls": the laughter, when the list of titles containing shojos is submitted to them, testifies to the incongruity or embarrassment for them to have read them.

Matthieu never read any shojo and thinks his friends never read any either. Ashkan tried to read a "slushy" manga she borrowed from a classmate, but "it pissed [her] off, I love it … that was the story, two girls who were in love with a boy … I don't read manga for that". As for Mickael, Nayir, or Noé, they just need to say that "it's a manga for girls" to close the subject. If a boy must read manga for boys he has to hate manga for girls, especially in front of his friends. As Octave says, "I can't imagine any boys saying: 'Ohhh, it's so sad!!!' If I see one starting to do that, yeah, I'll definitely make fun of him". Hacine learned this at his own expense, as he liked to read shojos, and was mocked by his classmates (see Portrait). Similarly, Nabil and Moussa, very good friends, are doing the interview together. Nabil's reaction when Moussa "admits" that he liked *Sailor Moon* is explicit about what's at stake in hiding the "gender troubles": "No, stop it, *Sailor Moon*, it sucked, stop it. It was my sisters watching that …" In the same way, when Moussa delivers his interrogations ("in fact I've always wondered, for example, in *Dragon Ball Z*, Bulma and Vegeta, I mean I wondered if they love each other. Well sometimes …"), Nabil punishes him with a "Are you serious?", bursting out laughing. As the 12-year-old Vincente sums it up, "I don't really like the stuff for girls because I find that … I find that … I don't know how to say it, it's for girls, let's say that it's each one his manga".

While Hacine has stopped reading shojos, Moussa resists his friend's remarks, and repeats several times that as a child, he really loved *Sailor Moon*. Moussa's parents are a doctor and a pharmacist, and Moussa is 18 years old. Hacine's parents are a textile company manager and a housewife, and Hacine is 15. The parents' age and capitals can thus be combined in those who all the same read shojos.

However, shojo never has the same place as shonen, and its reading is therefore part of a distinction strategy; supply is one of them: Félix specifies that he does not buy them, unlike shonen and seinen, but that it is his female friends who lend them to him. Madji (19, 11th grade, father a bus driver, stay-at-home mother) "watches them in anime", Laurent reads them in scans, admits that "it's nice, it's for a change", but also points out that he doesn't buy them, just like Octave, who borrows them, reads them in scans or at the FNAC, "when he has time to lose", because "it's less interesting" and that he wouldn't "buy a stuff for girls". Another strategy for recovering shojo is to highlight the characteristics that distinguish it from other manga. Thus, Noé (11, 6th grade, father a religious books publisher, stay-at-home mother) read *Miro Miro*, which is "a manga especially for girls but a little for boys. It's a manga for girls, but in fact there's a bit of a fight". According to Madji, "*Jigoku Shojo* [*Hell Girl*] doesn't look like a shojo at all", even though it falls into this category. Pierre believes that *Lilim Kiss*, that he reads, is classified as a shojo, and he thinks it should be classified as "dramatic or fantastic". Laurent or Octave emphasize the quality of the drawings and the precision of the details. As for Nathaniel, Pierre, Madji or Léo, their very status as experts in manga makes it necessary for them to read shojo, even without appreciating them, in order to improve their encyclopedic culture. Reading shojo is acceptable, provided that it in a detached and distant way ...

In these gender games, however, one category of manga remains taboo: the yaoi, which refers to manga written by women and featuring male homosexual relations. Even Pierre (17, 11th grade, father a postman, mother a retired schoolteacher), who argues that he has an encyclopedic knowledge of manga, and therefore wants to read everything, finds this goes too far for him. For young teenagers, homosexuality remains an extremely delicate and disturbing subject, which one can approach, as Matthieu does, only through lesbian relationships, described in *Blue*. Thus, Juliette (18, 12th grade, father a doctor, mother a pharmacist), who shares all her manga readings, and the practices related to them, with her older brother, remarks that "there are yaoi too, that he, strange as it may seem, doesn't like". Félix's comments on "those shitty stories", like Pierre's confusion, whereas he was very talkative during the rest of the interview, point to the mental block felt by the boys when it comes to this topic. Pierre's laspsus is moreover revealing, since he refers to the yaoi as a "manga for gay". However, while yaoi depicts sentimental and sexual relations between men, the yaoi readership is overwhelmingly made up of female readers, and in Japan, even some homosexuals violently opposed the yaoi (Brient 2012):

> A friend of a friend of mine is reading a gay manga ... That's the kind of manga I don't read. It's called yaoi, Y, A, O, I.
>
> *And what kind of story is it?*
>
> I don't know, I haven't even tried to find out. I've never opened any, I haven't even opened any.
>
> *Why didn't you?*
>
> Because I don't like it.
>
> *And how do you know you don't like it if you haven't read them?*
>
> Because I came across it once and I didn't like it. But I really didn't like it. It was really
>
> *What do you mean?*
>
> Well, I don't know, it's like this, it's me, I ...
>
> *But because what is it, the story, the drawings*
>
> No, it's the story. It's the story, and the drawings were very badly done, especially ... No, if the drawings were well done, I might have read it. But

> the graphic was very bad, the story really sucked. It could have been a guy or a girl, I would have deleted too. It's a guy who went to a boys' high school, and he met a guy and then I don't know (voice fades out). And then I didn't read further, but he wasn't in love yet. Anyway ... Anyway, I didn't like it from the start. That's it.
>
> PIERRE, 17,11th grade, father a postman, mother a retired schoolteacher

> *Nodame Cantabile*, yes I know, it's bad, I don't like it at all, bad drawings and a shitty story.
>
> *It's not the stories of love between men?*
>
> With music, something a bit psychedelic, I read one or two chapters, I really found it ... well, rotten.
>
> FÉLIX, 15, 11th grade, parents sculptors

These issues of construction of a masculine identity are also sensitive in another field, that of music. The lack of taste of boys for visual kei groups can be explained by the look of the singers, too androgynous, too effeminate ... Nathaniel (17, 11th grade, raised by his mother, an unemployement office employee) expresses his repulsion towards the male singers of Japanese groups, who abuse make-up. He prefers the Norwegian singers of dark metal bands: "I have some music, but I don't listen to it often. They scare me a bit. I mean, it's boys who do it, but it looks like girls, so it's a bit of a turn-off ... It looks weird when you watch the videos ... Their look, that's what's weird". About her 21 years old cousin, Kalaya puts in relation, shojo, j-pop and homosexuality ... ("But actually, my cousin is a real Asian, so he likes gay music like J-pop and all that. And so, he reads a lot of shojo strangely (laughs)").

Portrait of Hacine, "Manga Is Not for Sissies"

Hacine (14), described by his English teacher as "a slacker, but very nice", is the eighth child of nine and lives with his father. He is a 9th grade student, and he considers his academic level to be "average". He discovered manga in 6th grade, on the advice of a friend from his class, who told him that "it was quite short; there was a lot of action; it wasn't ... boring, actually. It wasn't always the same thing. Then he lent me one and it started that day". The manga in question was the first volume of *Naruto*, and Hacine, who used to read French comics (*Titeuf, Spirou, Largo Winch*), abandoned now because "too childish", became passionate about this manga, and buys them at the rate of one per month, because "it's better", even if he read the tome before, on scan or lent by a friend: "I prefer to buy them because I know they are mine, and I can come back to them several times, and two weeks later return them, uh, I'm not interested in that actually. I prefer to keep them, take my time, read. Understand the story. And then, yeah, keep them at home". He owns more than a hundred mangas and a good twenty figurines.

Hacine discusses with his manga friends, and there are about ten of them in his class who share this taste: comments on the new volumes published, reading advice, loans, are thus at the heart of their friendly sociability, marked in particular by the figure of two connoisseurs who have been "fans for a long time". These exchanges go beyond the simple framework of school, since Wednesday afternoons are also devoted to them, at the homes of one or the other: "we go to someone's home and we exchange books, we read them at the other's home, and we actually talk. We talk". During these afternoons, they also play video games based on their favorite mangas. If the discussions can lead to reading advice, they also function as reminders of order, particularly in terms of gender: for example, Hacine, after trying to defend *Fruits Basket*, of which he had read and enjoyed the first five volumes, agreed with his classmates, who mocked him on the grounds that it was a "women's thing". Hacine, likewise, admits to making fun of boys who read *Nana*, because "it's so lame". In his class, one of the girls is a fan of *Nana*, and "we don't tell her anything because she's a girl; but if it were a boy …". Similarly, he doesn't like the boys he meets in town who wear make-up to be in the spirit of manga.

If Hacine follows about fifteen series, and reads at the time of the interview *Naruto, Love Hina. Negima, Death Note, Kyo*. *Naruto* remains his favorite manga, for the action, for the drawings, but especially because the character reminds him of himself: "He does a lot of stupid things. Like me. And in fact, when I was young, I was rejected by my friends … like him. Now it's good". It is indeed the reading of manga that allowed him to make friends, first by this friend who introduced him to manga, then by discussions that made him enter a "gang", federated by manga, but also by sports (soccer, handball, basketball), and by "outings with buddies". If he identifies himself with Naruto, and appreciates the fact that Naruto went from 12 to 16 years old almost like him, his favorite character is nevertheless Sasuke, whom he admires for "his class" and "his calmness", as well as for his strength and his dark side: "He becomes mean, I liked that. I like it when there are not only good guys, because it is not boring". He has two costumes of Sasuke, especially the outfit he wears when he becomes a villain, which he wears at the manga costume parties organized by his cousin. In the same way, he likes to compare his friends to characters of mangas, that he nicknames according to this character: one becomes Luciole, in *Kyo*, because he is tall and has big legs, and another Akira, from *Naruto*, for his calm and thoughtful side.

However, even if he used to read it when he was younger, he doesn't like *Dragon Ball Z* anymore, "too old" for his taste, but he still follows it in anime: "Before, I didn't know it was old, I thought it was all new and everything. But in fact, it's too old". Hacine establishes differences between the various series he reads: *Kyo* and *Naruto* according to the style of combat (magic or sword), *Death Note* which is "darker", featuring a hero struggling with an inner demon. Hacine rejects the categorization "for girls or for boys", affirming that "manga is mixed" (while taxing *Nana* of "girls' stuff" nevertheless). He discusses manga with girls, with whom he also exchanges. Hacine says he is so "used to Japanese mangas" that he does not like French mangas, whose drawings are too "simple" and the stories "too basic" for his taste. For his birthday, his father took him to the Japan Expo in Paris, where he bought mangas and figurines of Naruto. Although his father would like Hacine to read more novels, he recognizes, according to his son, that reading manga has introduced Hacine to reading in general: since Hacine has been reading manga, he has the impression that he reads faster (two weeks, even three days, instead of four weeks before) and above all that he understands better the novels imposed by the school, even if this skill does not lead to a personal taste.

Hacine searches on the internet, with his friends, for the sequels of *Naruto*, and had himself created a blog, two years ago, to discuss mangas, a blog that he has since abandoned, notably because his cousin's blog is much better. This cousin, of the same age as Hacine, advises him, and poses as an expert figure, reading more than thirty mangas per month. Hacine has since created a group on Facebook, of "*Naruto* fans", which has exceeded the 2000 "friends", and thanks to which he has made new acquaintances, giving each other an appointment in the main city square to go shopping or play laser games (last time, there were 50 of them, and they had to split into several groups). Through this group, he met a "nolife", who learns Japanese, imports Japanese mangas, but who "still scares him a bit".

When he reads, Hacine imagines himself teleporting, like Son Goku from *Dragon Ball Z*, or spitting fireballs, like Sasuke from *Naruto*, but does not talk about it with his friends. He imagines himself to be the bad guy, "because being good is always a bit the same, saving the world … So being a bad guy is more fun, bad guys are stronger; they are more intelligent, more cunning". Hacine is never moved by a manga, since "mangas are not for sissies". He thinks that he has learned things from manga, especially about gastronomy, since Naruto loves to eat. He reads on Wednesday afternoons, in the evening, after homework; in the subway sometimes, in the bus, when he goes to his mother's house; on weekends; on Sundays. He likes "animated films": Pixar, Dreamworks (*Kung Fu Panda*), Walt Disney (*Nemo*) but especially Miyazaki, which is according to him "the best" and "mythical", discovered thanks to his cousin and of which he bought all the DVDs ... This cousin is also the son of the director of a cultural center in the region, and encouraged his father to screen *Princess Mononoke*. At his father's house, Hacine can read manga, his father's only remark concerning the budget invested in this passion. On the contrary, his mother is opposed to this reading, which she finds "vulgar". Hacine tried to get his parents to read mangas, without success, because his father thinks it is "for teenagers", while his mother rejects it on principle, which is beyond her son ... In 5th grade, he and five of his friends had started to write a manga: they drew the characters, but were blocked by the lack of a scenario, and internal dissensions: "Some wanted to do stuff about robots ... Some wanted to do stuff about ninjas and everything ...". The move of the "designer" put an end to this attempt ... More connected by "Rap, R&B, electro, hard style", he does not like the music of mangas, too rock for him. He also watches a lot of cartoons, *Naruto*, *One Piece* and *Death Note* on French TV as well as on the internet. He decorated his room with posters of Sasuke and *Death Note*, placed on his *Naruto* wallpaper. Nevertheless, according to him, he is only a "small fan", his cousin being "a medium fan", because contrary to the "big fan", who is "the one who goes to the exhibitions, who buys all the time the last manga that comes out on the first day, who has all the outfits, who knows all the stories by heart", his cousin "doesn't dress up as a manga character; he doesn't know how to draw; he doesn't always buy the last manga on the first day". Later, Hacine plans to do a vocational baccalaureate, in order to work in "domestic electricity".

4.2 *Diverse Models of Masculinity: Intelligence, Psychology, and Emotions*

While the taste for action manga brings together many male and female readers, and refers to a logic of honor associated with the valorization of physical strength, some male readers claim that they prefer another aspect of manga: the psychological or strategic dimension in the confrontations between characters, and not only the physical dimension of the fights. What is valued here is not so much the physical strength, fighting techniques or special powers of the heroes, but their "intelligence", their charisma linked to mental dispositions (strategy, perspicacity ...). *Death Note* is thus often one of their favorite manga, as it focuses essentially on this type of confrontations based on manipulation and stratagems, with a large part left to the dialogues and texts necessary for the characters to explain their strategies and motivations, with fewer spectacular scenes of combat and violence than in some other manga.

This hierarchy of the manga's and male characters's qualities male, which values complexity and dominance through intelligence, also refers to an ideal of masculinity distinct from the one mentioned above.[12] Matthieu (17, 11th grade) declares that his favorite series is *Death Note*, and he values the following qualities in the main character:

> *Death Note* is this guy's intelligence, it's ... he's crazy, he's crazy but he's incredibly intelligent. And the fact that he's always wondering what else he's going to come up with, what else is he going to come up with? It's great.
>
> *Do you have any favorite characters?*
>
> Yes, in *Death Note*, the main character, without hesitation. Here we go. Just for his intelligence. I think this manga, it is worth reading just for that.

The emphasis on the intelligence of the characters is thus characteristic of boys from privileged backgrounds. Their social background, their good marks at school and their age are combined, and the interest in the hero's intellectual capacities is also a way of distinguishing them from "children's" manga. Intelligence, but also, far from the excessive muscles, their physical aspect is much more "lanky", charcateristic of a boy who spends more time behind his computer than in the weight rooms ...

> For example, *Death Note* he makes his characters pretty ... They're pretty big, pretty thin ... They all look smart and stuff. While others, they all look like kids, they look like idiots, they're very small.
>
> PIERRE, 17, 11th grade, father a postman, mother a retired schoolteacher

> *Are there any other characters you like?*

12 This ideal is reminiscent of the model of virility favored by role-players from the middle classes analysed by Wenceslas Lizé (2004).

> *Full Metal Alchemist*, Edward, it's because he doesn't have a kid side, he's more mature you know. [...] And in *Death Note*, Kira is the hero, and then L would be the other hero because he's the super-smart detective, because they're always doing stuff ... they show you super talented people but with the strange side, like you get the idea of someone you know is really gifted but who doesn't really realize it, or who's in another world with the offbeat side. It's funny, just L, the investigator, he's a young guy, he's always walking around a bit curved like that, he's got jeans that are too long, a T-shirt that falls off, while all the investigators are in suits and ties next to him, and then when he sits on a chair he always sits like that. He always has weird reactions even though he seems otherwise very thoughtful ... and he thinks fifteen times more than everyone else.
>
> FÉLIX, 15, 11th grade, parents sculptors

Intelligent heroes, but also sensitive heroes ... for readers who would be just as intelligent? In his article dealing with the *Strange* readers' feedbacks, Éric Maigret describes how the letters sent to readers' mail show the difficult learning of a problematic masculinity, notably through the tension between the pole of "classic" and stereotyped, violent and brutal virility, and the more contemporary pole of tormented and psychologized virility, in "a process of role inculcation, but in a process of learning a complex and historically new masculine identity". This new stage of masculinity is articulated with the schooling and education of middle-class and privileged models in society as a whole: no longer supermen, but human beings, no longer—or no longer only—external forces, but struggles against their inner demons, no longer beings with protruding muscles devoid of any emotion, but heroes capable of sensitivity. Thus, "through the model of the hero, it is a masculine ideal that is sought, but a 'humanized' ideal: mastering the expression of an emotionality, generally controlling one's affects, one's behavior in public, becoming a reasonable and self-confident person without giving up understanding of others and tenderness" (1995, 92). Similarly, according to Matthieu, "the superhero side attracts me a little less", as does Alexandre, who now has "trouble with the untouchable character, who will always win", "without any human qualities".

However, the appreciation of the torments of the soul does not influence teenagers the same way regardless of their social background, and not everyone says they have felt emotion, even if social distinctions should not be seen in a Manichean and radical way. This psychologization of characters is both an echo and a stimulus to the expressive and empathetic faculties of readers.

Being able to say that one has cried, that one has felt emotions thus makes it possible to recognize oneself, to construct oneself according to these new norms of masculinity which combine with the distinction of the younger self, this child who was only interested in action manga. Thus, the ability to admit to having cried or to having been saddened, anguished or disturbed by such and such a scene varies according to age, and according to social background. Even if for Hacine, manga "is never moving, it's not for sissies", manga is undoubtedly a space where expressing one's emotions becomes possible, however "weird" (Maigret, 1995, 92). it may be, to use Nathaniel's term. As Dominique Pasquier writes, "these stories do not only make you dream, they also make you feel and help you express your feelings", whether it be feelings of love and interest in romance, or tears shed because the hero dies, or because the emotion is too intense ... While Nathaniel says he "almost" cried, Nabil, Moussa (who are doing the interview together) and Léo, for example, have no difficulties admitting it:[13]

> Sometimes I get the weirdest things. In *Love Hina*, at one moment, there's Motoko, she got a forfeit, she has to dress as a girl. So, at one point, she's crying, and I don't know why, in my head, I felt like hugging her, stuff like that, completely delusional. Sometimes I'm moved to tears. *Evangelion*, when Asuka ... It's just a barrier for me because when I see Asuka actually for a moment, she's in a bathtub, she's got dark circles, she's skinny. It's borderline scary actually ... I almost cried once when I saw her like that.
>
> NATHANIEL, 17, raised by his mother, an employment office worker

> I would say now, you need a little more emotion in manga. Before, it was only the fight I was watching, and that's all that's changed. I don't know, all kinds of emotions.
>
> MOUSSA, 18, 12th grade, father a doctor, mother a pharmacist

> I saw a manga, I suffered from depression for three days. [...] When I discovered the end, I remember that in the evening I couldn't eat (laughs). I had been depressed for three days, I was pouting all the time. It was quite moving because the girl is young. The relationship between the characters makes you get attached to the girls: it makes you think of a child you wouldn't want to see die, and suddenly it just falls on you, like that, on your arms.
>
> MADJI, 19, 11th grade, father a bus driver, stay-at-home mother

13 See supra.

Conversely, the total absence of feelings can lead one to turning away from a manga, as Alexandre says:

> But if you take a manga like *D. Gray*, where the characters are barely 15, 16 years old, they may have quite intense adventures, they have almost no feelings for each other, there's something missing a little bit, I think. … [*Berserk*] it's not the fact that it's violent that bothered me, it's mostly the character's tough side. […] *Samurai Deeper Kyo*, the main character is a little … I mean I would say far from being human almost. We don't really feel any feelings, we don't feel anything at all.
>
> ALEXANDRE, 17, 11th grade, parents schoolteachers

So, manga can work in a privileged way as a conveyor of emotions learning. For boys too, reading manga is an "emotional experience".

As we see with Ladji or Madji, the expression of feelings and emotions is not the preserve of boys from intermediate or privileged backgrounds. However, it must be said that while all the boys from the more privileged pole tell about episodes that moved or upset them, they are much rarer in the less socially privileged pole. So, we may wonder whether the silence or rejection of any idea of emotion among some, the youngest, children from the most popular backgrounds, is a sign of a more binding imposition of the stereotype of "traditional" virility, which may suppress any feelings, or whether it is more difficult for them to express it in an interview.

4.3 *The Little Nana Girls*

While the teenagers' reactions and preferences reveal the difficulties in becoming a boy, becoming a girl is not much easier, since one has to combine this gendered identity with one's social and cultural capital. While Fatou, Leila or Safya, who are from working-class backgrounds, describe a relationship to the shojos devoid of any complex, it is clear that afficher of the stereotyped "tastes of girls" for the shojo would be demeaning for girls from privileged backgrounds. In the same way that exhibting a passion for rock, hard rock or heavy metal, as opposed to R'n'B and singers who are too popular, too sexy and too "feminine" (Lahire 2004), they claim that they despise shojo, and that they like shonen, fighting and violence. The gender hierarchy, "the differential valence of the sexes" (Héritier 1996), thus provides a means of distinction for some readers, among the most endowed with cultural and educational assets, such as Nora or Célia, who, moreover, shared their childhood with older brothers, who made them familiar with them with manga, video games, etc., and who are now more likely to be able to read and write. This socialization through siblings or cousins is also very effective among other young girls from more popular backgrounds, such as Maureen, Sophie or Maeva, and once again reveals the strength of the hierarchy between men and women: no little brother of an older sister has indeed developed an immoderate passion for shojo, to the point of rejecting shonen, whereas the opposite is common. Nora (16, 11th grade, father a school teacher, stay-at-home mother) thus admires *Full Metal Alchemist*, *Death Note*, *Bleach*, and so stories of samurai, ninjas or warriors as well, and rejects shojo, which she considers "bothering". It is also through her two older brothers that she discovered manga, drawing from their collections, before becoming the most passionate of the three. She shares with them other 'masculine' tastes, such as fighting video games like *Fall Out* or *Doom*. Nora also makes fun of the "hysterical girls" she came across when she went to a manga convention in Paris:

> It's scary, those girls who dress all the time in cosplay, gothic lolita, stuff like that. It doesn't really annoy me, but I find, those girls, I don't know, I think, but poor people can't be easy every day.

Célia, who in general, exhibits "masculine" tastes and enjoys manga like *Jackals*, Gothic music, the band Rammstein and horror films, also expresses strongly her taste for fighting, her disinterest in "manga stuff with big-breasted girls, which frankly must cause back problems absolutely filthy". She prefers "shonen, so more intended fo young boys". Cécile, Maele and Marie are also very virulent against shojo and their female readers, and the recurrence of the verb "to annoy" expresses their fear of being identified to this form of "femininity":

> Well, it's ... Well, there's the ones with big eyes and little noses and little mouths, and it's ugly. And ... the stories that go with it are usually very, very, very silly. It's like, 'I love you, but you don't know that because I'm actually invisible'. And it's kind of boring. Usually, it's manga for girls called shojo that are drawn like this and it's horrible. Well let's just say that when they [her female friends] read their own manga, it's actually cute but it's really too dumb'.
>
> CÉCILE, 17, 1st year college student, father an executive, mother a private nurse

> I don't like manga for girls. For example, *Nana*, *Nuts* ... I don't really like love stories.
>
> *Have you tried reading any?*

> Yes, I tried, I read all the *Love Hina*. It's silly. The girls, they're often ... juggy. It lacks action. Always about 'he loves me, he does not love me, maybe'...
>
> *So, the manga that you like are more of a special kind?*
>
> Yeah, it's more like shonen.
>
> MARIE, 14, 9th grade, father an accountant, mother a cleaning lady

> *Sailor Moon*, I don't like the drawings either and the story is too ... mushy for me: 'Ah I love you', 'Ah I love you too'. 'Ah, but we love each other then!'. It's too pink for me. I can't stand it.
>
> MAELE, 16, 11th grade, father a teacher, mother a counsellor

> There's no point in love stories, they get on my nerves, after a while it's always the same thing! No, that annoys me!
>
> MAEVA, 18, 12th grade, father an electrician, mother an accountant, Jérôme's twin sister

> *And you for example, you have girlfriends who read manga?*
>
> I mostly have friends who read manga.
>
> *No girls among your friends?*
>
> Yes, yes, but not too many. They're more into romance novels.
>
> *And you don't read any?*
>
> No. No, no, I don't like that. I don't like it at all.
>
> MAUREEN, 15, 9th grade, father a worker, mother an administrative officer

The very girls who don't like shojo, or read them with a bad conscience, will hardly appreciate the characters of shonen girls, too "soft", too "silly" for their taste. This adjective comes up in all the interviews of these young girls, with the verbs "to infuriate" or "to drive mad". Estelle describes the female characters as "the classic style of the groupie, who is useless at the beginning, who is crying all the time. Who has pink hair on top of that". And Célia, once again, makes a formal accusation aimed at both the charcaters and the female readers, even imitating the high-pitched voice of the groupie:

> I don't know how to translate this word in French, in English we say obnoxious, it would be a character who does too much, it's too cute, too dumb, who tries too hard, I mean to be a favorite character whatsoever. [...] Everybody says: 'Oh but she's too cute, oh' (exaggeratedly high-pitched voice, laughs). It's a little bit to add the feminine touch or whatever, but I'm deeply annoyed. It's rather the girls that get on my nerves. [...] For

> example with my best friend, we compare ourselves to male characters. There's not really a female character that we compare ourselves to.
>
> CÉLIA, 17, 11th grade, mother an opera director, father a choreographer

The rejection of shojo takes many forms, and is more or less internalized. One might think that, rather than a strategy of differenciation, the preference for shonen could be due to family socializations, either masculinary, with brothers and cousins, or school socializations for the girls from scientific areas, or even media, the degree of violence in films having considerably increased in recent years, as shown for example by the *Twilight* series, or the contemporary way of capturing fight scenes. But both combine: in some interviews, we see that the acerbic remarks of some hide a knowledge and practice of reading shojo, even though these teenagers are kind of ashamed of admitting it. For those who nevertheless read shojo, as with the boys, "excuses" are needed: to be busy during a course at school, as with Cécile, to clear their heads, as with Kayala … ("When I want to empty my brain, I take a shojo and when I want to be interested in something, I take a shonen"), to want to know the end, as for Estelle, to like the "graphics" and the style of drawing, as for Élodie or Caroline, or to appreciate humor, in spite of and towards the love story. Cécile (17, 1st year college student, father an executive, mother a private nurse) says that she does read shonen, and rejects any interest in sentimental relationships. But she nevertheless reads shojo in class. According to her, she doesn't have much choice, since that's all her classmate has. Cécile nevertheless reads them (she could refuse or bring something else …), but will do everything to stand out from this reading, which she despises both because the characteristics of the genre as those of the female readers:

> Shojo is for girls (high-pitched voice), so the silly romance stories. […] It's a very closed circle, people who love manga. So, the one I'm sitting next to in class, she talks to me about manga. Except that she reads shojo. So sometimes, when I have nothing else to do in class, I read manga like that (sigh). It keeps me busy for a while. But it's really boring. But when I see the way she pounces on manga (high-pitched voice): 'So cute'. Oh, shut up!

Saving the shojo amounts to question the classification, as for Estelle with the nurse's after school:

> It was one of the manga that impressed me the most, I would say. I really liked it a lot.

> *It's a shojo?*
>
> I don't know if it can really be considered as a particular style because there are a lot of fights, there's fantastic, it's very dark. There's also a love relationship between the three main characters. It's very difficult to classify it.
>
> ESTELLE, 17, 12th grade, father a bank clerk, mother a school nurse

But standing out from girls and their shojo can also be done by exploring other genres in the range of manga categories. Categorization by age, as for boys with seinen vs shonen can help grow and develop. This is the case of Caroline (14, 9th grade, father a shopkeeper, mother an insurance trainer), for example, who appreciates josei, these manga for young adult women, while she is in ninth grade and her friends only read manga for schoolgirls. Élodie (18, 12th grade, father a biologist, mother a designer) also prefers "weird shojo" to rosewater shojos:

> *And weird shojo is* Happy Mania, *for example?*
>
> Yeah, it's the heroin, she's totally nuts. She's 26 years old, she absolutely wants to find a boyfriend. To begin with, the graphic design is very particular, well, the story is pretty crazy too, in the sense that she's not staid, she's a first-rate immature and she's absolutely looking for true love. She even goes so far as to steal her girlfriends' boyfriends. Anyway, it's pretty weird.

Above all, two genres will cause girls to be interested in the subtleties of sentimental relationships without running the risk of contempt associated with reading shojo: on the one hand, the manga of "vampires". *Vampire Knight*, which Marie loves because "it's extremely violent. There's blood spurting everywhere all the time. The first one I read, I almost fainted"... This kind of manga allows indeed to cash in on the long teeth fashion of the *Twilight*, to combine love and violence. Last but not least, yaoi and shonen-ai, the real taboo for boys, become a new form of romance acceptable for girls. Thus, the same people who used to proclaim their contempt for love stories about the shojo, suddenly become enchanted by the sentimentality of the yaoi, insisting that this genre is neither pornographic nor perverse.

> It's the story of a boy who wants to become a singer, who meets a writer and falls in love with him, if I remember correctly. It's often a sentimental story. How can I put it ... I thought it was very much in line with the general idea that we made love in comic books, the films and all that, it's

> really treated in a very different way, I found it really interesting. I found that sometimes there was a truer side to these stories, and then in general the love dealt with in comics is a bit like The Young and the restless manga version, and it gets annoying very quickly. I thought there was a more real side to those stories.
>
> ESTELLE, 17, 12th grade, father a bank clerk, mother a school nurse

> *Boys next door* … it's Kaori Yuki (Laughs) Let's see … an employee, a businessman who … It's been a long time … who loses something important and starts wandering around in dark, badly frequented alleyways … (Embarrassment) … really badly frequented and he comes across a young man, he's being exploited, and he finds within himself what he's desperately looking for, love for who he is … And finally, he's going to help him break free from his chains … It's a beautiful love story, too.
>
> MAELE, 16, 11th grade, father a teacher, mother a counsellor

> Some yaoi, I'm reading some yaoi. On the Internet. It's not really my … I prefer shonen-ai. Yaoi is pornographic. Shonen-ai, it's just love stories between boys, but that's it, that's all there is to it. Sometimes the stories, it's cute, it's a change from shojo.
>
> CAROLINE, 14, 9th grade, father a shopkeeper, mother an insurance trainer

> Shonen-ai, yes … (Laughs.) It's a friend who said: 'Here, read this, you'll like it'. 'So I read … Yes, it's nice. The shonen-ai, it's a homosexual relationship between two boys … It's light, it won't go further than a simple kiss, it's more the love part that's developed. It's not perverse.'
>
> MAELE

To the question "why do girls read yaoi?", the answers are diverse, and they probably vary depending on whether we look at the female or Japanese audience: girls would find, in these mostly androgynous male characters, an alternative to the overly silly and stereotypical female characters. These characters would allow them to identiy without running the risks of contempt associated with reading shojo, and without the complex of female characters with a perfect figure; yaoi, written by women and read by women, is seen as a revenge against male domination, since, in turn, they reify male bodies (Brient, 2012), etc. Janice Radway, in her book for women readers of romance novels, stumbled upon the following paradox: while these novels were staging a most stereotypical romanticism, the readers claimed a part of emancipation. Similarly, is the reading of yaoi a sign of poaching and subversion by young girls, who appropriate manga "for boys" by diverting the gender relations of the initial story? Or is "hiding behind the strangeness of homosexuality" only a "revival of romantic clichés, such as the slow progression of love before getting involved in a relationship, or of stereotyped patterns, with the reintroduction of an unbalanced relationship within the couple featuring a protector and a protégé" (François 2010, 20)? Beyond the nature of the couple, or a militant request for transgression, the yaoi, finally, for these young girls, would only be love stories like the others, but that they can, unlike the others, read—and write—without being accused of being mushy …

Reading manga thus allows one to learn one's gender, and to experience the troubles and disarrays associated with it: a type of masculinity where bravery must go hand in hand with intelligence and feelings for boys, and a type of romance that should not be too sappy for girls. Gender combines with cultural and social capital. While the "invisible barrier" identified by Éric Maigret still exists, which separates boys from privileged and popular backgrounds in the way they express their feelings, and girls from these backgrounds in terms of sensitivity to sentimentalism, the barrier is not so clear-cut: boys from popular backgrounds, such as Nayir, Madji or Ladji also tell about their tears, and girls from popular backgrounds, such as Alice, Maeva or Maureen, also reject the "pinkest" shojo. For boys, it's probably a matter of age, and it seems more difficult for a middle schooler than for a high schooler to admit to having cried or shuddered watching a love story. Similarly, gender or social origin are not sufficient to understand the girls' choices in terms of manga, especially when they were raised with older brothers whom they admired and whose practices they followed.

Finally, as Maele and Marianne put it, "seeing a girl take a shonen won't shock anyone. I think it's more shocking if it's a boy taking a shojo (laughs)". This discrepancy in the possible appropriations shows, just like the rejection of shojo by boys in general and by many girls, how much the "differential valence of the sexes" and gender stereotypes are still alive and weigh heavily on girls as on boys, suspected of deviance towards masculinity as soon as they dare to take a shojo, the positions around yaoi showing clearly the stakes involved concerning the notions of masculinity and virility on the one hand, but also around femininity and sentimentalism on the other.

5 Growing Up with Manga: Practical Uses

While Naruto is growing with the readers, the readers, too, say they are growing, improving, enriching themselves, mentally, intellectually and psychologically, all along their career as manga readers.

5.1 *Seeds of Knowledge*

Much like the female readers of romance novels met by Janice Radway, who, by reading novels whose plot mixed history and romance, said they were improving their knowledge of history, teenagers emphasize all they have learned from manga. Often, they have mastered a few Japanese words by now, and have fun, in anime or print, recognizing this small common repertoire of Japanese terms. However, this linguistic knowledge remains fragile and very fragmented, and for the majority of readers, learning Japanese is not a goal. However, this impregnation sometimes continues in a more voluntary, self-taught way: Nayir tries to learn words with the help of a friend, Estelle searches on the Internet and consults her girlfriend's copy of *Japanese for dummies*. Alexandre makes himself a lexicon and already has "a double-sided copy". Caroline has fun hiding the subtitles of the anime and has bought manuals and CDs. Annabelle, Maele, Marianne and Nathaniel are following an optional Japanese course at school. Nathaniel (17, 11th grade, raised by his mother, an unemployement office employee) has thus undertaken to learn Japanese, the manga's "original language". He first began to learn on his own with a Japanese learning book, before taking classes in an association when he was in middle school, and then enrolled in the only high school in the city offering Japanese courses.

More generally, manga is perceived as a metonymic element of a culture, which can thus be approached through reading. Whether through the details of daily life, mythological references or historical elements, manga allows, according to these readers, to acquire knowledge about a foreign world, or even to counter the stereotypes that are too widespread about Japan. Kader believes that he has learned elements of history, in particular "the medieval era of Japan" with *Samurai Deeper Kyo*, and Célia poetically calls these extremely varied elements of knowledge "seeds of knowledge", since they range from history to mythology, through gastronomy or the rules of Mah Jong, which she picks up as she reads them. Estelle is also proud to mention "a radio programme that once said that manga was very good for the general culture of children", and stresses the interest of the explanatory notes. Kalaya (18, 2nd year college student, parents executives) also liked the statistics presented in *Step Up Love Story*, "because in the corners, you have little boxes, statistics on

Japanese people, or on sex in general, how to do this or how to do that. [...] Just for the statistics it's worth it".

Some gains are even directly convertible into the school market, sometimes surprisingly: for example, Alexandre (17, 11th grade, parents schoolteachers) finds that his level in English has improved since he read the scans translated into English. Nayir and Bastien convert their pictorial essays into drawing lessons, Marianne (16, 11th grade, father a numerical control operator, mother a restaurant employee) was "very much ahead of the mythology program with *Sailor Moon*", Maele is inspired by the world of manga for her essays in middle school, just like Marianne ("I remember I did on *Sailor Moon*. We had to do something detective, so I thought: 'Here, I'll take up the same story again'. I just changed the names and a bit of intrigue, I made up a story about a lost necklace"). Arthur (18, 1st year college student, father an executive, mother an accountant) even reinvested his reading of *Full Metal Alchemist* in a philosophy essay:

> Ah yes, about science: could you blame science, or should you blame the men behind the science. So, with *Full Metal Alchemist*, there's one who says, I think it was Alphonse who said, 'Science should serve man, not the other way around'. So that, for example, I put it back in my ... not in the form of a quote (laughs) because otherwise, I don't know how she was going to react about it. But here's what, for example, to say that it's not the science that's to blame, but rather the men behind it, things like that.

Sometimes even a whole academic orientation can stem from reading manga or from the constellation of interests it relates to, as for Juliette in computer science, Arthur in chemistry (according to him, his educational orientation derived from his passion for *Full Metal Alchemist*), Alexandra, who wants to become a video game designer and wants to go to a school in Japan, Nayir who wants to become a mangaka, Maureen, Sophie and Nadia who would like to go to a graphic arts school, or Caroline, who would like to work in manga publishing ...

5.2 *Seeds of Life*

But manga can also make people grow morally and mentally, and provide life lessons, teachings that then bear fruit. Ethical-practical reading is thus dialectical: through identification, readers recognize themselves, but through the examples, they feel that they improve. The heroes grow up, become teenagers, young adults, but the readers are themselves caught up in this process of initiation, and manga then works as a coming-of-age novel. Thus, Maureen

(15, 9th grade, father a worker, mother an administrative officer) believes that manga, combined with the practice of martial arts, has helped her to channel her energy. Fatou (24, 12th grade, father a poultry farmer, mother a shopkeeper) thinks that she has learned to accept herself as she is. Yohanna (16, 10th grade, father an engineer, mother a sales representative) believes that he has become more respectful, "because it talks a lot about the same thing in the manga and then I tried to carry it out a little bit", just like Félix did, as a matter of fact. Madji learned to put things into perspective, and "that in life, despite everything, you shouldn't get depressed for nothing". According to him, "manga can bring beautiful things in real life, beyond what we think, beyond a reading, just as novels can change ways of living, ways of thinking too". Nabil also finds that "those who read manga are always a bit different. It's a minority, yeah. They will have better relationships with people, I don't know why, it's weird". As for Vincente and Océane, reading manga simply made them happier and more joyful. What more could you ask of a book after all?

> I liked ... techniques ... self-control. I really need it! They say I'm aggressive. So, it made it possible for me to channel my energy.
>
> *Who said you were aggressive? The teachers or the family?*
>
> Yeah, teachers, everyone. Because I'm nice, but I'm too impulsive. So, manga also helped me channel my energy. Actually, I also took karate because I liked manga and then it went into a crescendo.
>
> *And how did manga channel your energy?*
>
> Well, seeing as I was seeing fights and stuff ... I mean it got me ... I mean It's okay, I've calmed down. But it's true that I can get aggressive easily, though. But I can control myself now. A little bit. It doesn't look like it, but the breathing exercises, all that, as they show ... Because it's still an art, martial arts. It's true that compared to that, they manage to channel their energy, so I try to do the same.
>
> MAUREEN, 15, 9th grade, father a worker, mother an administrative officer

> *What did you get out of reading manga?*
>
> I'm a little happier because I wasn't ... I wasn't like that before. I'm more ... I'm happier because before I was shy, but now I'm not.
>
> OCÉANE, 15, 9th grade, father an electrician, mother a housewife

> At first, I was ... how can I say it, I was ... how can I say it too serious and then when I started to know more about manga, I thought it was good, and then I started to be ... I would say happier.
>
> VINCENTE, 11, 6th grade, father a garbage collector, stay-at-home mother

As for Nadia (14, 8th grade, father a worker, mother a secretary), who is passionate about cosplay, manga allowed her to accept herself from a physical point of view: for this rather shy teenager, the appearance, and especially the way she dressed, was indeed problematic. With an Algerian father, Nadia had to deal both with his remarks when her skirts were too short, but also with the more or less acerbic mockery of the pupils of her middle school, located in a sensitive district, as soon as her outfit was too feminine. Given the fact that she goes now to another middle school, she finds herself with children from much more privileged backgrounds. Manga, and the outfits that go with it, are thus for Nadia a real resource against adversity, a way of exhibiting with pride an eccentric appearance, and to some extent of claiming a different status, of transforming in some way the stigma she suffers from:

> They recognize me, they know my name. Everybody knows me now, even though I'm new this year, I'm quite … Everybody looks at me, every time I bring out something new.

Portrait of Nadia

Two interviews were conducted with Nadia, whose mother is a secretary in an institution of higher learning, and whose father is a skilled worker in a chemical company. Both are Algerian. At the time of the first interview, Nadia, 14 years old, was in the fourth grade, and at the time of the second, conducted a year and a half later, she was 16 years old and in the second year of high school. These two interviews allow us to reconstruct Nadia's reading trajectory and the evolution of her tastes.

During the first interview, Nadia has just discovered manga. She saw them while accompanying her parents and her younger brother, who is eight years younger than her, in a bookstore specialized in comics. Nadia had also browsed the manga sections of a supermarket, populated by teenagers absorbed in reading, which had aroused her curiosity. But it was the intervention of a friend from high school that encouraged her to start reading a manga series. Nadia started reading *Fruits Basket*, which she loved, and then asked her mother to buy her the manga *Nana*. Nadia continued to read manga lent to her by her middle school friend, read manga when her parents went shopping at the supermarket or mall, or when she went to specialty stores with her friends. Shortly after entering the third grade, Nadia also started to watch scans of manga or anime on the Internet, in streaming, and to download "music from Japanese bands". Nadia likes to reread the ten or so volumes of manga that she owns, or those that her friend lends her, especially before going to sleep. She has also started to lend her own mangas: "Yes, I lend them. I don't have many left, I don't even know where they are. I must have three left. [...] In fact, that's when I read them to sleep, but otherwise, they're there, because I lend them every time, and some leave, some come back, so there's always room". In order to understand certain mangas, Nadia is sometimes obliged to reread the "annoying" passages that she had "skipped". Nadia doesn't attach much importance to the news of manga or anime releases, in France or in Japan: "because I discover them all the time, so I know that I'll still discover a lot of them, so I don't rush too much for the moment, because afterwards, I know that if I read too much of them, it's going to irritate me. I'm always like that, when I do something too much, it starts to annoy me afterwards, so I'm going to go slowly, because I like it and I want to keep reading it". Nadia tries to keep up with every manga and anime series, and watches the latter "directly on the Dailymotion site, in Japanese with French subtitles". Nadia prefers to "watch the manga than to actually read it", first of all because it is "free", more easily accessible, and the subtitled anime are "ahead" of the plot developed in the manga published in French. But she reads the mangas after watching the animes nevertheless. Reading the manga makes it easier to remember the names of the characters, which Nadia sometimes finds difficult to read and remember in the scrolling subtitles. Contemplating images and characters' styles is also easier in manga, during the evening readings and rereadings that establish a more intimate relationship with her favorite series. Nadia reads the "back summaries" before choosing a manga, she flips through them "to see what's inside and everything, and then if I like it, then I buy it". She prefers to follow only one series at a time, "because afterwards, it gets mixed up, it's not very easy to manage in your head, lots of stories" and for the moment she concentrates on *Fruits Basket*: Nadia sometimes feels disoriented in front of an overabundant offer of manga ("I have to look for them because there are so many that it's hard to choose. It takes time") and often relies on the advice of five friends in her class who are "into it".

With her best friend, Nadia regularly visits a store that specializes in Japanese animation, derivative products, clothing and accessories related to manga. On the Saturday before the first interview, Nadia bought a *Death Note* bag with the money she received from her grandmother. She had come to buy a *Bleach* bag, but followed her friend's advice, and then sought to read the *Death Note* manga, which she loved. Nadia is the only one with a *Death Note* bag in her middle school, and thinks that "it looks good", "because they like *Death Note*, so they don't mind it too much". Nadia would also like to buy "a Ryu figurine" which costs "50 euros the small thing", or the DVD box set of the series, which also contains a small figurine. Nadia doesn't appreciate the parodies of this manga, like the Spanish series *Death Joke*, because "the story of *Death Note* is still good, it's stupid to spoil it". Finally, she says she knows a lot of other manga, "but the titles, they are hard to remember". Nadia's favorite characters are Zero from *Vampire Knight*, Nana Osaki from *Nana*, Ryuk from *Death Note* and Ichigo from *Bleach*. because she "likes the big monsters they have to kill, also the big sword he has. Also, he always gets blown up, but he's still alive actually".

Nadia's reading of manga is very much linked to an interest in Japanese music and fashion, to differentiate herself from the "no-styles" in her middle school. With a friend, starting in the 5th grade, she first adopted the "emo" style, which she often discusses on MSN. She defines it first as a style of music: "As music, it screams a lot, it screams more than metal. It can go from really high-pitched screaming, it's soft and everything and it can go, and it's often … There's emo-core and emo. Emo is softer, and emo-core is really, like, all over the place and stuff …" Nadia has also adopted a style of dress for herself and only knows of one other girl who displays this emo style at school, while the other students multiply the criticism against them. Nadia thus stands out in the symbolic economy of "styles" and "spectacular" cultures represented in her middle school (she lists "tektonik too, but that stuff sucks", and "fashion, the scum, with their own style"). She discovered the emo style through images on the Internet, and was drawn to it primarily by a hairstyle. Nadia thus changed her previously "classic" hairstyle and clothing. Mostly on MSN, Nadia has met other teenagers who share her interests and with whom she exchanges advice on music and hair styles. Nadia points out that although emo is not Japanese, it can be combined with Japanese styles, such as visual kei. Nadia finds pictures of emo hairstyles on the Internet and prints them out to show to her hairdresser. She tried a visual kei haircut: "it was like that up there, all spiky and everything, but I changed, because I was tired of it … I often get tired of hairstyles, quickly. And then it grew back so now it didn't look like anything. So, I left it like that and on Sunday, I'm getting a new hairstyle". According to Nadia, her mother is also "getting used to it", but her father is more reticent: "it bothers him a bit, he thinks I'm a punk and everything, he doesn't like it too much, even if I don't shave my hair". While walking in the city center, Nadia meets "little lolitas, well girls who dress like the girls there". She appreciates their style, made of "little dresses, yeah, cute little things, Japanese shoes with wooden soles", even if she "doesn't see herself in them".

In 10th grade, Nadia started listening to more and more Japanese bands, which she discovered on the Internet, especially thanks to the links exchanged on MSN in her emo discussion group. She likes An Café, Dio/DistraughtOverload, The Gazette, Versailles, and knows the dates of the Parisian concerts of some of her Japanese bands, even if she has never been there. Nadia appreciates the style, the hair and the hairstyles of the singers of these groups, as she evokes it about the group An Café: "I liked how they dressed too, their hairstyle, because they have too good hair, the Japanese. I have curly hair by nature, so to straighten it, it's not so practical and finally, I love their hair, because they can do many things with it". It was also Nadia's interest in the manga *Nana* that led her to explore a constellation of tastes and practices related to Japanese music. Nadia prefers the character of "Nana the rocker, the punk" and the "look" of the members of her music group, Trapnest: "I think to myself, I don't know, I've never seen people like that in France yet". Nadia also went to sites dedicated to *Nana* to "take wallpapers". She went three times to the Japan Expo, once to the Chibi Japan Touch and Paris Manga, and twice to the Japan Touch festival. There she meets the people she chats with on MSN: "It's ... The idea of liking manga and seeing those who like manga". Nadia wants to both "see more *Death Note* stuff", "see especially people's cosplays, how they're going to be". She herself would like to "do one" but "it's a long time to do it" and she started too late. One year before the second interview, Nadia's friends made a group cosplay from the manga *Ludwig Revolution*. She didn't feel strong enough to participate in quizzes and other knowledge games about the manga, but she did karaoke and attended anime and drama screenings with her friends. Nadia went once to the Japan Expo festival in Paris with a Japanese girl she met last year, and with whom she kept in touch "on the computer". She saw the concert of the band that does the opening credits of *Naruto*, and the one of the band X Japan, but "they only did two songs, I was disgusted, they did their star ...".

Nadia declares that she has "changed" in high school ("well yeah, I'm not in the same trip as before"). She notably abandoned the emo style and the "tomboy" clothes in favor of the *gyaru* style: "yeah but now, I don't know if you know, it's a style in Japan, it's called, it's gyaru: it's girls who are very interested in fashion and everything, they're all bleached, they do everything to have big eyes". Nadia has thinned her hair, which she wears long and straight, and similar contacts, ordered on the Internet, and says she has "started to dress like a girl", a look she was leering towards in college without really daring. She consults on Internet the scans of Japanese fashion magazines: "after I looked at their outfits, then I started to make me cuts like them, finally all like that then uh … After what, it came like that. I mean, when I'm in conventions, for occasions, I really dress with bows like that and everything". Nadia has thus appropriated some elements of this Japanese fashion: "there are the clothes, there are the nails too, well they do fake nails, something crazy, well there are sequins with pearls and everything, I bought some at the Japan Expo, uh they do what else? UV, but I didn't do UV, I'm glad I didn't, and that's it. But then they dress normally, they follow the fashion". Nadia also appreciates the "sweet Lolita", the "gothic Lolita" and the "*hime gyaru*". She bought herself a "doll dress", which she wears on certain occasions. It is a black dress, with flowers, "more a gothic lolita thing", bought 50 euros at the Chibi Japan Expo, but she lacks the shoes that go with it ("the same as in *Nana*"): "I also like the lolita style, I don't have the opportunity to dress like that often because uh I really dress for occasions or when I'm with people who are the same, because I have a dress and everything of doll like that, well I call it doll because it's really … but uh it really goes only to Japanese girls. … You have to be small in fact to uh really then there is a size … there is a cut of dress which uh which is specific and everything". Nadia has already gone several times for a walk in the city with this dress, in company of her friends. One of them buys "branded stuff", and has spent up to 300 euros to buy a lolita dress. She still often meets groups of girls dressed in "sweet lolita": "they are really well made, frankly they have pretty dresses, which must be worth a lot of money, it's uh Baby, the stars shine bright, that's the brand". Nadia finds it a nice style, "beautiful to look at", and people "looked at her from everywhere like that, it looks like a doll oulala, it's pretty, there are some who laughed at me but hey, I'm used to it".

Nadia also consults the blog of a lolita she saw at a local convention, and that she had noticed for her dress: "I think she is really pretty this girl. Moreover, she makes music and everything, she sings in Japanese and everything, she has a blogphotos I think, where there is everything finally full of photos of her. When she goes to conventions, she does concerts and everything, she sings. Yeah, well she has a whole list of songs. I saw she had a lot of amazing dresses, it's so beautiful to look at, I really like it". Nadia often goes to the Tokyo Fashion website to learn about "all the styles you see on the streets". She doesn't want to learn Japanese ("it's long to learn, it's hard to remember"), she doesn't know Japanese cooking, but she would like to go to Tokyo because she "likes their clothes, because over there, we're not so much criticized ... Well, they have a lot of looks and everything". Nadia recently saw a report on Tokyo, where "there were a lot of girls with the same hairstyle as Nana". She would like to buy the DVD of the "live" adaptation of this manga, especially to better appreciate the "haircuts" of the actors. Nadia also likes the websites and photos of young Korean teenagers, the "uzzlang", and other Asian "cyberstars", who put photos online and are voted on by Internet users, the most popular of whom can be seen in Kpop or dramas.

In 10th grade, Nadia bought *Paradise Kiss*, *Lolipop* and *Vampire Knight*. When her high school friend who used to lend her "lots of manga" moved to another high school, Nadia started buying some of the titles she had discovered in high school. She stopped reading *Naruto* because the friend who used to send her the links in middle school also left for another high school and she "didn't feel like downloading anymore": "I don't even know what's going on now, a lot of things must have happened". Nadia doesn't like the constraints of the "publication" and reading mode of the scans: "I had started to read *Nana* in scan, until volume 23, and uh after that, I stopped because it's annoying in fact every time to download, to search and everything. I don't like it, I prefer to have it directly, and even waiting for the mangas, I prefer to have them all at the same time. Nana, she publishes them every week in magazines, so it's not the whole volume". She reads and rereads *Detective Conan*, which she has also followed on television since she was little. She wanted to start reading *One Piece* but gave up due to too many volumes. The demons of the underworld of *Black Butler* or the vampires of *Vampire Knight* replaced the ninjas, and Nadia continued her exploration of shojo manga and the work of Ai Yazawa, whom she names as her favorite author. Nadia read and loved *Lolipop*, the story of a girl abandoned by her parents after they win the lottery, who falls in love with the "son of the house" in which they have placed her. Nadia also loved *Comme Elles*, whose author she knows, Fujisue Sakura. Nadia discovered this manga at a supermarket and she liked it so much that she bought it every time it came out: "it is really realistic about the love life of girls today." Nadia even thinks that "even boys should read it I think, really". It could really happen in real life. Nadia has become passionate about the story of these "two girlfriends who each have a different vision of love", and have to face the deceptions of their boyfriends, "I mean, it can happen". She opposes this "shojo like no other" to the "corny stories", especially thanks to the "maturity" of the characters.

Nadia read the five volumes of *Paradise Kiss* after having read *Nana*. She appreciates the drawings of the mangaka, and the world of fashion that is presented. She recognized herself in the story of this "intelligent" girl, who "thinks only about school and everything and then one day, someone sees her in the street to become a model". During her summer vacations, by the sea, Nadia, dressed in lolita fashion, was approached by a photographer who had noticed her style, and she happily lent herself to this impromptu photo session.

Nadia also reads "other stuff" than manga, like "big books", but she stopped reading French-Belgian comics, which are still associated for her with childhood. Nadia prefers "bigger books", especially "vampire stories", like Stephenie Meyer's *Fascination* and *Temptation*. In general, when it comes to novels or TV series, Nadia "prefers American stories, which are better than French stories, because you're less bored". Nadia also enjoyed the vampire stories featured in many manga and anime, such as *Vampire Knight*, *Rosario + Vampire*, *Blood +*. She doesn't consider these titles to be in the horror genre, but what she likes about vampires are their looks, their teeth, and "their powers". Nadia enjoys *Vampire Knight* because the series takes place in a middle school: "It would be cool if there were vampires that existed, I like vampires". While she read "a lot" in elementary school, Nadia dropped out in middle school, started reading novels again in high school and got good grades in French. Nadia does not play video games, unlike her younger brother. However, Nadia has been drawing frequently since middle school. She doesn't like to "copy" images or scenes from manga, but focuses on the hairstyles and haircuts of manga characters: "Actually, I do the heads from manga and then I do the haircut I want, because actually, I like to draw the hairstyles I want". Nadia would like to "study graphic design": "I prefer to draw on T-shirts instead. I'd like to draw stuff for T-shirts, because sometimes you can't find the T-shirts you want. And when you have my style, you want very specific T-shirts, with things you like ..." Nadia sought admission to a high school that offered art classes, but she was not selected and, like many of her classmates, was directed to 10th grace class in another high school. Nadia has since almost stopped drawing, but is increasingly interested in fashion.

Fantasy or adventure stories, police mysteries or sentimental romances between schoolchildren or boarders, love stories between men ..., manga allow the implementation of strategies from identification admiring or empathetic, real or metaphorical, and offer for most of their readers a reading grid to decode the world, their world. The "relaxation" they provide is therefore of crucial importance, at a time in life when questions often jostle each other, and when the definition of oneself and one's place, in one's family, in one's group of friends, or even at school, evolves. But reading these manga, like any reading in fact, can also help to fix pain and trauma, and provide resources to make up for absences.

Generally speaking, the manga publishing offer with its codified and gendered categories allows multiple appropriations: the title, the chosen series allow one to construct oneself as a teenager of this or that age, to claim a form of generational autonomy, by distancing oneself from the tastes and practices of the parents. In these games of distinction and identification, gender identities are also negotiated: learning a masculinity where "classic" virility remains necessary but is no longer enough for boys from more privileged backgrounds, and for others as they grow older, and must be combined with humor, intelligence, psychology and sensitivity; depreciation of an overly sentimental femininity, among girls from privileged backgrounds or socialized among brothers and cousins, who then use tricks to have the right to dream of love ...

The manga preferences make it possible both to reflect and build the readers' gender. The use of the term "strategies" should not lead one to believe that these are conscious manoeuvres or positioning: it is indeed the play of dispositions, activated, put on hold by the different levels and spaces of socialization that are revealed in the tastes and dislikes, which, very often, do not strictly follow the actual practices.

Manga, like other kinds of reading, allows identification, reparation, escape, self-construction, etc., and we could find the reading modes defined by Mauger et alii. But this would be forgetting that manga is not a reading like any other: for some teenagers, manga is associated with the stigma of "bad" reading, as they hear it from their parents, their teachers, but also from their non-reading friends. How do they manage, then, especially when their socialization predisposes them to legitimate practices and to reading corpus, if not scholarly and literate, at least recognized by the institution, to continue reading manga, between bad conscience and regained legitimacy?

CHAPTER 4

In Search of Lost Legitimacy

In the country of manga readers, everything would be fine, and to paraphrase the song used in the French opening credits of *Candy Candy*, "we have fun, we cry, we laugh …"

But there are hard times too: as a matter of fact, while manga is no longer loathed as it may have been the case in the 1980s and 1990s, while museums or cultural magazines open their doors and columns to some titles and authors, the words of teenagers, at times, reveal the conflicts of legitimacy they have to cope with. Cécile, Octave or Félix indeed express some aggressiveness towards the interviewer ("I don't know if you've read, I think you've read more novels than manga, sorry"); Cécile (17, 1st year college student, father an executive, mother a private nurse) denigrates her practices, anticipating the believed judgment with sharp remarks; Matthieu says he quit reading manga years ago even though during the interview it turned out that if he had stopped, it would only have been a few months ago, and still … The silences, the embarrassment, the acerbic remarks show how much manga is not, for these teenagers, reading like any other, like "real books", and how the conflicted dispositions can cause one to suffer. Faced with these difficult situations, either the manga reader's career is interrupted, or it moves on …

1 Conflicted Dispositions

1.1 *Parents, Teachers and Friends*

Manga does not have the same "value" according to the medium of origin. It will be remembered (see Chapter 3) that while some parents from working-class backgrounds would encourage their children to read manga, parents from privileged backgrounds, without vehemently opposing it, developed an attitude of pained tolerance towards their children's reading practices: manga are not "real" books, and their reading has no value on the market of cultural legitimacy. The parental stance reported by the two brothers Félix and Octave, or by Franck and Pierre, show how strong the stigma can be:

 | DOI:10.1163/9789004548312_006

> My mother complains, she doesn't call them real books, for her it's like comic books, she'd rather read a novel, she likes it but she'd rather we read more novels.
>
> OCTAVE, 17, 12th grade, parents sculptors

> My mother, she'd rather I read more novels, but hey, she's an old ... My father, he never says anything. ... sometimes people like my mother: 'Read, read some real reading'. I really make fun of him when he says things like that. Well, that's one point of view. Besides, she's an old one. They're obtuse.
>
> FÉLIX, OCTAVE's brother, 15, 11th grade

> *What do people around you say about manga?*
>
> My parents, they tell me it sucks, that it would be better if I read a normal book. Every once in a while, I tell my mother what I've just read. She's a little annoyed by that. It's true that my mother, she'd rather I read novels instead of manga.
>
> PIERRE, 17, 11th grade, father a postman, mother a retired school teacher

> *So, what do people around you say about reading manga?*
>
> Japaneseries.
>
> FRANCK, 17, 11th grade, father a cardiologist, mother a health network coordinator

> My parents are pretty much against it. My mother, she'd rather I read, just normal good reading (laughs).
>
> BASTIEN, 15, 10th grade, father an engineer, mother a biologist

The case of Matthieu (17, 11th grade, parents architects), who states that "daddy, he would prefer me to be very cultured", illustrates another parenting strategy: if their child reads manga, it might as well be manga chosen by them. Thus, in sixth grade, when Matthieu started reading manga, his parents, both architects, gave him a biography of Hokusaï, "the inventor of manga", and encouraged him to read books on Japanese culture ("daddy's books"). His grandfather, himself an architect, had offered him an art book on Japanese prints and the history of manga. His aunt makes him read Murakami's novels (*Kafka on the Shore* and *Chronicles of the Springbird*) and his father, a comic book lover who "buys comics just for the sake of it", is trying to replace the series of his son with "arthouse" manga. The effects are real since, in the interview, Matthieu denigrates his own readings and prefers reading more legitimate manga:

> Well, daddy, it annoys him when I read manga, but when he bought these, because he heard about them, he bought them because of the drawing, and he said, 'Instead of reading your shit, you should read this', and yeah, and I liked it very, very much.

The hierarchy may even be implicitly instilled into children, in addition to the parental contempt towards manga. Discussing with parents about literature or films, or even just seeing them reading 'scholarly' novels or arthouse comic books, can lead to classify manga as a paraliterature, an underproduction that is not considered worthy of sharing by parents. Thus, Matthieu discusses the novels he reads with his mother, who "introduces him to a lot of things", and to whom, conversely, he recently advised *Le Rouge et le Noir*, which he studied at school. He mentions *Salammbô* among his favorite books. Félix talks about "the philosophical discussions that spin out of control" with his parents.

In the school environment, some experiences are also sensitive, even though the majority of teachers and librarians are rather open-minded. Nayir (16, 9th grade, father a delivery driver, mother a housekeeper) discovered manga thanks to a librarian, to whom he keeps expressing his gratitude: while Marie's librarian only agrees to buy manga "without sex, without insults, without fights, without blood. Pfff", if Alexandre imagines the remarks that his French teachers could make, "because we don't try to go further, to read the classics", Estelle's teacher read *Monster*, Nayir's history teacher agreed to read it "and in fact he thought it was good. He found that it brought a bit of general knowledge".

Paradoxically, however, the most emphasized rejection does not stem from parents or teachers: to some degree, it is "normal", even functional, since it makes it possible to express generational belonging and autonomy through one's cultural practices.

The problem is precisely that the judgement comes from peers, friends who don't read manga. Madji's friends think that "it's too childish, it's money thrown away", that "it's for idiots", Théo's friends, "except for those who read manga", "say it's children's stories, that it's rubbish, that it's better to read a book. And they don't understand why you have to read in the other way round". Safya's friends say the same thing: "It's for kids". Some of Cécile's acquaintances stated categorically that "it was for the degenerates". Apart from Estelle's small group, "new people, they always hear us talking about manga, they sometimes call us geek or no life". Maele remarks that "there are plenty of people who have too much preconceived ideas about manga, those who stop at the fact that it's Japanese and therefore violent. So, the summary is violence, sex and blood". Annabelle (16, 11th grade, father a bank executive, mother a consultant) talks about "the people I meet in the hallways who hear me talking ... who say, 'Manga sucks' and leave". All regret these attitudes from young people who, most of the time, have never read manga, and who therefore, "can't really know what they say" (Théo), who "don't try, but criticize" (Madji). Matthieu (17, 11th grade) thus distinguishes between the reactions of adults and those of "young people", who are much less tolerant than their elders:

> So, when you say manga, it's either 'ah it's shit', or 'ah it's not bad', or 'oh it's good'. But it's really ... most of the time it's either really good or it's really bad. Not many people in between. And most of the time the ones who don't like it, I noticed they hadn't read any. ... but it's often people who didn't know what. ... Since they [parents] don't know, they don't judge too much. Whereas the young people, precisely those who do not like, they give an opinion without really knowing.

1.2 *Internalization*

These hierarchies of legitimacy are internalized by some adolescents, among the most endowed in cultural and social capital and academic achievement. Thus, for them too, manga reading is not on the same level as other "serious" readings. Manga is used for relaxation and leisure, but can in no way be put on the same level as "books".

Matthieu shares his father's opinion and believes that 'it's minor' and that he should have 'read a little more serious reading and a little less manga'. As for Bastien, although he loves manga, he is extremely critical:

> We're going to say that it's still ... by definition, it's more of a children's thing so (laughs) it's reading for fun, I mean you shouldn't do that either, because there's no point in just reading that. Because once we get a book, just because we read manga doesn't mean we can read a ... It doesn't add up to anything in reading. ... if I may give some advice, it's that I'm advising a book.
>
> *But not a manga?*
>
> Not a manga (laughs) because manga is ... It's not reading, all comics are not reading per se.
>
> BASTIEN, 15, 10th grade, father a biologist, mother an engineer

This lower value granted to manga is reflected in reading practices by both material and symbolic indicators, such as the importance given or not to personal possession of manga, compared to other categories of printed matter or cultural goods. Matthieu says he has a few manga at home, but "that are hidden under other books". Tom, whose parents are both teachers, says he doesn't have any, and only reads them by borrowing them from his friends: "I rarely store manga at home, in fact. When I have them, I read them all at once, and then I pass them on to someone else. It's true I never really told my parents about it. I'm not really a big, passionate reader who buys a lot", although the interview reveals that he watches … five series.

Ashkan also owns only a few manga (the ones his aunt has given him), and he mainly reads manga scanned on the Internet or in cultural department stores, without ever buying them. While manga is not a priority in his budget, it is primarily because he values manga less than book.

> I like to have a library with my books, manga, it's not serious … No (laughs), it's not that, it's that maybe, the lifespan of a book, maybe it's more profitable to buy a book than a manga, because the manga, I'll read it quickly, and the book, I'll take time, and I can reread it. I do not know why, but I am much more attracted by the fact of buying a book than by the fact of buying a manga.
>
> ASHKAN, 18, 12th grade, father a director of a clothing brand, mother a stylist

Thus, while owning manga revealed a commitment to reading and to the book as an object, in intermediary circles, unlike in popular circles (see Chapter 2), for adolescents from privileged backgrounds, or those with cultural capital, manga are not "enough" books to deserve to be bought … The challenge is also not to be considered as a "fan", manga is a hobby, not a passion, and the reader's self-portrait is that of a dilettante, certainly enlightened, but not of a passionate fan, of an "otaku" monopolized by this practice. Thus, Cécile (17, 1st year college student, father an executive, mother a private nurse), who throughout the interview kept marking a distance, in particular by ironic incisions making fun of the manga she reads, specifies that she is not a reader "with an overwhelming fanaticism", even if her answers show a great culture in terms of manga. Likewise, she, who "would not spend a euro in a manga", criticizes in a sharp manner the girlfriend who provides her with manga ("when she takes five out of a big bag, you're afraid! It's worse than cigarettes for her!") or the cousin who gives him posters, which "end up in the trash" or "all torn for three months in my bag".

2 Fans in Their Own Words: Self-Portraits

Bastien denies being a "big fan", because it's not his "favorite subject". Félix is not a "real fan", because he doesn't go to demonstrations, and doesn't spend "too much money on it". He feels that he "has a lot [of manga] but still moderately compared to what others can have", that he loves and knows a lot "but not very much compared to others who are completely hooked, deep down, who know everything about everything". Ashkan similarly tends to define manga as a simple "hobby", as opposed to "manga fans" who are much more personally involved in reading, sometimes seriously.

> I've had two guys in my class since middle school, and even now in my class I see four, five who are manga fans, they read a lot of stuff, different stuff … I mean much more than me. Me, I read once in a while … it's more leisurely what.
>
> *Isn't it a hobby for the others?*
>
> It's more that they are fans in fact, nearly addicted to it (laughs) … Manga for me, today, it's not my main goal anymore. That's it, it's pleasant, I still like comics, I'm not too choosy in terms of reading, I like it, but manga, it makes me laugh, it's nice.
>
> ASHKAN, 18, 12th grade, father a director of a clothing brand, mother a stylist

So, there's always more of a fan than you are. Being a fan just as it should be actually engages in a subtle quantitative and qualitative dosage, and is not everyone can be a "good fan" of manga. Thus, if reading manga can generate conflicts of cultural legitimacy, and detaching oneself from the fan's figure can be a way of partially resolving these, the fan posture is in itself a question of distinction, within the field of manga lovers. Some people position themselves by distancing themselves from the fan figure, but for them it is a question of better valuing themselves as 'real readers', amateurs and manga lovers. The division and the hierarchy they operate then makes a distinction between various manga readers, and not only manga fans and novel readers. For some, the term 'fan' is claimed and considered as a positive figure of connoisseur or disinterested enthusiast. Others tend to put this figure of the fan at a distance, associating it with the stereotypes of a pathological or excessive relationship to manga:[1] whether it is Hélène et les garçons (Pasquier 1999), the Beatles (Le

1 In the ethnographic survey she conducted in a shop specializing in the sale of manga, Clothilde Sabre also notes the "paradoxical status" of the term fan: "It is a positive designation when applied to people considered legitimate within the store space, which reflects the

Bart 2000) or manga, being a fan is thus a label, stigmatized or claimed, where the bad fan is "always the other":

> This leads to the construction of reading communities on the basis of the alleged existence of deviant reading and a nonsensical relationship [to television].
>
> PASQUIER 1999, 212

Between being a fan or not being a fan, being a "good" or "bad" fan, there are issues of distinction in terms of cultural legitimacy, age and gender positioning, which make it a real "identity strategy". As Christian Le Bart points out, the term "fan" is associated with a negative value, which teenagers are going to have to distance themselves from to make it an issue of "differenciation, of singularization, of distinction", while implicitly are emerging "the opposite (and shameful) figures of imitation, depersonalization and alienation" (2004, 284). In adolescents, according to their social, gender and age characteristics, how are these positionings translated?

2.1 Not *Being a Fan*

The fan label can thus be categorically rejected, tainted as it is with stereotypes of passivity and alienation. Of course, saying or identifying oneself as a fan also depends on one's degree of investment and attachment to reading and to the world of manga. But many teenagers whose entire interview shows a significant practice and enthusiasm in this area refuse to be seen as "fans". Célia (17, 11th grade, mother an opera director, father a choreographer) mocks the fans who "lack critical mind", only know the popular series, and are fascinated by Japan:

> The word fan, I don't know, I don't really like it that much. I like manga a lot, and I like the ones I read, for such and such a reason. But fan of manga no, because that would imply a little bit that I love manga in all its forms and that's not the case, there are genres that I absolutely do not like. But it's true that there are fans who absolutely do not know how to judge a manga, who absolutely do not know how to see the good and bad sides, because I know very well that there are bad sides also in Saiyuki

community link and implies sharing the same repertoire of references. On the other hand, 'fan' is a negative and pejorative designation when it applies to individuals who have been sidelined by virtue of a judgment that their exacerbated and hysterical attitude is detrimental to the image that the salespeople and the boss wish to portray" (Sabre, 2009, 149).

> and *D.Gray-Man*, there are exaggerations that can be made. [...] I mean the word fan implies that we like absolutely everything, and also without any judgment. I can say that I really like some manga, even within the same genre there are some I don't like ... A bad fan is like what I was saying earlier, it's someone who is not able to have a critical mind about what they like, and even about what they don't like, who are not able to make a judgment, who just absorbs, without anything coming out of it.

This logic also works in the "self-distinction of self" (Lahire 2004), insofar as some readers now distinguish themselves from the "fan" they themselves were a few years ago. Ashkan refers to his "teenage period", marked by the posters in his bedroom, and Maureen (15, 9th grade, father a worker, mother an administrative officer) thinks she was a fan "between 8 and 12–13 years old". The mocked fan is also the one who is so passionate about manga that everything becomes conditioned by it, including clothes: excessive attitudes are criticized, when "too much is too much". Jérôme (18, 11th grade, father an electrician, mother an accountant) thus evokes a girl who "thinks she's an animal, it's a trick for dogs, she walks around with a big dog tail, a fox tail ... She doesn't wear it every day, but it's her big trip when it's really too ugly". Maureen, likewise, has a female friend who "puts her hair in a bun", who loves Japanese, "wants to become familiar with their culture", has a website and Japanese pen pals: Maureen thinks "she's too much" ("Well, we can be inspired. But she's too much ... too focused on that"). Salim (19, 12th grade, father a mason, mother a cleaning agent) distinguishes himself from those who "are absolutely concerned by manga, they see that, they talk about it all the time, they live only for it", and Xavier (17, 11th grade, father a firefighter, mother a childcare worker) almost complains "these people who spend their time reading manga, they don't even leave to eat. They can't wait for the next one, they play it on their game consoles all the time. It's meant to have a good time, it's not meant to feel bad waiting for the next one".

The words "geek" and "otaku" are often used to distinguish onelself from it, insofar as that they must have been heard among these friends who stigmatize manga, or in reports that fuel moral panic in the media. Léo finds the fans ridiculous, "people who lock themselves up in this world, who don't know how to live outside of it. Well, that's my opinion, afterwards, I may be prejudiced but to me, these people have no life outside manga!". Only Félix and Estelle reverse the stigma and claim to be "geeks", individuals spending all their time on their computer, but without this identity meaning a fan relationship to manga, of which they are nevertheless big readers. We can see how "being a fan" goes beyond the objective measurement of time spent reading or watching anime.

It is a whole identity, personal, material and physical relationship to passion. Teenagers, when offered the words "fan" and "passionate", choose the latter, and their angry reactions show the risk they would have to be assimilated to these "fans". As Salim sums it up, "manga is not my absolute passion, it's just a passion like any other", and they all take care to specify that they have other activities, and above all, a social life.

> *Would you refer to yourself as a 'manga fan'?*
>
> Not that much, I would refer to myself as passionate, but not a big fan, because, well, I think the big fan, I think it's the one who goes out dressed in what's-his-name ... who goes to all the conventions, who follows all the time. I love manga reading. I follow all the series very carefully and my room is full of manga stuff. Manga is a passion of my life, but it's not the only one, I share it with other things.
>
> OCTAVE, 15, 11th grade, parents sculptors

> *Would you say that you are a manga fan, passionate?*
>
> Not a fan. Maybe passionate, but not really a fan. I'm not like my best friend who's totally into it. I like to read them.
>
> *What would you call a real manga fan?*
>
> Well, it's someone who knows everything about everything. Who read pretty much every manga. Knows everything about everything. Goes to the Japan Expo every time, goes to the shows every time ... Some people are fans, but too many. Cosplays are fun, but when there are people who ... who love a character too much, or who invent cock-and-bull stories sometimes.
>
> CORALINE, 17, 11th grade, father a worker, mother a cleaning lady

Stigmatization doesn't correspond to the logic of social demarcation, since Samuel (15, 10th grade, father a firefighter, mother a childcare worker), who also refuses to be considered as a "fan", Xavier or Salim are from rather popular backgrounds. It is rather a certain way of concurring with a fan posture that is rejected, a posture assimilated to childish (collecting figurines) or rather feminine (cosplay) practices: going to conventions and shows, like the Japan Expo, then becomes the characteristic of these overly passionate fans, who no longer see the difference between real life and leisure, and who give in to the sirens of an outrageous mediatization and commercialization. The collection of derivative products often symbolizes this "commercial aspect of passion", and specialized shops are sometimes the theater of confrontations between "commercial logic" and "passionate logic" (Sabre 2009, 131).

2.2 *Being a Fan*

Nevertheless, others claim a fan identity, especially among teenage readers from middle- or working-class backgrounds: Estelle, Alexandre, Théo are, or would like to be fans. In the same way, Marianne or Maureen admire those who are "really" fans, like Théo who believes he has read a lot 'but not yet enough to say that [I am] he is a real fan' and evokes "his master" in manga, a female friend who knows everything, has read everything, and "has reached a higher level than me, we'll say".

But "fan" does not have here the same definition, does not refer to the same dispositions. Being a "real fan" is thus based on mastering the manga field, and transcends the gender divide.

> I know someone in my neighborhood, I've known her since I was a little girl, and the good thing is that she watches absolutely everything. She is not really into any kind of manga, she's got everything, especially the new stuff. She's way ahead, actually. She comes and and she says: 'Look at this, it just came out in Japan', and she watches drama, animes, everything. I can discuss everything with her.
>
> MARIANNE, 16, 11th grade, father a numerical control operator, mother a restaurant employee

> *And on the other hand, are there readers that you admire and consider as good connoisseurs?*
>
> Yes ... I know a group of about three or four of them, where they devour manga all day long, they watch episodes that aren't even French; they take them on the Net, eh? And they're really into it, they follow it a lot ... well I have a friend: *Bleach*, *Death Note*, all that, all that, all that, he knows everything, all the adventures that are not even released yet, he's into it, he reads them, he talks about them, it seems he wrote them ... He even knows things that are not even released yet, because he follows the story so much ... For example, an episode that we watch together, and that he hasn't seen yet, he can say: 'You'll see, he'll lose because he always does this technique, this and that'. He's really into it. I listen to him, I'm all ears! Oh yeah, I like that!
>
> MAUREEN, 15, 9th grade, father a worker, mother an administrative officer

> *Would you say you're a fan of manga?*
>
> Yes, I would. Because I know that not a day goes by without me thinking about manga, without me reading manga, when I'm on the Internet,

> it's usually for that, to look for drawings, to watch episodes, to look for scans. And then, a lot of little details of everyday life. And after a while, by dint of watching manga, we start to adopt Japanese attitudes ... We bend down when we say hello, do that (she claps her hands) before eating. It's by dint of being into manga, that it's a little mania.
>
> ESTELLE, 17, 12th grade, father a bank clerk, mother a school nurse

Madji (19, 12th grade, father a bus driver, stay-at-home mother) regrets the fact that the word fan is "really misused" (see portrait). A fan, in his view, "is someone who really burns with passion for this precisely, and who would does not hesitate to sign anything, even if it is desperate or useless". Madji has launched a petition to the publishers of *Karakuri Circus*, whose publication had been discontinued. Christian Le Bart, in his article devoted to Beatles fans, identifies three stages, the ideal type character of which he specifies, and the entanglements when observed in each individual case: the adolesecent differenciation within the family group, made possible by the practice that sets one apart; the de-differenciation by the encounter with other similar ones; and the third stage, which again works as a differenciation process, but within the group of fans this time. It is this third stage that interests us here and that will unfold in the discourses of adolescents about the practices of "others", and which is always built in tension "in search of a pivotal point between monstrous singularity and alienated indifferenciation" (2004, 286).

In that respect, the bad fan is the reader who is captivated by an immediate reading, without any distance or criticism, of commercial titles promoted by fashion, and who, moreover, collects derivative products. The bad fan is the reader of *Naruto* or *Death Note*, which for Caroline (14, 9th grade, father a shopkeeper, mother an insurance trainer) is not "a real reader". Célia (17, 11th grade, mother an opera director, father a choreographer) doesn't care about *Naruto* or *Bleach* readers, "who say they're manga fans, fans of Japan, and that's often like 14-year-old who don't know how to make the difference between several genres ... and either they grow up, or they should be given a good slap in the face".

Océane calls herself a specialist, against those for whom "it's only ... only *Naruto*". It is thus a question of distinguishing oneself from those who only read the best known and most commercial series. "Fashion" and "marketing", of which *Naruto* is a typical example, act as real repellents:

> I think there was a fad about *Naruto*. Like, 'there was one reading and everyone started reading'. But there's always people who read because they like it. In middle school, a lot of people read manga and then they

stopped. I don't think they really liked it. It gets too much media attention sometimes even if it's not the manga's fault, it's our society.

MAEVA, 18, 12th grade, father an electrician, mother an accountant

And what do you think of the younger generation of fans?

Ah, the little things that run down the street … here, uh (laughs). I think they're stupid, yeah. I've got *Naruto* label pins actually, that I bought at Japan Expo, so it's fan-art but well …, that I've got on another bag. And often in the subway, there are little boys and everything: 'Wow, it's Naruto, it's Naruto'. I feel like slapping their faces, seriously. I think it's completely stupid because they usually know Naruto from the anime that's on Game One. So, when you know that the French version already, the dubbing is atrocious. It was made from the American version, which is censored, cut and so on, in short … In fact, the anime of *Naruto*, it's like a fanfiction of *Naruto* … I don't like it at all. For them, it's a fad. I think it is. Because there is no real passion whatsoever. They only know *Naruto*. I just hope that it's a fashion, that it will pass, that they will not visit fanfiction.net. That's all I'm saying.

ÉLODIE, 18, 12th grade, father a biologist, mother a computer graphic designer

And you consider yourself a real fan, then?

Pretty much. Because there are, then there are the fans who read manga that are very famous, like *Naruto*, things like that, they are fans. But they don't go further than what is fashionable, what they've heard about … what everyone knows like *Dragon Ball Z*

Whereas you …

Well, I'm trying to find new ones, to discover some …, to go on websites to see what's been released in Japan that worked a lot, to see if … new things what.

LUDIVINE, 17, 11th grade, parents tax officials

For example, with the *Naruto* phenomenon, I absolutely hate it. It's lengthened, it's commercial, and while, well, it makes me laugh when I sometimes read a little bit of volumes where they try to give something very philosophical, very deep, but where the characters are as hollow as a bowl, so after a while, it gets a bit on the nerves.

CÉLIA, 17, 11th grade, mother an opera director, father a choreographer

Thus, even popular manga can lose their value because they become too popular: Maureen stops *Naruto* because "I don't like it when everyone does what

I do and when everyone reads because it's fashionable, I don't like it". Léo continues to read *Naruto*, but refuses to buy it because he doesn't want to "fall into the *Naruto* cliché", "getting so much media attention". Félix (15, 11th grade, parents sculptors) follows him in scan, but no longer wants to read it in print, and while he "really likes to have the manga", "*Naruto* now, [he] doesn't care, there are ten or fifteen missing". Ludivine (17, 11th grade, parents tax officials), likewise, turns away from titles she liked, because everyone starts to read them and it "makes them merchandising", and fears that the titles she likes, like *Vampire Knight*, will become too popular.

Not to blend in with the anonymous mass of *Naruto* readers means developing knowledge and skills that make you an amateur. Here too, an age effect is involved: the period of "imitation" of peers, which is necessary in order to promote generational autonomy, is followed by the period of singularization in this same group. Reading manga that no one knows, untranslated manga, or returning to the very sources of manga, by reading titles from the 1980s or 1990s, makes it possible to establish oneself as a true connoisseur, a "specialist" as Océane claimed. For these teenagers born in the 1990s, the manga published in the 1980s and 1990s constitute "historical" references and cult manga, even if the history of manga is much older and many titles from the 1950s to the 1970s have been republished.

Salim (19, 12th grade, father a mason, mother a cleaning agent) thus appreciates "an old manga that was broadcast in the eighties, my mother watched it when she was younger". Against the stigmatized position of "fan" then arises the legitimate posture of the "aesthete" (Le Bart, 2004, 300). Nathaniel (17, 11th grade, raised by his mother, an unemployement office employee) contrasts the "fan" with the "otaku":

> *And are there fans or fan behaviors that annoy you?*
>
> Yes, usually it's the ones who say: 'I love manga', and when asked what they like, 'Well: *Naruto*, *Death Note*'. For me, the fans are the ones who just like the known stuff, so *Naruto*, *Death Note*, *Bleach*, *One Piece*. And then the otakus are the ones who know …, I mean who read everything, whether it's from the 80s, 90s, 2000s. Because generally, people, when you tell them: 'I love manga from the 90s', and when you tell them: 'This is a manga from the 90s', they get all pissed off. They say: 'Ah, the graphics suck, the stuff sucks', whereas it's much more interesting than the ones that are released now. They're just fans, because they don't want to go deeper into it. They just stick to what they know, they don't try to know other stuff. What I'm looking for is to discover unknown works, things like that. When I find a second-hand manga, for example *Seraphic Feather*,

when I find one, well I'm really happy. *You're Under Arrest*, it's the same, it's super rare to find one, and when I find one I'm happy, but most of them ... I mean, when I say that to a friend, he is like: 'But, what's the point?' Most of the time, yeah, fans are people who just watch *Naruto, Death Note*, well-known things, whereas otakus are people who know things that not everybody knows. Well for example, *Evangelion*, some people know it by name, but hardly anybody has a clue about what it really is. A lot of people say: 'Oh yes, I know, the thing with robots', but they don't know what it really is. There's *Akira* too, it's an old manga by Katsuhiro Otomo from the 90's, I think it was released in 1989, 88. So there's this ... *Ghost in the Shell*, which is very good. Then there's *Gundam* and stuff like that.

You know any fans?

Well, there's some in the class. And then in Japanese, when we talk about manga, it's always *Naruto* or *Death Note* that comes out.

Nathaniel then points to two other students in his class: Maele and Marianne, who have a fan posture, especially Marianne (16, 11th grade, father a numerical control operator, mother a restaurant employee) who collects posters, figurines and objects, and has art-books, but doesn't read them, because "in fact, an art-book is mostly for collecting when you're a big fan. For example, the only art-books I have are *Sailormoon, Death Note*" (Marianne). These are indeed girls, among the teenagers I met, and from popular circles, which occupy the pole of "fan culture" as it is stigmatized by others. Nadia (14, 8th grade, father a worker, mother a secretary) goes to trade fairs and conventions, where she buys figurines, posters, pins and bags. She was inspired by them for her hairdo and her style of clothing, whether she identifies them as *emo* or *visual kei* (see portrait). The principles of male and social domination that govern the depreciation of this mode of relationship to passion, that of "groupie", compared to a form of "idolatry" without distance, have been highlighted in other bodies of work, whether in television series (Pasquier 1999) or music (Le Bart 2004; Raviv, Bar-Tal and Ben-Horn 1996). Fleur (19, 1st year college student, father employee in a security company, stay-at-home mother) thus criticizes the "fangirl syndrome" (see portrait). To detach oneself from it is to learn the rules of one's gender, one's social background, or one's age. Élodie, who is a combination of age (18), cultural capital and schooling (last year of highschool), was thus mistaken once in a festival dedicated to "manga" ("Japan Touch"):

You don't like Japanese fashion?

Oh no, I hate it. All the girls ... I feel like I'm in ninth grade, so now it's annoying.

> *What did you like about the Japan Touch?*
> I liked nothing!

Félix (15, 11th grade, parents sculptors) doesn't like going to Japan Expo and co either because "the only person we're likely to meet is a 12-or 13-year-old girl, it's not going to be fun". Collecting figurines, or hanging posters, is another example of this relationship with passion. The fact of being a "fan" is actually doubly stigmatized: it involves the youngest and the girls, and it implies a naive, childish relationship to passion (Pasquier 1999; Le Bart 2004),[2] especially when it focuses on derivative objects, as Laurent(18, 12th grade, father an engineer, stay-at-home mother) describes it well:

> When we were younger, we collected them. We used to collect *Dragon Ball Z* stuff in particular, the little figurines and posters. But now less, we read more in manga than in derivative products.

Contrary to this passive and mercantile relationship, genuine passion implies being "active" in one's appropriation of manga, by multiplying activities, discussions, amateur and "creative" practices (fanfictions, drawings, fanzines …), and finally the stances taken to "stand up for" the cause of manga.

3 "Scholarly" Readings

3.1 *Reading as a Meticulous Task*

For these "real fans", manga becomes the support of elaborate readings, based on methods similar to those learned in school to comment on texts. Some people take manga seriously, as an object of knowledge that requires real work, and the same title can thus be the medium of identification and analytical reading. Nathaniel expresses very clearly his desire to master all the details of the *Evangelion* series, and prepares, by rereading the whole series, for the release of a new film in France, "just to know the story like the back of my hand". Nathaniel has developed his knowledge of the series by reading and rereading the various versions of the manga, as well as by watching the films and DVDs of which the manga is the adaptation, and specialized websites. His analytical reading results in the elaboration of "theories" and hypotheses on

2 There are, however, adult readers, collectors of figurines, models and derivative products, who display in this field an expertise far removed from these stereotypes and these childish or mercantile connotations.

this complex series with multiple extensions and variations. He has thus imagined a theory to explain the color of the 'Eva' (robots), according to the personality of their pilots.

Reading is then work and requires concentration, far from the stereotype of easy, light and purely entertaining reading. Nathaniel thus distinguishes between "pure jokes" manga, such as GTO, *Love Hina* or *One Piece*, and manga that requires "racking one's brain".[3] Moussa (18, 12th grade, father a doctor, mother a pharmacist) also believes that to "read it well, to enjoy it fully, of course, like everything else, requires concentration", and closes the door of his room when he reads. *Death Note* provides a good example of this need for reflection.

According to Estelle, *Death Note* is "very cerebral", and this manga has made Matthieu's head "spin".

> *Death Note*, it's psychological, at some point they're two fighting with each other, and then he says: 'Yeah, but if I tell him I know, he's gonna think I'm the bad guy, but at the same time if I tell him I don't know, he's gonna think it's because he knows I don't know he knows …', I know that I'm exaggerating a little bit, but there are passages where it's very concentrated, there's a lot of lyrics all of a sudden and if you don't pay attention, you reach the end of what he says and you think: 'I didn't understand everything'. It's a fight between two nerds, so keep up!
>
> MAELE, 16, 11th grade, father a teacher, mother a counsellor

This need to concentrate can even be discouraging for some, even from circles with cultural capitals:

> *Death Note* is a manga with a lot of writing, all the time, so when you read one you have to hang on to it, you must not be a little tired otherwise you fall asleep, because there are moments it's still long long explanations so you have to be motivated to read it.
>
> FÉLIX, 15, 11th grade, parents sculptors

3 Which can be, conversely, a reason to stop a series, as for Kader: "But there are times, in fact, I can't understand, I have to reread maybe two or three times the same passage, it's *Bastard*: oh dear, it really racks the brains. *Bastard* … It's a sick thing, forget it, it's too difficult … It's too much, it racks the brains too much. Yeah, I've noticed it, oh my God, that's sick."

> *Death Note*, because he's supposed to be a diabolical genius, so it's getting ridiculously complicated. There's a passage that I find almost burlesque, because in fact he's facing L., the bad guy, who pretends to be nice ... Well, they're playing tennis, it's ridiculous because he thinks: 'Ah, he thinks I'm Kira, so I have to let him win so he'll think I'm a bad guy, that I can't be Kira, that I'm not smart enough to win a match'. And I guy across the way he's like, 'Um, he knows I think it's Kira', and it goes on like that for three pages. 'Yeah, he's already thought that I know he knows I'm Kira, so actually I must lose the game', actually in the end after fifteen pages he goes back and you're confused, you went back four times on the page to see who thinks what, well he plays the tennis game and he gets thrashed, because he's bad (laughs).
>
> FRANCK, 17, 11th grade, father a cardiologist, mother a healthcare network coordinator

For these "scholars" of manga, there are "classics", including *Dragon Ball*, which thus escapes the stigma of commercial success, whereas these same readers despise a series such as *Naruto* due to its commercial success. Against the "fan culture", the "manga cult" (Le Guern, 2002) is then displayed. For Félix, *Dragon Ball* is a "myth", for Franck, it is the "cult manga", for Estelle, it is "the classic manga of reference". Élodie, who in one of the previous excerpts, wanted to "slap in the face" the little ones who rave about her *Naruto* pins in the subway, and says she is "passionate", is also distinguished by her extensive knowledge and the intensity of her passion for manga. She explains the corpus of "classics" that every fan should master:

> *Akira*, it's a must for me ... *Gunnnm* is nice too. And *Dragon Ball Z*, that's the basis, so ... I mean, it's still one of the great pioneer manga in France, so ... If you haven't started, I mean if you haven't read at least one volume of *Dragon Ball Z*, you can't really call yourself manga fan I think. For example, you have to have read at least one volume of *Sailor Moon*, to say: 'Oh, that was it'
>
> ÉLODIE, 18, 12th grade, father a biologist, mother a graphic designer

3.2 *Reading Skills*

The mastery of Japanese categories, of the names of authors, and much more rarely of publishers, obviously shows the skills invested in the field. It is strongly linked to the level of social, cultural and educational capital, which is compensated, for example, in Madji (19, 11th grade, father a bus driver, stay-at-home mother), by the desire to build an expert identity (see portrait). For example, Lydia and Clara believe that manga was originally written in Chinese. Océane (15, 9th grade, father an electrician, mother a housewife) does not have any favorite authors because "what [she] prefers is mostly manga", Maureen is completely unfamiliar with the terms "shonen", "shojo" etc. Yohanna (16, 11th grade, father an engineer, mother a sales representative) stumbles over the word seinen which becomes "senine or something like that", Maeva admits she's always mixing up the terms, and her twin brother Jérôme is also quickly lost in taxonomy …

Skills can be varied, and based on both the graphic side or the textual and narrative side of the manga. Because manga involves other skills than literary skills alone: it is also an object of drawing, and the quality of the latter also becomes a selection criterion, the mark of a "style". According to this criterion, the repellent is once again … *Naruto*. Fleur, who began her career as a manga reader because she had been attracted by the cover of volume 3 of the manga *Rurouni Kenshin*, has two art-books, one dedicated to the manga *Fushigi Yugi*, that she won in a drawing competition, the other she bought herself for her birthday ("*Salty dog II* by Minekura that I worship above all"). Fleur (19, 1st year college student, father an employee in a security company, stay-at-home mother) is very sensitive to the material aspect of art-books, to the pleasure of "having the image in large format with a beautiful cardboard cover".

> You can't understand the pleasure I get as soon as I take *Salty Dog II* in my arms like a relic, that I admire the drawings with pleasure, the lines and the rest, the sketches on the last two pages.

Fleur regrets that "publishers don't take great care of their publishing", and refers to the example of the *Saiyuki* volumes: "The *Saiyuki*, you open them, you hear the noise, they're there crrrriii … like that; the paper is yellow". Fleur regrets finally that "in manga, the colored drawing boards [in the original edition] are in black and white". Cécile especially appreciates the drawings in manga, Marie likes "graphics like Mari Okazaki for example, I mean the style of drawing, because it's thin, it's detailed", which she contrasts with *Naruto* ("too simple. Not very well done, a bit fast"). Ludivine and Élodie, in the same way, pose as experts, quoting this or that draftsman:

> The drawings. In fact, I attach great importance to the drawings of a manga. I would have a really hard time reading a manga the drawings of which I don't like. Even if the story is exciting. For example, there's *Vampire Knight*, the drawings, I like them a lot. *Black Butler*, it's great

drawings, with Victorian costumes … While *Dragon Ball* was really … I mean I didn't like it.

Do you have any favorite cartoonists?

One of them is Takeshi Obata. He's the one who made *Death Note*. His drawings are magnificent. Usually, when he releases a new manga, I look at it because he draws really well. Then there's Kaori Yuki. Same thing. The one who made *Vampire Knight*. I always look at his new manga. But it's mostly the ones from Clamp Studio. Four manga girls, manga artists. They're the most famous, there's been even an exhibition at the Grand Palais about them, not long ago, and they, each time they release a new manga, it's really the manga that are … where I look each time.

LUDIVINE, 17, 11th grade, parents tax officials

Yoshizumi Wataru, I read *Marmalade Boy, Mint Na Bokura, Ultra Maniac* …, I like the way she draws. If the drawings are ugly, I can't read, it's not possible. The … I don't know sometimes, there are characters that are drawn, if I don't find them beautiful. The lines, they have to be subtle and everything.

Are there any other writers like that you know of?

Yes, but I forgot her name … Obana Miho, the one who makes *Honey Bitter*. I've always liked her drawings, and it's only this series that was released in France, and the other series, I have trouble finding them on the Internet.

ÉLODIE, 18, 12th grade, father a biologist, mother a computer graphic designer

Célia (17, 11th grade, mother an opera director, father a choreographer) even deploys a true pictorial intertextuality, recognizing and comparing graphic styles. She manages to date the manga from the forms, the first ones of Tezuka being "rounder", while "it becomes square as the years go by", "so when we look at a manga, we can roughly locate the year". Pierre (17, 11th grade, father a postman, mother a retired schoolteacher) recognizes the drawers of the various mangas, Alexandre (17, 11th grade, parents schoolteachers) identifies the drawers by the outline of the figures ("we find characters who have the same physical appearance which you can come across however in very different manga. We find the main character of *Eye Shield 21* and *Reborn*'s one, physically it's almost the same. If you want, I have the two series, I can take two volumes at random, you'll see that the two characters are almost the same").

The attention to the drawings is coupled, for big readers, with a narrative intertextuality. It is thus a question of identifying narrative patterns and recurrences, such as the "struggle between the forces of good and evil" for Bastien, the principle of "love in a triangle" for Pierre, or the "pattern of the hero who fights, makes friends and whose enemies become friends" according to Franck. But intertextuality is also the ability to identify references: Félix thus identifies references to *Dragon Ball* in GTO, Jérôme points out the transversal pictorial codes, the "mimics that are often repeated", such as "the embarrassment, scratching behind the head with the elbow bent towards the sky". Caroline also likes to catch winks to other series, as in "*The melancholy of Haruhi Suzumiya*, since it is a manga for otaku, so fan of manga, video games". Célia is sensitive to the references to *Dragon Ball* and *One Piece* in the manga *Yakitate Japan*, Matthieu to the parodic quotations of *Jeanne and Serge* [*Atakkā Yū!*]. As for Madji, he draws in an elaborate way the games of influences and borrowings between manga:

> It's not done anyhow. Nothing is born out of nothing. *Tsukihime* is related to *Fate/Stay Night*, it's related to *Kara no Kyoukai*, it's related to other novels that the author has created. And all that creates a world and this world is just unique, I couldn't find better. For example, the heroine of *Kara no Kyoukai*, and the hero of *Tsukihime*, they have the same power. The author created rules that the hero, he doesn't get his power from anywhere, from anything, the world has a soul, each world is connected. For example, he created a manga, a novel, called *Angel Note*, which tells the end of the world. And it's all related to *Tsukihime*. And a lot of things like: it's linked by characters, it's linked by stories, it's linked by rumors. He created power relationships between characters and everything.
>
> *And it's not complicated to follow?*
>
> No, not at all. In fact, you just have to know it a little bit. You have to know where to start because, if you start with *Kara no Kyoukai*, you won't understand what he's talking about in there. The best is to start with *Fate/Stay Night*, for example, and then follow with *Tsukihime*, etc.
>
> CÉLIA, 17, 11th grade, mother an opera director, father a choreographer

The interest and taste for intertextual references or parodic allusions present in manga is strongly linked to the level of investment in reading practice. It is a real pleasure for the connoisseur, who masters the set of internal references to manga culture, the history of the mode of expression and the conventions that characterize it, a pleasure that is based on the feeling of "being a part of it".

Portrait of Madji, a Scholarly and Popular Manga Reader

Madji, 19 years old, is a 11th grade student (in a section dedicated to the "maintenance of industrial systems"), after having repeated two years, in a vocational high school of a city of 500 000 inhabitants. His father is a bus driver, his mother is unemployed, and he has a half-brother and a half-sister who are older (28 and 27). At the time of the interview, Madji was accompanied by his best friend, Aurélien, 19 years old, in his final year of high school in the same section (his father is a chemist, his mother a social worker). Aurélien wants to become a "maintenance electrician", but Madji is "a bit torn between bus driver and electrician: bus driver is quiet, electrician is more of a prison". As we shall see, Madji offers an interesting example of combinations of dispositions, both popular (admiration for an asserted and assumed virility against weak-willed heroes, taste for "hentai") and learned (in his way of reading and appreciating manga).

Madji defines himself as a "fan", a passionate person, and he distinguishes himself by the extent of his knowledge in manga and Japanese animation. He follows closely the news of Japanese releases in manga, animation, video games, and especially visual novels and *dojin* games. He acquired this knowledge by visiting many websites, blogs and specialized forums, but also a specialized store that he likes and whose sellers he knows. To list all the anime and manga he has seen or read, he has created a page on a specialized English-speaking website ("MyAnimeList"). His interest in Japanese animation was born at the beginning of high school, when he started to watch Japanese cartoons on TV with his father. He does not own any Japanese animation DVDs and downloads most of the titles he is interested in. Madji usually starts by watching anime, before eventually reading the corresponding manga, if it exists. For the past two or three years, Madji has built up a large personal collection of manga, and he buys them very regularly. He says that he owns "200, 230 or something like that, bought". Madji occasionally consults scans of manga that have not yet been released, and may not be released, in French ("generally, the manga that are released are not often the ones I like"). If he liked the scans, Madji bought the series when it was published in French. His parents giving him little pocket money and disapproving of this kind of spending ("money thrown out of the window"), Madji buys mostly manga with the money he earns while working.

Madji especially likes shonen and seinen. He quotes a lot of "trashy", "oppressive" and "gory" titles, like *Higurashi* (*Hinamizawa, the cursed village*), of which he describes a series of bloody scenes ("*Higurashi*, it puts in place kids, who, because of a disease, go crazy, that is to say it is total hallucinations in fact. For example, you see, some girls come to look for the hero, and in fact, he believes that he wants to hurt them, and in the end, he's going to massacre them with a bat"). But if Madji appreciates this kind of anime and manga, it is because "the story is worth it" and has a "tragic" dimension, sometimes reinforced by the "cute" graphics of the characters. Madji also appreciates sentimental and school comedies, humorous series such as *Bokudo*, *GTO*, *School Rumble*, "an essential manga in the comic genre". Madji is sensitive to the humor that deals with "the subjects of life", and assigns this comic function to manga rather than to anime. He has also read popular shonens, but does not appreciate long series like *D. Gray Man* or *Bleach*, whose interest decreases according to him with each volume. When he retraces his trajectory as a manga reader and anime fan, Madji puts at a distance his tastes as a schoolboy (the shonens *Shaman King*, *One Piece*, *Naruto* and *Love Hina*, judged childish and too "classic", "stereotyped" and "boring"). He started "with the most popular series, so necessarily the easiest to access, in terms of language and everything", and describes a typical trajectory: "so necessarily, people will start reading *Naruto*, they will say that it's the best manga, and then they will go somewhere else, and they will find something else, they will say that it's better. In the end, the more you advance, the more mangas you discover, the more difficult it becomes to understand". Madji establishes filiations between the shonen mangas, stemming from *Dragon Ball*, and quickly spots the clichés. He criticizes "popular" manga and anime, especially those that target "big fans of panties".

Madji is therefore sensitive to "well-constructed" plots and scenarios: "Well, I'm not really interested in the genres, it's mainly the story: the principle of a well-made, well-coordinated scheme, not too unrealistic stuff where, like, the hero draws his power from friendship, the hero who, like, his girlfriend is in danger, he goes to save her, and then he becomes super strong, he wins. I don't like that pattern, I prefer well-constructed patterns". Madji values the complexity of the plots that "give you something to think about". Like Aurélien, he appreciates *Death Note* because this manga allows him to "see the psychology of the characters, how they kill all their victims, under what circumstances, at what moment". Beyond the individual titles, Madji greatly appreciates the themes and intertwined plots developed by the Japanese studio Type-Moon, whose video games have been adapted into anime and manga. His reading of the manga *Fate/Stay Night* and *Tsukihime* is part of this constellation of media consumption. Madji first discovered anime through his cousin, before becoming interested in the original video game. The titles *Kara no Kyoukay*, *Fate/Stay Night* and *Tsukihime* are indeed "linked together" and form a "universe", the "nasuverse", governed by specific rules inspired by role-playing games ("it's linked by characters, it's linked by stories, it's linked by rumors"). Madji is finally sensitive to the political "message" of certain series, such as *Code Geass*, and retraces in social terms the clashes between the "peoples" and powers of this alternative universe: "And the end, in fact, it will be that the world will unite so that it never happens again, and that there will be fewer wars, that all the social advantages, like the bourgeois, like the British—it was the British people who colonized the world—will no longer have the privileges they had, that there will be no more deaths, no more terrorists, no more attacks, nothing". Madji also spotted a religious dimension in the *manga Death Note*: "In the end, if God or not exists, it was rather questions like that that were asked, to show that God was also a symbol before being an entity that sees everything, that knows everything". Madji thus appreciates certain battle scenes for their spectacular dimension, but its interest depends above all on their mythological, strategic or political background: "The fights between heroic souls are made to be really exciting, because they are heroic souls with superhuman powers. It's just following the rules of *Dungeons and Dragons*, so it's not really anything. So in the end, it's much better. *Naruto*, we know that the hero has a demon inside him, but in the end, where does his power come from? We don't know, we don't understand, it's not very interesting". Madji underlines the "inconsistencies" and the "unjustified" events that are scattered throughout the *Naruto* manga, which he stopped reading after volume 20 ("They abuse all the time by saying they are going to resurrect people, we don't know how. So when it's incoherent, I don't like it. Even if manga is a bit fantastic, there are certain limits"). In contrast, Madji appreciates *Tsukihime* and *Kara no Kyoukai* because these two series "get out of the classic scheme": "It's quite interesting because it's not exactly the panty/girlfriend scheme/the super strong hero but at the same time super indecisive. It gets out of the classic scheme and that's what I liked about it". In contrast to popular titles and the prevailing taste, his favorite manga, *Karakuri Circus*, is a series that "did not sell": "the French public did not like the drawings, so they went to other manga. However, the series is really the best I've ever seen". Madji also values the subtle use of language and humor in a manga like *Sayonara Zetsubo Sensei*, as opposed to *Naruto*. These two mangas differ in their target audience, the difficulty of the language level and the time needed to read a volume. Madji considers manga as a subtle universe, accessible only to connoisseurs.

Madji shows his preference for shonens and seinens, and his disinterest in shojo, which he "doesn't like at all". He opposes shojos, focused on love stories, to other mangas, more "versatile". When asked about mangakas, the first names that come to Madji's mind are those of "hentai" artists (Naruko and Tony Taka), which allows him to approach a production that he seems to know precisely. Madji was first drawn to pornographic parodies of popular manga: "At first I would watch it just to look at favorite heroes in the nude, or something like that, and then eventually I wouldn't find any interest in it". He has continued to explore "hentai" anime and now considers that it can be "just as exciting as normal anime". The fact that many anime titles are based on hentai video games reinforced his interest in the genre. As a connoisseur, Madji draws hierarchies within the field, between anime that "obviously has a storyline, with exciting characters sometimes", and anime that "sucks, just based on sex what". Madji also enjoyed the manga called *My wife is a student*. He also says that *Step Up Love Story* is "a great classic", which he finds "informative, but a little boring (laughs)".

Madji specifically mentions his preference for "GAR characters", a term used by fans to refer to characters whose masculinity is so ostentatious and exuberant that they inspire a sense of deference and worship, or forms of submission: "It's the character who's yelling for nothing, who's charismatic, who's super strong", for example Kamina in *Tengen Toppa*, "he's kind of the idiot, which is the guy who's yelling for nothing. (…) And in fact, the character, he imposes his style, he imposes his charisma and that's what makes the character quite powerful, in all his words, in everything he does. He even instills a movement on the level of the whole planet which makes the character become mythical. He is a legend in the genre". Madji likes precisely these characters "because they impose their style, they are unique", and thus distinguish themselves from introverted, tortured, timorous or indecisive heroes: "In fact, it's rare to meet nowadays precisely because the anime, they turn more on subjects that are not very focused on the character that is super charismatic or imposes his style. But it's more focused on the rather soft characters, the classics, like the shy guy who's in love with a girl but never says so". Madji has already imagined himself in the situation of this type of male character. He also can't stand one category of female characters, the *tsundere**, which he defines as follows: "Nahru Segawa in *Love Hina,*Tosaka in *Fate/Stay Night*, all these characters are called *tsundere*, they are characters who, in front of the man they love, they are really really shy, but in fact, they are really haughty as characters, and they do not hesitate to hit. They're annoying characters". Madji has little interest in female characters in anime ("usually they're all the same"), except when they are involved in the action and are "useful to the story". He has also enjoyed several manga where the main character is a young woman, endowed with supernatural powers and the object of every threat. Madji also expresses his emotion about the tragic fate of the heroine of the anime *Air TV*, and says that he "went into a depression for three days". He is also sensitive to the sentimental relationships and plots developed in shonen and seinen manga, but prefers when they are "suggested", unlike some popular titles, such as *Naruto*, where it is not well integrated into the story. Madji emphasizes the ethical dilemmas that the characters have to face, and he appreciates their evolution through the trials they go through, taking as an example the tragic friendship of the two heroes of *Tengen Toppa*, Simon and Kamina.

Madji invests a lot to defend the "cause" of manga and to make his friends discover titles, to "promote" them, as for *Karakuri Circus*, "because I'm really disgusted that the series stopped, while it is really so exciting. I'm lending it out a bit to encourage people to buy it. Anyway, people, once they read it, they buy it". Since they met at the vocational school, Madji has played the role of prescriber and initiator with his friend Aurélien, who recognizes his legitimacy in this field and emphasizes his charisma. Madji tries to adapt to the tastes of his interlocutors ("when I speak with the person, I can already know what he will like as a genre"). As opposed to those who would "passively" consume manga or anime, Madji indeed stresses the importance of discussions and conversations about the object of his passion ("otherwise, it's not interesting"). Madji also created a "manga club" in his high school, he read all the series bought by the club, but criticizes the relationship to manga of most of the members and high school students, their lack of care, curiosity and openness apart from the most popular manga, and he finally left the club. Madji has thus multiplied public speeches, debates and initiatives with his classmates and friends to encourage them to read manga, and to answer the criticisms of the laymen. He wrote and circulated a petition to protest against the stop of the publication of his favorite manga (*Karakuri Circus*).

Madji evokes the hostility and the contempt of his entourage towards manga and anime. His parents think that "it's too childish, it's money thrown out the window", and he also comes back to the negative reactions of some classmates. He considers that these "preconceived ideas" stem from a lack of knowledge about manga, which most people reduce to *Naruto*. Conversations with others sometimes lead to new "theories" or interpretations: "That's how I found out that *Death Note* was more about religion, because otherwise I would never have guessed". Madji likes to elaborate theories collectively, "during long hours", notably on the universe of *Fate/Stay night* ("I have already spoken to friends for more than six hours on this very universe"). If Aurélien is a daily partner of these reading sociabilities, Madji privileges the virtual sociabilities with manga connoisseurs. For lack of enough manga fans in his immediate environment, he uses specialized sites such as MyAnimeList, which allows him to establish "degrees of compatibility" by comparing lists of preferences, but also online games or general discussion forums such as MSN, where the choice of a pseudonym or an avatar from the world of manga constitutes a "signal". Madji frequents many forums and uses the *Final Fantasy*-inspired nickname he chose when he was nine years old, or new nicknames inspired by *Tsukihime*.

For two years, Madji's parents have allowed him to go to the Japan Expo festival in Paris. He enjoyed the cosplays, the concerts and "the Japanese girls". However, Madji is very critical of this festival, too much focused on "marketing, buying, buying, buying". He prefers to go to the Epitanime festival, "more friendly and smaller", and where people "tend to talk better". Madji is angry about the misuse of the term "fan" by readers whose knowledge is very limited and "who believe that *Naruto* is the best manga in the world". In contrast, he defines himself as a passionate person: "And a fan, for me, is really someone who burns with passion for it, and who wouldn't hesitate to sign anything, even if it's desperate or useless. A passionate person, a fan, a fanatic, for me, that's it. And yes, I consider myself a fan. When there is something I like in a manga, I don't let it go at all".

Madji has many tastes and practices related to the world of manga and Japanese animation. He started in high school by drawing inspired by manga, before "giving up the idea", especially because the friend with whom he had a relationship of emulation ("rivalry is what makes us progress") stopped this activity. Since he entered high school, he has started making "Anime Music Videos", *i.e.* video clips combining anime excerpts and musical titles. Madji has also written fanfiction ("only one, it was short"), but prefers to play as characters in "RP forums", which adapt the principle of role-playing games to discussion forums and are based on interactive forms of writing. If learning Japanese seems "too hard" to Aurelien, who already considers that he has difficulties in English, Madji expresses his determination to learn and master this language, mainly to know the end of the manga *Karakuri Circus*, whose French edition has been interrupted ("and if I have to learn Japanese, even if it takes me a year, two years, I'll learn it, because I don't want to finish the manga at volume 22 when there are 44 in Japan. I'm not decided to be like that. If I want the end, I'll get it"). The taste for Japanese animation and the attraction for the language are also combined in Madji's musical tastes, dominated by Japanese music ("At 98%, I only listen to that").

Madji's favorite subject at school is French, even if he is not a big reader of novels, and does not read Franco-Belgian comics since elementary school, which he considers uninteresting and repetitive: only the comic strip *XIII* could, according to him, compare with an "average manga". He seems to have some of the same expectations of novels as of manga, and thus values "fantastic" and "oppressive" authors and novels, *Le Horla* (which he attributes to Victor Hugo instead of Guy de Maupassant), and plans to read Edgar Poe, "a master of all that is stressful, oppressive". Madji was "hooked on video games" when he was a "kid", he "did all the consoles" and "had his period" in middle school (*Final Fantasy*, *Lineage 2*, *World of Warcraft*, *Ragnarok online*). Madji believes that he has now "done a bit of a tour", and is also holding back because he prefers 2D games, as 3D "loses its charm" to video games. Madji prefers *Final Fantasy*, because "it's the longest game, but it has an end: it's rare in a mmorpg, that's what's interesting. It is the only mmorpg where there is a story, where there is a beginning and an end. There are some after seven years, they still haven't finished the game. But the end, it is still close. It is they who do not want to finish it". In terms of television, Madji as well as Aurélien watch "only comedy series", like the French TV shows *Kamelott*, and the "small humorous things", like *The Simpsons*, *American Dad*, *Futurama*, *The Griffins*" ("the rest, it's not interesting").

Madji and Aurélien both answer that manga brought them first of all "pleasure", but for Madji, also "a way of thinking, a way of living", and a stimulation of his reflection and his intelligence.

Reading manga, and especially owning up to one's identity as a manga reader, is not easy, insofar as conflicted dispositions are deeply involved. Actually, whether adolescents from privileged backgrounds with cultural and social capital, or adolescents attending school with other schoolchildren, and especially high school students who are reluctant to this practice, the peer group, where advice and anecdotes can be exchanged within teenagers' inner circles", is not the only sphere of socialization. The sign of recognition can thus be reversed, and become a stigma. Various strategies are then put in place in order to have "the right distance" (Le Bart 2000, 209): minimizing, at least in the investigative situation, which is also sometimes experienced as a risk of delegitimization, one's taste for manga, and making as if was is only a hobby, a hobby without much affective investment or money; posing as a "real reader", as opposed to the figure of the shameful "groupie", the "fan" lobotomized by his passion, by developing real skills, by endowing manga with a story and cult works.

As a matter of fact, the particularity of manga, which combines drawing and narration, allows the implementation of scholarly and expert reading, academic skills such as intertextuality, literary history, recognition of recurrent narrative patterns or allusions and references. These strategies for distinction are all the more complex as they are not all outward-looking and are sometimes the tip of the iceberg in conversations between friends. For these "expert" teenagers, passion, in this case manga, has a strong identical role, where age, gender and alternative cultural capital are involved. Matthieu, whose reading pratice is monitored by his architect father, an enlightened comic book lover, is torn apart between his desire to read manga and the parental calls to order. When he compares his comic book and manga readings, "it's two ways, it's two ways and it makes me feel good that they don't meet", even if it's not without pain …

Conclusion

Working on comics from a psychoanalytical point of view, Serge Tisseron begins his study with the following observation:

> I therefore made the hypothesis that through their reading, young people try to give themselves representations of feelings, emotions and anxieties they experience in the face of the physical transformations of which their body is the object and the social mutations they are about to embark upon. In addition, these comics certainly allow these teenagers to socialize their experiences through the endless comments that they make about them among peers, a bit like the Pokémon among younger children today. With them, they 'kill two birds with one stone', as the saying goes, since they gain both pictorial representations of their inner states that are devoid of them and a socialization of their states, in short, both a 'better psychological integration' and a 'better social integration'.
>
> 2000, 2

This short preface is close to the conclusions of our study on adolescent manga reading experiences. Our study can actually, in a way, serve as a demonstration, through the words of adolescents in interviews, the writings and drawings posted on their blogs, but also their silences, the various intonations of their laughter, sometimes caused by embarrassment, sometimes by the memory of a humorous scene, sometimes by mockery, and the degrees of their voices, whispered allusions, whispered titles.

If manga are so successful, it is first of all because their reading is perfectly embedded in adolescent times: the narration, between scenes, episodes and narrative arcs allows indeed both a fragmented and crumbled reading during a school trip, a recreation or a boring course, as well as the rereading, in the evening before going to sleep, or the week-end before a new volume is released.

Manga also fits into the constellation of interests which, beyond an illusory "youth culture", is nevertheless characteristic of contemporary teenagers: music, multimedia, friendly sociability, while allowing the development of more "traditional" amateur practices, such as writing and drawing. "Young people's reading", often identified as such by adults who even technically are put off by reading "backwards", manga is also an opportunity to experience the tensions between the will, which functions as a necessity, to distinguish oneself from "adults" and "little ones", by being identiying and being identified as part of the peer group, while at the same time standing out from it,

 | DOI:10.1163/9789004548312_007

but not too much—the chronological sequence of these stages functioning as an ideal type. The first step is to read manga, both against the comics of childhood or parents, and also to read what others of one's own age read: the choice is then made of the most well-known, most consensual titles, which can be discussed with friends for long hours. Many people drop out after this communal moment, which is rather characteristic of middle school. For the others, who will continue to read manga in high school, belonging to the community is not enough: it is a question, within this community, of distinguishing oneself, of exhibiting one's "personal" tastes, of distinguishing oneself by the choice of less known, more state-of-the-art titles, and the contempt towards the readings of those who have then become the "smallest", the middle school boys, and this middle school boy that one has been oneself. Thus, manga are a support of sociability that makes it possible to define oneself among peers. Mangas engage a participatory reading, they make people laugh, make them cry, even if it is more difficult, especially boys, to recognize it, while at the same time they allow distraction, in the strong sense of the term, in times of life often marked by school, family, friendship and even love pressure.

Paradoxically, they are a way of escaping from oneself, but where finally one looks for oneself, and one finds oneself. Actually, teenagers find in manga representations of their emotions and anxieties, and manga is a support of identification and self elaboration, or even repair against adversity: meeting an abandoned, ostracized, and unhappy hero, whether it is about great mourning or small sorrows, but also a hero in love or a hero embarrassed by a body that betrays him allows, for lack of answers, to feel less alone with one's questions, and above all to be able to laugh about it.

Above all, reading manga allows one to learn and experience one's gender, one's way of being a girl or a boy: and the matter is much more complex than the publishing categorization into shojo and shonen might lead one to think, so much so that learning about masculinity and femininity is combined differently according to one's age and social origin. Between exacerbated virility and tormented introspection for some, sentimental romances and superheroes for others, the side paths are sometimes more surprising: the displacement of some female shojo readers to the yaoi as readers and as publishers is a striking example of this phenomenon. In these sentimental relationships between men, girls search for a form of sentimental romance, which they are the first to despise in its 'classic' form. While girls do show how much the stereotype of femininity is discredited, even among them, the violence of the taboo linked to yaoi, and beyond that to homosexuality, which is extremely vivid among boys in middle and high school, as well as the reluctance of these boys, once they are past the age of playground games, to put their bodies into play—even in the reserved spaces that are the cosplays—testifies to how much this differential sex valence goes beyond the mere dividing between girls and boys, and the extent to which the latter also really suffer from it.

However, the group of 'peers', amateurs or at least manga readers, is not the only one where teenagers evolve. While, as Michèle Petit writes, readers, especially children, can "pull out all the stops, whatever the cost, to save a space of their own, to construct meaning, to respond to their quest for words, stories, metaphors" (2008, 138), not every child does it the same way. Thus, on the market of scholarly legitimacy as well as that of the group of non-reading manga peers, this reading practice can be devalued, become a source of remarks, contempt and mockery.

The reader's career must then develop, create its own principles of distinctions, opposing the figure of the "true reader" to that of the "bad fan", of the "expert" to the "groupie", the hierarchies and principles of legitimacy thus acting as fractals, which are reproduced identically and infinitely …

Of course, these appropriations take different forms according to gender, age, social origin, educational capital or skills in the field of manga. These various characteristics are intertwined and interwoven. Being a middle-school girl from a working-class background involves a different relationship to manga from a high-school girl from a privileged background, but if both are "experts" in manga, the experiences can be similar on certain points, with distinctions being made in nuances, the choice of a title or the way of defining the same term, such as "fan", for example. Similarly, against distinctions in terms of gender or social origin, reading skills—here manga—can become a capital in its own right, which recomposes the forces at play, at least in the arena in question, however limited it may be (Albenga 2007). Let us thus attempt to draw a typology of these manga readers in this complex landscape:

The "fans": mostly schoolboys/girls, they grew up with the anime, which they later learned were adaptations of manga. They follow the "big" series, in manga, anime and sometimes in video games: *Naruto*, the humor and action of which they enjoy, *One Piece* and *Death Note*, which they read and reread, buy and exchange in a small community of friends, where they discuss characters and develop hypotheses. Reading manga and buying are part of a broader relationship to the digital culture: anime, scans, Internet, video games … Their collections are often impressive, up to a hundred or even hundreds of volumes and scanned episodes. Boys don't read shojos, or without their friends knowing. Some girls are also part of this group, rather of average and privileged background, reading shonen and some humorous shojo. These readers draw a lot, the girls write fanfictions, which they share online.

The "detached": This group is made up from middle school and high school boys. It includes teenagers with episodic readings who often favor anime. They borrow books from the library or from friends and see no point in owning them, especially because manga, for most of them, is not 'real' reading. Little investment, therefore, and little or no associated practices.

The "prevented": These schoolchildren discovered manga through a friend, or, more often than not, at the library, which is their main source of supply. From a working-class background, the girls belonging to this group are passionate about the sentimental intrigues of the shojo, and the boys about action and humor series. But the shortcomings in the collections offered by friends or libraries are a hindrance to sustained reading and practices such as rereading.

The "experts": They are older than the previous group. While some of their classmates stopped reading manga when they moved on to high school, they have continued to do so, notably by developing strategies for distinction in their reading career: having an encyclopedic knowledge, knowing the titles not translated in France, reading manga classified as seinen (for adults) … *Naruto* and the whole commercial industry of derivative products became their pet peeves[1] (they resold their collection, or more rarely developed scholarly readings of *Naruto*), as well as the "fans", identified in a caricatural way as young people and … girls. Often victims of depreciative judgements in the games of cultural distinction, they try to rehabilitate the reading and the universe of the manga, by developing scholarly, aesthetic, philosophical readings. They are boys or girls, most often focusing on scientific areas and having been socialized in masculine universes, particularly admiring an older brother or a cousin. These girls, extremely severe towards the shojo, their female characters and their readers, nevertheless find romance in the yaoi, these stories staging the emotions and frolics of young homosexuals. These readers do not want to be assimilated to the figure of the fan, devoid of social life and passive, but continue to associate the reading of manga with amateur artistic practices such as the writing of fanfiction and other modes of "active" appropriation of "non-commercial" manga. The girls, and a few boys, write fanfictions, listen to Japanese music, sometimes disguise themselves during cosplays. The most motivated members of this group are learning Japanese, have chosen this language as an option in high school, and want to work in world of manga.

"Those with hang-ups": These girls and high school boys, from privileged backgrounds endowed with cultural capital, while they appreciate manga,

1 Some, however, appreciate the figurines and derivative products dedicated to lesser-known manga, which they buy as imports, which is another form of distinction.

decide to stop reading it, or to read less of it, so much they internalize the criticisms and remarks of their close circle, parents and friends. These teenagers are thus faced with a conflict between their tastes and highly legitimistic judgements: they do not buy them but borrow them from friends, while denigrating this reading, and, all the while denying it, do not accompany it with ancillary practices.

As we can see, this typology deliberately does not take into account the ways of reading: actually, to have fun, identify oneself, think …, crosses the categories of readers and reading, and everyone picks "seeds of knowledge and life", to use the expression of one of the teenage girls: a few words in Japanese, a recipe, elements of Japanese culture or history, but also a certain tolerance and philosophy of life for some. It would be a mistake to smile at these remarks, just as it would be wrong to question the reasons for them. Just as reading manga serves both to distract and to "rack one's brains", to escape and to find oneself, metaphorically or empathically, whether on different titles or during the same reading session, successively or simultaneously ('racking one's brains' being a source of great pleasure for some), so too, the explanations put forward, which, in the course of the writing, are set out one after the other and in separate chapters, work in interrelation in so far as the effects of age, gender, social background cannot be isolated from one another.

While our survey is primarily devoted to adolescent experiences with manga in the fin 2000s, this should not obscure, as is the case in many media discourses,[2] the historical roots of manga reading practices and the existence of an adult readership that discovered them one to two decades ago. The analysis of these adult readers'careers makes it possible to shed light on the conditions for maintaining an interest in manga beyond adolescence, to understand some of the reasons why the passion for manga sometimes fades away, and to highlight the transformations in ways of reading and tastes in the course of the readers' biographical, familial and professional trajectories.

The longitudinal and biographical analysis of fans' practices and of the effects of growing older is a recent line of research within cultural studies and fan studies (Bielby and Harrington, 2010). To analyse the place of manga in the lives and trajectories of these readers, it is also possible to use the "two major models of articulation between cultural passion, professional activity and family life" that Olivier Donnat has identified from a secondary exploitation of the Life Stories survey carried out by INSEE (2009b). These readers have

2 Many reports only deal with manga in relation to young readers (the 'digital natives') or 'new media', and focus on the most spectacular aspects of the passion (cosplay and others).

experienced intermittent reading and variable forms of investment: the identities of "fan", "passionate", "otaku" or mere reader are more or less invested and relevant depending on the historical context and on biographical events, which give rise to new identities or priorities. Among the readers interviewed in the context of a sociology thesis (Vanhée 2019), we will limit ourselves to highlight a few cases. For readers who discovered manga as teenagers in the 1990s, in a very hostile context, access to manga and manga information, apart from popular titles, was an "obstacle course" and, before high-speed Internet was available, "fan culture" took the form of fanzinat, postal correspondence and insider conventions. Some of its first readers, especially those with educational capital, became professional in the specialized press, publishing, translation or "events" concerning manga, or even in the illustration and creation of manga. However, the paths to professionalization are narrow and uncertain, and for most of those who have continued to read manga regularly, it remains a "secret garden", disconnected from the professional world, but the object of a strong affective and material investment.

These readers have various ways of "adapting the constraints of adult life so as not to break the course of passion" (Donnat 2009b, 213) and escape or reverse the stigma of "otaku", the maintenance of a reading practice being made easier when both members of a couple share the same taste. For some readers with precarious jobs or living alone, reading and collecting manga, fan identity as it unfolds on the Internet or in conventions, testifies to "the importance of the micro-spaces of personal happiness that individuals build in the domestic or associative setting to resist the harshness of the working world" and social pressure, and allows "the promotion of a valorising self-image" among amateurs (Donnat 2009b, 82). Games of distinction with new generations of readers then sometimes take place. But the entry into working and family life often leads to a gradual "disengagement" from passion and practice, which becomes more occasional and selective, unless it is shared again with children. Finally, as we have seen with librarians, some have started reading manga as adults, for professional reasons, or by welcoming into their eclectic cultural repertoire manga authors alongside graphic novels or Miyazaki's films, or by plunging back into the series of their childhood, as the success of the "nostalgia market" testifies. Some of the teenagers interviewed in our survey have parents who knew and appreciated Japanese cartoons.

It is with emotion that we leave there *Naruto*, *Nana*, *One Piece*, *Tsubasa* and the others, and all those teenagers who, for hours, spoke to us about their passionate, nonchalant, nostalgic or enthusiastic reading practices, have taken us to those worlds where you turn into a sign of the zodiac, where pirates are scattering the islands in search of their dreams, where memories are feathers, where you change into a girl when it rains, where you just have to write someone's name in a notebook to kill them, where love triangles make you lose your mind.

To us, adults who were previously non-readers (or "weak readers") of manga, these young readers will undoubtedly have learned the necessity not to judge a genre "as a whole", and to appreciate the varieties and subtleties of the paths they follow and the variety of the appropriations they derive from it.

APPENDIX 1

Glossary: The Manga and Japanese Animation Universe

This glossary gathers terms pertaining to manga, Japanese animation, and more broadly to contemporary Japanese culture, which are used in this book, as well as terms linked to some cultural, media, and digital leisure activities used by the adolescents interviewed. Part of this lexicon concerns the modes of production, publication, and classification of manga in Japan: names of professions involved in manga production (*mangaka*, *tantô*...), distinction of comic book forms according to their medium and mode of publication (*mangashi*, *tankôbon* ...), classification of production according to the commercial and socio-demographic segmentation operated by Japanese pre-publication magazines (shônen/shôjo/seinen ...), terms referring to aesthetic trends or specific manga forms (story-manga, gekiga, yonkoma).

As far as Japanese publishing categories are concerned, it should be kept in mind that the real manga readers do not necessarily match the age and gender criteria of the targeted readership, and that the use and extension of these categories in France are not the same as in the Japanese context. The specialized vocabulary specific to Japanese animation is made up of a large number of Japanese terms derived from English (chara-designer, OVA ...). Some of these terms from the Japanese language are commonly used in France, as in most countries where Japanese manga, cartoons or video games are distributed, which shows the globalization of the Japanese media culture and its lexicon. These terms are widely used by professionals in the sector, publishers, specialized journalists, but also by the readers and teenagers interviewed, and some of them have made their way into the dictionaries. The term 'manga' has thus been present in most dictionaries for nearly twenty years, even though its meaning has varied: some definitions, and still today some uses, encompass under this term, in an indifferentiated manner, Japanese comics and cartoons, but this meaning is most often perceived as improper and a stricter definition is now tending to impose itself ("Japanese comic strip").

The use of a specialized vocabulary, while not yet "officially" recognized, is tending to become more widespread as manga and related cultural products become part of the leisure activities of successive generations of fans: the term anime (or anime) is thus widely used to refer to Japanese animation series or films (see Berndt 2010).

As manga is at the heart of the Japanese entertainment industry, a second set of Japanese terms refers more generally to the whole of Japanese media and popular culture: vocabulary linked to the musical field and to the various modes and styles that characterize it (idol, J-pop, J-rock, *visual kei*, gothic lolita, *kawaii* ...), or to other modes

 | DOI:10.1163/9789004548312_008

of expression or media, such as television (drama). Some terms refer to amateur practices (cosplay, *dôjinshi* ...), categories of fans (*otaku, fujoshi* ...) or types of characters (*coodere*, GAR ...). Finally, a series of terms used in the interviews are not specific to manga but refers to uses of the Internet and modes of consumption and distribution of manga and anime, and more broadly of television series and music: fansub or scanlation practices, multiple forms of subtitling, downloading, sharing.

This glossary, which combines English and Japanese terms related to manga or new technologies, is per se the product of a story and intense intercultural circulation, which establishes the emergence of Japan as a major cultural pole. It is also the result of codification work first carried out within fanzines or specialized press titles, such as the magazine *AnimeLand*, and then widely spread in the form of educational and encyclopedic works, such as the *Dico Manga*, an "encyclopedic dictionary of Japanese comics" (Finet 2008), or, in English, the *Otaku Encyclopedia* (Galbraith 2009). The lexicon is based on these various works and quotes them.

Anime A Japanese term, short for *animēshon*, a transcription of the English animation. In Japan it refers to cartoons. The term is used in France to refer more specifically to Japanese cartoons, including animated series produced for a television broadcast or for the video market, and sometimes to animated feature films. The term "japanimation", sometimes shortened to "japanim'", a contraction of "Japan" and "animation", has also been in use since the 1990s in France to refer to Japanese cartoons.

Anime comic "A comic book offering the adaptation in printed form of an animated work previously created in the audiovisual format (television series, OAV, animated film) While manga often constitute the matrix from which multiple derivative products are made, it is here the audiovisual work, through its commercial impact and/or its cultural influence, that pre-exists the book and gives rise to downstream comic book adaptations. The images are taken from the film and the dialogues are added. The page layout is built like that of a manga, giving the impression that it is a color comic book" (Finet 2008, 32).

Art-book the art-book is "an often luxurious and large-format work presenting the graphic work done by an author or a team" (*AnimeLand* 2003, 128). A monograph or thematic collection, it allows an author or a publisher to showcase various images, previously published or not, from a manga: album covers, chapter openings, sketches, character sketches, illustrations of all kinds. These books may also include articles, biographies and interviews (Finet 2008, 44–45). The art-books are very widespread in Japan but are much less so in French-language publishing. Nicolas Finet brings some art-books closer to the tradition of the artist's book, especially those which are centered on the graphic universe of an author and which present original illustrations.

Bishônen "Handsome young man", tall, slim, androgynous in appearance, who can be encountered manga for girls (shojo and yaoi) (*Manga 10000 Images* 2010, 224). This ideal of male beauty is also noticeable in some manga for boys and, beyond that, in the appearance of Asian singers or actors. This term is sometimes abbreviated to "bishi" or "bishie" (in France).

Bunko A type of paperback with high pagination and good quality paper (Bastide and Prezman 2006, 276), bunko is a standard in Japanese publishing that allows for the reprinting of old series, classics or bestsellers at reduced prices, previously published in more luxurious versions (AnimeLand 2003, 128). This format is used in France for some prestigious editions, notably for some manga by Osamu Tezuka.

Chara-designer The contraction of the English word "character designer", the term chara-designer is used in Japan to refer to the professionals in charge to the morphology and appearance of manga, anime or video game characters (Finet 2008, 124). The chara-designer thus has a specific place within the very advanced division of labor that characterizes the production of manga or anime, and ensures a "standardization" of the characters' graphics.

Coodere A type of manga or anime character who practically expresses no emotion and remains silent and cold. This term is mostly used by anime and manga connoisseurs.

Cosplay The term cosplay comes from the contraction of the English terms costume and play. Cosplay consists of dressing up as a manga, cartoon, or video game character (or any fictional character whose image is known, whether from comics, French-Belgian comic books, novels, films, or series). Cosplay can also be inspired by real people, actors or singers (especially visual rock). Practiced at gatherings, conventions and festivals, 'free cosplay' consists of walking down the aisles, wearing the clothes and accessories of a particular character in public. During cosplay contests, the "cosplayers", individually or in groups, perform small choreographies or scenographies inspired by a manga. The personal creation of costumes is valued by amateurs, but "ready-to-wear" cosplay costumes and accessories are also marketed. While this term was primarily associated with the world of manga, anime and Japanese video games, it refers to a practice (the masquerade), born in the American conventions of science-fiction fans. Cosplay inspired by the world of manga and anime appeared in France in the early 1990s.

Dôjinshi Dôjinshi refers to the very numerous fanzines, magazines and amateur manga magazines in which artists, most often non-professionals, exhibit parodies, pastiches and caricatures of famous series or characters (*animeparo* are thus parodies of anime), but some of these comics are original creations. By extension, the term refers to all amateur comics in Japan (Finet 2008, 134). The erotic or pornographic parodies are one of the components of dôjinshi, which contributed to the emergence of the yaoi and lolicon genres. These creations are the work of many amateur circles and associations, which are very well represented in high schools and universities, and some of them can be very successful. Many authors now known and published in France have started to publish in the universe of dôjinshi (such as the collective of authors Clamp), or are becoming famous both in the world of professional publishing and the universe of amateur manga. Dôjinshi are distributed informally in France, imported from Japan or available in scanned form on the Internet. More broadly, many French manga enthusiasts have been creating fanzines of amateur manga, either parodic or not, or fanzines made up of articles on manga and Japanese animation since the 1990s. While the digital era caused the emergence of webzines and multiple forms of online creation and spread of amateur drawings and manga, printed fanzines are still represented at conventions and festivals (*AnimeLand* 2003, 129).

Drama Japanese term from the English "television drama", which refers to a television series in Japan and in many Asian countries. Many manga are adapted more or less freely in the form of drama. Japanese and Korean dramas have been increasingly successful in France since the early 2000s and are mainly available on the Internet in subtitled versions (fansub).

Ecchi Japanese term that means indecent, lewd, salacious. In Japan, it refers to narrative content of an erotic and pornographic nature. It is originally a transcription of the Japanese pronunciation of the letter H, the first letter of the term hentai. The letter H in Japan has a meaning close to the letter X used in France to classify pornographic films. The expressions ero-manga or seijin manga (manga for adults) are also used to refer to this pornographic production. In France, the terms ecchi and hentai refer to relatively distinct types of contents. Unlike the term hentai, which applies to the same field, the term ecchi does not have a perverse connotation (*AnimeLand* 2003, 129) and is often used to label manga or anime intended for a male audience, featuring scantily clad female characters or multiplying textual or visual allusions to sexuality. It also refers to works with more explicitly erotic and pornographic contents.

Ending The ending of an anime.

Fan Art The English term for any drawing made by a fan, as a tribute to a series or a manga.

Fanfiction A term derived from English for fan-written stories, short stories or novels, set in the universe of their favorite series. This amateur writing practice, which is highly feminized, involves devising scripts or dialogue featuring the characters or the fictional universe of one or more series. The main websites devoted to fanfiction have attempted to codify this practice, issuing rules, advice, and prohibitions (the need to respect the personality of the characters used, or else write 'out of character' fictions, for example), and proposing forms of evaluation and classification (some contents are not recommended for younger children, depending on the degree of eroticism). Among the categories of fanfictions, there are, for example, death fic (a story imagining the death of a character) or slash or yaoi fanfictions (a story imagining a romantic relationship between two characters of the same sex). Mary-sue is a genre of fanfiction that consists in the author putting himself or herself on stage alongside his or her favorite characters. It may still involve imagining a sequel to a manga, an alternative version, or a crossover between several series. The stories appropriated by fanfics authors are far from being limited to manga and Japanese animation.

Fan service Characteristic of a manga or anime that multiplies winks, stereotypes or staging to please the audience of fans of a particular genre, without these graphic references having a scenaristic necessity. They can be shots on the underwear or the breasts of the female characters, on the design and the fights of giant robots (for the fans of the genre), allusions to sentimental relationships between men (for the fans of yaoi) or the presence of a character from another manga or anime. It is thus necessary to satisfy the alleged expectations of the fans and to insert intertextual references known by the connoisseurs.

Fansub The abbreviation of the English term fansubbing, a contraction of 'fan' and 'subtitle'. This amateur practice consists of subtitling and translating the dialogues of television series, cartoons, or films, which are then made available on the Internet. This work is often done collectively, with the 'fansubbers' sharing the tasks of retrieving the original series, translating the dialogues, correcting them, inserting the subtitles using computer software, and putting them online … In the case of anime, the series are often translated from English, or directly from Japanese. Most of the time, these activities do not abide by thelaw on intellectual property and copyrights, but they have allowed, especially in the 1990s, to make Japanese production available (in the form of subtitled videotapes). While some fansub sites focus on little-known series not distributed in France, others broadcast the latest episodes of popular series every week and sometimes run up against the legal offensive of the publishers who acquired the rights. Some publishers have recently embarked on the practice of simulcasting, which consists of putting translated episodes of certain series online, legally and for a fee, shortly after they were broadcast in Japan.

Gekiga A trend in Japanese comics born in the late 1950s, which differs from children's comics featuring only stereotypical characters, whimsical situations, and using comic effects. Yoshihiro Tatsumi (b. 1935) and Masahiko Matsumoto (b. 1934) published realistic stories with a dark tone during this period. In 1957, Tatsumi created the term gekiga to refer to this new category of comics: the ideogram geki suggests intensity, vehemence, impetuosity, and the term gekiga is often translated as "dramatic images". Gekiga is thus originally the claim of an adult, realistic comic strip (Finet 2008, 173–174) and more specifically refers to comics created between the 1950s and the 1970s within the lending bookstores or avant-garde magazines such as Garo, by authors such as Saito Takao, Tsuge Yoshiharu, Hirata Hiroshi, Koike Kazuo … The works of some of these artists have been reprinted in Japan, and many French publishers of the 2000s drew their inspiration from this trend to present an 'alternative' offer, close to the graphic novel. From the end of the 1960s, gekiga also influenced the main pre-publication magazines and contributed to the diversification of the publishing offer intended for teen and adult readership (Finet 2008, 207).

Goodies All derivative products related to a cultural product, and in particular to the world of manga and animation: keychains, models, posters, figurines …, which can be encountered in specialized stores and at the stands of conventions. French publishers tend to develop the publishing of calendars or diaries, and sometimes give derivative products as part of promotional operations for the purchase of a manga or anime. Some of these products, imported from Japan, such as robot models or character figurines, have brought together communities of fans (Finet 2008, 189–190).

Gothic Lolita Japanese clothing fashion that appeared in the early 1990s, which combines baggy skirts and dresses, petticoats, lace, ribbons and headbands, and refers to the appearance of Victorian dolls. This fashion was popularized by some music bands, and gave birth to clothing lines and stores, which have also been present in France since the mid-2000s, especially during festivals such as Japan Expo.

Guide book a type of book dedicated to a manga which, in the form of an illustrated booklet with maps, characters sheet and a glossary, offers a complete exploration of the manga universe. This type of accompanying discourse extends, enriches and illuminates the work to which it is dedicated. As a rule, only long series that have reached a certain level of complexity are given a guide book.

Hentai A Japanese term that means "pervert". In Japan, it refers to all forms of sexual deviations and perversions, but does not specifically refer to a category of manga. In France, this term is used to refer to the production of manga and pornographic anime, especially for the male public, the ecchi/hentai distinction overlapping in some uses the eroticism/pornography opposition. Some hentai are original creations, while others are parodies. French usage sometimes makes the term hentai a synonym for erotic or licentious, whereas its Japanese meaning is much more connotative (Finet 2008, 273). Contrary to the term ecchi, which is associated with eroticism and situational comedy, hentai is also used to refer more specifically to extreme pornographic works (sadomasochism, violence, staging of "tentacled" monsters …) (Gomarasca 2002). There are also hentai productions aimed at a female audience.

Kawaii Literally 'cute', this term is often used to describe the curvaceous, ingenuous, and innocent world that characterizes many manga (Kinsella 1995). It refers in particular to "touching" characters, objects, or pets that "look adorable" (Finet 2008, 250–251). The term was coined in the 1970s to describe a type of writing saturated with hearts, stars and exclamation marks, and a childlike way of speaking that was popular with teenage girls and young women. It then refers to the aesthetics and design of a whole range of accessories, clothing and merchandise, the emblem of which is the Hello Kitty mascot.

Josei Literally "adult woman", this term is used in France to refer to manga intended for adult female readers, active women, as opposed to shojo, intended for young girls or teenagers (*AnimeLand* 2003, 130). The use of this label in France hides the complexity of Japanese publishing categories (Finet 2008, 322) and refers mainly to the works of a few mangakas: Q-ta Minami, Kyôko Okazaki, Moyocco Anno, Sakura Erikazawa … These manga offer a more realistic and psychological description of human relationships, a sophisticated type of drawing and sometimes an explicit sexual dimension. Ladies' comics are another category of manga for adult women, born in the 1980s, with erotic and sexual scenes. The emergence in Japan of manga for teenage girls with erotic scenes has blurred these distinctions, as well as the pre-publication in fashion magazines of manga targeting teenage girls and students, such as Paradise Kiss, by Ai Yazawa. Between shojo and josei, the category 'mature shojo' is sometimes used in France to refer to erotic manga for teenagers or young women.

J-pop A contraction of "japanese popular music", this term refers to a wide range of contemporary Japanese musical creations, as opposed to traditional musical forms. The term encompasses many musical genres, from Japanese rock (referred to as J-rock) to variety to rap, but more specifically refers to Japanese variety bands, pop singers, girl bands or boy bands, as opposed to English or "international" bands and musical styles.

Lolicon This Japanese term, often pejorative, is a contraction of "Lolita complex", an expression built upon the name of the eponymous 12-year-old heroine of Vladimir Nabokov's novel Lolita. It refers to the attraction or fascination for young girls, teenagers or little girls and more specifically refers to a category of erotic or porno-graphic manga or anime featuring such characters and the readers who are fond of them. It also refers more broadly to the sexualization of the appearance of juvenile female characters in any type of manga or anime.

Magical Girl This term, borrowed from English, is used to refer to the characters of young girls with magical or supernatural powers, who often transform into teenagers. Since the creation of shojos in the 1970s, the success of "magical girls" stories has meant that the term has come to refer to "an aesthetic, a thematic field and a narrative vocabulary, to finally constitute a genre in its own right" (Finet 2008, 327), with its specific graphic codes.

Manga Japanese comic strip. *Manhua*: Chinese comic strip. *Manhwa*: Korean comic strip.

Moé Japanese term literally meaning 'bud'. Moé refers to the feelings and desire for protection aroused by certain manga and anime characters, young girls and boys portrayed in their everyday lives, without explicit sexual scenes. By extension, it refers to a type of character and a category of manga targeting an "otaku" audience (*AnimeLand* 2003, 129–130).

Mangaka Author of manga, whether scriptwriter or cartoonist. In Japan, this term refers to "the person who signs his or her work with his or her name. Other artistic collaborators, such as assistants, do not benefit from this qualifying term".

Mecha Contraction of the English word mechanical. In anime, a mecha refers equally to a vehicle, an artifact, or a robot. There are two types of robots: the human-looking one, and the giant robot (Finet, 2008, 382).

Nekketsu A Japanese term that literally means "burning blood". It has become a qualificative in the world of manga, and is applied to shonen works and series: in France it is associated with the ideas of going above and beyoind, courage, and even sacrifice (Finet 2008, 411).

OAV The Initials of the English expression "Original Animation Video", which refers to anime produced exclusively for the video market and medium, without prior broadcast by television or cinema. These animes can be stand-alone or linked to a TV series and often benefit from a larger budget and better animation quality than series diffused on TV.

One-shot A one-shot is a manga the story of which is completed in a single volume.

Opening Opening credits of an anime.

Otaku This term refers to an enthusiast, regardless of the field. It derives from a Japanese word meaning either "home" or a polite "you". An otaku is an enthusiast, a "fan", dedicating all of his or her leisure time to the object of his or her passion: comic book characters, cartoons, TV series, singers, computers, and technological objects (Kinsella 2000; Satomi 2007). The term has a very negative connotation. The term has a very negative connotation in Japan and refers to a pathological form of addiction and confinement. Japanese dictionaries and research on the subject associate otaku with communication difficulty, withdrawal, and even an escape from the responsibilities of working life, while the Japanese media evoke otakus when murderous stories are on the news, and sometimes associate it with the lolicon genre (Galbraith 2010). The connotation of this term has however evolved during the 2000s and otakus are presented in a more favorable way by some Japanese critics and by certain mangakas who have made them endearing characters: the otaku is also perceived as an expert and a connoisseur in a particular field, as a consumer and an economic force, even as a positive figure of Cool Japan, promoted by the government. In France, these various connotations are also present: the term is very often used, and claimed, in a positive sense to refer to manga and Japanese animation enthusiasts, but it can also be used pejoratively and be synonymous with nolife.

RPG The initials of the English expression "role playing game". In Japan, the term RPG is used to refer to a video game genre that transposes the rules of role-playing games to the tabletop, and in which players embody and develop characters in a particular environment. It is one of the specialties of the Japanese video game industry, with titles like Final Fantasy. One variant of the RPG is the MMORPG, or "massively multiplayer online role-playing game". An MMORPG "allows a large number of people to interact simultaneously in a virtual world that is also a persistent world, meaning that it continues to evolve when the player is not connected. The player is represented by an avatar, a character that he or she creates and then progresses through a fantasy, science-fiction or superhero inspired virtual world, involving a lot of adventures. In doing so, he interacts with the environment controlled by the program and with other players" (*AnimeLand* 2003, 130).

Tankôbon A manga is pre-published in a pre-publication magazine (mangashi), then published in a collection of several chapters. These thick volumes, which have between 160 and 250 pages, are called tankôbon. It is this format that we find in our bookshops and to which we refer in France as manga (Finet 2008, 478–479).

Tsundere A type of manga or anime character who is at first eccentric and combative, but who turns out to be finally affectionate and sensitive (article on Wikipedia, accessed 10 March 2011).

Scantrad A French term formed by contraction of "scan" and "traduction", on the model of the English term scanlation (from scan and translation). It refers to a widespread practice among manga fans, which consists in "scanning" the pages of original Japanese comics, translating them and circulating them via the Internet, most often before these manga are published by traditional channels. This practice shortens the time it takes for a manga to become available in a given language, or provides access to rare and untranslated manga (Kinsella 2000, 46).

Seinen A Japanese term meaning "young adult male". The term seinen- shi, despite its connotation of "youth" describes a part of Japanese pre-publication magazines aimed at adults. Some magazines target adults in their thirties to fifties, while young seinen magazines target an audience of high school students and young adults. These young seinen extend the themes of shonen manga, often with a greater degree of violence or sex, complex plots or psychological or philosophical themes. The seinen also refers to information manga, manga featuring various employees or interests, from sports to history. Besides seinen manga, another category of manga for adults includes pornographic manga (*narunen-shi* and the majority of *seijin-shi*), whose content is considered inappropriate for young people (Allen and Ingulsrud 2009, 15). In France, seinen includes manga intended for a readership of older teenagers, young adults and adults, as opposed to the categories shonen and shojo, which are intended for children, boys and girls (Finet 2008, 501).

Shojo A common noun used exclusively in the written Japanese language, this term means "girl" (Prough 2011, 7–11) and initially describes the stages between childhood and adulthood. Today it refers to girls of school age in the Japanese equivalent of elementary and middle school, while the term gyaru (from English girl) is used to refer to teenage girls and young women. By extension, the term shojo in Japan refers to manga published in magazines aimed at a readership of young girls, from elementary school to high school: the magazines *Ribon*, *Nakayoshi*, *Ciao*, and *Hana to yume* target girls aged 10–11; the magazines Margaret, Shojo friend, Shojo Comic, and Lala target middle school girls; the magazines *Cookie*, *Dessert*, and *Bessatsu Shojo Comic* target high school girls or students (Bastide and Prezman 2006). In France, shojo-type manga are published in magazines that are not published in the Japanese equivalent of elementary and middle school. In France, shojo manga are also manga intended for young female readers, from primary to high school. Julien Bastide and Anthony Prezman distinguish, among manga for girls, those that are available from age 11, 13 and finally 15 respectively (Finet 2008, 502). The category of "mature shojo" is sometimes used to refer to manga for high school girls with an erotic dimension (it corresponds to certain josei, young josei or teens love manga in Japan).

Shonen This term used only in the written Japanese language means "boy" (*AnimeLand* 2003, 130). In Japan, it refers to manga magazines aimed at young boys and teenagers, from the end of elementary school to middle school, sometimes up to high school (the category of young seinen manga is also aimed at male readers from high school on). Similarly, shonen manga in France are aimed at boys from elementary school to high school.

Spoiler A term derived from the English verb "to spoil". The spoiler refers to a summary that is so accurate that it reveals the highlights and sometimes even the end of the story (Finet 2008, 519).

Super Deformed A Japanese term derived from the English, which refers to a way of representing characters and expressing the intensity of their emotions and feelings by an outrageous deformation of their features, their morphology and their face. The characters are then often represented, in a parodic way, with a big head and a small body.

Story-arc Narrative arc.

Tankôbon Collection of several chapters or episodes of a manga pre-published in a periodical. Intended to be diffused in bookstores and not in the press network, tankôbon is characterized as a rule by a better quality of paper than that of prepublication magazines. The tankôbon is most often an album in pocket format, with a soft cover and a dust jacket. It is in this format that most of the manga are published in France (Finet 2008, 542).

Tsundere A type of manga or anime character who is at first eccentric and combative, but who turns out to be finally affectionate and sensitive (Wikipedia, accessed 11 March 2009).

Visual Kei The name of a Japanese music genre that emerged at the end of the 1980s, practiced by rock bands whose visual identity and aesthetic appearance are highly valued and influenced by glam rock, punk, or gothic.

Yaoi Yaoi refers to a category of manga depicting sentimental and sexual relationships between male characters. The genre appeared in the 1970s and is mainly written by female authors and aimed at a female audience (it is considered as a sub-category of shojo manga and is distinct from manga aimed at a gay audience, known as bara manga). The Japanese term shonen ai ("love between young men") also refers in France to manga featuring sentimental relationationships between men, without the sexually explicit dimension of yaoi. This type of manga, shonen ai and yaoi, is referred to in Japan by the generic term Boy's Love, or BL.

Yonkoma Comic strip set in four boxes, generally with a humorous tone, quite close in its principle to the Anglo-Saxon strip. This very compact format was originally designed to appear in the daily press (Finet 2008, 610).

Yuri Manga featuring sentimental and sexual relationships between girls.

APPENDIX 2

The Manga Readers Interviewed and Their Characteristics

To conduct the interviews, the investigators multiplied the modes of "recruitment" of manga readers, in order to obtain a diverse population from the point of view of levels and forms of investment in the practice of reading (from the fan and connoisseur to the more occasional reader). We also included readers from a diversity of social backgrounds and school training. The schools were one of the ways of entering the field: high school and middle school students were contacted through their teachers or parents, but the interview was most often conducted at the reader's home. These schools are located in a wide variety of municipalities: two elite high schools in the centre of Lyon, two high-schools in disadvantaged areas of Lyon, middle and high schools in a rural area in Normandy, etc. Once contact was made with some of the students, they were able to point out other readers who were known and recognized in the school, or among their relatives or peers. For example, six boys belonging to the same group of friends and attending the same schools were interviewed. Several members of the same sibling group were interviewed successively (Clara and Lydia, Félix and Octave, Samuel and Xavier, Maeva and Jérôme). Some collective interviews took place with two friends (Nabil and Moussa, Madji and Aurélien, Maèle and Marianne), which offered the opportunity to capture the interactions between these two manga readers, the jokes, the laughter, the mutual mockery, etc. This way of finding repondents and conducting the interviews allowed us to highlight the links between sociability and cultural practices, and the cultural socialization within peer groups and sibling groups. Interviews were also conducted with readers of local libraries.

A second way of contacting readers was by attending conventions and various cultural events related to manga (distribution of small questionnaires), and by using discussion forums or Internet sites specialized in manga and animation. Interviews were also conducted by students who took a Sociology of Culture and Reception seminar in the sociology department of the Ecole Normale Supérieure de Lyon. Nine students in sociology have carried out interviews by recruiting readers among their personal acquaintances or their local family networks: Elise Benchimol, Marie Du Boucher, Raphaël Colombier, Lucie Jégat, Adrien Michon, Cécile Noesser, Cécile Rodrigues, William Taverny, Marine Trégan.

The age distribution of the readers surveyed covers the entire middle and high school years, and there is a slight over-representation of boys. These readers come from diverse social backgrounds, according to their parent's occupations.

 | DOI:10.1163/9789004548312_009

1 Summary Table About the Manga Readers Interviewed

First name	Age and educational stage	Father's occupation	Mother's occupation
Noé	11, 6th grade student	Publisher (religious books)	Stay-at-home-mother
Clara (Lydia's sister)	11, 6th grade student	Technical executive	Baker
Vincente	12, 6th grade student	Garbage collector	Stay-at-home-mother
Kevin	13, 8th grade student	Machine driver	Secretary-accountant
Marie	14, 9th grade student	Accountant	Cleaning lady
Caroline	14, 9th grade student	Shop manager	Instructor in an insurance company
Philippe	14, 9th grade student	Management assistant (road transport company)	Private nurse
Nadia	14, 8th grade student	Skilled worker	Secretary
Alice	14, 9th grade student	Skilled worker	Computer assistant
Félix (Octave's brother)	15, 11th grade student	Sculptor	Sculptor
Léo	15, 10th grade student	Commercial executive	Librarian
Jennifer	15, 8th grade student	Veterinarian	Stay-at-home-mother
Lydia	15, 8th grade student	Technical executive	Baker
Bastien	15, 10th grade student	Biologist	Engineer
Hugo	15, 10th grade student	History teacher (middle-school)	Nurse
Samuel (Xavier's brother)	15, 10th grade student	Firefighter	Childcare assistant

First name	Age and educational stage	Father's occupation	Mother's occupation
Maureen	15, 9th grade student	Worker	Administrative agent (in a police school)
Safia	15, 9th grade student	Assistant nurse	Stay-at-home-mother
Hacine	15, 9th grade student	Director of a textile company	Volunteer in an association (assistance to the elderly)
Océane	15, 9th grade student	Electrician	Stay-at-home-mother
Tom	15, 10th grade student	Electrotechnics teacher (high-school)	English teacher (middle-school)
Théo	15, 10th grade student	Instructor in a public transportation company	Bank employee
Leila	15, 10th grade student	Unemployed	Janitor (in a hospital)
Yohanna	16, 10th grade student	Engineer	Sales representative
Ariane	16, 12th grade student (applied arts section)	Metal worker	Secretary (real estate agency)
Nayir	16, 9th grade student	Delivery driver	Surface technician
Annabelle	16, 11th grade student (scientific section, Japanese language learning)	Bank executive	Consultant (social and family economy)
Marianne	16, 11th grade student (literature section, Japanese language learning)	Numérical control operator	Restaurant employee

First name	Age and educational stage	Father's occupation	Mother's occupation
Maele	16, 11th grade student (literature section, Japanese language learning)	Schoolteacher	Consultant (for assaulted and demotivated staff)
Nora	16, 11th grade student (literature section)	Schoolteacher	Stay-at-home-mother
Célia	17, 11th grade student (literature section)	Former professional dancer, choregrapher	Former profesional dancer, director of an opera house
Matthieu	17, 11th grade student	Architect	Architect
Franck	17, 11th grade student (scientific section)	Cardiologist	Healthcare network coordinator
Xavier	17, 11th grade student (technological section)	Firefighter	Childcare assistant
Alexandre	17, 11th grade student (scientific section)	Schoolteacher	Schoolteacher
Coraline	17, 11th grade student (laboratory science and technologies)	Worker in a linery and farmer	Housekeeper
Estelle	17, 12th grade student (scientific section)	Bank employee	School nurse
Octave (Félix's brother)	17, 12th grade student (scientific section)	Sculptor	Sculptor
Cécile	17, 1st year college student (osteopathy)	Executive in a maritime transport company	Private nurse
Nathaniel	17, 11th grade student (literature section, Japanese language learning)	Unknown father	Employee in an employment center
Pierre	17, 11th grade student (industrial section)	Postal worker	Schoolteacher

First name	Age and educational stage	Father's occupation	Mother's occupation
Ludivine	17, 11th grade student (literature section)	Tax official	Tax official
Élodie	18, 12th grade student (scientific section)	Biologist	Computer graphic designer
Laurent	18, 12th grade student (scientific section)	Engineer	Stay-at-home-mother
Moussa	18, 12th grade student (economics and social sciences section)	General Practitioner	Pharmacist
Arthur	18, 1st year college student (chemistry)	Commercial executive	Accountant
Ashkan	18, 12th grade student (scientific section)	Fashion brand manager	Stylist
Kalaya	18, 2nd year prepa courses student (physics and chemistry)	Executive	Stay-at-home-mother Real estate
Sophie	18, 12th grade student (technological section)	Cook	Restaurant-owner
Kader	18, 10th grade student	Industrial painter	Stay-at-home-mother
Ladji	18, 12th grade student (vocational training)	Electrician	Stay-at-home-mother
Nabil	18, 12th grade student (economics and social sciences section)	Employee (former manager of a car dealership)	Home-nurse
Maeva (Jérôme's twin sister)	18, 12th grade student (scientific section)	Electrician	Accountant
Jérôme	18, 11th grade student (scientific section)	Electrician	Accountant

First name	Age and educational stage	Father's occupation	Mother's occupation
Juliette	18, 1st year college student (engineer school)	General Practitioner	Pharmacist
Salim	19, 12th grade student (computer science section)	Mason	Cleaning agent
Madji	19, 11th grade student (vocational training)	Driver	Stay-at-home-mother
Aurélien	19, 12th grade student (vocational training in electricity)	Chemical engineer	Social worker
Fleur	19, 1st year college student (Japanese and English)	Employee in a security company	Stay-at-home-mother
Mickael	19, 12th grade student (literature section)	Executive	Executive
Fatou	24, 12th grade student (technological section)	Poultry farmer	Hardware shop manager (in Togo)

APPENDIX 3

Summaries of Some Manga Titles by Those Who Read Them

These summaries highlight differences between readers in the way they put their reading experience into words. Jennifer thus tends to relive the action and to string together the narrative of the highlights and episodes of a series, without putting them into perspective, with a succession of juxtaposed sentences ("and then …, and then …"), whereas other readers contextualize the manga they are talking about more precisely, presenting the general framework of the plot, the characters, in a narrative with a more scholastic form (Schatzmann and Strauss, 1955).[1] We find here the inequalities of educational capital, but also of age and of more or less lasting investment in the passion.

"*Ayashi no Ceres*, it's a much older series, it dates back to before 1999 I think … because it was republished in 1999. And it's the story of a girl who, in fact she's called Aya and she's in a family called Mikage in fact, and she has a twin brother called Aki and on her 16th birthday, she goes to see a fortune teller who tells her that her life is going to be completely dark, I mean it's nice … And when she comes back, she's going to spend the birthday with all the family, and the grandfather arrives and he takes out a hand and the hand, in fact, is that of one of the ancestors who was killed by a nymph whose feather dress was stolen so that she couldn't go back to heaven and, when she sees the hand, Aya sees images and Aki is wounded, he has cuts … And we learn that Aya is in fact the reincarnation of the nymph who almost destroyed the Mikage family and Aki is the reincarnation of the descendant of the ancestor, and so, afterwards, they are going to oppose each other and, in turn, Aya and Aki, they are going to change personalities because, as soon as Aya sees Aki, Aya goes back to being the nymph and, similarly, the ancestor takes Aki's place, I mean it's quite complicated (laughs) …" (Annabelle, 16, father a bank executive, mother a consultant)

"*Bleach*, in fact he is a boy who is able to see spirits and has a very strong psychological strength and so his house gets attacked once by a hollow, they are supernatural creatures, and in fact, they feed on the souls of people. And as his soul, it is very powerful, well they want to kill him. And at this moment, there is a shinigami who arrives, it is some kind of samurais against the hollows, who comes and who is beaten by the hollow and he, he recovers the sword and he kills the hollow in one blow, and after he

1 American sociologists Schatzmann and Strauss highlighted similar social differences in the way tornado witnesses constructed their narratives.

 | DOI:10.1163/9789004548312_010

starts to train and he becomes a great shinigami." (Théo, 15, father a trainer in a transport company, mother a bank employee)

"*Blood*, a hyper bloody thing, there you can say that it is violent. In fact, the argument of the story is that there are some people who have the ability to have invisible arms. The story begins, one of these people escapes, she had a helmet on to prevent her from using her arms, and she's walking around naked, the girl, and she's got pink hair, blood red, and no summons, we see her, she's shot at with machine guns and heavy weapons, and strangely enough no bullets hit her, you see the bullets ricocheting around. At one point, there's a silly girl—because in manga you always have patterns like that—completely silly that comes out and her head turns in front of the other girl, and you have more than just her head hanging off. Something pretty violent, and you know it's a hand because, when he passes the head of security, who didn't want to shoot on sight, you have the door opening, you have blood getting on the doorknob, and you have a hand, which, which, you have a handprint on the back of the head, who is one of the only survivors." (Franck, 17, father a cardiologist, mother a healthcare network coordinator)

"*Chocola & Vanilla*, the story is about two girls who are witches in their world and they want to become the queen, and then they're going to say, 'You're in competition. To become queen, you have to collect as many hearts as possible from boys, they have to fall in love with you. The more pink the heart is, the more points they get. But to do that, you have to go to the human world'. So there you have it. The queen of the witch world is Vanilla, her mother. Chocola's mom, she's going to … Chocola, we don't talk about her parents at first. It's in the end it's … Chocola and Vanilla go back to the human world. That's it. And then, they meet a man named Lovin I think. Afterwards, he's going to tell them how it's going to work. He's going to say, 'I'm your tutor from now on in the human world'. After that, they're going to be in a school, in a middle school and that's it, then after … After … the more the days go by, the more … After we discover that the witch world, it's in danger. Because there are … the … the … for the world … There are the ogres, they are evil people. Then they want to conquer the world of magic and after the queen, she will do everything but she will need the help of all the people of the magic world. Then after that, there is one of the villains called Pierre who enters the human world to try to conquer it. But he tried but he won't be able to because Vanilla and Chocola will stop him. But then, as the episodes go on, Chocola will fall in love with him. Afterwards he's going to do a lot … Afterwards Pierre is going to try to do everything to get his heart back because that's actually when you … in their world, when you get a witch's heart back, that person becomes powerful, they have a lot more power and he wants that, the power … And there are lots of problems like that." (Jennifer, 15, father a veterinarian, stay-at-home mother)

"*Chrno Crusade*, ah! well, a girl in the class over there lent it to me last year … And this is the story of a girl who has made a pact with a demon and is looking for her brother actually. And every time she uses ... actually, she has some kind of watch and every time she uses the demon's power, her life time, it goes down, and actually, in the end, she dies (laughs)." (Annabelle, 16, father a bank executive, mother a consultant)

"*Chrno Crusade*, it's about a 16-year-old nun, who is an orphan, or whatever happened to her, who befriends a demon, and together they go hunting other demons. It turns out that they fall in love, etc., and the demon that she's attached to is very powerful and the others are looking for him. And, so this is the story of their fight against the bad guys (smiles)." (Kalaya, 18, parents executives)

"*DNA* is about a man who meets someone from the future who tells him that in the future he is a sex symbol, that he will have more than 100 children in Japan. In fact, she's going to shoot him to change his DNA so that he doesn't become a mega playboy. And so, in fact, unfortunately, there is a manipulation in the future that makes him become a mega playboy. In fact, it is on five volumes. But he realizes that he knows how to handle it, he knows how to control ... He has superpowers at the same time, that he can control. So, he already knows his future and he's going to change it." (Coraline, 17, father a worker, mother a cleaning lady)

"*Darren Shan* is about a kid who loves spiders. He has a friend who also loves them. At one point, he's on the street, it's night, he meets a man who gives him a flyer about a freak show, and he goes with his friend. And the person who gave him the paper, he does a show for him. He is a spider trainer. The hero's friend, he would like to turn into a vampire. And whoever has the spider, he's a vampire." (Marie, who has a spider tattoo on her arm ..., 14, father an accountant, mother a cleaning lady)

"*Death Note,* in fact basically the idea is: there are the gods of death, who are called shinigami. And I think it's funny, I call them sewer clowns because they're hideous, they have big scars, big eyes, pale skin, leather armor, they're scary. In fact, they have the 'Death Note', it is a notebook where they write the name of a human, and this human dies just afterwards. And a bored shinigami—because they're not allowed to kill anyone, there are rules—uh ... deliberately loses his notebook in the human world, and a human finds the notebook. A guy, who is an ordinary student in a high school that must exist, in Tokyo I think, finds this notebook, tries. At first, he does it in the name of justice, for example on TV, he sees a terrorist, he writes down his name in the Death note, the terrorist dies within thirty seconds. At the beginning, he does quite commendable things, like that, he gets rid of the ... the criminals, but very quickly, you realize that he starts to think he is a god, since he has the right of life and death. Normally, we judge this kind of people ... And he deviates, he starts to kill uh, several people ... When the shinigami comes to him, he tells him: 'You're making a carnage'. He thinks that the shinigami is going to kill him, but in fact, it amuses him, he had done it for that, to see the chaos. And the guy has a rival, who wants to catch him, uh, he's the only one he can't kill, his nickname is L., he's kind of a detective." (Franck, 17, father a cardiologist, mother a healthcare network coordinator)

"*Detective Conan*, he's a teenager named Shinichi, he's Japanese. He wants to become the greatest detective in the world in modern times. And then one day, he was with a friend, her name is Ran. He went to an amusement park. Then he discovered a dead man. It's mysterious then after, and he followed them. Afterwards, he found out that there were gun traffickers. There was money and everything. He was going in and then another person hit him on the head, then afterwards gave him a poison, the poison of their organization. Then he forced him to drink it and then he drank it. After that he felt very bad, he felt very bad, his eyes split and he became a child of seven years old. Afterwards, he did everything to find out who gave him this poison. Then there is a man, he has several gadgets, glasses, a bow tie that transforms the voice, a lot of stuff. And at the same time, he … with the help of one of the victims even if he is not very well known, he is Ran's father. And then he too, thanks to him … he solves cases. And afterwards, as he is bad, the one who is bad, he takes his place with his voice, he sums it up and afterwards, it's as if he's the one who's talking but in fact it's Conan. That's it. There are lots of adventures like that." (Jennifer, 15, father a veterinarian, stay-at-home mother)

"*Devil Devil*, it's a new collection that just, you know, it just, it's the first volume. Basically, it's an angel and a demon, you know, who have been fighting you know since the beginning of time. And they meet, then, you know, they fell on earth, and they killed two kids … And actually, they went into the bodies of the two kids, and you know, now, they're trying to find a way to get out of the bodies, and go back … There you go, and frankly, it's good, it's fun. There you go." (Kader, 18, father an industrial painter, stay-at-home mother)

"*D.Gray-Man*, he's a young man with a gun in him. His left arm, well, he has a crucifix on it. It kind of leads to religious stuff. This guy, he met a marshal. Marshals are the ones who command a tower. They're exorcists, actually. Because in them there are demons that only turn when they are hungry. When they are hungry, they eat other people. And then they have stage one, stage two, three. And when they get to the ultimate stage, they have much more power, and they kill many more people. They can think. Because when they're at stage one, they don't think too much, they destroy everything in their trail. And so the young man, he wants to enter the congregation of the shadow, that's the name of the clan that will allow him to develop his soul, and know how to use it to the fullest to destroy, I mean purify the Akuma. He wants to become an exorcist to help the world." (Nayir, 16, father a delivery driver, mother a housekeeper)

"*D.Gray-Man*, it's in a XIXth century a little bit parallel, a little bit dark, gothic, but still with some humor, so it's quite nice. And so, they are exorcists who fight against the millennial Count who, seven thousand years ago, was responsible for the flood, and who is … The millennial Count creates what we call Akuma, which are some kind of killing machines, that he creates due to the despair of people when they have lost a loved one. He offers to bring their loved one back to life, but finally, that loved one becomes an Akuma, and takes the body of the person who called them to join the humans, and so it makes a little bit of a mess, since the more they kill, the more they evolve, so … So that's the job of the exorcists, who are people who are compatible with innocence, and so that's their job, and they're the only ones who can kill Akuma." (Célia, 17, mother an opera director, father a choreographer)

"*Full Metal Alchemist* is the story of two little boys, they lose their mother, and in fact they make alchemy to try to make her live again. Unfortunately, it doesn't work. So, there's the big brother who loses his leg and his arm, and the little brother who loses his body completely. He will gather in an armor, and the big brother, thanks to one of his friends, will make a mechanical hand, a mechanical arm, and then a mechanical leg. They're going to look for answers, and at the same time they're going to do a little bit of alchemy to help themselves and to help others; they're going on the road to get to the final goal, which is to revive their mother." (Coraline, 17, father a worker, mother a cleaning lady)

"*Fullmetal Panic!* Uh … it's completely silly (laughs) … It's the story of the girl … I mean, it's a girl that's a little more mundane but apparently has a memory … a repressed memory and there are people who are interested in it so … she's given a bodyguard who is very good at missions but absolutely not good at social life so he shows up on the first day of school with a gun in his bag … There's a lot of stuff going on like that. He spies her on a date … and he gets a plush costume except as soon as he puts the plush costume on, it's actually a kind of Bonta, it's a hamster actually, and every time he talks with the Bonta thing, he starts talking fumoffu, basically. And it's incomprehensible, but he likes the suit, so finally, he keeps it on and he puts mecha stuff in it, so he can shoot enemies … And every time he puts it on, he's forced to change his voice, so he talks in fumoffu … It's just that he makes noises like that and … At one point he meets a guy who's a little weird, he was sad that he didn't see a ponytail anymore and so he was tying the hair of the girls in a ponytail with barbed wire and glue and he actually has a pony costume, he's a pony … And there's a moment where the two characters are talking fumoffu and pony and you're skeptical watching this because you don't understand anything (laughs) … There you go. It's silly so I like it." (Annabelle, 16, father a bank executive, mother a consultant)

"*Fushigi Yugi*, it's about a girl in fact, she has … She goes into a book, she goes to the library, she looks at a book like we look at and then I don't know, she talks through this book, then she encounters a world I don't know an imaginary world and everything where she … In fact, she's a priestess and everything in the book, it's a super beautiful story, I mean at least I liked this story very much." (Lydia, 15, father a technical executive and mother a baker)

"*Gunslinger Girl*, it's about a secret society in Italy, where basically it's little girls that were either raped or half-dead … so they were … or cybered. So, there you go, it was going around, and the girl was victimized by this kind of stuff. So, they were taking people who were dead so to say, they rebuild them, they turn them into cyborgs. And the little girls, they fight the mafias where … In short, they're in the service of the government. And what's the … I mean it's not the most interesting thing, but what's nice is that they're all related to what's called 'their brother', who's a normal government man who takes care of them. And what's weird is that the little girls, they lose the memory of their lives before and so they get attached to their brother very quickly and it's weird. They have a little bit of a strange relationship and that's what's really fun." (Kalaya, 18, parents executives)

"*Icarus*, he's a baby that's born and he levitates. And so, they put him in a research center, and he, well, what he dreams about is seeing the sky, being able to fly as he wants. And he ends up running away with a … well with one of the scientists who helps him escape. And it's a nice story." (Matthieu, 17, parents architects)

"*Imadoki*, that too, it's actually, it's a girl, she made a pact with another girl, with another girl she made a pact that finally one day there's … some kind of … well a demon, I don't know what, a monster, it came to her, it killed her parents and she, afterwards, to defend herself and everything, she made a pact with it and everything: he gave her ten years to live and one day, she had to live only ten years. Afterwards, she met a little boy and everything, he helped her, in fact he's a magician, this little boy is a magician, and he helped her to uh how to say, he has powers, he killed the demon that … that had taken her life and then bah! she could live her whole life." (Lydia, 15, father a technical executive and mother a baker)

"*Inu-Yasha* is a high school female student who lives in our time. She accidentally falls into a well, which takes her back to the time of feudal Japan. And there, everyone believes that she is the reincarnation of a priestess, whereas apparently, it is not only a simple reincarnation. And she frees a half-demon from a spell that has imprisoned him for fifty years." (Bastien, 15, father a biologist, mother an engineer)

"*Jackals*, in fact, is an orphan who was taken in by his uncle, and he becomes a hitman. In a city where it's terror, there are two gangs that control the city, the police are corrupt, the mayor too." (Bastien, 15, father a biologist, mother an engineer)

"*Kekkaishi*, in fact, is the story of a young man who must defend a school. Because underneath this school, there is a shrine. From his grandfather's lineage, from father to son, who have to protect this place. There's a rival family, too. It's only girls, it's from mother to daughter. And also who have to protect. The grandfather of the little one, and the grandmother of the little one, well they are rivals, while the two little ones, they help each other every time. Then there are monsters that come to attack the place, and the two little ones have to protect it." (Nayir, 16, father a delivery driver, mother a housekeeper)

"*Kenichi* is the story of a boy who was being abused and wanted to become strong in fact, because he met a girl, whom he fell in love with, and he wants to protect her. But by trying to protect her he meets powerful opponents and … it makes for a great story.

Summarized like that, it sounds rather silly and simple but you have to read it afterwards, to get an idea. You can't judge a manga by its cover (laughs)." (Pierre, 17, father a postman, mother a retired schoolteacher)

"*Last quarter* is a story between a girl, a girl named Eve and a guy. And on the day they're supposed to meet, the girl, she's been in a car accident, and the boy the same way has been in a car accident while picking up his cat I think. And then, I don't know, they're ... Nobody's found them yet but uh, I think the story goes ... They're both in another world, in two different worlds, but they're trying to find each other actually." (Fatou, 24, father a poultry farmer, mother a shopkeeper)

"*Love Berrish,* it's in two volumes and she's a girl who keeps getting knocked back (laughs). She's a high school student, I think she changed high schools so that her reputation wouldn't follow her, and she actually wants to live a normal life and, unluckily, she ends up in the sophomore council, if I remember correctly, and the problem is that they're all a little bit weird ... And so, all of a sudden ... It's a bit of a special school with weird rules, like there's a girl dormitory, a boy dormitory, and the girls and the boys aren't allowed to meet, that's kind of normal but ... And so, there are stories going on, they're trying to solve conflicts, well it's kind of fun (laughs)." (Annabelle, 16, father a bank executive, mother a consultant)

"*Love Hina,* the story is quite funny, it's a boy who fails all his studies actually. He wants to enter the Todai, and every time he fails. So, he goes to boarding school, to his grandmother's boarding school, to be the director, except that it's a boarding school for girls, so uh (laughs) ... At first, the girls don't accept him. It kind of makes for accidents, with the bathing (laughs): he gets in, he ends up with girls, and then he gets hit, that's it." (Nathaniel, 17, raised by his mother, an unemployement office employee)

"*Love Hina* was half a love story, two kids who promised each other that in a few years they would end up in the most prestigious university in Tokyo. The problem is that the boy was a real idiot, that he took the entrance exam three or four times without ever passing, and he finds himself, since he has no money, in a boarding house for young girls that he inherited from his grandmother, and he has to more or less manage it with the six girls who live in it. And it's a pretty difficult management because he's a very clumsy person, and not very smart. And all the while there's this story behind it, he's trying to find the girl that he made the promise to, it's really quite funny actually." (Estelle, 17, father a bank clerk, mother a school nurse)

"*Mär,* it's quite complicated because it's about a young man, he's at school, and every day he has a dream of another parallel world, where animals don't exist and everyone has superpowers. And that's it, and when he tells his dreams, everyone doesn't believe him except for one friend of his. And then, one day, while he was in class, a door will open to enter this world." (Noé, 11, father a religious books publisher, stay-at-home mother)

"*Marmalade Boy*, it's a teenage girl who finds out that her parents want to break up. Then afterwards, they say here, her parents, they invite other parents ... The parents of the girl, her name is Miki, they want to get to know each other and everything, and they want to get married actually. But she, her parents, they want to be separated. Then after, she finds there, they have a child. After she sees, after he is called Yuu I think, she falls in love with him. Then, after her parents, they tell her: 'You must not fall in love with him' and everything. After that it's difficult, because, from one day to the next, they tell her, 'We're not breaking up' but she doesn't understand why. Then there are other issues: her best female friend, she falls in love with her homeroom teacher who is young but there is ... There is a difference of age between the two. Then afterwards, she discovers that the school, they are shocked. At first, she's not going to understand but then she's going to understand her. Miki, she will understand her friend. That's it. Afterwards, the boy, Miki, when she fell in love with him, afterwards he will also fall in love with her. But then, he does everything to find his father because he discovered that they were not his real parents. So, he will do everything to find his father. After there are clues, he discovers a boy called, I don't know what his name is. His friend, he has a father and he's going to tell him: 'Are you my father?'. He's going to tell him: 'No, I'm sorry, I'm not your father. I knew your parents very well' and all: 'It's another man who is your father'. Then afterwards, there are lots of problems like that because it's difficult. And then there's a point where he's going to find out, he's going to believe that she's actually his sister. And he's going to see pictures because his parents, they were with Miki's parents, they were together and everything. And then he's going to say that means I'm his sister. So after that, he's going to do everything to forget about it and everything. But he's going to hide the truth from Miki. Then she'll say, 'Why? It's because of me' and everything? He says: 'I'm sorry. Then she couldn't take it. Afterwards, at one point, he said: 'I'm fed up, I have to tell you the truth, I can't take it anymore' and he told her. She says: 'It's not possible'. They went to their parents, explaining the situation. 'Why did you lie to us all these years?' And then he says, 'No it's not true, you're kidding yourself'. Afterwards, he explains the situation to them, 'We know we're brothers and everything.—No, she's not your sister. You can go on loving her' and then that's it. It's a family story really. I like stories like that." (Jennifer, 15, father a veterinarian, stay-at-home mother)

"*Miss Oishi, twenty-eight years old and single*, she's a girl, a normal young woman who ... who works and she's still single like all people, like all women her age, she still hasn't found love so she's looking, she's looking for true love I mean, but sometimes she finds some but it doesn't work out and then, etc., etc. Afterwards, there will be drama about it and everything." (Fatou, 24, father a poultry farmer, mother a shopkeeper)

"*Nana*, well, you'll think it's a little weird at first. Well, it's two girls, they're both called Nana, they met on a train. Yeah, that's right, they met on a train. They were sitting next to each other. Well, afterwards, as they are the same age, they talked a lot together. Afterwards, they were going to meet again, they were going to share a flat, it was chance that made them share a flat. Afterwards, one of them is a singer, she is very famous. And the other one … Well, she's a girl who works, like everyone else. And then, there are lots of stories. She'll meet people from the girl's group and everything. And there will be a long story." (Leila,15, unemployed father, mother a janitor)

"*Naruto* is the story of a young boy who lost his parents during a battle with a demon called 'the nine-tailed fox'. And in fact, he doesn't know that the demon has been locked inside him. So, he realizes that people are not very nice to him. So, he wants to stand out from the others, and become hokage, that is to say a great master of magic. And ninja. A great ninja. So, in fact, we are going to follow his adventures, with three other people: his master, Sakura, and then I don't remember … Sasuke. So, in fact, we'll have all their adventures. It's quite funny, as it can be very hard sometimes." (Coraline, 17, father a worker, mother a cleaning lady)

"*Negima*, actually, he's a little 10-year-old boy who has magician powers. In fact, he is doing a kind of internship in Japan. He has to teach English to Japanese girls in a high school. A whole series of hilarious and spectacular adventures are about to happen to him." (Hacine, 15, father a textile company manager, stay-at-home mother)

"*Paradise Kiss* is the story of … children … teenagers in high school, in a … in fashionable places, a normal student from a basic senior high school, I must say, who meets students from fashionable high schools, and that's where the story begins … a love story: a group has been formed, and in the middle of the group there is a love story." (Fatou, 24, father a poultry farmer, mother a shopkeeper)

"*Rave*, he's a kid who also wants to follow in his father's footsteps, and in fact, his father he thinks that he was attacked by an evil brotherhood. And in fact, he's going to fight them but the problem is that he realizes that he's the one who created it but left it, and with his father, he fights the leader of this big guy and he kills him, but he learns that the other leader, it was his father's best friend and that he had a son who is very powerful, but on the side of evil. And, basically, they are the two opposites." (Théo, 15, father a trainer in a transport company, mother a bank employee)

"*Reborn* is the story of the mafia in fact. And the boy in question is the tenth godfather. He's the future sponsor of a crime organization. And he's sent a … private tutor, to teach him. And this tutor is a baby, named Reborn. A baby. A baby assassin. Yes, it's quite, quite special, yes. And in fact, the baby, he is able to kill him with a bullet of last will. If he doesn't have a will at that moment, he dies. If he has a will, his will comes true. So, there you go. It's pretty special. So, at first it was really lame. And then it was good." (Pierre, 17, father a postman, mother a retired schoolteacher)

"*Rose hip Rose* is kind of a police action series. It's a young girl, Kasumi, who was in fact an ally in a paramilitary organization, but illegal and which was fighting against the power. And so, since her early childhood, she was educated by the paramilitaries, which makes her have overdeveloped reflexes, an incredible capacity for destruction. And she is hired by the police to fight against terrorists, because precisely, she ran away, because she was tired of brainwashing. So afterwards, she left. And so, the police recruited her to fight against terrorist organizations, except that she has somewhat muscular methods, so there is always destruction, but she never kills anyone, because she uses plastic bullets, because she values human life in fact … So, there you have it … And then in the end …, it finishes, she meets up with a female childhood friend, and they live happily ever after (laughter)." (Nathaniel, 17, raised by his mother, an unemployement office employee)

"*Sakura* is a fifth-grader who discovers a mysterious book at home. It is a book, then it makes strange noises. She enters the library room, she discovers a book. Then it's a book of cards. It's called Clow. Then she opens it, then she says a for-, she didn't know, she says a magic formula. She repeated it, repeated it out loud. And it happened, the books started to move and the cards flew away. And in fact, they have a lot of power and they were locked in a book. Then afterwards, there is a guardian, the guardian of the animal. Afterwards, she says to him, 'What kind of animal are you?' and everything. He said, 'I'm the keeper of the book. You have to become a card captor'. Afterwards, at first, she wanted to say, 'No no, I can't, I'm a little girl' and everything. He said 'You have to'. So then there's her best friend, she's going to tell him, she says, 'That's great', and everything. And they have to you know, they have to save the world actually. The cards afterwards, they do a lot of the … They cause a lot of trouble to the earth. To the planet that's it." (Jennifer, 15, father a veterinarian, stay-at-home mother)

"*Samurai Champloo*, it's a girl who is a waiter in a tea shop, in a city in Japan, and one day there are important guys who come … I mean they are people who are a bit … it's the son of a how to say? Of the governor for example, who comes with his escort and I don't know what, and like, she spills tea on him, and he wants to cut her hand off. So, there's a guy who comes in, with a very bestial look, his name is Mugen, and he looks at her … Oh no! before she spills the tea on him, he says to her: 'If you want me to get rid of these guys, you give me three hundred rios', that was the currency at the time, very expensive too, 'and I'll get rid of these guys'. And she says no to all that, she leaves, and the guy wants to cut her hand, she says: 'Ok for three hundred rios', she has the sword there and she says: 'Ok'. So he gets up and he dismantles everyone, in short he dismantles them and he says: 'You guys are too lame for me, bring me a guy who can really fight'. And so, he starts counting on the fingers of the governor's son by breaking each finger like this (he mimes) and so they run to find a guy, a samurai who was very strong, but these samurais, they got dismantled by another guy, so they put him down too, and there, there's this guy who comes back to the tea house to drink (laughs), and there, they both see each other, he goes: 'Ah you're the guy, no I'm out of here'. And anyway, they both start fighting and the tea room burns down. The girl gets out, and they all die, the others, and in the end the two of them, they get caught by the police and they manage to escape, and they end up the three of them together. She says, 'Yeah, since I managed to get you to escape, and you burned down my tea shop, you have to help me find my father'. And so, the three of them start going on the road and there, that's where the whole story starts. There's some good plots, because it's a journey, it's fun." (Ashkan, 18, father a director of a clothing brand, mother a stylist)

"*Seraphic Feather*, it's very old, I mean it dates back to the nineties. It's a science-fiction story, set on the moon. Humans have discovered stones, three special stones in fact, the emblemsides, which develop tele-psychic powers on certain human beings, and so ... The story is very confused, because afterwards there is a struggle precisely to take back the emblemsides, and at the same time, there is a struggle on the moon precisely for the moon's independence. The Selenites want to be independent, while the Earth wants to keep the moon as a colony, so there is a small war. The emblems are used in this war because they increase the tele-psychic powers, so there is a person in the shadow who manipulates other human beings, who creates attacks everywhere on earth. So there you have it. The story itself is quite confusing, so it's quite difficult to explain, but ..." (Nathaniel, 17, raised by his mother, an unemployement office employee)

"*To Love Trouble* (To Love Ru) is about an alien who falls to earth, and her father wants her to get married. And she hides in the house of a human, without doing so on purpose, and this human protects her. And as time goes by, she falls in love with him and everything, and she doesn't want to leave. But this human in question, he's in love with a girl from his class. And there you have it, it's full of little stories like that. And every time, he tries to express his love to this girl, and ... Then everyone realizes, everyone knows that he's in love with her, and she doesn't know it. And she's in love with him. So, there you go. There are often love stories like that, triangle loves, we'll say that. So, there you go. It's such and such a girl loves such and such a guy, and that guy loves another girl and ..." (Pierre, 17, father a postman, mother a retired schoolteacher)

"*Tsubasa Reservoir Chronicle*, it's not the same at all, this is a shonen this time. It's, it's spread over ... There must be twenty-four volumes ... and it's the story of a princess in a country ... Well, in the manga, there are several worlds, and in each world, we find the same people who have the same appearance, who have the same soul but who don't have the same actions. It's the same background but it doesn't come out the same in each one. And the princess, in fact, opens the ruins and she acquires the power to travel in dimensions except that there is going to be a kind of accident and in fact, she had feathers in her back that appeared, they are going to scatter and it is her memory and so ... There's a boy who's in love, who's going to go looking, in different dimensions, for her memory ... But in exchange ... uh ... To allow her to travel in different dimensions, he has to give away the memories that Sakura has of him, so, he ends up bringing back the feathers for a girl that he loves and who will never love him back, actually." (Annabelle, 16, father a bank executive, mother a consultant)

"*Ueki's law* is a boy, normal, a schoolboy like all the others, except that one day, one of his teachers gives him a power, it's a bit weird, to recycle garbage into trees. And in fact, his teacher gave him this power to participate in a contest where all the participants are young people who have powers like that, and the winner, he gets the ultimate power, something like that, he can have all powers, and the teacher becomes God. It's kind of weird (laughs)." (Nora,, 16, father a school teacher, stay-at-home mother)

"*Vampire Knight,* it takes place in an academy that has classes during the day and classes at night. During the day classes, it's normal students and during the night classes, it's vampires. And we follow the story of Yuuki, she is a girl who has amnesia, she doesn't remember when she was three years old … and everything that happened before … and in the snow, there is a vampire who saved her from another vampire who wanted to kill her and she goes to the academy … The vampire who saved her is called Kaname and he knew the director of the academy so he brought her to him, he gave her as a girl in fact, and here it is. And we also follow the story of Zero Kiryu … He's actually a vampire hunter, he's the descendant of a family of vampire hunters, and his parents were killed by a vampire and, so the two of them, Yuuki and Zero, so they're in charge of the protection of the daytime students … to bridge the gap between the daytime class and the nighttime class … since they're actually extremely good looking so all of the girls chase after them …" (Annabelle, 16, father a bank executive, mother a consultant)

"*X* by Clamp, it's the story of dragons and angels. So, I think it's the Seals, it's the Seals and the Angels. The Seals must, want to save the human beings, while the Angels want to save the earth, because the human beings do not have their place on the earth because they are destroying the ecosystem, etc. And in fact, basically, there are supposed to be seven of them, except that there is one who has to choose whether he wants to be a Seal or an Angel, and so in fact as he has a female friend that he loves madly, etc., he wants to become a Seal and he wants to protect the human beings. And the brother of the female friend he's in love with, in fact, is his alter ego, so if he becomes an Angel, he becomes a Seal and vice versa. So, it tells the story of the choice and how he's going to save the world. He chooses to be a Seal throughout the series, but in the end, he chooses to be an Angel. And as a result, he manages to save human beings, in the series." (Kalaya, 18, parents executives)

"*Zetman* is the story of a young man who has a power, he can turn himself into a demon. This demon, it was built by people and it was put in the body of a child. And now, the people who built it, they are looking for it to try to make several more to create the perfect child. But this child, he's not going to let himself be made, because as time goes on, he grows up, and he understands why nobody likes him and all that. There's the kid who wants to defend himself, but on the other hand, he kills everyone, even those around. Even though they know that the kid is helping the others, he kills them all. He is violent. Except that when he transforms, he's another person, so he can't control himself anymore and that's it." (Nayir, 16, father a delivery driver, mother a housekeeper)

APPENDIX 4

Graphs and Tables About Manga Publishing in France

1 Manga Series and Print Runs of Over 25,000 Copies

de 50 000 to 250 000		de 30 000 to 40 000		de 25 000 to 28 000	
Naruto, t . 46, Kana	250 000	D.Gray-man, t. 18, Glénat	40 000	Blazer Drive, t. 2, Kurokawa	28 000
Naruto, t . 47, Kana	250 000	D.Gray-man, t. 19, Glénat	40 000	Dernier maître de l'air, Ankama	25 000
Naruto, t . 48, Kana	250 000	Pluto, t. 1, Kana	40 000	Switch Girl!!, t. 7, Akata/Delcourt	25 000
Naruto, t . 49, Kana	250 000	Pluto, t. 2, Kana	40 000	Switch Girl!!, t. 8, Akata/Delcourt	25 000
Naruto, t . 50, Kana	250 000	Pluto, t. 3, Kana	40 000	Switch Girl!!, t. 9, Akata/Delcourt	25 000
Naruto, t . 51, Kana	250 000	Bakuman, t. 1, Kana	40 000	Kilari Revolution, t. 4, Glénat	25 000
Twilight, t. 1, Pika	250 000	Bakuman, t. 2, Kana	40 000	Kilari Revolution, t. 5, Glénat	25 000
Fairy Tail, t. 10, Pika	100 000	Black Butler, t. 4, Kana	40 000	Kilari Revolution, t. 6, Glénat	25 000
One Piece, t. 55, Glénat	95 000	Pluto, t. 4, Kana	40 000	Kilari Revolution, t. 7, Glénat	25 000
One Piece, t. 53, Glénat	90 000	Bakuman, t. 3, Kana	40 000	Kilari Revolution, t. 8, Glénat	25 000
One Piece, t. 54, Glénat	90 000	Pluto, t. 5, Kana	40 000	Kilari Revolution, t. 9, Glénat	25 000

 | DOI:10.1163/9789004548312_011

de 50 000 to 250 000		de 30 000 to 40 000		de 25 000 to 28 000	
One Piece, t. 52, Glénat	85 000	Black Butler, t. 5, Kana	40 000	Détective Conan, t. 61, Kana	25 00[illegible]
Fairy Tail, t. 11, Pika	80 000	Bakuman, t. 4, Kana	40 000	Détective Conan, t. 62, Kana	25 00[illegible]
Fairy Tail, t. 12, Pika	80 000	Doubt, t. 3, Ki-Oon	40 000	Détective Conan, t. 63, Kana	25 00[illegible]
Fairy Tail, t. 13, Pika	80 000	Doubt, t. 4, Ki-Oon	40 000	Mashima-en, t. 1, Pika	25 00[illegible]
Fairy Tail, t. 14, Pika	80 000	Saint Seiya: Hadès, t. 10, Kurokawa	40 000	Mashima-en, t. 2, Pika	25 00[illegible]
Fairy Tail, t. 15, Pika	80 000	Soul Eater, t. 12, Kurokawa	40 000	Tsubasa, t. 26, Pika	25 00[illegible]
Fullmetal Alchemist, t. 23, Kurokawa	75 000	Vampire Knight, t. 11, Panini	40 000	Tsubasa, t. 27, Pika	25 00[illegible]
Fullmetal Alchemist, t. 24, Kurokawa	70 000	Vampire Knight, t. 12, Panini	40 000	Monster Soul, t. 1, Pika	25 00[illegible]
Bleach, t. 35, Glénat	60 000	Monster Hunter Orage, t. 1, Pika	40 000	Monster Soul, t. 2, Pika	25 00[illegible]
Bleach, t. 36, Glénat	60 000	Monster Hunter Orage, t. 2, Pika	40 000	Tsubasa, t. 28, Pika	25 00[illegible]
Bleach, t. 37, Glénat	60 000	Monster Hunter Orage, t. 3, Pika	40 000	The Legend of Zelda, t. 5, Soleil	25 00[illegible]
Bleach, t. 38, Glénat	60 000	Monster Hunter Orage, t. 4, Pika	40 000	The Legend of Zelda, t. 6, Soleil	25 00[illegible]
Bleach, t. 39, Glénat	60 000	Dragon Ball Z: Cycle 3, t. 1, Glénat	38 000	The Legend of Zelda, t. 7, Soleil	25 00[illegible]
Soul Eater, t. 7, Kurokawa	55 000	Dragon Ball Z: Cycle 3, t. 2, Glénat	38 000	The Legend of Zelda, t. 8, Soleil	25 00[illegible]
Soul Eater, t. 8, Kurokawa	55 000	Saint Seiya: Hadès, t. 11, Kurokawa	36 000	The Legend of Zelda, t. 9, Soleil	25 000

de 50 000 to 250 000		de 30 000 to 40 000		de 25 000 to 28 000	
Soul Eater, t. 9, Kurokawa	55 000	Negima!, t. 23, Pika	35 000		
Dofus, t. 13, Ankama	50 000	Tsubasa, t. 25, Pika	35 000		
Dofus, t. 14, Ankama	50 000	Negima!, t. 24, Pika	35 000		
Les Années Douces, Casterman	50 000	Saint Seiya: Hadès, t. 12, Kurokawa	34 000		
Hunter X Hunter, t. 27, Kana	50 000	Saint Seiya: Hadès, t. 15, Kurokawa	34 000		
Soul Eater, t. 10, Kurokawa	50 000	Saint Seiya: Hadès, t. 13, Kurokawa	32 000		
Soul Eater, t. 11, Kurokawa	50 000	Dofus Goultard Bazar, Ankama	30 000		
		Maliki, Ankama	30 000		
		Dofus Monster, Ankama	30 000		
		Switch Girl!!, t. 10, Akata/Delcourt	30 000		
		Les Gouttes de Dieu, t. 11, Glénat	30 000		
		Les Gouttes de Dieu, t. 12, Glénat	30 000		
		Les Gouttes de Dieu, t. 13, Glénat	30 000		
		Dragon Ball Z: Cycle 3, t. 3, Glénat	30 000		
		Les Gouttes de Dieu, t. 14, Glénat	30 000		
		Dragon Ball Z: Cycle 3, t. 4, Glénat	30 000		
		Les Gouttes de Dieu, t. 15, Glénat	30 000		

de 50 000 to 250 000		de 30 000 to 40 000		de 25 000 to 28 000	
		Les Gouttes de Dieu, t. 16, Glénat	30 000		
		Black Butler, t. 2, Kana	30 000		
		Black Butler, t. 3, Kana	30 000		
		Pandora Hearts, t. 1, Ki-oon	30 000		
		Pandora Hearts, t. 2, Ki-oon	30 000		
		Pandora Hearts, t. 3, Ki-oon	30 000		
		Pandora Hearts, t. 4, Ki-oon	30 000		
		Blazer Drive, t. 1, Kurokawa	30 000		
		Saint Seiya: Hadès, t. 14, Kurokawa	30 000		
		Negima!, t. 25, Pika	30 000		
		Negima!, t. 26, Pika	30 000		
		Negima!, t. 27, Pika	30 000		
		Negima!, t. 28, Pika	30 000		
		Dragon Ball Perfect, t. 6, Glénat	30 000		
		Dragon Ball Perfect, t. 7, Glénat	30 000		
		Dragon Ball Perfect, t. 8, Glénat	30 000		
		Dragon Ball Perfect, t. 9, Glénat	30 000		
		Dragon Ball Perfect, t. 10, Glénat	30 000		
		Dragon Ball Perfect, t. 11, Glénat	30 000		

2 Chronological References. The Progressive Positioning of the Comics Publishers in the in the World of Manga

1990		*Glénat* (created in 1969)	Publication of *Akira*, by Katsuhiro Otomo
1994		*Tonkam* (created in 1994)	Bought by Delcourt in 2005 (Tonkam is maintained as a distinct manga inprint)
1995	Mangas	Casterman (created in 1777)	Stopped in 1998
1996	J'ai lu mangas	J'ai lu (created in 1958)	Stopped in 2006
1997	*Kana*	Dargaud (created in 1943)/ Média Participations	
2000		*Pika* (created in 2000)	Bought by Hachette Books in 2007 (Pika is maintained as a distinct manga inprint)
2001	Génération Comics (*Panini Manga* from 2006)	Panini (created in 1961)	
2002	*Akata*	Delcourt (created in 1986)	
2002	*Ecritures*	Casterman (created in 1777)	
2002		Végétal Mangas (created in 2002)	Bought by Soleil publishing in 2003
2004		Asuka (created in 2004)	Bought by Kaze Video in 2007, which itself is bought by the Japanese publishers Viz Media Europe in 2009.
2004		*Ki-Oon* (created in 2004)	
2004	*Sakka*	Casterman (created in 1777)	
2004		*Le Lézard noir* (created in 2004)	
2005		*Cornélius* (created in 1991)	
2005	*Kurokawa*	Univers poche (created in 1962)/Editis	
2006	Doki Doki	Bamboo Editions (created in 1997)	
2010	*Kazé Mangas*	Viz Media Europe	

In bold are indicated the publishers active in 2011 and which dominate the manga market (among them, the most important are Kana, Glénat and Kurokawa). In bold italics, the publishers active in 2011 and who publish occasionally manga by authors or graphic graphic novels. Most of them are publishers of "alternative" comics born in the 1990s and 2000s, literary publishers (Le Seuil), or comic book publishers who have developed collections of manga by authors (Sakka, at Casterman). In italics, are indicated publishers who have stopped publishing mangas, manhwas or manhuas.

This table clearly shows a first increase in the number of manga publishers in 1994–1996, and a second explosion in 2002–2006. It also shows a significant number of publishers (especially those specialized in manhwa), a phenomenon of publishing concentration (through buyouts and shareholdings) and the development of "author's manga" from 2002 onwards.

Finally, it should be noted that this chronology does not take into account the few rare mangas published in France before 1990 France before 1990: *Gen d'Hiroshima* published, in an abridged version, in 1983 by Les Humanoïdes then, in 1990, by Albin Michel, under the title *Mourir pour le Japon*, or the mangas pre-published in the magazine *Le Cri qui tue*, founded in 1978.

3 Frequency of Publication of the Series

If the average publication time of a volume of a series is two months and some series can reach more than forty forty tomes, the average series comprises from ten to twenty volumes, while other titles are isolated. Some series have a sustained series are published at a steady pace, with six to seven volumes published each year, which is which is much higher than the rate of publication of Franco-Belgian series. In contrast to the logic of publication in series which holds the reader in suspense over several years (nine years for *Naruto* whose publication is not finished), we can thus underline the positioning of manga publishers who prefer the publication of isolated titles (one-shots), or (one-shots), or collections. This is the case of the collection Écritures at Casterman which favors short series, collections or one-shots (*La Montagne magique* by Jirô Taniguchi released in 2007), Lézard Noir, Vertige Graphic or Cornélius, which publish manga for an adult audience at a rate of a few titles per year (these publishers have respectively published two, three and five titles in 2010).

Title	Publisher	Date of publication of the first volume (French edition)	Date of publication of the last or latest volume (in 2011)	Duration of the publication in months	Number of volumes published	Average periodicity for the publication of a volume (in months)
MW	Tonkam	March 2004	July 2004	5	3	1,6
Baki	Akata	May 2005	August 2010	64	31	2
Beck	Akata	July 2004	July 2010	72	34	2,1
Naruto	Kana	March 2002	November 2011	117	54	2,2
Jackals	Ki-Oon	September 2008	December 2009	16	7	2,3
One Piece	Glénat	September 2000	October 2011	133	58	2,3
Nodame Cantabile	Pika	January 2009	August 2011	32	13	2,5
Fullmetal Alchemist	Kurokawa	September 2005	July 2011	71	27	2,6
Vampire Kngiht	Panini	June 2007	November 2011	54	14	3,9
Nana	Akata	November 2002	October 2009	95	21	4,5
Fruits Basket	Akata	August 2002	November 2007	87	23	3,78
Quartier Lointain	Casterman	September 2002	June 2003	9	2	4,5

Bibliography

Albenga, Viviane. 2007. Le genre de "la distinction": la construction réciproque du genre, de la classe et de la légitimité littéraire dans les pratiques collectives de lecture. *Sociétés contemporaines*, 2(24): 161–176.

Allen, Kate, and John Ingulsrud. 2009. *Reading Japan Cool. Patterns of Manga Literacy and Discourse.* New York: Lexington Books.

Allison, Ann. 2006. *Millenial Monsters. Japanese Toys and the Global Imagination.* Berkeley: University of California Press.

Amsellem-Mainguy, Yaëlle, and Arthur Vuattoux. 2020. *Les jeunes, la sexualité et internet.* Paris : Les Pérégrines.

AnimeLand hors-série 5. 2003.

Azuma, Hiroki. 2008. *Génération Otaku.* Paris: Hachette.

Bacon-Smith, Camille. 1992. *Enterprising Women. Television Fandom and the Creation of Popular Myth.* Philadelphia: University of Pennsylvania Press.

Bahu-Leyser, Emmanuel, and Steve Naumann. 2008. Le shonen nouveau est arrivé !. *AnimeLand XTRA hors-série* 1 : 8–9.

Bakhtine, Mikhaïl. 1968. Rabelais and His World. Cambridge: MIT Press.

Barker, Martin. 2005. The Lord of the Rings and "Identification". A Critical Encounter. *European Journal of Communication* 20 (3): 353–378.

Bastide, Julien. 2004. Le manga adulte : BD réalité. *Bang!* 7: 83–88.

Bastide, Julien, and Anthony Prezman. 2006. *Guide des mangas.* Paris : Bordas.

Baudelot, Christian, Marie Cartier and Christine Détrez. 1999. *Et pourtant ils lisent.* Paris : Seuil.

Baudot, Anne. 2010. Le manga en bibliothèque publique. *Bulletin des bibliothèques de France* 3: 62–66.

Beaty, Bart. 2007. *Unpopular Culture: Transforming the European Comic Book in the 1990s.* Toronto: University of Toronto Press.

Becker, Howard. 1963. *Outsiders. Studies in the Sociology of Deviance.* New York: The Fress Press of Glencoe.

Béliard, Aude-Marie. 2009. Pseudos, avatars et bannières: la mise en scène des fans. *Terrains & Travaux* 1(15) : 191–212.

Benrubi, David-Jonathan. 2009. Et nous ? Enquête sur les consommations culturelles des bibliothécaires. *Bulletin des bibliothèques de France* 4: 6–16.

Berndt, Jaqueline. 2009. Manga and manga. Contemporary Japanese Comics and their Dis/similarities with Hokusai Manga. In *Civilisation of Evolution, Civilisation of Revolution, Metamorphoses in Japan 1900–2000*, edited by Arkadiusz Jabłoński, Stanisław Meyer and Koji Morita, 210–222. Kraków: manggha/Museum of Japanese Art and Technology.

Berndt, Jaqueline (ed.). 2010. *Comics Worlds & the World of Comics: Towards Scholarship on a Global Scale*. Kyoto Seika University: International Manga Research Center.

Besson, Anne. 2004. *D'Asimov à Tolkien. Cycles et séries dans la littérature de genre.* Paris: CNRS Éditions.

Bielby, Denise D., and C. Lee Harrington. 2010. A life course perspective on fandom. *International Journal of Cultural Studies* 13(5): 429–450.

Boilet, Frédéric. 2001. Manifeste de la Nouvelle Manga. Frederic Boilet's website (boilet.net). http://www.boilet.net/fr/nouvellemanga_manifeste_1.html (accessed 5 June 2008).

Boltanski, Luc. 1975. La constitution du champ de la bande dessinée. *Actes de la recherche en sciences sociales* 1(1) : 37–59.

Bosche, Marc. 1996. L'invisible colonisation japonaise. *Le Monde Diplomatique* 513 : 25–26.

Bouissou, Jean-Marie. 2009. Le rire du manga. *Lecture jeune* 130 : 19–22.

Bouissou, Jean-Marie. 2010. *Manga. Histoire et univers de la bande dessinée japonaise.* Arles : Philippe Picquier.

Bouquillard, Jocelyn, and Christophe Marquet (ed.). 2007. *Hokusai Manga.* Paris : Bibliothèque nationale de France/Seuil.

Bourlès, Ludovic, and Yann Nicolas. 2022. *Note de conjoncture*, n°1, Ministère de la Culture.

Bourdieu, Pierre. 1996 [1992]. The Rules of Art. Genesis and Structure of the Literary Field ... Stanford: Stanford University Press.

Brient, Hervé (ed.). 2012. Le yaoi. *Manga 10 000 Images* 1.

Brienza, Casey. 2015. *Global Manga: "Japanese" Comics without Japan?*. London: Routledge.

Brienza, Casey. 2016. *Manga in America. Transnational Book Publishing and the Domestication of Japanese Comics*. London: Bloomsbury.

Brougère, Gille (ed.). 2008. *La ronde des jeux et des jouets*. Paris: Autrement.

Burgos, Martine, Christophe Evans, and Esteban Buch. 1996. *Sociabilités du livre et communautés de lecteurs, trois études sur la sociabilité du livre.* Paris : Éditions de la Bibliothèque publique d'infor- mation/Centre Pompidou.

Cahen, Gérard (ed.). 2001. *Livres de chevet. Pour une nuit, pour une vie*. Paris: Autrement.

Cha, Kai-Ming, and Calvin Reid. 2005. Manga in English: Born in the USA. *Publishers Weekly online*. https://www.publishersweekly.com/pw/by-topic/industry-news/comics/article/29378-manga-in-english-born-in-the-usa.html (accessed 2 February 2004).

Chartier, Roger (ed.). 1985. *Pratiques de la lecture*. Marseille : Rivages.

Chedaleux, Delphine, Myriam Juan and Thomas Pillard (ed.). 2020. Dans l'intimité des publics. *Théorème* 32.

Cicchelli, Vincenzo, and Sylvie Octobre. 2018. *Aesthetico-Cultural Cosmopolitanism and French Youth. The Taste of the World.* London: Palgrave.

Cicchelli, Vincenzo, and Sylvie Octobre. 2021. *The Sociology of Hallyu Pop Culture: Surfing the Korean Wave*. London: Palgrave/MacMillan.

Cino, Carla, Nicolas Penedo, and Méko. 2010. Young seinen. *AnimeLand* 158 : 53.

Cino, Carla. 2009. Le shojo, un marché dans tous ses états", *AnimeLand* 154 : 91.

Cino, Carla. 2008. Le Yaoi. Harlequin au masculine. *AnimeLand* 141 : 45.

Cino, Carla. 2007. Collection Lolita, un péché original. *AnimeLand* 127 : 90.

Collovald, Annie, and Erik Neveu. 2004. *Lire le noir. Enquête sur les lecteurs de récits policiers*. Paris : Bibliothèque Publique d'Information.

Cotelette, Patrick, Christine Détrez, and Charline Pluvinet. 2007. Lectures des filles et des garçons: à propos du Seigneur des anneaux. In *Les jeunes et l'agencement des sexes*, edited by Henri Eckert and Sylvia Faure. Paris : La Dispute.

Court, Martine. 2010. *Corps de fille, corps de garçon: une construction sociale*. Paris : La Dispute.

Dagiral, Éric, and Laurent Teissier. 2008. 24 heures! Le sous-titrage amateur de séries télévisées. In *Les arts moyens aujourd'hui, volume II*, edited by Florent Gaudez, 107–123. Paris, L'Harmattan.

Dayez, Hugues. 2004. *La nouvelle bande dessinée*. Bruxelles : Nifle.

De Muelenaere, Michel, and Martine Vandemeulebroucke. 1997. Dragon Ball affronte la morale et le Code penal. *Le Soir* (online archive). https://www.lesoir.be/art/%252F des-mangas-oses-incitent-a-la-pedophilie-dragon-ball-af_t-19970326-ZoDH8J.html (accessed 22 February 2010).

Détrez, Christine. 2002. *La construction sociale du corps*. Paris: Seuil.

DiMaggio, Paul. 1987. Classification in Art. *American Sociological Review* 52(4): 440–455.

Donnat, Olivier. 2009a. *Les pratiques culturelles de Français à l'ère numérique. Enquête 2008*. Paris : La Découverte/Ministère de la Culture et de la Communication.

Donnat, Olivier. 2009b. Les passions culturelles, entre engagement total et jardin secret. *Réseaux* 1(153) : 79–127.

Duval, Patrick. 1991. Opération Manga. *Télérama* 2141 : 28.

Elias, Norbert. 1969.The Civilizing Process. Oxford : Blackwell.

Eloy, Florence (ed.). 2022. *Comment la culture vient aux enfants : repenser les médiations*. Paris : Ministère de la culture/Presses de Sciences Po.

Erickson, Bonnie. 1996. Class, Culture and Connections. *American Journal of Sociology* 1(102), 217–235.

Evans, Christophe, and Françoise Gaudet. 2012. La lecture de bandes dessinées. *Culture Etudes* 2.

Evans, Christophe (ed.). 2014. *La bande dessinée, quelle lecture, quelle culture ?*. Paris : Editions de la BPI.

Finet, Nicolas (ed.). 2008. *Dico Manga*. Paris : Fleurus.

Flandrin, Laure. 2021. *Le rire. Enquête sur la plus socialisée de toutes nos émotions*. Paris, La Découverte.

François, Sébastien. 2009. Fanf(r)ictions. Tensions identitaires et relationnelles chez les auteurs de récits de fans. *Réseaux* 1(153) : 157–189.

François, Sébastien. 2010. Slash, Yaoi, Boy's Love: subversion ou renouveau du romantisme chez les adolescentes?. *Lecture Jeune* 136 : 12–16.

Gabilliet, Jean-Paul. 2005. Du comic book au graphic novel: l'européanisation de la bande dessinée américaine. *Image and Narrative* 12 http://www.imageandnarrative.be/inarchive/tulseluper/gabilliet.htm (accessed 3 March 2010).

Galbraith, Patrick, Thiam Huat Kam, and Bjorn-Ole Kamm (ed.). 2015. *Debating Otaku in Contemporary Japan*. London: Bloomsbury Academic.

Galbraith, Patrick, and Thomas Lamarre. 2010. Otakuology: A Dialogue. *Mechademia* 5: 360–374.

Galbraith, Patrick. 2009. *The Otaku Encyclopedia*. Tokyo: Kodansha International.

Galland, Olivier. 2006. Jeunes: les stigmatisations de l'apparence. *Économie et statistique* 393–394 : 151–183.

Glévarec, Hervé. 2009. *La culture de la chambre*. Paris : Ministère de la Culture/DEPS.

Gomarasca, Alessandro. 2002. *Poupées, robots, La culture pop japonaise*. Paris : Autrement.

Granjon, Fabien, and Philippe Cardon. 2002. Eléments pour une approche des pratiques culturelles par les réseaux de sociabilités. In *Le(s) public(s). Politiques publiques et équipements culturels*, edited by Olivier Donnat, 93–108. Paris, Presses de la Fondation Nationale des Sciences Politiques.

Granjon, Fabien, and Clément Combes. 2007. La numérimorphose des pratiques musicales. Le cas des jeunes amateurs. *Réseaux* 6–7(145–146) : 291–334.

Gravett, Paul. 2006. *Soixante ans de mangas*. Paris : Éditions du Rocher.

Groensteen, Thierry (ed.). 1993. *L'univers des mangas*. Bruxelles : Casterman, 1993.

Guilbert, Xavier. 2011. Numérologie 2010. Website Du9.org. http://www.du9.org/Numerologie-edition-2010 (accessed 4 June 2011).

Guilbert, Xavier. 2021. *Panorama de la BD en France. 2010–2020*. Paris : Centre National du Livre.

Hammou, Karim. 2012. *Une histoire du rap en France*. Paris : La Découverte.

Hébert, Xavier. 20099. Le style Tezuka: un modèle de narration visuelle. *Manga 10000 Images* 2: 37–76.

Hee, Kyung-Lee. 2009. Between Fan Culture and Copyright Infringement: Manga Scanlation. *Media, Culture and Society* 31 (6): 1011–1022.

Hellekson, Karen, and Kristina Busse. 2006. *Fan Fiction and Fan Communities in the Age of the Internet*. London: Mac Farland & Co.

Héritier, Françoise. 1996. *Masculin/féminin I, La pensée de la différence*. Paris : Odile Jacob.

Ito, Mizuko. 2010. Mobilizing the Imagination in Everyday Play: The Case of Japanese Media Mixes. In *Mashup Cultures*, edited by Stefan Sonvilla-Weiss, 79–97. Berlin: Ambra Verlag.

Ito, Mizuko, Daisuke Okabe, and Izumi Tsuji (ed.). 2012. *Fandom Unbound. Otaku Culture in a Connected Age.* New Haven: Yale University Press.

Jauss, Hans Robert. 1978. *Pour une esthétique de la réception.* Paris : Gallimard.

Jenkins, Henry. 1993. *Textual Poachers: Television Fans and Participatory Culture.* New York: Routledge.

Jenkins, Henry. 2006. *Convergence Culture: Where Old and New Media Collide.* New York: New York University Press.

Julé, Vincent. 2005. Le triangle amoureux. AnimeLand website (animeland.fr). https://animeland.fr/dossier/le-triangle-amoureux/ (accessed 3 march 2010).

Kameniak, Jean-Pierre. 2009. Le rire adolescent. *Lecture Jeune* 130: 5–8.

Kern, Adam. 2006. *Manga from the Floating World. Comicbook Culture and the Kibyōshi of Edo Japan.* Cambridge: Harvard University Press.

Kinsella, Sharon. 1995. Cuties in Japan. In *Women, Media and Consumption in Japan*, edited by Skov Lise and Brian Moeran, 222–225. Richmond: Curzon Press.

Kinsella, Sharon. 2000. *Adult Manga. Culture and Power in Contemporary Japanese Society.* Richmond: Curzon Press.

Koyama-Richard, Brigitte. 2007. *Mille ans de manga.* Paris: Flammarion.

Lahire, Bernard. 2004. *La culture des individus. Dissonances culturelles et distinction de soi.* Paris : La Découverte.

Lardellier, Pascal. 1996. Ce que nous disent les mangas. *Le Monde Diplomatique* 513 : 29–30.

Le Bart, Christian. 2000. *Les fans des Beatles : Sociologie d'une passion.* Rennes : Presses universitaires de Rennes.

Le Bart, Christian. 2004. Stratégies identitaires de fans: l'optimum de différenciation. *Revue française de sociologie* 45(2) : 283–306.

Le Goaziou, Véronique. 2006. *Lecteurs précaires.* Paris : L'Harmattan.

Le Grignou, Brigitte. 1999. *Du côté des publics.* Paris : Economica.

Le Guern, Philippe. 2002. *Les cultes médiatiques. Culture fan et œuvres cultes.* Rennes : Presses Universitaires de Rennes.

Lesage, Sylvain. 2019. *L'Effet livre: métamorphoses de la bande dessinée.* Tours : Preses universitaires François Rabelais.

Lizardo, Omar. 2006. How cultural tastes shape personal networks. *American Sociological Review*, 71(5), 778–807.

Lizé, Wenceslas. 2004. Imaginaire masculin et identité sexuelle. Le jeu de rôle et ses praticiens. *Sociétés contemporaines* 3(55) : 43–67.

Lozerand, Emmanuel. 2005. *Littérature et génie national. Naissance d'une histoire littéraire dans le Japon du XIXe siècle.* Paris: Les Belles Lettres.

Lurçat, Liliane. 1981. *A cinq ans, seul avec Goldorak*. Paris : Syros.

Lurçat, Liliane. 1994. *Le jeune enfant devant les apparences télévisuelles*. Paris : Desclée de Brouwer.

Lurçat, Liliane. 1995. *Le temps prisonnier: des enfances volées par la télévision*. Paris : Desclée de Brouwer.

Macias, Patrick, and Izumi Evers. 2007. *Japanese Schoolgirl Inferno. Tokyo Teen Fashion Subculture Handbook*. San Francisco: Chronicle Books.

Mac Lelland, Mark, Kazumi Nagaike, Katsuhiko Suganuma, and James Welker (ed.). 2015. *Boys Love Manga and Beyond*. Jackson: University Press of Mississipi.

McRobbie, Angela. 1989. Second Hand Dresses and the Role of the Ragmarket. In *Zoot Suits and Second-Hand Dresses*, edited by Angela Mc Robbie, 23–49. London: HarperCollins Publishers.

Maigret, Éric. 1995. Strange grandit avec moi. Sentimentalité et masculinité chez les lecteurs de bandes dessinées de super-héros. *Réseaux* 13 (70) : 79–103.

Maigret, Éric. 1999. Le jeu de l'âge et des générations: culture BD et esprit manga. *Réseaux* 92–93 : 241–260.

Mauger, Gérard, Claude Poliak and Bernard Pudal. 1999. *Histoires de lecteurs*. Paris : Nathan.

Mercklé, Pierre. 2017. *Une traversée de l'adolescence. Culture, classe, réseaux*. Mémoire de recherche original, habilitation à diriger des recherches.

Metton-Gayon Céline, Fatima Aziz, Hugues Paris, and François Jost. 2009. Internet, cinéma et télévision. De quoi rient les adolescents?. *Lecture jeune* 130 : 13–16.

Mitchell, Claudia, and Jacqueline Reid-Walsh. 2008. *Girl Culture: An Encyclopedia*. Westport: Greenwood Press.

Miyamoto, Hirohito. 2003. The Stratyfing Process of the Notion of Manga: From the Early Modern Age to the Modern Age in Japan. *Bijutsushi. Journal of the Japan Art History Society* 52(2): 319–334.

Montmasson-Michel, Fabienne. 2020. Les toupies *Beyblade* et la *Reine des Neiges* à l'école du langage : fabriques du genre et des rapports sociaux de classe à l'école maternelle. *L'orientation scolaire et professionnelle* 49(2) : 313–337.

Murakami, Haruki. 2006. *Kafka sur le rivage*. Paris : Belfond.

Monnot, Catherine. 2009. *Petites filles d'aujourd'hui. L'apprentissage de la féminité*. Paris : Autrement.

Moulin, Caroline. 2005. *Féminités adolescentes. Itinéraires personnels et fabrication des identités sexuées*. Rennes : Presses Universitaires de Rennes.

Nouhet-Roseman, Joëlle. 2011. *Les mangas pour jeunes filles, figures du sexuel à l'adolescence*. Toulouse : ERES.

Octobre, Sylvie, Christine Détrez, Pierre Mercklé and Nathalie Berthomier. 2010. *L'enfance des loisirs. Trajectoires communes et parcours individuels de la fin de l'enfance à la grande adolescence*. Paris : DEPS.

Octobre, Sylvie. 2014. *Des pouces et des neurones. Les cultures juvéniles de l'ère médiatique à l'ère numérique*. Paris : La Documentation Française.

Pasamonik, Didier. 2007. Japan Expo est une fenêtre ouverte sur la culture asiatique. ActuaBD website. http://www.actuabd.com/Jean-Francois-Dufour-Japan-Expo-est-une-fenetre-ouverte-sur-la-culture-asiatique (accessed 2 February 2011).

Pasquier, Dominique. 1999. *La culture des sentiments. L'expérience télévisuelle des adolescents*. Paris : Maison des sciences de l'homme.

Pasquier, Dominique. 2005. *Cultures lycéennes. La tyrannie de la majorité*. Paris: Autrement.

Passeron, Jean-Claude. 1991. *Le raisonnement sociologique*. Paris : Nathan.

Penedo, Nicolas. 2011. L'art délicat de l'achat de mangas. *AnimeLand* 176 : 66–67.

Penedo, Nicolas. 2010. Le yaoi en France. Un an après. *AnimeLand* 165 : 66.

Petit, Michèle. 2008. *L'art de lire, ou comment résister à l'adversité*. Paris : Belin.

Petit, Aurélie (ed.). 2021. *Anime Streaming Platform Wars*. The Platform Lab: Concordia University Research Group.

Pigeat, Aurélien. 2012. Le scantrad aujourd'hui : Mafia Blues ?. In *Les Acteurs du livre*, edited by Sylvie Ducas, 24–36. Paris : Nicolas Malais éditeur.

Pham, Bruno. 2011. Le manga au féminin: shojo/josei, la frontière floue. *Manga 10 000 Images* 3 : 81–92.

Piault, Fabrice. 2005. Les pièges de la course aux droits. *Livres Hebdo* 602 : 23–24.

Proulx, Serge. 1998. *Accusé de réception. Le téléspectateur construit par les sciences sociales*. Paris: L'Harmattan.

Prough, Jenifer. 2011. *Straight from the heart. Gender, Intimacy, and the Cultural Production of Shōjo Manga*. Honolulu: University of Hawai'i Press.

Radway, Janice. 1984. *Reading the Romance. Women, Patriarchy, and Popular Literature*. Chapel Hill: The University of North Carolina Press.

Ratier, Gilles. 2011. *Une année de bandes dessinées sur le territoire européen, rapport annuel*. Paris : Association des critiques et journalistes de bandes dessinées.

Raviv, Amiram, David Bartal, ALona Raviv, and Asaf Ben-Horin. 1996. Adolescent Idolization of Pop Singers: Causes, Expressions and Reliance. *Journal of Youth and Adolescence* 25 (5): 631–650.

Raynal, Marie-Saskia, Mathias Hayek, and Méko. 2004. La distinction des genres. *Le Virus Manga* 3.

Reinhard, CarrieLynn D., Julia E. Largent, and Bertha Chin. 2020. *Eating Fandom: Intersections Between Fans and Food Cultures*. London: Routledge.

Renard, Fanny. 2011. *Les lycéens et la lecture: entre habitudes et sollicitations*. Rennes: Presses universitaires de Rennes.

Roueff, Olivier. 2013. *Jazz, les échelles du plaisir. Intermédiaires et culture lettrée en France au XXe siècle*. Paris : La Dispute.

Roure, Benoît. 2021. Manga : la nouvelle euphorie. *Livres Hebdo*, (en ligne : https://www.livreshebdo.fr/article/mangas-la-grande-euphorie).

Sabre, Clothilde. 2009. Être vendeur, être fan: une cohabitation difficile. L'exemple d'une boutique spécialisée dans le manga. *Réseaux* 1(153) : 129–156.

Sabre, Clothilde. 2016. Holidaying in Japan, Falling in love with Japan. From pop culture to tourism imaginary. In *Tourism Imaginaries at the Disciplinary Crossroads: Place, Practice, Media*, edited by Maria Gravari-Barbas and Nelson Graburn, 163–179. New York: Routledge.

Sakai, Cécile. 2000. *Histoire de la littérature populaire japonaise*. Paris : L'Harmattan.

Satomi, Ishikawa. 2007. *Seeking the Self: Individualism and Popular Culture in Japan*. Bern: Peter Lang.

Schatzmann, Leonard, and Anselm Strauss. 1955. Social class and modes of communication. *American Journal of Sociology* 60: 329–338.

Scott, James. 1990. *Domination and the Arts of Resistance: Hidden Transcripts*. New Haven: Yale University.

Sigal, Den. 2003. Animes et épopées. *AnimeLand* 90 : 63–67.

Sigal, Den. 2006. *Grapholexique du manga*. Paris : Eyrolles.

Singly, François de. 2006. *Les Adonaissants*. Paris : Armand Colin.

Steinberg, Marc. 2012. *Anime's Media Mix. Franchising Toys and Characters in Japan*. Minneapolis: University of Minnesota Press.

Suvilay, Bounthavy. 2004. Robot géant, de l'instrumentalisation à la fusion. *Belphégor* 3(2).

Suvilay, Bounthavy. 2006. Comédie sentimentale. *AnimeLand hors-série* 10: 167–168.

Suvilay, Bounthavy. 2019. *Réceptions et recréations de Dragon Ball en France: manga, anime, jeux vidéo. Pour une histoire matérielle de la fiction (1988–2018)*, thèse de littérature française comparée, Université Montpellier 3.

Tamba, Akira (ed.). 1997. *L'esthétique contemporaine au Japon*. Paris: CNRS Éditions.

Tisseron, Serge. 2000. *Psychanalyse de la bande dessinée*. Paris : Flammarion.

Vanhée, Olivier. 2019. *L'appropriation du manga en France. Enquête sur la genèse d'un univers culturel spécifique, la constitution et l'expression des goûts et des manières de lire, les parcours de lecteurs et lectrices adultes*, thèse de sociologie, Université Lyon 2.

Vicky. 2006. Le shonen manga. *AnimeLand hors-série* 10 : 243–247.

Vincent Gérard, Armelle, Cécile Chaniot, and Maëlle Lapointe. 2020. *Les Français et la BD 2020*. Paris: IPSOS/Centre National du Livre.

Walter, Anne-Laure. 2011. Mangas. Les éditeurs contre-attaquent. *Livres Hebdo* 871 : 63.

Walter, Anne-Laure. 2010. Le temps de la maturité. *Livres Hebdo* 826: 71.

Ward-Black, Rebecca. 2009. Just don't call them *cartoons*: the new literacy spaces of anime, manga, and fanfiction. In *Handbook of research on new literacies*, edited by Julie Coiro, 583–610. New York: Routledge.

Index of Authors

Index of Subjects

www.ingramcontent.com/pod-product-compliance
Lightning Source LLC
Chambersburg PA
CBHW072056020426
42334CB00017B/1529